2/07

MAE WEST

Also by Simon Louvish

MAE WEST

It Ain't No Sin

SIMON LOUVISH

Thomas Dunne Books / St. Martin's Press

New York

THOMAS DUNNE BOOKS.
An imprint of St. Martin's Press.

www.thomasdunnebooks.com
www.stmartins.com

Library of Congress Cataloging-in-Publication Data

Louvish, Simon.
    Mae West : it ain't no sin / Simon Louvish.—1st U.S. ed.
        p. cm.
    Includes bibliographical references and index.
    ISBN-13: 978-0-312-34878-6
    ISBN-10: 0-312-34878-9
    1. West, Mae. 2. Motion picture actors and actresses—United States—
Biography. I. Title.

PN2287.W4566 L68 2006
791.4302'8092—dc22
[B]

                                                            2006047494

First published in the United Kingdom by Faber and Faber Limited

First U.S. Edition: November 2006

10 9 8 7 6 5 4 3 2 1

Contents

CONTENTS

PART FOUR

Belle of the Thirties

PART FIVE

Herself Alone

EPILOGUE

APPENDICES

List of Illustrations

PROLOGUE

Come Up and See Me

Things I'll Never Do – By Mae West (Undated)

1 Take another woman's man. Not intentionally, that is. Even though all's fair in love and war and it ain't no sin.

2 Try to be anything but myself at all times, publicly and privately, except on the stage or screen, for that's where acting belongs.

3 Cook, bake, sew, wash dishes, peel potatoes, eat onions, or bite my nails.

4 Wear white cotton stockings or join a nudist colony.

5 Like opera, number thirteen, yodelling, cold spaghetti, rats, snails, men who shave their necks, or over-ripe bananas.

6 Care for people who whistle in dressing rooms or checks that bounce as high as the stratosphere.

7 Play mother parts, sad parts, dumb parts, or a virtuous wife, betrayed or otherwise. I pity weak women, good or bad, but I can't like them. A woman should be strong either in her goodness or badness.

8 Go nuts about classical music, sandwiches, cigar smoke, places that smell like hospitals, and black nail polish.

9 Get excited over night clubs, contract bridge, fan dancing, bobby sox, the stock market, badminton, or bust developers.

10 Be thrilled to death by orchids, anonymous love letters, souvenir post-card folders, earthquakes, slave bracelets, or beds with hard mattresses.

11 Be bothered by Scotch money-lenders or boys who lisp.

12 Believe the worst about anybody without complete proof nor will I believe that it's useless to struggle against so-called Fate – the phony!

13 Walk when I can sit, or sit when I can recline. I believe in saving my energy – for important things.

14 Write a story that is unsophisticated, because I believe that innocence is as innocent doesn't.

15 Marry a man who is too handsome, a man who drinks to excess or doesn't carry his liquor like a gentleman, a man who is easy to get, easily led into temptation – unless I do the leading.

From the *Boston Herald*, 29 April 1938:

CLUTCHING, SQUEALING CROWD GREETS MAE WEST
WITH MOB SCENE HERE

Complete with the publicised curves and husky, slurring accents that have made her practically a symbol of what she is pleased to call 'the sex personality,' Mae West crashed into Boston yesterday morning through a clutching, squealing crowd of 3000 eager admirers who turned the South station into a mob scene.

Cries of pain mingled with shouts of 'There she is!' and 'Give us a smile, Mae!' as the mob, in a surging onslaught, trampled on toes and barked shins to get closer to the object of it all. The plump blonde actress, in a trailing satin dress, with make-up thick on her features and a huge bunch of orchids clutched in a heavily jeweled hand, gave them the smile and was taken off to the Ritz-Carlton, where she is staying while appearing in person at the RKO Boston Theater this week . . .

Mae West: 'sex personality', film star, women's icon, all-round celebrity, familiar and at the same time utterly mysterious and elusive. Many men had, reputedly, 'come up and seen her', but no one seemed to have quite pinned down the person hidden behind the mask – if there was, indeed, anyone there apart from the magnificent construct that her life on stage and screen had fabricated. By 1938, she had already appeared in eight feature films that had propelled her from the status of a notorious Broadway trouble-maker to that of the movies' greatest comedienne. Her personal appearance tour continued to cause ructions throughout the eastern states of the US: in Hartford she was the subject of a dedicated 'Mae West Safe Driving Week', a parade which, upon the star's appearance, 'created one of the wildest and maddest crowd scenes here in several years. Not since Lindbergh came to town has there been such a tumult.' Traffic was disrupted, and the police were overwhelmed by a turnout of over 30,000 fans. From Connecticut Mae moved on to New York, where Loew's State Theatre opened its doors at 8 a.m. and the jam of backstage 'autograph hounds' was so heavy that extra cops were deployed throughout the day.

The fans' enthusiasm did not diminish. In 1946, after years of war and the Royal Air Force's adoption of her name for their buoyant 'Mae West' life-preserving jackets, her appearance in her own play, *Come On Up*, continued to awe both public and critics. One breathless columnist, for the *Los Angeles Times*, had to resort to ellipses:

Being invited to 'Come up and see me' . . . Not just sometime . . . But after the show at National Monday night . . . by the lady who originated that seductive phrase . . . Mae West no less . . . I did see her . . . but as through a fog . . . of human beings . . . lined up out to E Street and around corner . . . getting her autograph . . . door to her dressing room was a bottle-neck . . . as they neared 'the presence' . . . everyone craned their necks . . . some of the sailors and GIs got so flustered they dropped their programs . . . their eyes bugged out . . . was she real? She was . . . and a real lady . . . dashing off her signature with a pleasant smile . . . lift of her big blue eyes . . . still with their heavy mascara 'window shades' . . . thick tan make-up on her face . . . her body unconsciously giving those seductive twists . . . which have such devastating effect on males . . . on the stage and off . . .

In 1951, presenting a regular revival of her greatest stage hit, *Diamond Lil*, the glittering image knew no limits, as she appeared 'encrusted with what is said to be $1,175,000 worth of platinum and diamonds loaned for the performances by Harry Winston Inc., diamond merchant of 7 East 51st St. The jewelry is brought to the theater under guard, Miss West is guarded while wearing it and after the show it is returned to the Winston vaults . . .' The ornamentation included 'Seven part waist decoration, $500,000; necklace, $100,000; three bracelets, $200,000; 46-carat emerald-cut diamond ring, $300,000; 30-carat oval-cut diamond ring, $75,000 . . .'

To the hordes of pop-eyed journalists, Mae would purr: 'Men and jewels are my hobby'; and to the query of one Joe DeBona, of the *Connecticut Sunday Herald*, in 1952, 'If all the men in the world suddenly died, would you want to go on living?' she replied – or was reported to have replied – 'No, there would be no sense in it,' as she waved in the reporter's eyes a '22-carat diamond as large as a golfball on one of the fingers of her right hand'.

Her stock in trade, as the years went by, was to appear for ever ageless. Sceptics were given short shrift, as Earl Wilson, of the *World Omaha Herald*, reported in 1949, under the heading: MAE STILL HAS ALL HER TEETH:

Mae West opened her mouth and invited me to look down her throat, an offer which I was too gallant to refuse.

'Look,' she smoldered, 'Uh got all muh own teeth. Yuh ask me muh age – Uh'm over 21.'

Miss West, in this gay, confident mood because her show, 'Diamond Lil,' is a hit again after 20 years, had overestimated me if she thought I could tell her age by looking at her teeth. When I was a farm boy in Ohio, I might have been able to achieve it . . .

'Tell me,' I said, facing Miss West there in her dressing room as she waggled about restlessly, 'what difference is there between the two productions – between the Mae West now and the Mae West 20 years ago?'

Miss West was wearing one the lowest-cut flamin' red dresses this side of the South Sea Islands.

'Have you grown any larger?' I asked.

'No,' she said, 'they're the same. Muh measurement is 38 bust, 38 hips and 28 waist.'

'Have you added any new lines to the show?'

'Yeuh. The one about "Goodness, what beautiful diamonds," and I say, "Goodness had nothing to do with it." That was in the picture, but not in the original show. I got some yells outa that.'

'Won't you be getting married?' I asked . . .

' . . . Uh'm still lookin' for the right man,' she said. 'Muh trouble is, Uh find so many right ones, it's hard to decide.'

But, to her female fans, Mae West often presented a completely different image, building on the experience of the transgressive plays which had made her name – before the movies beckoned, in the late 1920s – and her battles with convention and censorship. Presenting herself as an early sex educator, in 1929 she wrote, for *The Parade*, under the title 'Sex in the Theater':

I have often been accused both by the press and individuals of deliberately appealing to the salacious and evil-minded. One can readily see how wrong this is, when you consider that I have played to more than ten million people in the United States drawn from all walks of life, from the highest and the most intelligent to the lowest and poorest. Ten million Americans can't be all salacious and evil-minded. When one can please the masses one must essentially be right.

But what few people realize is that my work has had a deliberate plan and purpose . . .

It is usually long after the death of pioneers that their work is respected and the truths they stood for recognized. Because of narrow-minded censors and silly taboos the people are unable to learn truths they are starving for. Think of it, thousands of women have asked me the most personal questions about their husbands and love life. In many cases I have been forced to suggest food tonics and the like to help the poor, love-starved wives. They know nothing about sex at all, for the subject is hidden from children, kept out of books and schools and education.

The wonderful medium of theatre, Mae suggested, was ideal to bring those hidden educational truths home to ordinary people and to cast light on such concealed realities as the lives of prostitutes and the even less known facts of homosexual lives and loves. In three plays, *Sex*, *The Drag* and *Pleasure Man*, written by herself, Mae had attempted to bring these lives to the attention of her eager audiences, only to be met with banning orders, court cases and, in the case of *Sex*, an actual spell behind bars. Nevertheless, Mae vowed: 'I realized the problem and devoted my career in the theatre to the education of the masses. I shall boldly continue to do so, in spite of criticism, insults and narrow-minded bigots.'

The movie Mae West, however, had to fight a different kind of challenge, both to her material and to the very persona she had built to lure those legions of fans. A hard bed in the cells was no longer threatened, but her capacity to be what the fans now demanded came under growing pressure. Her 1934 film *Belle of the Nineties* became the test case for the newly fortified 'Hays Code', which was deployed to tame Hollywood's firebrands – the directors, producers, writers and performers who threatened to kick over the traces. Their battle was lost, but the fight was a stubborn one, with unexpected heroes.

Mae West's career in movies as a major star was not, in fact, a lengthy one, if one counts the seven-year period between 1932 and 1939 when the films by which she is remembered were made, most of them for Paramount Pictures. Her last undisputed classic, her great double-act with W. C. Fields, *My Little Chickadee*, was released in 1940 by Universal. A rarely viewed straggler, *The Heat's On*, was made in 1943. Her last two films, the most eccentric comebacks in all of movie history, were committed decades later: the amazing and scandalous adaptation of Gore Vidal's *Myra Breckinridge*, released in 1970, and the lesser known *Sextette*, the last hurrah of the ageless sex goddess, produced in 1976.

In between, though Mae made no new films, she continued to groom her unique image through a non-stop stream of stage appearances. She performed in new plays, razzle-dazzled Las Vegas and all points north, south, east and west, emitting endless interviews and homilies. Mae West on Health and Beauty, Mae West on Sex, Love and Marriage, Mae West on New Year Resolutions, Mae West on Extra-Sensory Perception and, ever and anon, Mae West on Men. But these published writings were but the tip of a very large iceberg, a ceaseless lava flow of projects for both stage and screen. From the 1920s, Mae became known for her authorship of her own plays and, later, of three raunchy novels, versions of her favourite stage hits, as well as her autobiography, defiantly titled *Goodness Had Nothing to Do with It*. The archives of the Library of Congress in Washington, the formal repository for copyright materials, contain manuscripts for twelve plays attributed to Mae, some with co-writers. Three of her best-known plays from the 1920s – *Sex*, *The Drag* and *Pleasure Man* – have been published for a new generation. But recently donated archives, at the Academy of Motion Picture Arts and Sciences in Los Angeles, provide a unique insight into the writer Mae's workshop. Long known for scorning the nightspots, cabarets and clubs where scandal was brewed and decanted, eschewing the Hollywood or Broadway gala premières – apart from her own productions – Mae West had an unguilty secret: she stayed home, night after night, and endlessly wrote, learning her craft by a slow painstaking process of trial and error, redrafting and recycling notions and themes. This was not the way she wished to represent herself as a creator, as she recounted to gullible reporters in 1928:

Mae West's formula for writing a play: 'hire a room in a hotel, lock yourself in and go to work for as many hours as you can stand the pace. Then you grab a little sleep, get up and resuscitate yourself with a few tons of cold water and start all over again. And so on until the play is finished a few days later . . .' That's the way Mae West wrote 'Sex.' That's the way, in fact, she has written all her plays, including her latest, 'Diamond Lil . . .'

There are lies, damn lies, and publicity . . . 'STAR CREATES PLAYS WITHOUT WRITING A LINE,' headlined the *San Francisco Examiner* in 1929, recounting yet another Maesian tale of creation through rehearsals alone. What Mae, like many modern playwrights and scriptwriters, performed was a labour that put her original drafts through many permutations and versions – often dependent, in the case of her five produced plays, on the casting and input of her various actors, much as improvisers like John Cassavetes and Mike Leigh have done in our own time for movies. In movies, however, Mae's input was different, as we shall see in due course.

I am fortunate to have had a first sight of this archive that sheds new light on Mae West the writer, one which transforms our outlook on Mae West the performer and actress. She remains, as well as these, a feminist icon, attracting attention as a precursor of the modern woman, determined to preserve her independence of thought and of action, financial power and sexual desire.

'THE TROUBLE WITH MEN IS GETTING RID OF THEM' an essay about her was headlined as early as 1933, in *Movie Mirror*, written, alas, by the very male Marquis Busby: '"Men?" repeated Mae West in a puzzled voice, for all the world as if she has never heard of the darned things. "Oh, you mean MEN! I haven't time for them now. I'm in Hollywood to make a success in pictures, and you can only do one thing at a time."' Nevertheless, the name of the game was still getting your man, rather than ignoring him only to inflame his passions.

It should come as no surprise that someone born in the last decade of the last century but one should still harbour some old-fashioned notions. Many things claimed as *sui generis* for Mae West, like her adoption of black music and styles, were more a matter of combining existing trends and forgotten modes – some less attractive than others – that have dropped out of our collective memory.

So my brief in this book is to give an all-round picture of a unique twentieth-century performer, an American and feminist icon, no doubt the movies' most famous female star, one who was universally recognized – and not only as a floating appendage to save air-force pilots from a watery grave. She was, like many of her contemporaries – the juggler W. C. Fields, the four Marx Brothers, Charlie Chaplin, Buster Keaton, Stan Laurel, Fanny Brice, *et al.* – a vaudeville baby, schooled in the five-a-day world of non-stop performances, the rough hustle of the quick-change stage, where a fifteen-minute slot had to grab the audience before it called for the next act; competing with one-legged unicyclists, trained seals and giants like Houdini and Eva Tanguay, her role model and precursor. From these hardy roots, in the first decade of the last century, to her remarkable swansongs in the era of flower-power, gay rights and gender-bending fantasies, she remained a once-only phenomenon. Like her sole comedy equal, W. C. Fields, she carved her own identity out of a patchwork of influences, which then faded into an invisible backdrop, leaving the self-made creation to inhabit its own singular world, to challenge and disrupt, by sheer force of personality, our easy assumptions about life and art.

PART ONE

Rap Rap Rap

I

More Sunlight and Less Smoke

Mae West wrote:

The Brooklyn I was born in, near the end of the 19th century, was still a city of churches, with their great bronze bells walloping calls to the faithful from early dawn, and a city of water-front dives where the old forest of the spars of sailing ships was rapidly being replaced by funnels and the Sand Street Navy Yard already had a reputation for girl chasers. Gentlemen, and deer, ran wild in Prospect Park . . . A world of more sunlight and less smoke than now, a world of ringing horse cars, ragtime music, cakewalks and Floradora Sextets, and a sense that the coming century would be the biggest and the best . . .

Brooklyn was indeed, before its incorporation as a New York City borough in 1898, a suburban town that moved at a more leisurely pace than the great sprawling mass it is now. Grown from the status of a village, it had also become a powerhouse both of work and leisure, known for its waterfront commerce and the world famous Coney Island pleasure park. Victorian villas nestled in leafy avenues, the new elevated railroad marched up Fulton Street towards the hub of City Hall, and the construction of the Brooklyn Bridge over eleven years, from 1870 to 1880, tied the suburb to the island of Manhattan with bonds of steel. In 1892, the Brooklyn City Railroad Co. was planning to extend the railways in all directions: up Morgan Avenue, from Flushing to Nassau, from Bushwick Avenue to Flushing, up East New York Avenue and along Vanderbilt Avenue, from the Plaza to Prospect Park. The early 1890s, however, were seeing a dip in the apparently unstoppable advance of prosperity, as the local clarion, the *Brooklyn Daily Eagle*, revealed in its headlines on the day of Mae's birth, 17 August 1893:

'BREAD AND WORK' THEIR CRY – FIVE THOUSAND HEBREWS
HOLD A RIOTOUS MEETING IN NEW YORK

Unemployed garment workers were venting their fury, and two major enterprises, the *Eagle* reported – the Oliver Iron and Steel Company, 'one of the largest business concerns in the country', and the Standard Wagon Company – had gone into receivership on the same day. On a positive note, the paper covered the jollifications of the Firemen's Banquet, 1,100 'good men and true', stout and boisterous Irishmen in the main, assembled in the Sea Beach palace, with two big bands vying with each other: 'Nobody Heard a Word of the Speeches, and Nobody Cared.'

Despite the recession, life was already speeding up towards the century of new opportunities and hazards. A Mrs Jacob Lablen of Riverhead was run into and injured by a bicycle ridden by a Mr Orville Young. A seven-year-old child was injured while jumping off a Greenpoint trolley car, near Navy Street. Concerns about the new mechanical transport was a perennial subject for columnists' debate and gossip: '"I tell you . . . the horse car is less likely to run down pedestrians than the trolley, not only because it does not go so fast . . . but also [because] the horses, whether their driver does or not, always have their eyes open, and before they are upon a body they will, either by stopping or shying to one side, draw his attention . . ." "Well, there's no use fault finding," says his interlocutor, "we have got the trolley and had better make the best of it . . ."'

Politics was an enduring source of controversy, with members of an Independent Citizens' association gathering in the nineteenth ward to unseat the incumbent Republican – 'Ready to Knife Worth,' as the *Eagle* put it. Residents of Rockaway were also gathering to protest against the garbage-dumping station established off their beach. Even New York's mayor agreed with them: 'The present system is not the right one. The garbage is brought on old fashioned scows managed by Italians, and the vessels are dumped at ebb tide.' Entertainments, too, were matters of hot debate in the *Eagle* of 17 August, particularly regarding the audience's sacred right to hiss. 'It is a radical question of independence,' noted the editorial writer, 'does not common sense say that the right to praise what you like carries with it the right to condemn what you don't like? . . . The exaltation of the hiss would promote more intelligent audiences and a more robust race of actors.'

The robust race of actors was indeed being reinforced that day by a formidable new arrival at the home of Matilda and John Patrick

West, on Bushwick Avenue, Greenpoint. No birth record is extant, but later census records verify the year. She was named Mary Jane West, after her paternal grandmother, Irish-born Mary Jane Copley. She was not her parents' firstborn, as there had been a baby sister, named Katie, who died at the age of three months. In 1898, a sister, Mildred, later named Beverly, and, in 1900, a brother, John Junior, were added to the family.

Legend has preserved John West Senior as 'Battlin' Jack', a one-time prizefighter, bouncer and man-about-town who was tame enough by the 1890s to own a livery stable business, sending carriages and coaches out for hire. Mae described him in her 1959 autobiography as 'an epic figure in Brooklyn . . . all knobby with muscles . . . once captured two robbers single-handed . . . He had been a catch-as-catch-can street fighter, and had fought in the ring since he was eleven years old.'

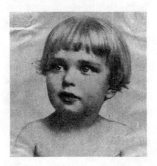

Baby Mae, Battlin' Jack and Tillie West

There is scant record of 'Battlin' Jack's ringside prowess, prize-fighting being, even in the 1880s, an illegal sport in many states. A rare early record of the name John West appeared in a *New York Times* report of 25 July 1886, which noted that 'pugilists "Nitchie" Golden and John Grady, Referee James Ryan, and Timekeeper John West' were arrested in Philadelphia, charged with 'aiding and participating in a prize fight' in Delaware. Whether this was our John West or another, who can tell? Upon his marriage, the tale goes, 'Battlin' Jack' rested his fists, at least in the professional mode.

Mae claimed for her pa a long pedigree of Irish and English descent stretching back to 'Long Grendon, Buckinghamshire, England', ascending to America in the 1700s. His own father, John Edwin West, had been a seaman working on whaling ships, by some accounts as a captain, who had later dealt in real estate. Among his respectable, college-educated siblings, 'Battlin' Jack' West was something of an admirable black sheep, the way his daughter told the tale. But in an interview with writer John Kobal, conducted in 1970, Mae's memories of her father were somewhat less gushing:

I was crazy about my mother. But I never liked my father much when I was small. I don't know why, 'cause he never laid a hand on any of us, you know, and he always provided good for us. The only reason I can think of now why I wasn't crazy about him was that he smoked those big cigars. To this day I haven't been able to stand cigars. He was a prize-fighter in the beginning, and later he had a detective agency and then his own hansom cab business.

In the parlance of our time, he was a taxi-cab owner. But there had been other jobs along the way, according to city directories: 'mechanic' in 1889, the year of his marriage; 'bridle maker' in 1891; 'laborer' or 'watchman' in 1898. The profession entered in the 1900 New York census is a somewhat indecipherable handscrawl: 'Policeman's (unreadable)'. Mae's claim about his detective agency is borne out by the 1910 census, which clearly lists John West as 'Detective'. This has an odd echo in her own early annals. Battlin' or not, he was clearly a Jack of many trades. Despite Mae's claim that she had been brought up in prosperous circumstances, with a carriage always available or a 'deep fur-lined sleigh' kitted out for winter jaunts, the family may not have been wholly immune to the downturn of the 1890s business cycle.

If John West provided the combative can-do, up-and-at-'em attitude that was to mark his eldest surviving daughter, her mother Matilda, better known as Tillie, was the originator of her love of finery, her penchant for expensive clothes and fashion. Matilda Delker or Doelger – Mae used both names in her own account – was a German-born immigrant to the United States, arrived in 1882, with a family of three sisters and two brothers; her father Jacob had a cousin who had founded a now prosperous brewery in New York in the 1840s. Mae often referred to her French origins on her mother's side, probably deriving from her grandmother Christiana Brimier's ancestry in Alsace. Tillie's 'Frenchness' might have been a reference to her work before her marriage as a model for corsets and other fashionable items.

The earliest folder in the newly acquired Mae West collection at the Academy of Motion Pictures library contains a set of *Harper's Bazaar* magazines dating from 1885 to 1897, kept and preserved by her mother. The illustrations in the magazine are the familiar drawings, with the women's faces often bearing a strong Mae Westian look, fanciful as it may be to try to identify Matilda Delker's visage amid the 'postilion basques', the 'ladies' summer wrappings' and 'jetted silk pelerine', or under the 'pagoda parasols' which 'are seen again on the streets this spring'. She might have been the lady on the cover of Saturday 10 July 1886, twirling a parasol daintily as she consorts with a natty young gentleman on a rocky beach above the title 'Students of Geology'. Or she might have modelled the 'security corset', advertised by the Weedsport Skirt and Dress Company, which 'conforms to the body of the wearer in the most trying positions'. The last issue in the set, from 20 February 1897, has models displaying the 'Paris Hat from Virot, and Sable Cape, with various Spring Hats within'. In the gossip section, we learn that 'Professor Chakravarti . . . has come to this country to represent the Indian section . . . in the Theosophical Convention to be held in Chicago this month . . . ,' an occult strand that will recur, in later years.

By this time, Mary Jane West would have been just three and a half years old. The earliest extant photograph of 'Baby Mae' shows a pair of big wide eyes gazing out of a chubby blonde face. For such early years one has only Mae's own testimony, in which she reports that her mother later described her as 'a child that has to be humored and can't be forced or ordered. She resents even an unfavorable tone of voice.' One of Mae's earliest memories was her desire to have her picture taken with a dog, a very particular dog, with long white hair, a black eye and black ear, which she had seen 'around the corner'. One of her uncles was delegated to bring the elusive canine in. There was always only one thing that could be right for the child; whether in dogs or dolls, she had to have her way. As she told interviewer Charlotte Chandler: 'We went to a store and there were a hundred dolls. Everyone thought all the dolls looked alike. The one I wanted was on the highest shelf no one could reach. Everyone in the store thought I just wanted that one because I was difficult. But I wanted her because she had a mauve dress, a beautiful mauve dress. If you see the difference and other people don't, they think you're just being difficult. I always knew what I wanted. My mother never questioned it. She made them get a ladder and get me the one I wanted.'

In another recollection, gathered for but omitted from her *Life* magazine interview of April 1969, Mae recalls her Brooklyn child-hood in 'a fine residential section', near a block of 'those single build-ings, one story high and all French', housing a barber shop, a millinery shop and a hairdressing parlour, all with 'mirrors in the doors and windows, long fancy work at the bottom, and I'd pose as I'd walk along and I'd look at myself this way and then that way ... In the window of a jewelry store there used to be a big diamond hanging on a black velvet bust and I'd say to myself, "I've got to have a diamond like you and then I'd be absolutely more than happy." Diamonds, you see, are the best things a woman can have. It never loses its value, the shine of it, when a man gives you one, it lifts your ego.' A most precocious, perhaps wishfully thought, predilection.

We have only Mae's word, too, about her earliest stage appear-ance, as 'Baby May – Song and Dance', at a Sunday concert at the Royal Theatre in Fulton Street, Brooklyn, at the age of seven, 'going on eight'. Wearing 'a pink and green satin dress with gold spangles, and a large white lace picture hat', with pink slippers and stockings, she sang 'Movin' Day' to great audience applause and won a gold medal from the Elks.

'I heard the applause,' Mae recalled, 'applause just for me, and I knew they really liked me, and I knew then there wasn't any other place I ever wanted to be.'

2

Made Ready for the Footlights

Mae told John Kobal:

I had a natural singing voice and my mother took me to singing and dancing schools. Nobody else in our family had ever been in show business, but she had wanted to go on the stage when she was a young girl. Her parents wouldn't let her, they were very strict like that. But she loved me being in the theater . . . When I was twelve, I had gotten too mature for children's parts, so I went back to living at home in Brooklyn till I was sixteen, when I could get a work permit and go back on the stage.

Mae's stage career had begun, she related, after dancing lessons with a 'Professor' Watts on Fulton Street, and then continued with a stock company of dramatic players formed by the actor Hal Clarendon. This timing hits an awkward speed bump. Clarendon, a local Brooklyn boy, was of a distinguished stage family. Both his parents had been actors, and one of his aunts was Mrs Minnie Maddern-Fiske, grand New York diva. As a child actor, he had played 'some 200 different characters in as many plays'. However, his own Stock Company was not formed until 1907, as announced by the *Brooklyn Daily Eagle* on 15 April of that year:

Hal Clarendon, of the Spooner Stock Company, and who successfully managed the Bergen Beach Casino last summer, will form a new company under the name of the Hal Clarendon Stock Company, opening at the Gotham Theatre, April 29, in the play 'Northern Lights.'

Mae's own timing would have fitted her creative alteration over two decades later of her birth date to 1900, adjusting her age for the attentions of the movie camera. The highly publicized details of her hidden marriage – of which much more anon – forced her true age into the headlines in the mid-1930s. This leaves us with seven years unaccounted for before Mae could have realistically claimed to have joined the Clarendon Company, at the age of fourteen. The timelines of history, therefore, inexorably alter Mae's own presentation of herself as an instant child prodigy, never out of the spotlight from the age of eight. We have to assume that 'Baby Mae' most probably performed at amateur shows and talent evenings or matinees, under her mother's firm tutelage, until 1907, and proper, mundane schooling took place throughout that period.

The listings of the Hal Clarendon company bear this out clearly. Stock companies were, in fact, enjoying an 'astonishing revival' in 1907, according to the *New York Dramatic Mirror*. They were, in the words of one veteran stage director, Paul Scott, 'the school for our future actors and actresses. Without good stock companies I don't see where the future generation of capable, experienced people will come from.' Unlike the sister category of 'Repertoire' companies, which toured extensively, stock companies remained local, and indeed the record shows that the Clarendon troupe stayed in Brooklyn, playing first at the Gotham, then at the beach resort Bergen Beach Casino through the summer, and folding at the end of August. Mae was therefore playing close to home, and in the autumn of that year most probably returned to school.

This makes sense, given Mae's proven ability in future years to wield the pen and demonstrate her eloquence and wit both verbally and on the page. If we are looking at the period around the turn of the twentieth century, with its still massive discrepancies between rich and poor, we should appreciate that there were two modes of education: the schoolhouse or the street. If one learned to read and write, one learnt 'proper' in the formulaic teaching of the time. As Mae herself was to comment in her 1940 role as Flower Belle Lee in *My Little Chickadee* while appraising a blackboard: '"I am a good boy. I am a good girl." What is this, propaganda?' But Mae's presentation of herself as a rough, unschooled, on-the-road stage baby is, alas, pure bunkum.

It is not clear at which point the birth name Mary Jane became 'Mae', particularly as 'May West' continued to be an alternative spelling into her early vaudeville years, though most probably in error. Biographer Emily Wortis Leider has dug into common usage to find that 'May' was often used for 'Mary', quoting a popular song of the era, sung by Lydia Barry: 'Her Christian name was Mary / But she took the R away / She wanted to be a fairy / With the beautiful name of May.' Though how we got from 'y' to 'e' is somewhat more vague.

Mae's comment to Charlotte Chandler, that the downward curve of the 'y' offended her because 'I don't like anything downbeat', is an amusing fancy. Up to the census form of 1910 she is still listed as Mary J. West.

We do not know how her name was spelled at Hal Clarendon's Stock Company, as she appears to have fallen too far down the list to be credited. We have to assume she was taking part in such productions as *The Silver King*, which played in June 1907, or *Dr. Jekyll and Mr. Hyde*, in July – 'the popularity of Mr. Clarendon's company is increasing with the progress of the summer. Every member of the organization works hard for success, and the result is generally pleasing,' quoth the *Dramatic Mirror*. *The Bowery Newsgirl* followed later in the same month, *Who's Your Wife* and *The Great Well Mystery* in August. According to Mae's own account, she played in Shakespeare plays, English drama and French farce, and an 'authentic old photograph' shows her dressed as 'Little Lord Fauntleroy', eight years old according to the caption, but in reality clearly older. These standard popular plays, potboilers and melodramas provided an essential theatrical education, as she learned the tone and pitch of these dramatic narratives, tales of 'lost heirs, lost virtues . . . seduced barmaids . . . Murder, rape (done offstage of course), forest fires, wrecks of famous river boats, crooked jockeys and forged wills'. One such play, *The Ranchman's Daughter*, by Joseph Byron Totten, was robustly described by the *Brooklyn Daily Eagle* in 1907: 'The Eastern Detective, his hands bound behind him, awaits death from five kegs of powder, about to be ignited from as many slow burning fuses. With his hands still bound behind him, the detective manages to draw his revolver and shoot out, one at a time, the burning fuses.'

This would have been a decidedly more exciting influence than the normal domestic examples set at that age for little girls, though she was growing up in a period which provided another role model for imaginative girls: Dorothy in Frank Baum's Oz books, the first of which, *The Wonderful World of Oz*, was published in 1900. But with Hal Clarendon Mae was being exposed to male characters other than tin men, straw men or cowardly lions.

It was an age, too, of many other hearty entertainments: down at Brighton Beach, not far from her own stage, she may well have had her first encounter with the 'humorous juggler' W. C. Fields, playing the week of 6 July 1907. The magical world of Coney Island presented

'Little Lord Fauntleroy', 1908

the Luna Park, featuring The Trip to the Moon, where 'a beautiful girl is met at every turn', while the Mountain Torrent, the Kansas Cyclone, the Shipwreck and the Tickler provided rib-crushing physical thrills. Steeplechase Park offered performing dogs and seals, as well as 'King Pharaoh, the Educated Horse'. In the same summer, Buffalo Bill's Wild West Show, fresh from its sensational European tour, opened in Brooklyn, with its massed ranks of riders, 'more than two hundred Indians, Cowboys, Cossacks, Mexicans and soldiers, gaily accoutred . . . on mounts peculiar to each'. The centrepiece of the show was the grand reconstruction of the Battle of Summit Springs, fought on 11 July 1869 in Colorado, with Colonel Buffalo Bill Cody, himself then Chief Scout for the 5th US Cavalry, ranged against Chief Tall Bull. (Colonel Cody had, according to this version, dispatched Tall Bull in person.) Further afield, in Manhattan, the taller bull of the capital of burlesque, vaudeville and musical revues beckoned.

At some point, though Mae does not date the event, her mother enrolled her in Ned Wayburn's Institute of Dancing. We do not have archival evidence of this, and she does not figure in the famous Class of 1907, which featured the graduates of Wayburn's spin-off 'College of Vaudeville', including the Astaire children, Fred and Adele, then eight and ten years old, and the 'Marks boys' Julius and Milton, later to be Groucho and Gummo, who were then seventeen and fifteen years old, respectively. As Ned Wayburn played his part in putting Mae West on the stage a few years later, her participation in his dancing classes is credible, more than likely following her season with the Clarendon company.

Unlike the journeyman Clarendon, Ned Wayburn was a major show-business figure whose presence was ubiquitous from the late 1890s until well into the 1930s. He was born with a silver spoon in his mouth and never quite lost it, despite his enterprises' occasional bankruptcies. He was the son of one Wilbur C. Weyburn of Chicago, 'inventor of the duplex knitting machine'. Becoming a 'ragtime pianist' in 1897, he rose through the ranks, with the help of family cash, to become a producer and theatrical mogul, with his chief area of expertise being the training of young girls for shows.

Wayburn called his school of dancing his 'squab farm' – 'the Place Where Chorus Girls are Taught to Dance and Sing from the Raw Material, and Made Ready for the Footlights'. This was by all accounts no fun at all but a tough process, as Wayburn drove his charges before him with a 'crook-handled cane . . . He uses a whistle now to start and stop the dancing. He had a bell one time. One ring, stop; two rings go ahead'; but the girls going home from rehearsals and the theatre used to cause confusion on the street cars when tired and distraught by bursting into song and dance and as suddenly stopping when the conductor signalled to the motorman, so that Wayburn took up the whistle. 'I have girls that have been dancing since they were tots of ten,' Wayburn told the *New York World* (8 July 1906). 'The demand is great, but the supply keeps up with it. When I need a bunch of eight girls or more for a vaudeville production, or when I am called to put a rollicking chorus into a musical piece, I know just whom I want and where to get them.'

Within a few years he became the 'chief picker' for Florenz Ziegfeld's sumptuous annual Follies, which paraded the girls like so many cogs and wheels in a grand theatrical machine: 'It is system, system, system with me,' he declared. 'I believe in numbers and straight lines. I learned to value both when I was a mechanical draughts-man and I apply my knowledge of them with what I believe good results . . . Can you imagine a spontaneous military parade?' And to *Theater Magazine*, in May 1920, he described his idea of the epitome of the female role in show business:

The text of a musical show is woman. Woman – of all sorts, of all sizes, all temperaments, all attractions – woman. The chorus girl is the principal part of this text . . . She is a creation as completely thought out, moved about, wired and flounced, beribboned and set dancing, as any automaton designed to please, to delight, to excite an audience . . . to invent groupings of girls that could be moved artistically, to set them climbing up golden stairs, or dancing and marching about on a huge [turn] table, constantly increasing the procession of beautiful girls so that they will overwhelm the imagination of an audience with sheer sensuousness of spectacle, and dazzle it with the universal text of the theater woman.

Wayburn's ideas echoed the words of industrial theorist Frederick W. Taylor, whose advocacy of 'scientific management' by the assembly line was at its most popular while Ziegfeld's extravaganzas were flourishing. 'In the past the man has been first,' Taylor wrote in 1911, in his *Principles of Scientific Management*, 'in the future the system must be first.'

These then were some of the limits of the opportunities available to

Ned Wayburn and his 'squab farm' girls – cartoon from 1907

Mae West and thousands of stage-struck girls like her who ventured starry-eyed into the world of show business in the first decades of the twentieth century.

3

In Dahomey

Despite Ned Wayburn's 'taylorized' view of the theatre, American vaudeville was a vast, chaotic field of distinctive and eccentric personalities. Mary Jane West's teenage years coincided with the golden age of this mass popular entertainment, at a time when its inheritor to be – the motion picture – was still struggling to find its place and form. There were over two thousand variety theatres around the US, fitting George Burns's assertion that you could play for five years all over the circuit and not appear in the same theatre twice. From great 2,000-seat chandeliered palaces to local fleapits, audiences could thrill to the magic of Houdini, gasp at the humorous antics of W. C. Fields, enjoy The Happy Tramp Nat Wills, the yiddish accented Joe Welch, not to speak of the thousand and one small-time acts, from Blatz the Human Fish to Fink's Trained Mules and a troupe of young kids called The Four Nightingales, dressed by their mother, Minnie Marx, in ill-fitting sailors' uniforms. Acts sang, yodelled, trilled and crooned, one-legged unicyclists tore across the stage, not-quite-trained monkeys deposited their ordure from the high wire, dogs leapt through hoops, mice clung to the backs of cantering cats, ethnic groups told Irish, 'Dutch', German, Jewish, Italian jokes, monologuists tried to hold the attention of veteran audiences, pickled in *déjà vu*, for the mere ten, fifteen or twenty minutes which the average act was allotted on the stage, with only the benefit of their natural, unamplified voices to breach the smoky fog of the halls.

This was a daunting, if exciting, life to contemplate for a teenage girl of good, if not quite genteel, family who craved attention and applause. With all the testosterone-fuelled delights of variety, there was also no shortage of feminine examples. Far above the massed ranks of chorus girls or the young singers who turned up in twos, threes or fours, cast by the booking agents to the wolves, there were glittering stars, appearing in glamorous costumes or, sometimes, the most minimal drapery that they could get away with in times which were still straitened, if not downright puritanical.

First in the front ranks was Lillian Russell, who first appeared at the age of nineteen at Tony Pastor's pioneering variety theatre, soon inaugurating his new 14th Street theatre with her pastiche of Gilbert and Sullivan, *The Pie-Rats of Pen-Yan*, in 1881. More a queen of the 'legitimate' theatre than vaudeville, Russell nevertheless moved back towards the 'vaud' stage with Joe Weber and Lew Fields's touring company. Shows with names like *Hoity-Toity* and *Woop-Dee-Doo* took her into the new century. She inaugurated the high-glamour character of the woman whose life was carefree both on and off stage, coasting through four marriages and drawing attention for rumoured affairs with the strongman Sandow and the gangster Diamond Jim Brady. She was to ease out of a life of show business by marrying a Republican politician, Alfred P. Moore, in 1912 – a vintage year, as we shall see, for Mae West.

Mae herself, in her autobiography, mentions a number of women whom she names as 'big feature acts' of the day: Evelyn Nesbitt, hardly a proper role model, had become popular at the halls after her lover, the millionaire Stanford White, had been shot by her husband Harry K. Thaw. Mae commented: 'Murderesses (found not guilty) were also stellar attractions for a while, and one female killer who was fired after one week asked, "What can I do to get back on?" The manager said, deadpan, "Go out and kill somebody else."'

A more standard route to fame was followed by Annette Kellerman, a renowned beauty who often cavorted in a one-piece bathing suit and was to become a Ziegfeld star. The other two women Mae mentioned, Gertrude Hoffman and Eva Tanguay, 'were both doing Salome dances, but after the sixth veil fell the patrons whistled for more and didn't get it'. Thus far the limits of vaudeville.

Eva Tanguay was without doubt the primary role model for the young aspiring Mary Jane West. Sometimes known as 'The Girl Who Made Vaudeville Famous', she headlined at the turn of the century and was soon a major draw. By 1910 she was earning $3,500 per week, a sum unheard of for an actress. She sang, she danced, she threw herself about the stage and disrobed as far as the proprieties allowed and a little further; the titles of her songs said it all: 'I Want Someone to Go Wild with Me', 'Go as Far as You Like', 'Nothing Bothers Me', 'I Love to Be Crazy' and her theme 'It's All Been Done

Before but Not the Way I Do It'. Billed as the 'Cyclonic Comedienne', 'The Evangelist of Joy', she had learned from the example of Lillian Russell to exploit the power of the gossip-hungry press. She excelled in the manufacture of scandals – a skill perfected in a previous generation by the master showman P. T. Barnum in the deployment of his star, Anna Held. Tanguay was forever being 'kidnapped' before appearances and losing her jewels, a trick which Mae West would later prove to have learned well. Her entire success, Tanguay declared in an interview quoted by vaudeville chronicler Douglas Gilbert, was 'due to the exploitation of her personality. "That's all there is to it," she said. "As a matter of fact, I am not beautiful, I can't sing, I do not know how to dance. I am not even graceful."' But she had the knack of projecting her boundless energy and self-confidence to hordes of fans.

Other women climbing up the ladder of vaudeville as Mae West simpered in child roles included Elsie Janis, another ex-child actress, a mistress of gentle impersonations and popular songs who would continue at the top for decades; Nora Bayes, a great singer and dramatic actress, who was to perform in and out of the Ziegfeld Follies and emulate Lillian Russell's run through multiple husbands on her way to superstardom; and, from abroad, there were guest appearances by the queens of British variety, Vesta Victoria and Vesta Tilley, male impersonators *par excellence*.

Topsy-turvydom, the gleeful overturning of conventions, was a staple of English music hall, though less common in the American medium still known as 'Polite Vaudeville'. Mae West writes of Julian Eltinge, the foremost female impersonator of the age, who carried on a tradition of cross-dressing familiar from time immemorial, 'even doing Salome's dance and not getting hissed or driven off the stage for it'. Other acts she chose to remember were Joe Cook – 'unicycling and ragtime piano' – Jimmy Savo the juggler, and the 'first great Negro star, Bert Williams'.

The relationship between Mae West and black African-American performers, their acts and their music has been central to some accounts of her life, culminating in the claim by biographer Jill Watts that her appropriation of African-American music, movement, dance and humour constitutes the core of her style. Watts goes so far as to speculate that Mae's grandfather, the seaman John Edwin West, might have been – or one of his forebears might have been – an escaped black slave who passed for white. The biographer writes:

'While no documents substantiate that John Edwin did, similarly none prove that he did not' – a somewhat hazardous form of enquiry.

During the last year of her life, Mae recalled to interviewer Charlotte Chandler that her father had once brought Bert Williams home for dinner, prompting a tantrum from the little girl, who didn't recognize the light-faced Williams without his dark burnt-cork make-up. 'I rushed in, looked at this man, and screamed, "It's not! It's not!" My mother told me my father wanted to go up to me, but Bert Williams stopped him. He said, "I'll do it." He stood outside my door and started to sing. Then I knew and came right out of my room and we all had dinner.' Curiously, Mae does not choose to tell this tale in her 1959 autobiography *Goodness Had Nothing to Do with It*, although she has no reservations about describing the influence upon her, some years later, of the black couples who danced the 'shimmy-shawobble' in cafés on Chicago's south side.

It would certainly be significant, if it were true, that Mae's father Battlin' Jack brought home African-American friends for dinner at the turn of the century, famous or not. But Mae, like every other show-business personality, told so many tall tales of her past that reminiscences in her declining years, however detailed, might be taken with the usual pinch of salt. As we shall see, Mae's relationships with black people – whether they were her peers or her maids – were complex and ambivalent, as was the connection between her art, as it developed, and the sources from whence its manners, tones and techniques stemmed.

A central problem in the exploration of these sources concerns the taboo, in current cultural discourse, on the major influence and indeed practically the whole history of the popular mode of American entertainment known as 'Minstrel'. This formulaic form of blackface jollity was, in fact, white America's foremost stage amusement from its inception in the 1830s till well after the Civil War. Overtaken by other ethnic forms of variety, such as Harrigan and Hart's Irish whimsies, and the industrialized vaudeville of the 1890s, it lingered on in the shape of large blackface troupes such as Lew Dockstader's or Al G. Fields's Minstrels or the double-act of McIntyre and Heath, which provided W. C. Fields with his first non-juggling stage part in 1905. (Radio's Amos 'n' Andy and the 'Two Black Crows', Moran and Mack, took the genre into the 1930s and beyond.) The vagaries of 'political correctness' and severe cultural discomfort among show-business historians have meant that this half-century of American cultural life has been swept firmly under the carpet until recent years, when a number of scholarly writers have sought to re-examine the residue.

The essential argument now being conducted over these unsightly remains is the following: does American popular culture derive, almost in its entirety, through ragtime and jazz, from an appropriation amounting to a cultural theft of black rhythms, music and themes, enriching American life while leaving its originators to suffer all the degradations first of slavery, then of discrimination and prejudice? In this context, as we shall see, a related question could be asked of Mae West: did she appropriate 'black' in order the better to be 'white', or is she a genuine heroine, as some of her chroniclers claim, of a cultural desegregation, an 'Icon in Black and White', to use Jill Watts' subtitle?

There is nothing so fierce as academics locked in a battle over moribund forms, although the echoes of this long quarrel can be heard today in arguments over both popular music and Hollywood. Most modern audiences would be strongly repelled, I have no doubt, by the grotesque physical appearance of nineteenth-century Minstrel: white performers, blacked up, with great exaggerated lips, dressed either in the ragged rube costume of the iconic 'Jim Crow' or the dandified 'Zip Coon', delivering 'nigger' songs and comic monologues in a set pidgin-English mode, such as in this typical preacher's parody:

Belobed black brodren, me tend to dress my scorce to you dis nite on de all imported subject of language, an de various tongues ob difern nations and niggars, libbin and dead, known and unknown, an in so doing me shant stan shilly shally bour preface to de subject, but run bang at him at once like mad bull at 'dam haystack . . .'

In historical terms, it was a white clown and comic-song writer named George Nichols who reputedly first wrote down the antics of 'an old darky in New Orleans' nicknamed 'Old Corn Meal', and it was another white performer, Thomas ('Old Daddy') Rice, who first danced the step known as 'Jim Crow' back in 1830. The first minstrel troupes were considered to be Dan Emmett's quartet of Virginia Serenaders and Edwin Christy's Original Christy Minstrels, in 1841. There were soon dozens, and later hundreds of minstrel troupes performing all over the US, and the Virginia Serenaders toured Europe and serenaded Queen Victoria in Windsor Castle, spreading the craze far and wide. Dan Emmett composed many of Minstrel's distinctive songs, such as 'De Boatmen's Dance', 'Dandy Jim from Caroline', 'Root Hog or Die', 'Turkey in de Straw' and many more, including what became, somewhat to his chagrin, the South's anthem, 'Dixie', which Emmett wrote as a slave's dream of a mythical land of freedom: 'Den hoe it down an scratch yoa grabble / To Dixie Lann I'm bound to trabble / Whar de rake an hoe got double trigger / An white man jiss as good as niggar!'

New historians of Minstrel, such as William J. Mahar and Dale Cockrell, have shown that early minstrel performers had a complex and ambivalent relationship with their sources and material, and, in the early years of the genre, deployed their acts to satirize and lampoon white attitudes as well as black foibles, real or imagined. George Washington Dixon, a circus performer, began highlighting the dandy character Zip Coon in the 1830s, turning the black caricature around to refer, as his audiences grasped at the time, to the grievances of poor whites. Zip Coon as President was as bizarre a notion as the economically depressed whites aspiring to high office and power. The burnt-cork white also reminded audiences of the prevalence of racial mixing among the lower classes of society. Midway through the nineteenth century, Mahar notes, New York's Five Points district was the 'most racially integrated milieu in antebellum New York', and he quotes a contemporary cleric who observed 'a motley multitude of men and women, yellow and black, black and dingy, old and young . . .' The word 'yellow' referred, in this context, to persons of mixed race. The further presentation in Minstrel of blacked-up men playing black or mixed-race women in drag, and their songs of courtship, failed marriage and death, could make the experience of watching Minstrel disturbing rather than necessarily reassuring white audiences about their superior status, in this image of the world turned upside down.

As for the musical sources, Dale Cockrell, a Professor of Musicology, demonstrates with sheet music of the period that the tunes played by minstrel performers derived not only from slave songs with identifiably African rhythms – which would later become sources of the blues – but also from European material – celtic jigs and Italian popular operas – which these acts often lampooned. The slaves' own music often carried influences from white immigrant tunes, and blackface frolics themselves had more antecedents than purely the African, resembling also masquerades and the 'Lord of Misrule' revels of Dutch and German rituals. As ever, music has no 'pure' origins but is more often than not syncretic, a mixture of sources, influences and the individual likes and quirks of composers and performers.

This is significant, if we want to understand the type of music, dance and popular entertainment prevailing during the period in which Mae West grew up. As far back as we wish to go in American variety, we find the minstrel chords echoing loudly. In the 1890s and into the new century, the predominant musical form was ragtime. Everybody was at it, from the headliners to the closing acts of vaudeville shows. The ubiquitous Ned Wayburn, back when he spelled his name with an 'e', in 1897, was introduced as a 'singer of Negro Melodies and "Rag Time" Pianist', the *Milwaukee Daily News* announcing: 'Ned C. Weyburn sings a number of negro songs to rag-time music, which, by the way, is attracting considerable attention nowadays . . .' In the same year, star performer May Irwin was reported to have engaged 'that past master of the science of syncopation, Ned Wayburn, to play the piano accompaniments of her coon songs'.

It should be noted that in the period of Minstrel black performers appeared, too, as 'Ethiopian' troupes, inaugurating the peculiar convention, which allegedly so confused little Mae West, that even black actors and actresses had to black up for the stage. The Brooker and Clayton Georgia Minstrels was an all-black troupe active in the 1860s. Black people also formed enthusiastic audiences for minstrel shows, whether performed by whites or blacks. As Minstrel waned and ethnic shows, with dialogue and music, subsumed it, black performers began forming companies along the lines of Harrigan and Hart. Performances of Harriet Beecher Stowe's *Uncle Tom's Cabin*, predominantly by blackface whites, began featuring black players, musicians and singers around the 1870s. The Hyers sisters, Anna Madah and Emma Louise, produced a number of African-American stage plays, such as *Out of Bondage*, although the language spoken was still close to the minstrel patois. White theatrical showman Sam T. Jack formed a black Creole Burlesque Show in 1890, with a male impersonator, Florence Hines, as interlocutor – an inversion of the minstrel inversion.

In 1901, the august *New York Times* was discussing, under the heading of 'Americanism in Music', the proposition by no less an authority than Antonín Dvořák that 'we adopt as ours the melodic idiom of the negro song. There is merit in the suggestion,' wrote the author, W. J. Henderson, 'in so far as it touches upon the truth that this idiom has grown up in this country, partly from assimilation of elements to be found in European and Asiatic music, and partly from the natural musical tendencies of the negro, inherited from African ancestry. Furthermore, the characteristics of negro music have a potent fascination for the American mind.' Consideration of black music by white intellectuals was therefore already present, and black classical musicians, such as the Englishman S. Coleridge Taylor, described in *The Times* as 'leader of the Handel Musical Society', championed the cause of 'original negro' melodies and denounced American 'coon songs' as 'the worst sort of rot'.

In New York City, with a population of 60,000 African-Americans in 1900 and a small black middle class, a few black entertainers rose to general prominence. Bob Cole and the Johnson brothers produced *A Trip to Coontown* in 1897, and the aforementioned May Irwin popularized a number of their songs in white vaudeville. Cole and Johnson presented a vaudeville act in which they sang a German song, played Paderewski's Minuet, performed soft-shoe dances and then played their own material. Another cross-over success was Ernest Hogan, who performed as 'The Unbleached American' and won fame and fortune with his 1895 hit song 'All Coons Look Alike to Me'. The terminology strikes us as pretty dreadful, but it was at the time favoured over the pejorative 'nigger'. Hogan was a mentor to two younger black performers, Bert Williams and George Walker, who performed their celebrated double-act Williams and Walker between 1898 and 1908. It was in this format that Mae West would have encountered Williams, if she encountered him at all before he joined the Ziegfeld Follies in 1910. At that point, Williams became a major star, thrust forwards by the inveterate Ziegfeld against the objections of many of his white actors, although Williams still had to use the tradesmen's entrance to enter the hotel in which the players stayed.

Bert Williams's signature tune was 'Nobody', which he performed with a melancholy thrust that survives in the scratchy recordings of his time. He participated in the Follies' signature sketches with the likes of Will Rogers, Eddie Cantor and W. C. Fields, but he was most known for his solo deliveries, either of song or monologue, standing stock still in the centre of the stage with a spotlight upon his made-up face. As Williams and Walker, the duo also produced a series of musical plays: *The Sons of Ham* in 1900, *In Dahomey* in 1902, *Abyssinia* in 1906 and *Bandanna Land* in 1907.

In the evolution of popular music, Williams and Walker's shows provided a synthesis between old European styles of operetta and the new music which would come to be known as 'jazz'. Black musical theatre was a form in which African-American performers sought to break away from Minstrel, not by returning to primary ethnic roots but by the familiar mixing of styles.

This world of black theatre may well have been distant to Mae West, although the plays had long runs, supported by white as well as black audiences, during the years when she was learning her craft. But it was no coincidence that her early vaudeville career, as covered in the stage press from 1912 onwards, was based on a repertoire of ragtime songs. On 25 May 1912, *Variety* noted of her first solo act that she 'sings rag melodies and dresses oddly'. Her songs included 'Parisienne', 'Dancing-Prancing' and 'Rap Rap Rap'. In October, she sang 'Everybody's Ragtime Crazy' at the major hall of Hammerstein's, New York. The critics had seen it all before. 'She's one of the frank persons on the vaudeville stage,' wrote 'Sime' Silverman of *Variety*, 'where freakishness often carries more weight than talent, but Miss West should be coached to derive the full value from her personality.'

It was as unusual, therefore, for Mae West to sing black music as it is for present-day white youngsters to stockpile black hip-hop CDs. Among vaudevillians, as we have seen, it was the norm. But it was what Mae made of these all-pervasive influences that marked her, soon enough, as something special.

'I Always Wanted Attention . . .'

Matters of great cultural moment were not, however, weighing down upon the sixteen- or seventeen-year-old Mae West contemplating a professional life on the stage. Encouraged and spoiled rotten by her mother, the girl who would only accept the one doll in a hundred or sent her uncles out on a neighbourhood raid to net the only dog she fancied must have been quite a handful at home. Papa John West does not seem to have put up much resistance to his daughter being allowed to work out her own life, though we are told that he threw verbal fits when Mae stayed out at night to play with the boys. Despite the stench of the cigar fumes and his quick temper, Mae wrote that 'he was never in any way unkind to us . . . and never laid a punishing hand on any of his children.' Battlin' Jack reserved his testosterone moments for hammering such local pests as 'the Iron Man of Dutchtown . . . beat him so terribly that the man had to have thirty-two stitches taken in his iron head'.

It is the bane of biographies, which are supposed to be factual, that skimpy material culled from often shaky memories is too often filled in with fictional speculation in order to make sense of inconvenient lapses. Were Mae West's parents that understanding or so lax in an era of strict parental concern? Could there have been economic circumstances that, despite the veneer of relative wealth, required the elder daughter to earn her way as soon as she was qualified to do so? We do not know. What we do have are snippets of personal information granted by the later, famous Mae West to newspaper and magazine writers.

One of the earliest clippings is from the September 1928 issue of *The Brooklyn Home Builder*. There, adhering to Mae's contemporary dating of her birth to 1900, the article repeats the claim that 'at eight she joined the Hal Clarendon Stock Company at the Gotham Theatre in East New York, and got her first contract for five years.

She was to play whatever child parts there were . . . Imagine, if you can, Mae West playing little Eva to a grease-painted Uncle Tom . . .' As this clipping is from Mae's own personal files, the annotations are often significant. A reference further on in the article to Mae having learnt 'acrobatics in vaudeville' has been crossed out by her own hand. Many years later she was not so meticulous, telling various tales of her physical prowess, such as lifting 500-lb weights. But it was not till the point of her highest fame in movies, in 1934, that Mae began loosening up about her teenage years, most convincingly to interviewer Ruth Biery in *Movie Classic* concerning that difficult period in which 'Mae began to turn from child to woman':

'I was neither one thing nor the other. There's no place on the stage for that in-between age. My mother took me to Ned Wayburn for dancing lessons, and she got private teachers for me.

'Of course there were boys. We were just kids. To tell you the truth –' she stopped to think – 'not one of 'em made enough impression on me over the other to remember anything particular about 'em.

'I always wanted to be admired. I was crazy about admiration. I wanted 'em all to like me and I guess they did. In school, there had been a schoolteacher. He was awful handsome. He got me to stay after school. I helped to correct paper and things. I was too young to feel anythin', you know. But I liked it because he was payin' me attention. I always wanted attention.'

In her autobiography, and later confirmed to John Kobal, Mae gave the name of her first boyfriend as Joe Schenk (or Schenck). She told Kobal: 'He was about seventeen and I was fourteen. He was a pianist and he had his own ragtime band, and Saturday nights they'd come up to our house to rehearse. But I had an awful lot of boyfriends in those years at home, Joe was just the first in long pants. I always had maybe one girlfriend at a time, but I wasn't much of a woman's woman. Even then. My sister, Beverly, was a lot younger than I was, so we never had much in common as children. But later we were very close.'

Young Joe was later to become one half of a famous vaudeville act, Van and Schenck. He was not the same Joseph Schenck who, as a booking manager for Loews theatres, was later said to be an ardent but unsuccessful suitor. In her autobiography, Mae gave Joe's age as nineteen and dated their liaison to around the time she was deciding to go on the stage with an older family friend, thirty-year-old actor William Hogan. Mae's mother Tillie, Mae claimed, advised her to 'divide my attention among several boys . . . "I don't think, Mae, that you should become too serious, or go too steady, with any one boy in particular."' 'Yes, Mama,' replies Mae. In this department, she was only too happy to oblige.

The next boyfriend 'in long trousers' was named as Otto North, a young light-heavyweight boxer who, Mae said, belonged to a local gang, the Eagle's Nest. A subsequent fight with a rival gang, the Red Hooks, drew her father into the fray. 'Poor Otto couldn't kiss good for a week,' Mae wrote. 'As Papa said, he forgot to duck.'

The pattern of her life, Mae wrote, was established, the male sex crowding round her 'without so much as my having to raise my voice. This is not ego, saying this; just a fact.'

That much we can truly believe. We cannot be certain exactly when Mary Jane West, the Stock Company actress, became a fully fledged vaudevillian, though the New York census of 1910, which shows her still domiciled with her parents and lists her profession as 'actress, vaudeville', indicates a date prior to April that year. The name of William Hogan, alas, does not figure in the published lists of vaudeville or burlesque players and acts in the stage weeklies of the era. There was a William Hogan in the 1920s, a musician in black jazz groups in Chicago. But chummy as he might have been with big stars like Bert Williams, it is not credible that John West or his wife Tillie would have sent their seventeen-year-old off with a black performer, nor would such a mixed act be possible at that time – or decades later, for that matter – in America.

The chronology suggests that Mae launched into professional show business some time in 1909, when, as she mentioned before, she was sixteen years old and could legally perform. The earliest available printed mention of her name, however, dates from 3 June 1911, in a *Variety* review of the 'Big Gaiety Company', which was 'organized in January to open the new Eastern Burlesque Wheel theatre, Columbia, Chicago. The Censoring Committee or some other people concerned,' wrote 'Sime' Silverman, *Variety*'s founder-cum-editor-cum-chief reviewer, 'switched the show's opening at the last minute to Cincinnati, on the ground that the show was not eligible to have the distinction of inaugurating an important new theatre.'

This was emphatically not the big time. The centre of the show, *Variety* reported, was a 'two-act piece called "A Florida Enchantment,"' which was, all in all, 'pretty bad . . . The cast has no principal women to talk about. The only likely looking one is May West, who joins with Fred Wallace in an olio turn. Miss West may develop. The first step towards that end would be a course in enunciation. Of the songs sung by her and Mr. Wallace, no words were distinguishable. They have a neat enough act for the environments, although they draw "The Draggy Rag" pretty close to the line in the style of execution. Miss West's tights worn in the acts are superfluous in this show. The chorus girls wear tights pretty steadily. The dressing of the sixteen choristers is the single point that seems to have received any attention. The clothes look ever so much better than the girls in them.'

Burlesque was classified apart from vaudeville as traditionally the rougher, tougher and more risqué form of popular theatre, performed to less discerning crowds. In social esteem, it stood somewhere between 'Polite Vaudeville' and the cruder form of the freak show or 'Dime Museum', which was still prevalent at the turn of the century. Bearded women, 'dog-boys' and 'missing links' vied with geeks or 'wild men', among whom the young Ehrich Weiss, who morphed into Harry Houdini, plied his early trade. Burlesque was the domain of extravagant melodrama, plays and sketches which had to feature teams of high-kicking girls, fully-fleshed and buxom, the Burlesque queens who could be collected on cigarette cards, sometimes with *commedia dell'arte* costumes or with as scanty a costume as legally possible. Burlesque featured Sandow the strongman and 'Little Egypt', real name Fahreda Mahzar Spyropolos, who introduced the traditional oriental belly dance as the 'hootch', thus providing one of amateur-night Mae's alleged song offerings: 'Mariutch Make-a the Hootch-a-ma-Kootch'. But burlesque also showcased and introduced many of America's later-to-be-great entertainers, from W. C. Fields, whose first long run was as a juggler with Fred Irwin's Burlesquers, through Will Rogers, Ed Wynn, Bert Lahr, Leon Errol, Jimmy Durante and many more. Eva Tanguay had passed through burlesque in the Salome dance craze, which led to burlesque's eventual mutation into the modern striptease.

The dearth of records of Mae West's career in this period from 1909 to 1910 is reflected by the lack of material in her own newly available archive, which contains very little data preceding her Broadway plays of the late 1920s. It is said that folders and scrapbooks of this early period were damaged beyond repair when her

apartment in Los Angeles was flooded at some unspecified date. There is indeed evidence of water damage to some early scrapbooks, but we are left to speculate that Mae might have destroyed these records, choosing only to keep the evidence of her more successful years. Her concealment, until 1935, of her early marriage to fellow performer Frank Wallace might have played a part in this disappearance, as early records might show the extent of their joint life on the stage.

It is clear, however, that Mae never forgot the burlesque choruses, the mighty 'Beef Trust' ladies, who were to appear in the very first scene of her 1934 movie *Belle of the Nineties* and to cause connniptions in the censorial Hays Office. And the plays of her auteur Broadway period reveal many echoes of that brawling, vivid, seedy and sometimes dangerous world of women performers at the bottom of the ladder. In December 1910, *Variety*, approaching Christmas, reflected about the fate of burlesque in the coming season through 1911:

To the majority of burlesque managers there is credit due for making the effort to uplift burlesque to a plane where it belongs . . . There will always be a demand for a suggestiveness, or possibly the use of double-meaning talk, risqué business, or blue songs, so long as the houses devoted to burlesque cater to stag audiences. It is not necessary to 'clean up' burlesque, however, to the extent of absolute purity to bring it under the caption of a clean show. In many cases it is the manner in which such material is used that makes it unclean. The uplifting of burlesque has been more noticeable among the shows of the Columbia Amusement Circuit, or what is known as the Eastern Burlesque Wheel . . .

'Advanced' or 'clean' burlesque was a holy grail which reformers were continually pursuing, usually against the grain of audiences, who largely adored the 'blue' stuff, just as audiences thirty years later made Paramount Pictures richer the more they received the less adulterated, less censored Mae West. For the moment, however, the new burlesque showgirl was still struggling to find her voice.

William Hogan, according to Mae's own reminiscences, was playing a juvenile act, dressed up as 'Huck Finn', with an old German-style comedy red wig and 'painted freckles . . . blacking out his two front teeth'. Mae joined him as a 'Sis Hopkins' character: 'I was the girl friend – sunbonnet, lace drawers and all – I screamed when he showed me his worm.' There is no trace of this act in the records, but it may well have been one of the thousands of small-time acts that never registered on the formal Vaudeville Route lists.

During one of these tours, Hogan and West shared the bill at the Waldo Casino in Canarsie with a young song-and-dance man named

Frank Szatkus, performing under the name of Frank Wallace. Mae and Frank took a shine to each other and began to tour together, leaving William Hogan to imitate Huck Finn in a red wig alone. On 11 April 1911, Mae and Frank got married in Milwaukee.

Of the foregoing two paragraphs, only the last sentence is firmly rooted in fact. Our only knowledge of the genesis of Mae and Frank Wallace is due to the unravelling of Mae's subsequent concealment and then denial of her marriage for many years. This subterfuge ended in April 1935, at the height of Mae's Hollywood fame, when Frank Szatkus/Wallace emerged out of obscurity with a marriage certificate to claim his dues as the husband of the great film star and eventually sue for half her fortune. The succession of court cases and intense press coverage of the story lasted for over three years.

The fullest description by Wallace of his meeting with Mae is contained in a clipping from her 1935 scrapbook (by this time Mae was keeping everything):

Back in 1909 I was playing a single at the Canarsie Music Hall in Brooklyn on the Fox circuit. Joe Leo, now a Fox executive, was the head of the circuit.

One day after my performance a swell-looking woman came around back stage and told me she had a daughter who was a comer. She had seen my act, she said, and thought I could help her kid.

Well, she brought the kid in, and I want to tell you she was one classy little dame. The brunette youngster was Mae West. Her mother talked with a German accent.

Mae was a sweet little kid, a brunette about 16. I took her mother up and we went into rehearsal – in the cellar of her Bushwick Avenue home.

She worked hard. She did a song and dance, and the first song she did was 'Lovin' Honey Man.'

She also sang the song, 'When My Marie Sings My Chiddee Biddee Bee,' and also the song 'Jealous,' which aided her climb.

After a few weeks' rehearsal we went on the Fox circuit. Later . . . we were playing at the Gaiety in Milwaukee when Mae and I decided to make it double. Ada Woods, who worked with Gus Fox, was the bridesmaid. Ada made that line famous – 'I drink my sandwich and eat my beer.'

A newspaper woman in Milwaukee said we were two of the cleanest kids seen in that town for a long time. That was in April, 1911.

We got along swell for a year and were back in New York when Mae (who was good) was offered a single act contract at $350 a week. She asked my advice. I said, 'Take it. Go on up the ladder and good luck.' Then

I went back to my single and I was doing a single until six years ago when Miss La May and I teamed up . . .

Mae and I got along very well. We were deeply in love. At least I was and still am. But she was kept traveling. We were only kids. I was a dance man. She liked to sing and dance. I liked Broadway. She liked to travel and they kept her going, always breaking in new acts. She got better prospects and we just drifted apart. There was no part for me. I suppose there still isn't.

There is some good reason for taking Frank Wallace (not Fred as he was erroneously called by *Variety* in their review of the 'Big Gaiety Show') at his word, as he was desperately trying to present as convincing and credible a case as he could in the full glare of the press and the witness box. During the months of publicity, one element of Wallace's story was particularly odd, his description of Mae as a brunette. Could it be that the Queen of Sex was not a natural blonde?! Critics seized on this to pooh-pooh the whole story. William Morganstern, producer of Mae's play *Sex*, claimed he was certain that 'Mae never was in Milwaukee in 1911,' and added: 'Don't forget there was a different Mae West in burlesque. I knew her. She was a brunette – weighed about 135 to 140 and was about twenty years old in 1913.' Of course, since Mae was telling everybody she had been born in 1900, such a confusion was possible, though, as research has discovered, there was a wholly separate May West in burlesque, active in the mid-1920s. 'Mae of the movies was never a brunette,' insisted Morganstern. 'Why don't you ask Ned Wayburn? He taught her to dance.' The intrepid interviewer trotted over to Mr Wayburn, who responded to the query of whether Mae was blonde or brunette: '"Neither." He pointed at a girl. "Oh, Miss! You in the corner. Stand up please." The girl rose. "That's just about the color Mae's hair was. Judge for yourself." The girl's hair could have been called either very light brown or rather dark blonde. But she certainly wasn't a brunette.'

Of course, there was the confusion of the two Frank Wallaces, one of whom later performed in Mae's *Diamond Lil* – or were they one and the same? It was nevertheless odd for Wallace to claim the Mae he married was not blonde when he was trying to convince the world of his *bona fides*. Over the long passage of time, the prosecution wavers and drifts. Photographs of the time are not conclusive. And some women's secrets are sacrosanct . . .

The fact of the marriage, however, was not in doubt, and Mae – faced with the published marriage certificate – eventually had to come clean, admitting in July 1937 that the nuptials were genuine. The local registrar, F. A. Kraft MD, and County Clerk Martin Plehn certified that Frank Wallace and Mae West were 'joined in Marriage on the 11th day of April 1911 in accordance with the laws of the State of Wisconsin', witnesses being one Arthur Shutkin of Milwaukee and one Etta H. Wood of Newark, NY. Both bride and groom gave their domicile as Brooklyn, NY, and their occupations as Actor and Actress. Frank's parents are given as Joe and Anna Wallace, both born in Russia. Mae's parents' birthplaces are given as New York for John West and France for her mother, whose name is spelled Matilda Dilker. Frank was twenty-one years old and Mae eighteen.

Frank Wallace described the happy day in a gushing interview with the *New York Daily Mirror* published on 12 May 1935:

I couldn't sleep the night before I married Mae West. She had promised herself to me. Tomorrow we were to be man and wife . . . All I did was dream and then I would suddenly awake with a start. Flashes of – Mae; the future; a home; children; I could stand it no longer, I jumped out of bed . . .

Breakfast took on a festive air. As we feasted on our doughnuts and coffee, she said:

'Are you happy, Frank?'

'How could you ask, Honey?' I replied.

'If you feel the same way as I do,' she whispered, 'then I'm sure you are.'

'Hurry, Mae,' I urged. 'I can't wait until we see that preacher . . .'

With that we left our coffee and hurried downtown. I must admit that I was nervous. The clerk seemed to understand our feelings and tried to make things as easy as possible for us . . .

When all the questions were answered, the clerk gave us a license and told us that we could be married right away . . .

We rushed to the theatre to get back in time for a rehearsal of some new numbers . . . After the rehearsal we sought our mutual friend, Etta Woods . . . 'You lucky kids,' she cried, 'come let's hurry to the city hall or we will be too late . . .'

Breathlessly, we rushed into Judge Cordes chambers. 'Will you marry us?' gasped the three of us.

The judge looked at us funny and we looked at Etta and we all laughed . . . 'Which of you girls is going to marry this man?' joked the judge.

'Me, me,' said Mae, seriously.

The judge arose from his chair, taking his time, adjusted his glasses, took a black book in hand and beckoned us to stand in front of him . . .

'Do you take this man, to be your lawful wedded husband?' he asked of Mae.

'I do,' she replied as sweetly and tenderly as though she were telling me that she loved me.

'Do you take this woman to be your lawful wedded wife?' the judge directed at me.

I couldn't answer, the words were stuck inside of me. I finally managed: 'I do, I do.'

'I now pronounce you man and wife,' said the the judge.

'Oh, I'm so happy,' I heard her say.

'So am I,' was what I whispered to her.

But youth's wedded bliss did not last very long.

Frank Wallace and Mae, 1911

34

'There is Never Enough Hot Water in the Dressing Rooms

In the 1930s, the revelation of Mae's marriage to Frank Wallace was a blow to her image on two counts. First was the legal tangle that arose from the fact that they had separated but never divorced. This could be dealt with by parting with the appropriate legal fees. The second blow was more damaging: the combined revelation of Mae's true age, with seven years added to the previous estimate, and the demolition of the myth of Mae as sexually mature, carefree and free-loving from the start, the *sui generis*, worldly-wise temptress.

Speaking of some unnamed beau in her four-part extended interview for *Motion Picture* magazine in 1934 before the whistle blew, Mae had told Ruth Biery: 'He wanted to marry me. He didn't want me to work. You know, he wanted *all* of me. I was so young . . . I wanted both – marriage and a career. For the first time in my life, I couldn't have my own way . . . My mother said he wasn't good enough for me . . .' This swain was not in the acting profession, Biery wrote, 'he was tall and dark – connected with some firm in the sales branch, Mae once told me. All about her were men of importance in her own profession. Men who loved her, who wanted her. Men have always wanted Mae West. She was *born* that type of woman . . . She ran away from New York, she ran away from love. She ran away from herself . . .'

She ran away from reality. This was par for the course in show business. It should not surprise anyone to realize that, aged eighteen, Mae had no idea of the myths she would eventually weave. On the road, in burlesque, with a much older partner, it is not unreasonable to accept that Mama West would have preferred proper matrimony with a young man her own age or that Mae should have fallen in love with a brash young blade who obviously knew the ropes in the business.

Of sex, her great expertise to come, Mae told John Kobal, in 1970, more candidly than she had spoken before: 'We never used any swearing or discussed sex at home . . . I never talked about sex with my parents. Even today I don't like to discuss sex with my sister . . . I'd feel dirty. The way I heard about sex first came from a friend of mine when I was nine. Her mother was a doctor, and we were playing in her house one day and there was this book lying there on the table and after I read it I had a funny feeling about my parents. A peculiar feeling – disgust, you might say. It took a long time for me to get over it. They suddenly weren't gods anymore. Ohh, I wish they wouldn't teach sex in the schools. They should teach health. *Health* is what's important.'

Well, it certainly is more important than sex when you're seventy-seven, though Mae claimed that her concern with the well body did derive from early days, telling *Life*'s interviewer that 'I never cared to drink or smoke. As a child I used to see in a drugstore this face, one-half filled out nice, with hair and everything, and the other half all down in lines and everything from smoking. Very indelible impression.'

Mae told Kobal that she had had 'lots of affairs' before she married Frank Wallace, 'but they were just love affairs, not sex-love affairs . . . Not till I got married. Probably one of the reasons I did get married then was because of sex.' Against her own myth, Mae West, like so many women before and after her, married the first boy she had sex with.

On the road with the show, out of sight of her parents, Mae claimed that her marriage was kept secret from her mother 'till the day she died'. This directly contradicts Frank Wallace's own testimony and appears unlikely. But as Tillie West died before the 1934 revelations, we cannot pin down the truth on that line. We can only return to a reasonably convincing image of Mae, conventionally accompanied by a *bona fide* husband in the burlesque world of rough and tumble.

Bernard Sobel, show-business press agent from Ziegfeld to Hollywood, has provided one of the most vivid descriptions of the typical burlesque performance:

As soon as the doors of the theatre open, everyone rushes in, crowding, shoving, cussing, laughing and adding his personal share of uproar to the general hurly-burly.

The ushers, alert to any emergency, quickly show patrons to their seats, and a policeman or two keep their eyes open for anything that might happen.

Suddenly the tumult gives way to a respectful silence when the candy butcher – whose wares also include music, pornographic literature and pictures – walks up the aisle and takes his place at the center of the theatre in front of the orchestra railing . . .

Sometimes it was necessary for the omnipresent cop to rap the railing with his billy club to get the audience to simmer down, particularly during the performance when the chorus girls pour on the stage:

Everyone goes into a paroxysm of catcalls, hooting, jeers, applause, wolf whistles and growing admiration.

At first glance the ladies appear to be visions of beauty. More critical observation, however, reveals heavy coatings of lipstick and rouge, copious applications of hair dye, and somewhat shaggy facial assets.

The opening chorus goes something like this: 'College girls, college girls, we are the college girls . . .'

Or, as portrayed in Mae's own *Belle of the Nineties* of 1934, going back to the 1890s and the 'Beef Trust Chorus' girls kicking high their massive thighs, belting out their song:

> *Here we are*
> *The beauties of the town*
> *The suckers buy us wine*
> *In cabarets we dine*
> *We sit and chat*
> *And what comes after that?*
> *Pom Tiddley Om Pom*
> *Pom Tiddley Om Pom*
> *Pom Tiddley Om Pom Pom!*

Even Joseph Breen of the Hays Office understood where this was leading and had it cut short on the screen. Mae's own act with Frank Wallace came on, as the Big Gaiety review revealed, in the 'olio', the section of the show usually performed after the interval in front of the curtain. As Sobel wrote:

The audience listened reverently while the vocalist sobbed out one of the many sentimental songs which were the popular musical fare of the day . . . how a beautiful, virtuous girl was undone by a predatory villain, while the sickly sweet picture showed her dying, with her illegitimate child nestling in her helpless arms.

Oddly enough, although almost every man in the audience was concerned with actually, imaginatively, or vicariously getting one of the dames in the show into bed with him, the story of the virtuous girl's downfall reduced most of the gentlemen to tears . . .

'Added Attractions' also included the hootch dancers, 'coon shouters' and retired prizefighters like Jim Jeffries or James Corbett, who presented monologues on their most famous fights or re-enacted them on the stage. 'The Sensational New Hula Hula Dance and Jack Johnson, Champion of the World' was a typical sample.

The more rarefied world of vaudeville was a considerable step up from this, but even there, as Mae herself noted, quoting the famous Nora Bayes, who commented about the changing nomenclature from 'Polite Vaudeville' to 'Advanced Vaudeville' to 'Fashionable Vaudeville', 'No matter what they call it there is never enough hot water in the dressing rooms.'

Secured from unwanted 'Pom Tiddley Om Pom' by her marriage with Wallace, Mae toured the burley-cue circuits through the summer of 1911 with the 'Big Gaiety Show'. The company eventually arrived to play in New York, and Mae was obviously eager to find some way to climb further up the show-business ladder. In her own account, she went to see the great Florenz Ziegfeld, who 'had a fine show in the New York roof and he said he wanted me in it. But I didn't like this type of theatre. It's too big, too wide, there isn't much chance for a personality . . . I wouldn't be seen to my best advantage by the entire audience at the same time.' This account is what is known as 'hutzpah', to be filed in the 'if only' department. More credibly, Mae wrote that she visited her dancing teacher, Ned Wayburn, who was producing the show. Even here Mae pours on the olive oil, relating how she examined the West 46th Street Fulton Theatre to see if it matched her standards. Its gilt balconies, deep red boxes and intimate atmosphere fitted the type of place she had played in the stock companies. 'The theatre is fine and I'll be in your show,' Mae told Wayburn.

In reality, the show that gave Mae her début on the legitimate stage, *A La Broadway*, was not a Ziegfeld show but an independent production, mounted by Henry B. Harris and Jesse Lasky and written by William LeBaron. Both Lasky and LeBaron would be key figures in Mae West's future. Within two years of this theatrical encounter, Jesse Lasky, in alliance with his brother-in-law, an ex-glove salesman named Shmuel Gelbfish, a. k. a. Samuel Goldfish, soon to be Goldwyn, and the playwright Cecil B. DeMille were to found a movie-making company which, in merger with Adolph Zukor's Famous Players and distributor W. W. Hodkinson, was to become the Paramount empire. In 1911, Lasky was a vaudeville producer who had begun his theatrical life playing the cornet and had most recently presented a 'snappy musical comedy', *The Photo Shop*. Lasky had raised money to open a new enterprise, named after the Paris *Folies Bergère*, in the centre of Manhattan's theatreland, the house that so impressed Mae West with its red plush and gilt balconies. (This theatre became the Fulton, later named the Helen Hayes, and is today the site of the Marquess Marriott hotel.)

William LeBaron, who wrote the show's centrepiece, was another young man heading upwards. Born in Elgin, Illinois, in 1883, he had studied at universities both in Chicago and New York, where he was 'bitten by the writing microbe and ... never got over it'. Making his living in advertising, he began to write plays, churning out the annual varsity show. The fourth of these, *The Echo*, was adopted by impresario Charles Dillingham for LeBaron's 'legitimate' theatrical début, after which he won a contract from Jesse Lasky to write 'all of his one-act comedies for vaudeville'. In 1916, he would become famous for a play called *The Very Idea*, a satire on the popular pseudo-intellectual fad of eugenics, based on the notion that 'only people who are physically and mentally fit should become parents'. He then followed Lasky into his Famous Players Lasky company and on into Paramount.

A La Broadway gave Mae West her first credit on the 'legitimate' stage, albeit at the bottom of the cast list. She played Maggie O'Hara, an Irish maid who gets planted on a rich family by a writer who wants her to take notes on their behaviour. Without the text, it is not possible to verify her claim that she spiced up the character, adding her own lines and cracks. The reviews were mixed. The *New York Dramatic Mirror* noted that 'the burlesque satirizes musical comedy in general by converting the usual love affair into a melodic narrative ... It is embellished with numerous songs and dances and with considerable wit. The idea, however, is not utilized to the best advantage, and the performance won only a modicum of approval.' Other notices, however, singled out Mae West, 'who played the part of a wise, flip maid. She danced in Turkish harem trousers in a most energetic, amusing and carefree manner.' The *New York Times* wrote: 'A girl named Mae West, hitherto unknown, pleased by her grotesquerie and a snappy way of singing and dancing.'

Alas for Mae, her début show only lasted for eight performances. Lasky and Harris's idea, to combine the theatre with a restaurant, did not attract enough paying guests. As *Variety* noted on 30 September:

FOLIES BERGERE EXPERIMENT REACHING
AN END TOMORROW

The new Revue at the Folies Bergère will close Saturday night. The revue production will be sent to the discard, with the exception of 'Hello Paris,' which may be seen in vaudeville . . . While it is claimed that the restaurant portion of the enterprise has yielded a profit, the scheme has proven itself impracticable owing to the limited seating capacity of the house under the present policy.

Lasky's 'intimate house', which had so impressed Mae as a venue, could not compete with the mass processing of Broadway's formula revues. Co-partner and investor Henry Harris took over the conversion of the house to a 'regular theatre'. Jesse Lasky was out, and *A La Broadway* with him. The show did, however, provide a hitherto unnoticed footnote to the annals of Mae West. Lasky had, he later wrote in his autobiography *I Blow My Own Horn*, scoured theatres in Europe for performers for his extravaganza, and:

At the Wintergarten in Berlin I found the Pender Troupe, eight acrobats on stilts, including a ten-year-old boy, whose stilts were so high that he had to be put on and taken off them from a ladder, and bend down to show his head under the proscenium. The lad's name was Archie Leach.

This sprite was to remain in the US and later change his name to Cary Grant, the unknown actor whom Mae West later claimed to have plucked from obscurity and set on the road to stardom, never having set eyes on him before. But, Lasky wrote, 'In later years when we were both working at RKO, Cary Grant reminded me that the ladder on which he started his climb to fame in this country was the one he used on forty-sixth street to mount his stilts.'

6

Very Violetta, Et Cetera

And what of Frank Wallace, the newly minted husband? We can recall his own account that he and Mae were together as a married couple for a year, from April 1911, until she was offered $350 a week for her single act. Mae claimed the split had gone the other way: a dancing job opened up with a 'big act' for the United Booking Office circuit, taking Frank out of her life for forty weeks. Either account would do. The primal passion had certainly cooled. Was it the sex? The love? The money? Mae told John Kobal in 1970: 'Frank kept on pressing me, making demands, wanting me to live with him instead of at home, but I wanted to be free. So I made up this story that my mother wanted me to do a single act 'cause she thought it would be good for my career . . . I had really gotten this offer to work for the Shuberts in a show.' This would date the break to the autumn of 1911, a bare six months after the marriage.

'Marriage and one man for life is fine for some people,' Mae told Kobal, 'but for me it wasn't any good. Every time I look at myself, I become absorbed in myself, and I didn't want to get involved with another person like that.' Besides, marriage meant children, and, as Mae said, 'I was my own baby. I had myself to do things for.'

As indeed she did. Despite her initial setback, opportunity soon knocked again for Mae. Within a few weeks of losing *A La Broadway*, she was cast again in a small part in another Broadway revue, a show named *Vera Violetta*.

Broadway, in the second decade of the century, had three principal popular formats: the annual Ziegfeld Follies and spin-off revues, rich in Ned Wayburn-style robot-girl choruses; European operettas, with composers like Victor Herbert and Rudolf Friml importing the fantasy Europe of Johann Strauss and Franz Lehar to America; and the robust flag-waving shows of George M. Cohan, most containing 'Broadway' in the title. Serious plays were, then as now, the domain

1

of 'off-Broadway' theatres, such as the Hudson, which had show-cased the Irish radical George Bernard Shaw, whose *Man and Superman*, in 1905, prompted Police Magistrate William McAdoo to declare that 'there was no room in New York for a play that ridiculed marriage'. The New Theatre at 62nd Street and Central Park West provided Shakespeare, Galsworthy, Sheridan *et al.* but would soon fail to pay its bills, becoming yet another venue for musicals.

These musicals provided an escape, in the words of Broadway chronicler Brooks Atkinson, 'into a never-never-land of innocent snobbery and bounteous wealth', an escape from the pressures and uncertainties of the new America of rising 'skyscrapers', Henry Ford's mass-produced 'Tin Lizzie', the promise, as yet unfulfilled, of new freedoms exemplified by women smoking, playing tennis and demanding Equal Suffrage, and unrest by male workers demanding their share. Divisions of race and class were as wide as ever, with newspaper headings of WOMEN SHOW PET DOGS IN WALDORF-ASTORIA vying with DIES OF STARVATION, TOO PROUD TO BEG.

There were home-grown playwrights at work of serious intent like David Belasco, or the brothers William and Cecil de Mille, who – like William Le Baron – would make their main mark elsewhere. The radical transgressions of Eugene O'Neill were not yet a gleam in the eye. The 'legitimate theatre' was safe for *The Prince of Pilsen*, *Mlle. Modiste* and *Piff! Paff! Pouf!!* – the latter two sporting the as yet unknown Mack Sennett warbling in the male chorus – or *Naughty Marietta*, the hit of 1910, inaugurating 'the Italian Street Song'.

In this vein the newly opened Winter Garden, built for theatrical moguls J. J. and Lee Shubert, was looking forward to its new winter extravaganza, combining *Undine*, a play by Manuel Klein, and the German Leo Stein's frothy *Vera Violetta*, adapted by Leonard Liebling and Harold Attridge.

The story of *Vera Violetta*, set originally in Paris, tells of a Russian princess who has lost all her property but is determined to live the high life in spite of a charmless, boring marriage:

VERA: I am a woman of fire – passion – temperament – and I married a piece of fromage . . . If only he would kick over the traces, flirt – show some signs of life – I'd forgive him, but it can't be done – he's a dead one.

This was not, alas, a role for Mae West but for Gaby Deslys, the French Eva Tanguay, who had, the *New York Dramatic Mirror* noted, 'acquired enough English to act and sing intelligibly in the language'. This was the least of Miss Deslys talents, as she already enjoyed a rapturous following in Europe since her Paris début in 1902. Like Lillian Russell, she was famous both on and off the stage, having reputedly enjoyed an affair with the King of Portugal, Manuel II. His gifts of fabulously expensive jewellery, her elaborate costumes and ornate hats inflamed the press and fashion magazines. *Variety*'s women's columnist 'The Skirt' waxed euphoric at her Winter Garden appearance: 'Gaby Deslys in "Vera Violetta" at the Winter Garden, shades all the women . . . A silver gown lined in emerald was a marvel but later when a coral colored gown completely covered in a bead fringe was worn, Gaby made every one sit up.'

Among the bedazzled was young Mae West, who could not fail to be impressed by the European star's lush wardrobe. In keeping with her status, La Deslys was suitably mercurial and jealous of her billing partners, to the extent that the show itself kept getting postponed, as *Variety* noted on 16 September:

The new Winter Garden show with Gaby Deslys as the star, will probably not open Sept. 25 as announced. Rehearsals are behind schedule, owing to several defections from the cast.

Among those to quit were Frank Tinney, William Simms, Louise Dresser and Leeds and Lamar, all having objected to the small parts assigned them. Outside of Mlle. Deslys, whose turn will consume over an hour, no one will have a part of any size. The new comers are Maud Raymond, Lydia Barry, Kate Elinore and Harold Crane.

And Mae West, who no doubt owed her booking to these mass defections and, once again, to Ned Wayburn, choreographer of the show. He had arranged a special ragtime dance for Miss Deslys and her dancing partner Harry Pilcer, the 'Gaby Glide', which would soon become a famous dance style, even performed, two decades later, by Mickey and Minnie Mouse. Another late engagement for the Winter Garden show was a new rising star, Al Jolson, plucked by the Shuberts from Lew Dockstader's Minstrels, where he had learned the blackface trade. Jolson provided 'his usual share of fun', crooning 'That Haunting Melody' and 'Rum Tum Tiddle'. He was, as yet, no threat to Mlle Deslys (whose real name, hidden in the folds of history, was the more prosaic Marie-Elsie-Gabrielle Claire).

Mae was hired to play Mlle Angelique, a cheeky dancer who

gives lessons in love-making. But, alas, the jinx of *A La Broadway* was active again, in a new form. The show was booked for an out-of-town preview at the Hyperion Theatre in New Haven, Connecticut, on the same weekend as a Yale–Princeton football game. At the Friday night show the Yale fans packed the theatre, whistling and cheering for the famous French star: 'With her famous rope of pearls dangling about her neck, Gaby conquered,' wrote the *New Haven Evening Register*. Some members of the audience were less enthusiastic and complained to the police that the play was 'vulgar and suggestive'. Demands were made to 'cut out the parts played by Gaby Deslys and May West', and there were 'other parts objected to on account of the clothing worn, which, I was told, wouldn't furnish material enough for a pocket handkerchief'. The show's producers agreed to cut some of the acts, and Saturday night's performance went ahead. The Yale fans, alas, had lost their game that afternoon and by nightfall were fairly well pickled. Their response to the show was so rowdy that stagehands tried to cool them down with a fire hose. This misfired and soaked some of the women attending in their weekend gowns, infuriating one young lady to the extent that, as the *Evening Register* put it, 'a wet hen was never madder. She decided to do something on her own hook and so started ripping out the seats in her row . . . other women joined in the destruction of the theatre property . . .' The police, however, moved in on the students, including those congregated outside the theatre, and New Haven rang to the merry sound of cop's clubs rapping against youthful craniums.

Some accounts related the cause of the students' rowdiness to confusion arising from Mae West's unexpected appearance in a costume imitating La Deslys' couture, which made the fans mistake her for the star. When the real star came on, the fans were confuddled, and when the show was cut short, they smashed the footlights and threw chairs on the stage. When the show arrived in New York, *Variety* noted:

After seeing 'Vera Violetta' at the Winter Garden, one can hardly blame the Yale boys at New Haven for having torn up the furniture of the Hyperion theatre there last Saturday . . . Yale lost to Princeton in the afternoon, and at the $3 price in the evening, the Yale boys were losers again.

THEATER WRECKING CASES ARE CONTINUED-DEAN JONES INSISTS THE STUDENTS DIDN'T DO IT ALL

At Odds Over Actions of Police in Theater Riot

CHIEF COWLES
Who Defends What His Men Did Saturday Night.

DEAN JONES
Who Declares Students Were Not Entirely to Blame.

M'NAY, AUTO RACER KILLED AT SAVANNAH

MAN WHO SMASHED LIGHTS WASN'T FROM COLLEGE, HE SAYS

Mayor Rice Declares He Will Investigate—Chief Cowles Tells Why He Didn't Police Theater and Eldridge Says He Will "Be the Goat."

MANY THREATS OF SUITS FILL THE AIR TODAY

Increasing probability of suits against the Hyperion by women, whose gowns were ruined by the stream from the hydrant turned on by stage hands, and of a suit by the Shuberts against the city, alleging lack of police protection; a continuance of all the student cases until Saturday in court, with rumors that a *nolle* might be entered then; a statement by Dean Jones, declaring that outsiders did as much damage as the students, if not more, word from Mayor Rice that he will make a thorough investigation of the affair, and a renewal of the argument between Chief Cowles and Manager Eldridge, were a few developments in the sensational wrecking of the Hyperion theater Saturday night. Although a large force of carpenters worked all night Saturday and all day Sunday, the theater could not be repaired sufficiently to allow for the staging of "The Wedding Trip" there tonight and it was postponed until tomorrow.

WHAT MAYOR SAYS

"I will make an investigation of the trouble and will have a conference with Chief Cowles as soon as possible. After this I will decide what to do."—Mayor Rice's statement today.

MGR. ELDRIDGE'S STATEMENT

"If New Haven wants a goat, I'll have to be it, I suppose, as everybody connected with the affair has gone." He further stated that the failure to announce the end of the performance lay with the manager of the company, as Mr. Eldridge had told him to do so before the show started.

"I tried to get to the stage before the trouble got started, but was met at the door by several men who knocked off my hat, nearly tore the clothes from my back and prevented me from getting back of the curtain."

DEAN CHITTENDEN WAITS

Director Chittenden of the Sheffield Scientific school said in regard to the trouble at the Hyperion:

"I am making no particular investigation of the trouble at the theater. I am waiting to see what the city court does in the case of Mr. Bomeisler of this department."

The cases of the eight men, six of whom were arrested after the roughhouse, were continued this morning in city court until Saturday, as the result of a conference last night between Assistant City Attorney Ierardi. Dean Jones of Yale and the men who were arrested took part.

The men held are as follows, with their bondsmen:

Walter J. Burns—Policeman Hoffman; bondsman, T. R. Blakeslee, 84 Norton street.

Charles H. Ridder—Policeman Stanford; bondsman, T. R. Blakeslee, 84 Norton street.

John L. Doggett—Policeman Kerrigan; bondsman, C. A. Bissell, 230 York street.

Louis Connick—Policeman Stanford; bondsman, T. R. Blakeslee, 84 Norton street.

Joseph N. Ewing—Policeman Stanford; bondsman, T. R. Blakeslee, 84 Norton street.

Norman H. Read—Policeman Kerrigan; bondsman, Alexander Troup, 80 Center street.

Louis Bomeisler—Policeman Kerrigan; bondsman, Alexander Troup, 80 Center street.

Samuel A. Dyer—Policeman Newberg; bondsman, Alexander Troup, 80 Center street.

The bonds in all the cases were fixed at $150, and when their cases were continued, this morning the bond was allowed to remain the same. All of the men arrested were charged with breach of the peace but Read and Connick, who are charged with obstructing policemen while in the performance of their duty.

NEW DEVELOPMENTS.

Many interesting incidents came to light today when the parties in the case were interviewed, not the least of which was that of an irate young lady who was wet by the stream from the fire hose, which Manager Eldridge declared was turned on by the stage hands without any orders from the management.

The young lady in the case got the

CLIPPING

45

The cast list reveals, however, that Mae West did not appear at the Winter Garden on opening night. *Variety*, on 25 November, published a brief note: 'Mae West, with the Winter Garden show out of the town, did not open in New York, having been stricken with pneumonia upon arriving in New York. She is expected back in the show before long.'

But though *Vera Violetta* ran for 112 performances, Mae West never rejoined the cast. Given Miss Deslys' history of jealousy, it is possible, as was rumoured, that Mae's *lèse majesté* in upstaging the star had got her sacked, turning her second try at the 'legit' theatre into another missed opportunity.

Gaby Deslys continued her starry trajectory in America and back to Europe's music halls. Her life story was to take a peculiar and dramatic turn during the First World War, when she apparently worked as a spy for the French government. She died in Paris of a 'throat infection' in 1920 at the age of thirty-nine.

Such were the circumstances surrounding the first riot allegedly provoked by Mae West – certainly not to be the last.

Mae returned, undaunted, to the grindstone. From *Variety*, 20 January 1912:

MAE WEST AND GIRARD BROS. SONGS AND DANCES. 10 MINS.
ONE. FIFTH AVENUE

She is now trying out a vaudeville act with the Girard Brothers, who are also said to have been in the Folies Bergère show [*A La Broadway*]. Miss West exhibits a nice wardrobe, wearing a nifty harem outfit at the close. She works hard. The boys dance well but their voices hold them back. Miss West is a lively piece of femininity but a cold prevented her from doing her best work. Miss West and the others need a lot of 'pop' circuit and 'big small time' work to put them in any kind of stride for faster company. The present frameup is not the strongest arrangement possible.

Mae had escaped burlesque, but only to put her foot on the lowest rung of standard vaudeville. The 'Girard Brothers', later the 'Gerard Boys', were, in fact, two young hoofers called Bobby O'Neill and Harry Laughlin. In her own account Mae had little to say about them, except for: 'I liked the boys. They were my type – men.' The important man in Mae's life at this point, however, was neither of these but her first proper theatrical agent, Frank Bohm.

In burlesque one might make one's own way under the umbrella of the big burlesque 'wheels', but vaudeville had long been a more streamlined business, controlled by the major circuits – Keith's, Poli's, Pantages – and their central booking agents. Frank Bohm, Mae wrote, had been recommended to her as a person with contacts and pull. He sat in his office, 'like a broken greyhound at his desk', with 'a slouch hat pushed to the back of his head'. The trick with the hat, Mae revealed, was typical of agents who kept lists of their acts and various memos tucked into the inner hatband. 'His attitude,' she wrote, was 'of a man who practiced complete indifference to everything,' though he was not, she related, indifferent to her. This was the period, Mae claimed, in which she enjoyed the romantic attentions both of Frank Bohm and his rival booking agent, Joseph Schenck, later to be the Hollywood producer of, among much else, Buster Keaton's silent films. She chose neither suitor, but, to use her own phrase, was calm and collected – a diamond ring from Mr Bohm.

The first tryout of the new act, Mae recalled, was in South Norwalk, Connecticut, another college town. 'The act went over very big,' she wrote. From the *New Jersey World*, 19 January:

The real surprise of the bill was a May West and Company. No one seems to have heard much of her, and inquiry showed she was new to the stage. But Miss West has a style and a willowy abandon that is intoxicating . . .

In March, the act reached New York, playing the American Roof, where a more detailed look at the new Mae in the limelight was offered by the stage journal *The Player*:

Mar 29 1912 – Mae West, late of the Folies Bergère, was seen at the American music hall in her new sketch, for which she herself wrote the lines and some of the music, and staged. She is assisted by two young men. It's a singing and dancing specialty strung together by witty lines and timely quips . . .

The little comedienne wore some stunning frocks. The first one was a black velvet, narrow skirt, bordered with black maribou; the corsage was of Persian silk and the slashed sides of the skirt revealed pink trouserettes. A black velvet bonnet with maribou band and shaded pink feathers high at the back, pink stockings, and gold slippers completed a dashing costume for the little blonde lady.

The second gown was of silver cloth draped up the front, bordered with silver fringe; it was a low-cut back and one shoulder left sleeveless, with the other a mere strap. Red trouserettes were worn and red satin slippers.

The last change was to a cloth of gold costume, also worn with red satin trouserettes and red slippers; this gown had a red satin high girdle with flat

Jap bow in the back and a gold bandeau was worn with it. But best of all, Miss West has natural style and a good understanding of stage effects.

Trailing the little lady to her dressing-room, I found her quite original and interesting. She talked freely and humorously, taking it seemingly as a joke to be interviewed. She told me:

'I have always lived in Brooklyn – I was born there; though my mother is a French woman. While fond of a stage life, I don't inherit the liking for it, as I have no relatives in the profession . . .'

It is interesting to note, at this point, the physical presence: Mae was always, despite the accretions of legend, a small woman, standing five feet five inches in flat shoes, and somewhat plump into the bargain. As audiences and critics would note, she had an ample bosom. The 'ideal' measurements of feminine pulchritude would be achieved either by the constraint of costumes or by the retouching of publicity photographs. Meanwhile, at the American Roof, *Variety*'s 'Sime' Silverman also caught up with the show, giving Mae a cautious welcome to the pantheon:

May West Monday evening was as far above the heads of the American Roof clientele as the roof was above the street. May is there. She's a wiggly sort of the rough soubret, who can let herself out, or keep herself in, and get it over. The wiser the house, the better May will go. The Gerard Boys are a couple of tall well dressed fellows (in evening clothes) who merely serve to surround Miss West, also fill in when she is changing. The three did a 'rag' on chairs that was a peach, and funny, but it will never show at Keith's, Philadelphia, though the remainder of the turn may get in there . . . What they did give however should get them a date at Hammerstein's.

A glance behind the scenes of the act is provided by Lew Garvey, manager of the Palace Theatre in New Haven, Connecticut, writing two decades later, in *Screen Play* magazine (September 1933):

The girl, I remember, was a tiny blonde, full of pep and vigor . . . At the Monday performance . . . things began to happen. The audience was composed mostly of Yale students and the trio was received with mild interest up to the very finale of the act . . . The finale was a song number, with the girl seated between the two boys on a bench. What they called in those far off days a 'rag' number.

As the song progressed through the verse, the three merely swayed in unison but as they swung into the chorus, I noticed the girl had begun a hip movement that quickly had that audience of Yale boys in a panic. It was something new to me and I realized that it was far too hot to ever get by in staid New Haven . . .

One would have thought Mr Garvey would have been aware of Mae's previous New Haven exploit, but, he wrote, it was the circuit manager, Mr Poli, who ordered 'the little lady to cut out the bench stuff and also to wear a dress a little less revealing in front. When I told her, she smiled and quietly agreed to comply. But at the evening performance, the news had spread and it seemed that every student at Yale was in the audience. The girl, inspired by such appreciation, forgot herself and cut loose again, hotter and hotter. The audience brought down the house, but I was furious.'

Mae noted this performance in her autobiography with the quoted headline: 'HER WRIGGLES COST MAE WEST HER JOB. Curves In Motion Shock Lou Garvey at Palace. Whole Act Fired.' 'I immediately removed her from the act,' wrote Garvey. 'I can see her yet, standing there contrite, dressed in a little tailored suit with her hands in her pockets and her little impudent face turned up to mine.

'"My dance is too far ahead of the time for you yokels," she said, "but you just wait. Some day they'll eat it up and I'll be famous."'

Meanwhile, during the same period as Mae's act with the Gerard Brothers, a rogue clipping from the 24 February 1912 edition of the *New Jersey Morning Telegraph* found in the Performing Arts archive suggests some strange antics in Newark:

SHOW GIRL . . . HEARD SMACKS – NEWARK N.J. FEBRUARY 23
May West, a former show girl, now a detective, figured prominently as a witness in the hearing today before Vice-Chancellor Stevens in the cross-suits for divorce brought by George M. Rusling and Nettie R. Rusling. The husband alleges infidelity and the wife charges abandonment. Rusling names A. D. Tooley, a Brooklyn restaurant keeper, as correspondent.

According to Miss West's testimony last March she was called upon to don her gum-shoes and solve a deep mystery. She was employed in the Rusling home, – 58 South Thirteenth Street, as a maid. Mrs Rusling, according to the testimony, didn't know that Miss West was a sleuth or she would have fired her in a minute.

Well, Miss West kept her ears open and, she said, heard loud smacks on several occasions.

Miss West yesterday produced a panel picture showing a man and woman kissing. It was entitled 'The Soul Kiss.' She testified that Mrs Rusling had directed her to hang it up, remarking that was the way she and the restaurant man kissed each other. Rusling alleged that on the evening of March 28 last, he and two men detectives hid in his garage until they got [a] signal from May West. They then entered the Rusling home . . .

Recalling the listing of Mae's father John West in the 1910 census as 'Detective', this raises the intriguing concept of Mae moonlighting for her father's business in a manner hitherto undiscovered. No other hints or indications of such activity have been found elsewhere, and this might-have-been career fizzled out.

Whatever else occurred early in 1912, it seems Mae was not yet convinced she should abandon her dreams of Broadway revue for vaudeville, as she is listed in April among the cast of *The Winsome Widow* at the 'Moulin Rouge' (formerly the New York Theatre, at Broadway and 45th). This was, at last, a Ziegfeld show, produced with impresario Charles Dillingham, a reworking of an 1891 play by Charles Hoyt called *A Trip to Chinatown*. The plot was clearly too slight to mention in the reviews – 'unnecessary grist for the Moulin Rouge', notes the *Dramatic Mirror*, highlighting instead the ice carnival and ballroom scenes, the gorgeous colour-coded costumes and the dancers who 'all appear to be fully qualified acrobats, for they do all the wiggles and twists permitted by the limitations of human anatomy'. Mae, wiggling with the rest, was sharing the stage with major players like Frank Tinney, Leon Errol and Emmy Wehlen ('the official prima donna'), although her role was another minor one, that of a 'baby vamp' named La Petite Daffy.

Critics gave the first night a mixed reception, the *New York World* calling it 'a tip-top show . . . never marred by unpleasant suggestiveness', but the *Dramatic Mirror* called it 'vagarious and disjointed', giving Mae the brief accolade of 'Mae West assaults the welkin vigorously.' *Variety*'s 'Sime' was much more grumpy, complaining about 'a poor performance, at least forty minutes too long, draggy, with superfluous people and songs and dances'. On our heroine, 'Sime' noted that she sang 'Piccolo' – 'a pretty melody, spoiled in the singing by Mae West, a rough soubret, who did a "Turkey," just a bit too coarse for this $2 audience'.

This time, Mae skipped voluntarily without being pushed – an odd decision, as the show continued for 172 performances. She appeared to have been following the advice of Frank Bohm, who had, as 'Sime' predicted, booked her into the prestigious vaudeville venue of Hammerstein's Victoria Theatre, minus the 'Gerard Boys'. Bohm celebrated her advent into the 'big time' with a half-page ad in *Variety*:

MAE WEST, LATE OF ZIEGFELD'S 'MOULIN ROUGE',
DIRECTION OF FRANK BOHM –
'THE SCINTILLATING SINGING COMEDIENNE'

'Sime' once again noted her arrival:

Mae West is a 'single' now. She has been about everything else, from a chorus girl in the Folies Bergère and head of a 'three-act' to principal in a Ziegfeld show. That she escaped from the latter evidences some strength of character and this becomes apparent in a way during the act at Hammerstein's. The girl is of the eccentric type. She sings rag melodies and dresses oddly, but still lacks that touch of class that is becoming requisite nowadays in the first class houses . . . There's enough of the act just now for it to pass, if Miss West can be taught how to 'get' an audience . . .

She was certainly not going to lack for experience over the next seven years.

PART TWO

The Low-and-Behold Girl

Looking Pretty and Saying Cute Things

'I believe I'll go to Paris and get myself a king. See my diamond pins. Gaby has nothing on me with her pearls.

'I think I'll get me a young trunk for all these music publishers' cards. They take up certainly too much room around here . . .'

'You have been on Broadway?' 'Yes,' demurely. And I asked the little lady: 'For how long?' With a rippling little laugh she replied, 'I opened and closed in one week.' Fearing I was keeping her from supper, as it was that time of evening, to my apology she said: 'Oh, sometimes I don't eat at all. Playing three-a-day, you can't have time to eat much.'

Noticing that she made her face up a bit, pulled her hair over the ears and adjusted a brown velvet hat carefully at the right angle, I remarked: 'How is it that you dress from the top down?'

'Oh, it's just a little habit of mine'; and I left the cunning, bright little girl in a happy mood, as it seemed to be the most natural to her. She is surely jolly little Mae West.

Unsourced clipping, early 1912

The early glimpses into Mae's publicity efforts show a slow and rather hesitant curl towards the construction of her own particular myth. Like everyone else in show business, she created her mask, her on-stage character, from a variety of pre-existing sources. Her clash with Gaby Deslys might have deprived her of an open door to Broadway, but it definitely, to use her own phrase, gave her ideas. Mae had seen Eva Tanguay on stage, but this was the first time she had experienced the full blast of an international star's razzle-dazzle from behind the scenes. Gaby Deslys entered a room always expecting to be the centre of attention. In her business, she expected to be the only game in town, the diva, the prima donna, the wow. The key was both in the moves and costume, body language and décor. This is what you came to watch, not the shadow people in the background. The spotlight has to be on Me.

This was quite a tall order for La Petite Daffy, although her role model, Eva Tanguay, was as compact, a ball of fire, energy igniting on the stage. Looking at her idols and at herself, Mae must have wondered, like so many in those early stages of their profession, how do I get from here to there?

In her later mythology, Mae insisted that she never looked back, never hesitated, never changed her basic style: 'I am captive to myself. It or I created a Mae West and neither of us could let go of the other, or want to.' It certainly required formidable will power to start that arduous climb. 'I had to learn it all firsthand,' she wrote. 'I didn't get it out of books.'

Variety's 'Sime' Silverman described the path of the 'single act' from 'small time' upwards through the critic's eye:

> The man single has two ways of getting over: singing and talking . . . The young woman, all alone on the big stage, with a few or more people in front, must sing. And she must change her clothes.
>
> The style of a 'small time' single woman is stereotyped. There must be at least three songs and three changes. You sit back and watch them . . . You wonder if the girl is getting $10 per song per week or is she among the $13.50 class, which would make her a '$40' single.
>
> The first thought though is where she came from. First you look at her hands. She is having trouble keeping them down by her side. She's new: some try-out, probably? Then where did she get her dresses, for the three look like $135, cash, if not rented from a Third avenue costumier . . .

Mae's stints, short as they were, with 'legitimate' Broadway probably gained her a much better deal. She claimed a fee of $350 a week for her show with the 'Gerard Boys', with $50 apiece for the boys. They were dropped, she claimed, because she wanted more spare money for the clothes, and Frank Bohm told her she could get as high a fee on her own.

Now that Frank Wallace was out of the way, Mae could concentrate on her own course. Every ounce of that determination would be required. The vaudeville road was long and rocky. The touring schedules were punishing – one week or a 'split week', meaning three days here, four days there, rushing in trains from New York to Baltimore to Indianapolis, Louisville, Philadelphia, Chicago, across the Canadian border to Ottawa and Montreal. Long-term survivor Fred Allen has, as ever, the best description of the peculiar life of *homo vaudevilliens*:

The elements that went to make up vaudeville were combed from the jungles, the four corners of the world, the intelligentsia and the subnormal. An endless, incongruous swarm crawled all over the countryside dragging performing lions, bears, tigers, leopards, boxing kangaroos, horses, ponies, mules, dogs, cats, rats, seals, and monkeys in their wake. Others rode bicycles, did acrobatic and contortion tricks, walked wires, exhibited sharp-shooting tricks, played violins, trombones, cornets, pianos, concertinas, xylophones, harmonicas, and any other known instrument. There were hypnotists, iron-jawed ladies, one-legged dancers, one-armed cornetists, mind readers, female impersonators, male impersonators . . . singers and dancers of every description, clay modelers, and educated geese: all traveling from hamlet to town to city, presenting their shows. Vaudeville only asked that you own an animal or an instrument, or have a minimum of talent or a maximum of nerve. With these dubious assets vaudeville offered fame and riches. It was up to you . . .

Life on the road was particularly hard for the married women, who, Allen wrote, 'foaled on trains, in dressing rooms, in tank towns . . . the show must go on . . . The smalltime vaudeville mother had the endurance of a doorknob. She did three or four shows a day as part of the act. She cared for the baby on the road and prepared its food. She did the family washing: there was always a clothesline hanging and dripping away in the dressing room and the boardinghouse, and the sinks were filled with diapers . . .'

One does not need much imagination to realize why Mae West, after her first aborted partnership, chose to remain 'single', both on and off the stage. It may have been a lonely life, despite the conviviality of the show folk, who also had their own union, the Society of White Rats (named after the British Grand Order of Water Rats), founded in 1900. Although actors were in the main keen to appear apolitical, the ladies of the species were more often than not supporters of the suffragist cause. Mae appeared in her act at one of their theatrical functions, the 'Suffrage Act in Vaudeville', mounted on New Year's Eve 1912 at Keith's Union Square Theatre, presenting 'songs and impersonations which won the applause of a crowded house'. Most of the time, however, she was representing no other cause but her own. The *Atlanta Journal*, 25 February 1913:

Mae West, the comedienne at the Grand this week, has won a real hit. She does not pretend to be a vocalist or anything but just Mae West. Her act consists of looking pretty and saying cute things and that fact has won a hit for her . . .

She also participated in another part of the bill, an impersonation sketch named '"The Movies," a delightful take-off on the motion pictures craze,' which 'has been accepted as one of the best things of the season . . .'

At about the same time, Mae also began using a byline which could drum up more press interest, calling herself 'the Original Brinkley Girl'. This referred to the cartoon drawings of artist Nell Brinkley, the successors to the previous fad of the 'Gibson Girl', an image of the liberated, freewheeling young woman of the day. The 'Brinkley Girl' was 'lithesome and willowy . . . a thing of continuous curves and shapely lines', her mouth a-pucker and her hair all tangled, blowing 'down her face and neck'. Mae was not, in fact, that lithesome and willowy, but she could make audiences believe that she was. There is no evidence that she was 'the original Brinkley girl model for the famous artist', as the *Baltimore News* claimed when she appeared there in June 1913; but, as the newspapers continued to enthuse, she made herself popular 'by singing a repertory of "I Don't Care" type of songs and appearing in a dazzling series of low-and-behold gowns'.

The songs Mae was singing were a medley of popular tunes which, as the opening clipping in this chapter shows, she picked from the music publishers' cards that littered every singer's dressing room. Biographer Emily Wortis Leider includes in her account sheet-music covers for 'Cuddle Up and Cling to Me', sung with the 'Girard Boys' in 1912, 'Good-night Nurse', also of 1912, and a song which she made notorious, 'And Then', of 1913. The words to 'Good-night Nurse' are tucked in the archive of her last agent (and biographer) Stanley Musgrove. A somewhat innocent ditty, the song was written by Thomas J. Grey, with lyrics by W. Raymond Walker:

Now Sam McKee was sick and he was taken to a hos-pi-tal,
And there he met a swell nurse gal
And right away – our Sam got gay
He forgot about his ills
Made love when she brought him pills
Every night when she would go off duty
Sam would holler out: 'Come here my cutey.'

Chorus:
Good night nurse,
Tell the doctor I'm no better,
Good night, nurse . . .

This would not have irked the censors too much, though 'And Then' was somewhat more suggestive: 'Mother said Good-night – and then / We turned down the light – and then . . .' This attracted serious opprobrium at the Temple Theatre in Detroit on 26 August, the critic of the *Detroit News* huffing that 'it hardly seems possible that Mae West will be allowed to sing her song, "And Then," the rest of the week by the Temple management, usually so careful to eliminate the objectionable'. Despite her act being 'the big hit of the bill' – or possibly because it was – the critic complained that 'Mae West . . . is plainly vulgar. This woman is all that is coarse in Eva Tanguay without that player's ability. Yet the audience howled for more.'

As well they might. Even in puritanical Philadelphia, at the Broadway theatre in September 1914, the critics noted that that 'nut comedienne styles herself "the Original Brinkley Girl" and makes good'. Another title Mae was sporting at the time was 'The Firefly Girl', as she was dubbed in Tulsa at the Nixon Theatre, where 'she amply lived up to her evanescent title in a pot-pourri of pleasant personalities'.

By this time, we now know, Mae was no longer alone, as she had found herself a partner both for the long train journeys and the boarding-house stops. Along the way – in Detroit, according to Mae – she met up with a young man on the same bill 'with a terrific personality and sensual Latin charm', whom she coyly named in her autobiography as D. His name was Guido Deiro.

Deiro has been acclaimed as the first star of the piano-accordion and had been the first accordionist to perform in vaudeville, in 1910, when *Variety* noted him among December's 'New Acts':

DEIRO – ACCORDIONIST. 13 MINS.; ONE. FIFTH AVENUE
Deiro will have no trouble in holding his own amongst the several accordion players now in the varieties. The man plays what seems to be a different arrangement than the usual. It has a keyboard similar to that of a piano. His manipulation is interesting together with the playing. Deiro has also shown rare judgment in his picking of selections. Instead of sticking to the heavys or the grand opera he opens with a solid number, devoting the rest of the time to 'rag' with which he does a few gyrations à la Travato . . . Placed 'No. 4' on the program he drew down a solid hit that came from all parts of the house.

Deiro and Mae were soon playing in tandem on the vaud circuits and were presented in another half-page ad by Frank Bohm in

Variety in December 1914: 'DEIRO, THE MASTER OF THE PIANO-ACCORDIAN; MAE WEST, "THE ORIGINAL BRINKLY GIRL" – Engaged Jointly as Headline Features.' This was a booking for a forty-week tour on the Loew circuit, whose chief booking manager was the aforementioned Joseph Schenck. Since Mae claimed both Schenck and Frank Bohm were wooing her, it was a little odd perhaps that they were so happy to send her out with her new beau, from whom she also collected a diamond. But Mae was already quite persuasive.

Deiro knew nothing about Frank Wallace and, Mae wrote, reconciled himself to waiting to marry her, having properly broached the subject with Mother. Mae quotes D. as commenting: 'For a man who wants to marry, waiting is hard' – which might well be one of Mae's early double entendres. He was a great lover, she said, though typically jealous, if attentive: he 'used to sit by my side and curl my hair with iron curlers while I was in bed'. Though he was not, it appears, as prodigiously talented in the boudoir as another performer Mae later claimed to have bedded in vaudeville, a 'xylophone player' mentioned in dispatches in Mae's 1973 volume *Mae West on Sex, Health and ESP*: 'This guy had quite an act. He came on stage in a Scottish kilt and really worked it out on that xylophone . . . He came around and asked me for a date, and I accepted. What started out as a night on the town ended up as a quiet evening at my hotel – but we still managed to hit all my hot spots. In fact we hit them for nine hours straight! I've always said that too much of a good thing can be wonderful, and that guy must have felt the same way. I asked him, later on, if he always gave such lengthy performances, and he told me that usually – in fact up till our night together – he had what I'd call a vaudeville schedule: two a day . . . He was one xylophone player who knew how to ring the chimes!' But this was too much even for Mae. One assumes Deiro was somewhat more moderate. But he, too, had some hindrance to a long-term relationship, namely his first wife, Julia Tatro, a teenage pianist from Spokane, Washington. Divorce may or may not have taken place by the end of 1914.

Aficionados of Deiro claim that he and Mae were formally married, but there is no evidence that such nuptials ever occurred. Newspapers occasionally referred to Deiro as Mae's 'fiancé.' The *Columbus Ledger,* on 14 March 1914, even quoted her describing him as 'Count Guido', though, the scribes added, 'he ain't no such animal'.

Nevertheless, Deiro was Mae's longest-lasting companion to date, lasting well into 1916. It was her parents, Mae wrote, who urged the final break-up, concerned about his fits of jealousy and the danger of 'those Italian knife tricks'. Mae dumped him and left for Chicago. But there might have been another crisis that caused that wrench: the untimely death of agent Frank Bohm. He succumbed in March 1916 to a 'tubercular condition of the spine, with complications', at the unripe age of thirty-two. He had been, for a time, both sick and in financial difficulties, *Variety* reported, having lost $30,000 trying to promote 'Singer's Midgets'.

'No Vulgarity Whatsoever!'

Rather than going to Paris and getting herself a king, Mae had gone to Detroit and got an accordionist. Things were not, in fact, looking good. There was another waif picked up on the way, some time later, according to Mae's own account, 'a spoiled, rich, baffling young man, in Chicago'. She named him 'Rex', which seems more appropriate for a pet. We know nothing about this featured lover – 'handsome, from a socialite family, a character out of F. Scott Fitzgerald'. This might have been the man she mentioned to interviewer Ruth Biery who was, more prosaically, 'connected with some firm in the sales branch'. He wanted her to settle for a domestic life. But once again, Mother championed freedom: 'Mother pointed out other married couples to me . . . Showed me how their lives were wasted. She never did. But when I saw her face – how unhappy she was, I couldn't get around that . . .' But she still pined: 'I wouldn't go out with a man who didn't remind me of him. And then I'd rush home before the evenin' was over because he did remind me of him.'

People talk such nonsense to magazine writers. Or have nonsense made up about them. Mae was at this time, between the ages of twenty and twenty-five, at the peak of her physical energy and drive, learning to make her way in the jungle, picking and choosing among the fauna and also learning, we must assume, how to avoid the pitfalls of unwanted pregnancy, motherhood or abortion. If there were any hiccups along this trail, we have not heard their echoes, despite a slightly suspicious loss of the route track in 1917 (and then again in 1925 . . .).

Research tracks the movement of vaudeville performers by the route lists published every week in the stage magazines: *Variety*, the *New York Dramatic Mirror*, the *New York Clipper* and the *Billboard* usually cover most eventualities. These lists will often temper oral accounts and gossip with the cold touch of facts and chronology.

When a performer falls out of these lists, however, one is returned to speculation. The act may be 'resting', unemployed, ill or back home on an extended family break; the act might have been booked on one of the smaller independent circuits that are not necessarily covered every week; or 'none of the above'. Clues can be found, too, in general trends and events affecting the performers' lives and work.

Her love life apart, an equally nagging issue for Mae West – as for all her peers on the vaudeville stage in this period – were the rumblings of 'industrial' unrest. In October 1914, vaudeville's managers notified the actors' agents that they were going to require cuts in salaries. A general depression, affected by the war in Europe, was impinging on all of show business. The vaudevillians' union, the White Rats, girded itself for what would turn out to be its final epic battle with management. The dispute would persist, with peaks and troughs of discontent, until a strike was called in the autumn of 1916. The managers, meanwhile, determined to snuff out the actors' rebellion, had formed their own 'union', the Vaudeville Managers' Protective Association.

Mae remains eminently trackable from 1913 to 1915, performing on the Keith circuit – through Philadelphia, Atlantic City, New York, Baltimore, Rockaway Beach, Detroit, Rochester, Richmond (VA), Newark, Harrisburg (PA), Utica, New York, Ottawa, etc., etc. After her Detroit hit with the vulgar 'And Then' in July 1915, a strange note appears in *Variety* on 20 August, on the Moving Pictures gossip page: 'MAY WEST IN PICTURES: May West, the vaudeville comedienne, has signed a contract with the U to go to the coast for four weeks.' This tantalizing glimpse of a possible silent Mae West picture is all we have; nothing follows this sighting. The 'U', Universal Pictures, was signing up all and sundry at this time; in September they apparently signed Sarah Bernhardt, but this turned out to refer to her French-made film *Jeanne Dore*, which was shipped from Paris to New York. As we noted, Mae began touring at this point with Deiro. The only other clue consists of a book preserved in Mae's personal archive, *How to Write Moving Picture Plays* by William Lewis Gordon, published in 1915. This includes a listing of 'Film-producing Companies' the aspiring playwright might submit texts to, including Edison, Essanay, Gaumont, Kalem, Keystone, the Lasky Feature Play Co. and Universal. There are, alas, no surviving samples of any writing by Mae from this early period.

After the death of Frank Bohm, Mae was left agentless, though Bohm's acts were preserved by his company, Frank Bohm Inc., which was incorporated by a consortium that included Joseph Schenck and Emil Bohm, Frank's brother. The other agents agreed not to poach any of Bohm's 110 registered acts. Nevertheless, every performer wants the personal touch, even without the diamond collection. Schenck was not going to fill the gap, as he was personally directing Eva Tanguay, with her guaranteed $3,000-a-week salary, never mind his day job as the Loew circuit's chief booking manager. (He would also, despite his plug-ugly looks, soon be engaged and married to Norma Talmadge, one of Hollywood's hottest beauties, whose sister, Natalie, would later wed Buster Keaton. Mae West was left far behind in these stakes.)

Mae soldiered on under the corporate arrangement for a while. On 2 June 1916, *Variety* ticked her name among the participants in a 'special entertainment for the prisoners' at Sing Sing, on the occasion of 'Decoration Day'. The artists were guests of the Mutual Welfare League, an early example of Mae's involvement in prisoners' rights, a persistent interest, as we shall see. A month later, in July, she reinvented herself yet again, appearing on stage in a new double-act, which drew an unusually hostile review from *Variety*'s chief sourpuss, 'Sime':

NEW ACTS THIS WEEK – JULY 7
MAE WEST AND SISTER – SONGS. 18 MINS.; ONE. FIFTH AVENUE.
Mae West in big time vaudeville may only be admired for her persistency in believing she is a big time act and trying to make vaudeville accept her as such. After trying out several brands of turns, Miss West is with us again, this time with a 'sister' tacked onto the billing and the stage. 'Sister's hair looks very much like Mae's, and there the family resemblance ceases in looks as well as work, for 'Sister' isn't quite as rough as Mae West can't help but being. Unless Miss West can tone down her stage presence in every way she just as might well hop right out of vaudeville into burlesque.

This working out new acts, buying new wardrobe and worrying will get to Miss West's nerve in time (but it will probably be a long time). Miss West, in the first number, 'I Want to be Loved in the Old Fashioned Way,' follows her sister (who sings the first verse straight) with a second verse telling how Miss West would prefer to be loved, in the modern way, auto ride, plenty of wine and so on.

Mae West and sister Beverly in later life

At the end, Mae 'reappeared in man's dress with silk hat, the couple doing "Walkin' th' Dog" with dance for the finish'. The act did very well at Keith's Fifth Avenue Theatre, 'Sime' had to admit, and Mae responded to the applause with a speech: 'I am very pleased, ladies and gentlemen, you like my new act. It's the first time I have appeared with my sister. They all like her, especially the boys who always fall for her, but that's where I come in – I always take them away from her.'

'Sime' was not pacified. 'Perhaps if Mae West would wear men's dress altogether while upon the stage and would stop talking,' he grouched, 'she would appear to better advantage. With "Sister" they could do a boy-and-girl "sister" act.'

One wonders what it was that got so far up the veteran reviewer's nose. An inveterate pirate, 'Sime''s name was almost synonymous with the journal he had founded and published from 1905 until two years before his death in 1933, aged sixty. A flamboyant, larger than life man – remembered for his green bow ties, trench coat and slouch hat, and hacking smoker's cough – he ran *Variety* as a personal crusade. His likes and dislikes were mercurial, often quite visceral. He

65

loved actors, but hated to be disappointed by them. He was far from unfamiliar with male impersonators, or vice versa, or cornily suggestive songs. Yet something in Mae's manner – her lack of respect for the boundaries of the medium – put him in a malicious mood on this occasion.

As in the other stage journals, everything in *Variety* was neatly pigeonholed: Vaudeville here, Burlesque there, Legitimate, then Cabaret, Music, Outdoors, alongside Moving Pictures and later, Radio. Burlesque now seemed to be a kind of sinkhole to which the uncouth should be condemned, despite the continual efforts by the burlesque circuits themselves to 'clean up' their act – 'Empire Directors Weigh Question of "Cooch" Dances – Elimination of the Wrigglers,' as reported back in 1912. We can recall the castigation of Mae's own wriggles, with the 'Girard Boys', at New Haven. In October, *Variety*'s front page headlined 'VAUDEVILLE MUST "CLEAN UP": UNITED BOOKING OFFICES ORDER.' Managers were 'Enjoined Upon Utmost Severity for "Blue" Matter and All Swear Words. No Vulgarity Whatsoever.'

Perhaps 'Sime's outrage can be linked to his consistent use of quotation marks around the 'sister', i.e., he thought the act was overtly lesbian. There was a thin line that professional impersonators, male and female, were shrewd enough not to cross. Coded signals to those in the know could cover for what the public wished, in its happy innocence, to ignore. But it was, in truth, Mae's sister Beverly up there with her on the stage.

At this time, Beverly was eighteen years old. She has left us a few reminiscences about her sister, and nothing of great value about the early years, apart from the claim that it was Mother Tillie, not Mae herself, who chose her 'extreme' clothes: '(Mother) was French and had worked as a stylist, so she naturally believed in dressing originally. Mae was always voluptuous looking, even as a little girl, so mother told her to wear clothes that showed off her figure.' Not that Mae required much encouragement. Of course, when Beverly was speaking in the 1930s about her sister, she had to fit her recollections to the creative shift of Mae's birth to 1900. Any mention of a younger sister in vaudeville might have pushed the charade a little too far, leaving them both to have performed in pushchairs.

Later presentations of Beverly, as in *Screen Play* magazine of 1933, portrayed her as a precocious starlet, just like Mae, who had begun as 'a child singer on the Loew circuit . . . progressed in vaudeville, until at the age of sixteen she had an important act in her own right'. But 1916 was her first appearance, and her own act was to come much later.

Mae West and Sister was not long lasting. 'Sime's killer review apart, the heat was being turned up in the vaudeville dispute. To counter the White Rats, the Vaudeville Managers' Protective Association had formed a rival union, the National Vaudeville Artists. Two million dollars had been allocated to breaking the White Rats once and for all. The target of the managers was the Rats' most potent weapon, which was also its Achilles heel in a period before any labour protection was afforded by government: the closed shop. In September, the Rats began calling a series of strikes. *Variety*, under 'Sime', had always championed the Rats, having survived a long blacklisting imposed by the theatrical moguls Keith and Albee, when 'Sime' had challenged their outrageous percentages. But 'Sime' was growing wary of the strong-arm, closed-shop tactics of the Rats' new leader, Harry Mountford, and was getting ready to embrace the new power. Mountford, a demagogic Englishman, mounted a shrill defence of his union, warning strike-breakers, in a lurid *Variety* statement, that they would be damned as 'blacklegs and scamps'. 'Poverty and disgrace,' ranted Mountford, 'is their living portion . . . sudden death pursues them with unrelenting feet, and the shadow of the hangman's noose is ever over them.' The vaudevillians, however, from Houdini and Eva Tanguay to the minnows, ignored the hyperbole and deserted in droves to join the managers' union. The White Rats sued the managers' association as a 'trust' but lost the case and faced bankruptcy. On 13 April 1917, they admitted defeat and called off the strike. The rump of actors who had stuck with them loyally were left to suffer a ferocious boycott.

It is difficult to pinpoint Mae's part in all this. Political commitment was hardly to be expected from 'jolly little Mae West', though we can gauge from her interviews with the Rats' house journal *The Player*, back in 1912, and her general defence of the underdog, that her sympathies were with the union. While she does not seem to have been blacklisted by the managers during the strike, there is evidence of an ingenious flanking manoeuvre on her part, as indicated by one of *Variety*'s tantalizing small items, dated 17 November 1916:

MAE WEST'S NEW NAME AND ACT

An act written by Blanche Merrill will return Mae West to vaudeville under another name and as a male impersonator.

A later item, on 24 November, casts some doubt on the reliability of Miss Merrill, who was being sued by another actress, Josephine Davis, for a written act contracted but not received on time – sum claimed: $250. She would later become known for a song co-written at the dawn of the so-called 'Roaring Twenties' – 'Jazz Baby'. Mae might have been seeking a refuge from 'Sime's attack on the 'sister' act or just making a satirical point or finding a subterfuge to avoid appearing while not actually showing her hand as a striker.

Mae did disappear for several months, and when, on 30 March 1917, *Variety* published a full list of members of the National Vaudeville Artists, Mae's name was nowhere to be found. Yet, the moment the strike was over, she popped up again, on 25 April, in New York, back as a 'single' and with a new repertoire, as reported by the *New York Clipper*:

THEATRE – PROCTOR'S TWENTY-THIRD STREET
STYLE – SINGING COMEDIENNE
TIME – FIFTEEN MINUTES
SETTING – ONE

Mae West bills herself as 'The Different Type of Songstress.' Her opening song is about a 'Wild Woman,' in which she is clad in a tiger skin robe, with her hair arranged 'à la Tanguay.' Her enunciation is poor, and she sings her numbers with a nasal twang. Her gesturing throughout the number is of a very suggestive nature, and leaves nothing for the imagination, executing her work in a risqué manner . . .

Clad as a chappy in a walking suit, she sings a song about being 'The Wisest Guy of All.' And for a finish does a dance with a 'prop' dummy. Should the average 'cooch' dancer try to present such an offering, she might be interfered with by the police.

The police and the rest of the nation, however, had other concerns at this time than climbing onto the stage to separate Mae West from her prop dummy, as on 6 April 1917 the US had declared war on Germany. *Variety*'s pages were soon filling up with the names of male actors being drafted. Ben Kahn, of the Union Square Theatre, organized his burlesquers for service, drilling them in the theatre courtyard in regulation Home Defense uniforms. George M. Cohan's song

'You're a Grand Old Flag' – 'Professional Copies and Orchestrations Now Ready' – was about to be sung at every street corner.

America mobilized. Women were not called up for combat, but many enlisted voluntarily as clerks and nurses and filled the work places left by the men sent out to 'win the war for democracy'. Women manned factory assembly lines, ploughed the fields, fixed automobiles and made gas masks. Even at home the ladies could contribute: 'OUR BOYS NEED SOX – KNIT YOUR BIT,' called the Red Cross. Teenage boys, too, were photographed sheepishly wielding the knitting needles.

In this context it was not surprising that striking unions would get short shrift, as children marched down Main Streets all over America with banners proclaiming '100 PER CENT PATRIOTS.' In vaudeville, German acts were boycotted. Most had already mutated to 'Dutch acts' after the liner *Lusitania* had been sunk by a German U-boat in May 1915, prompting one German-dialect comedian, Groucho Marx, to switch overnight to a Yankee patter.

Mae West, as far as we know, did not knit sox for the troops or join the Red Cross or rush to drive rivets. Hearsay, and her own account, place her in Chicago during much of the war period, putting 'some flag-waving into my act to match the torso waving', discovering the rhythms of jazz and the black dance craze – the ultra-wriggly 'shimmy-shawobble'.

'I planned a new act and a new romance,' she related.

Enter, stage right, Mr James A. Timony.

Of Jimmy and the Shimmy

It is not clear at which date exactly Mae encountered Jim Timony for the first time. He is introduced in her own book as initially her mother's attorney, already 'a power in politics, a hard man in court'. Mae wrote: 'He was big, handsome, with the build of the football player he had once been.' Later images of Timony show him to be, in the parlance of the time, no oil painting, but he was a good prototype of Mae's favourite male standard in later years – the hunk. As she later wrote:

Personally speaking, lots of different men have always interested me. Athletes and weightlifters have always been on my list. There's something to be said about well-developed men with hard muscles – I guess it's that a hard man is good to find.

Hard or soft, James Timony would be Mae West's longest-lasting male partner, though the precise nature of their personal relationship remains uncertain. It is, when one thinks about it, quite astonishing that Mae managed the trick of thrusting her persona into the public gaze at every possible opportunity – in her years of fame – while keeping her private life hermetically sealed. Mae described Timony as the man 'who was to help guide most of my mature show business life'. But though she writes that of course 'he was infatuated with me', she would only reciprocate with 'I got to like him very much.'

We can assume that Mae and Timony began as lovers. But the fact that he remained both friend and mentor is significant for our understanding of the hidden nature of the woman behind the mask. He was, after all, hardly a 'Svengali', a much older man teaching a young girl the ropes. Born in Massachusetts in 1886, a practising lawyer in Brooklyn by 1910 (according to the New York census), Timony was thirty-one years of age in 1917, when Mae was twenty-four. In terms of theatrical know-how, she was then already a veteran of six or seven years' prior experience. But it was clear he had a nose for business and a genuine feeling for the kind of theatre that could suit her talents best. Where Mae was hesitant, in these early years, about her future, Timony always believed in her star. And, as time went by, he forged the connections that enabled her to strike out in new directions and break out of the vaudeville rut.

In 1916, he had the unenviable job of legal counsel to the White Rats union, as well as, from October of that year, counsel to the separate Actors' Guild. The *New York Clipper* item announcing this refers to his 'extensive practice among theatrical folks', which involved handling various internal lawsuits and copyright claims. These concerns, the *Clipper* stated, had 'caused him to refuse a judicial nomination'. He did not, however, last the course of the strike. When the union began haemorrhaging both members and money, he jumped ship, later suing his employers for legal fees amounting to $3,000. By the time the union crumbled, he was in business on his own, advertising, on 11 May 1917, in *Variety*:

ACTORS, LISTEN TO THIS!

If I were to offer you a country home which is situated on the north shore of Long Island, overlooking the bay and only a 3-minute walk to the railroad station and to the restricted bathing beach, and only a 25-minute ride from Times Square, and ask you to make a small payment and the balance to be paid off in rent, would you consider it? . . . There is bathing, fishing, hunting and motoring at this ideal spot. In order to prove these statements, I will ask you to kindly call at my office at any time you please, and I will drive you down in my car and show you this wonderful place. It must be seen in order to be appreciated.

James A. Timony – Real Estate Investments, 1472–1480
Broadway (Longacre Building), New York

This does not sound like the sort of man who, at this stage, as Mae claimed, was prominent enough to own a baseball club and Hawthorne Field in Brooklyn. But he evidently had what Mae required.

The hard fact, for those who wish to present Mae West as a *sui generis* feminist icon is that, at this time, it was not feasible for a single woman to thrive or even function in show business without the obligatory male patron. Mae's path to her evangelizing role as the 'sex educator' was convoluted, beset by dubious turnings and blind alleys. Those with an ideological bent often put the cart before the horse: Mae did not become an independent force because she was a feminist; she had to become a feminist, and a boldly committed one, if she wished to carve her own way.

Again, we do not know at which point certain ideas, notions, ambitions, intentions came into play in Mae's mind. For most of her first decade as a working performer she seemed preoccupied, like anyone else in her position, with the sheer grind of survival. As a vaudeville baby, she was well aware that survival could be served by a certain minimal skill. As George Burns wrote about getting into the business: 'There was no radio, no television, no talking pictures . . . You really needed only one thing to break into the business – desire. You had to want to do it very badly . . . Believe me, if a wrestling cheese could work, I knew I'd never have to worry about getting a job.' Once in, as long as you had ten or fifteen minutes' worth of your own material, sketch, dance or spiel, you could keep it going without a change for decades. Captain Spaulding ate molten lead on stage for over twenty years. Fink's Trained Mules demonstrated their training. Eva Tanguay sang the same songs. The Marx Brothers performed the same sketches for years on end. W. C. Fields juggled hats, cigar boxes and billiard balls. Buster Keaton got thrown around the stage by his dad. Houdini got out of handcuffs.

But Mae was restless. The life was not good enough. The songs became a drag, even though some, like 1913's 'I Wonder Where My Easy Rider's Gone?' by Shelton Brooks, would be recycled later in her movies. How many changes of clothes could you make? And when she tried to vary her show, as the 'sister' act, she got shot down.

Broadway had spewed her out. She was not, after all, the most beautiful woman on the 'Great White Way' or, in fact, in the top hundred. Gorgeous girls were lining up in Ned Wayburn's studio, stunning, young and pouting. A new batch of publicity photographs, taken some time in the late 1910s, shows Mae trying to look the full glamorous part. But other thoughts were stirring.

Much has been made, in previous accounts of the 'missing' period of 1917–18, of Mae's sojourn in Chicago, frequenting African-American nightclubs, turning onto the new sound of jazz and learning the 'shimmy-shawobble'. This was a dance Mae claimed to have seen in 'a low colored Café' on Chicago's South Side. There were two cafés, the Elite 1 and 2. In No. 1 'big black men with razor-slashed faces, fancy high yellows and beginners browns – in the smoke of gin scented tobacco to the music of "Can House Blues" . . . got up from the tables, got out to the dance floor, and stood in one spot, with hardly any movement of the feet, and just shook their shoulders, torsos, breasts and pelvises. We thought it was funny and were terribly amused by it. But there was a naked, aching sensual agony about it too.'

As cultural historians who are worth their salt know, it is fairly difficult to pinpoint a moment when some new move or sound manifests itself, despite various claims that this or that performer initiated the form directly out of their gut. Mae, of course, laid her claim to the 'shimmy' as a white dance picked out of black dives. Other sources pick out singer Gilda Grey, who shook her 'chemise' while singing. Among blacks Haitian voodoo shaking was said to be the origin. Certainly, by 1918 it was becoming a craze, the latest of many dance crazes that swept through the clubs and dance halls. Restaurant-cabarets were big business, and 'matinee' dancing was castigated by moral guardians who warned about 'women of the streets and crooks' mixing with the wives of husbands whose life savings were pouring out of their loose spouses' feet. The Turkey Trot, the Bunny Hug, the Texas Tommy, the Castle Walk, the Shika, Black Bottom, Gaby Glide, the Cootie-Tickle and, to top them all, in the 1920s, the Charleston, soon to set the world ablaze. By armistice time, November 1918, they rocked to 'Ev'rybody Shimmies Now', sung by 'hundreds of vaudeville artists', 'the Biggest Knockout Razz Jazz Blue Shimmie Song ever written . . . the Song with a Hundred Laughs':

> Brother Bill, Sister Kate, Shiver like jelly on a plate,
> Shimmie dancing can't be beat, Moves everything except your feet,
> Parson Brown, Sister Burch, Shake the shimmie on their way to church,
> Honey would you show me how, 'cause ev'rybody shimmies now . . .

Mae might have picked the shimmy up in 1917, but it was certainly not her first taste of the song-and-dance life of Chicago or the new sound of jazz. In Chicago she could have heard and seen Freddie Keppard's Creole Band or the Original Dixieland Jazz Band, which recorded its first disc, 'Livery Stable Blues', in New York City in February of that year. The Elite Club, the scene of her dance epiphany, had hosted Jelly Roll Morton in 1914, and the Original Creole Band lit up Chicago from early 1915. Tom Brown's Dixieland Jazz Band, 'Direct from New Orleans', was a white band, recommended to Lamb's Café in Chicago by Charlie Mack, white blackface

showman, later to be half of Mack and Moran, the 'Two Black Crows', who were active into the 1930s. The 'loud, slapstick, comedic nature of the music of the early Dixieland groups', writes jazz historian Alyn Shipton, was 'in many ways as two-dimensional a representation of the new African-American music as blackface white singers were of what lay behind the old minstrelsy traditions'.

Disentangling cause and effect, as we have seen, is a highly arguable endeavour. Veteran songwriter Perry Bradford recalled in his memoir *Born with the Blues* that the jazz that was supposed to have been born in New Orleans could have been heard as early as 1905 in Chicago, or in 1912 in Harlem with the children's 'Jenkins Orphan Band'. By 1914, these early 'jass' sounds were tinkling around the cafés and bars of black downtowns everywhere. In Los Angeles, the young men and women of the movie colony sneaked into these meeting places, where they could pick up their weed or cocaine, later to make the sound the hidden – and often not so hidden – background to the flow of images, and certainly the jagged, frenetic action of the Keystones and other comic films. It was, in fact, a seamless process, from the 'ragtime' craze of the 1890s to Bert Williams and the all-black shows of the 1900s through to a young white kid named Irving Berlin, who began in 1911 to write the 1,500-plus songs that would make black rhythms into white America's most popular tunes. In Mae and Frank Wallace's appearance with the Big Gaiety Show in the same year, the *New York Clipper* noted that the duo sang 'several coon songs'. In 1912, at Hammerstein's, in her first solo, the *Clipper* reported that Mae West closed her act 'while seated in a chair and manipulating the old time minstrel "bones."'

'Jazz suited me – I liked the beat and the emotions,' Mae wrote, 'the low husky blues – the wild shouting laments of love and pleasure – the sad bounce of lovers and jazzmen and the music of honky-tonks and hot spots.' In 1917, she would not have heard the first recordings of blues singer Mamie Smith, whose first record with 'Mamie Smith's Jazz Hounds' was made by Okeh in 1920, nor Bessie Smith, who recorded a little later, but she could have witnessed their acts live on the black vaudeville circuit. Whether she had jazz players in the band for her own act, as she claims for this period, cannot, from the sources, be proven. By 1919, when Mae was back in the saddle as a *bona fide* star, jazz was all over the place, and the Original (white) Dixieland Jazz Band was even touring Europe.

The vaudeville route lists tell us nothing about Mae's trajectory from the summer of 1917 through to the early autumn of 1918, America's First World War years. Attempting to pin her down in Chicago is particularly fraught, as the local press is preoccupied by patriotic calls, tales of the soldiers who 'Thrive on Life in the Trenches', 'Women Who are Called to Salute the Flag', and the 'treason' of labour union 'pacifists' who 'give aid and comfort to the enemy'. Meanwhile, suffragists of the Women's National Party were arrested for picketing the President's national army parade in Washington. There were ample reasons for a jobbing actress to lay low. But in October 1918, one month before the guns fell silent in Europe, Mae broke the surface of public attention once again, returning, after an absence of seven years, to the world of the 'legitimate' musical and this time headlining as a star in her own right.

MONTHS

'What Do You Have to Do to Get It?'

Song: 'What Do You Have to Do?' (Mayme)
I'm getting awful fed up on the way this world is run,
Some girls have men to throw away and some girls can't get one,
It really is discouraging when all is said and done,
To plainly see your finish start before you have begun.
I see those pink and perfumed pets sink in their limousines
Without a single thought in life above their mezzanines,
I wonder why these dames can reign as lobster palace queens,
While I go home and o'er the gas, warm up a can of beans . . .

Chorus:
What do you have to do to get it? . . .
My life is one darn waiting.
It's really aggravating!
What do you have to do to get it?
What do you have to do?

From *Sometime*, 1918–19

Well, one answer to the above question is, get picked by producer
Arthur Hammerstein for the season's hottest musical comedy. Arthur
was the son of William Hammerstein, Broadway's most flamboyant
entrepreneur, who booked the notorious Evelyn Nesbitt, wife of her
lover's killer, Harry Thaw, in the week of her lethal husband's escape
from jail; Willie made an $80,000-a-week profit on that show. He
booked belly dancers, famous athletes, 'freak' attractions, Don the
Talking Dog (who could just about say the words 'hunger' and
'küchen') and anyone who could pull a crowd to his purpose-built,
lavish theatre. Son Arthur mounted his new show, *Sometime*, at the
Shubert but appeared to have inherited his father's liking for screwball acts. He had long been producing musicals scored by froth-meis-
ter Rudolf Friml, and this play (book by Rida Johnson Young) was to
be no exception to the general rule of the genre: a young maiden,

played by Francine Larrimore, finds her lover in a compromising position and dumps him without giving him a chance, until . . .

The structure of the piece was notable as an early instance of the influence of the movies, the whole tale being told in cascading flash-backs told from the standpoint of a theatrical troupe. The main draw of the production turned out, however, to be the story's second string, the tale of a chorus girl 'in search of temptation, but never finding it'. Arthur, remembering Mae West's successful and sassy runs at his father's theatre, cast her in this role, as Mayme, with another young comic screwball, Ed Wynn, as a property man who knows all the angles.

As the show entered rehearsals, it seemed that, once again, the Mae West jinx would strike her down before opening night, as the sudden influenza epidemic of that autumn spread its pall of terror. This virulent strain of the 'Spanish flu' was cutting down not the usual elderly victims but swathes of young people in their prime. (It was later surmised that a weaker epidemic of the same strain, in the 1880s, had immunized the older generation.) Theatres and motion-picture houses were major casualties of the epidemic, as people shunned close-quarter contact and shut-in places. Hammerstein's *Sometime* opened on 4 October, at the height of the epidemic in New York. Tolstoy's *Redemption*, a more fitting play for the times, opened at the same time, starring John Barrymore. But it was *Sometime* that endured, against all the odds. By November, the epidemic was ebbing as fast as it had begun, leaving the show to capitalize on the relief of Armistice Day, 11 November, when the Great War ground to a halt. *Sometime* ran for 283 performances, and more out of Broadway, on tour, though Mae had left the show by then.

The production allowed Mae West to play herself and tuck her own persona into the written character, Mayme. She made the best of it, adding her own wisecracks and, as *Variety* noted, finally capitulating to her risqué movements: She 'bowled them over with her dance . . . known in the dumps as "The Shimmy Shawabble," and coming under the heading technically for the better houses of a cooch above the waist. The cooch, otherwise, in times past, has been barred, but the days go by and the people want newness that children can think over at matinees, so here's the "Shimmy," not alone given in the Hammerstein show, but in other places where the old-fashioned cooch may be barred. But Miss West, with the assistance of what sounded very much like a well-placed clacque, stopped the show with it, then made a speech, and then made another.'

This mode of packing the house with her fans, learned from the Yale students' ruckus of New Haven, was an old trick of Mae's, most probably assisted by Timony and the young men of the bar. But Mae need not have worried, as she had certainly learned, since 1912, to 'get it over'.

Ironically, the role of Mayme was an inversion of the worldly-wise, man-eating character Mae was to become famous for later on. Mayme is, to our hindsight, a wannabe Mae West:

> *I was born a scamp,*
> *Meant to be a Vamp*
> *If I'd had the chance I could have did*
> *Theda Bara tricks,*
> *Paralyse the hicks!*
> *Nothing could have stopped me but the lid!*
> *But somehow my style has got a cramp,*
> *I can't find a single soul to 'Vamp'.*

And the refrain:

> *Won't you be my cave man for tonight?*
> *Please.*
> *You can drag me by the hair and pound me.*
> *Won't you hear my cry*
> *Once before I die*
> *Let me think I've got a man!*

Hardly the ideal of the suffragette movement. Mayme's desperation is coolly mocked by propman Loney (Ed Wynn):

MAYME: Every year I live makes me more suspicious of every man. What I want to know is this. If a gentleman was to enquire for me at the stage door, you wouldn't be low enough not to tell me.

LONEY: If a gentleman were to enquire for you, I wouldn't have the power to tell you. The shock would rob me of speech.

MAYME: You needn't get nasty . . . (*Mayme muses*) Men liked pep in those days. But now, I don't know what they want. I see all these dames getting their Packards, but I can't land even a Buick. What do you have to get it?

And cue song. Mayme plays the coquette with Loney, who is, in fact, scared of girls, and at one point the chorus girls pursue him all over the stage. Perhaps it's no surprise the audience preferred this to coughing up their lungs in a hospital bed, waiting for the angel of death, or even watching John Barrymore as Tolstoy's tortured Fedya committing suicide to save his bigamous wife from disgrace. 'Sime' Silverman loved the Barrymore play and noted, on the same page of *Variety* as his own review of *Sometime*: 'And if . . . the public don't want that, why not then give them the hokum, in characters, business and dialog that perhaps they do want – and are getting elsewhere at $2.'

Hokum or not, it was all grist to the mill of a country moving towards a new era of licence and fun pitched against ferocious reform. As the flu departed, and the war ended, and soldiers came home to tough prospects, and Prohibition begat empires of crime and the culture of the speakeasy fuelled by bootleg liquor, the public mood behind the noise of the 'Roaring Twenties' was nevertheless deeply conservative. While women who had experienced the independence of wage-earning kept a foothold on the job market, and a new generation of writers and critics, some scarred by the war, looked for new voices and sounds in the jazz joints of Times Square and Harlem, the presidential elections of November 1920 bade farewell to Democrat Woodrow Wilson and ushered in the new Republican administration of Warren Gamaliel Harding. Wilson had just managed to sneak in women's suffrage under the wire, in August 1920, but he had opposed Prohibition to no avail.

In the age of the 'flapper', the new fun-loving young woman who now not only smoked but drove motor cars, one would have expected Mae West to thrive. She herself, oddly enough, saw more of a threat than a promise in this new generation, as she kept reiterating, one decade later, telling vaudeville chronicler Douglas Gilbert in 1933:

Women much prefer to be feminine, believe me . . . Why, I couldn't spot a woman, three years ago. They got headed away from their natural lines, and I think what did it more than anything else was their addiction to sports and the silly idea that they looked well, by appearing mannish, in sports styles. Naturally, this lead to rough manners and general carelessness in attitude. Good Lord, if there's anything more awkward than a woman draped over a bar! You see, the speakeasy influence. Sit at a table, dearie, I always say. And don't forget your frills and ruffles and anything else that feminizes you. It's the icing on the cake for a gal. See what I mean?

Mae is always confounding us when we look to her for a role model of the 'progressive' woman, the leader of the pack. But these contradictions are, as ever, characteristic of show people, who develop a high degree of caution, even a terror of new ideas which might run ahead of the general paying public. As the 1920s loomed, Mae was still looking for a way into the front ranks of the traditional Broadway revue. But, despite the success of *Sometime*, there were no new immediate offers of stardom. When the show closed in the summer of 1919, Mae announced that she would rest 'for a few weeks' and then return to vaudeville.

Interestingly enough, this once again enabled her to avoid taking part in industrial strife, as actors of the 'legitimate' stage downed greasepaint in the Great Equity Strike of August 1919. Vaudeville performers were not part of this crucial dispute, which saw stars like Eddie Cantor and W. C. Fields, now in the 'legit' Ziegfeld Follies, coming out in support of stage extras and chorus girls whose right to be paid in rehearsals was one of the main bones of contention. This was the first actors' strike in America that was won by their union. By September, the actors were back at work, and on the nineteenth, again according to 'Sime', Mae West had ceased 'resting' and was back in the saddle:

MAE WEST. SONGS. 16 MINS.; ONE. FIFTH AVENUE
Mae West has returned to vaudeville after an absence of two years with an entertaining routine of pop numbers, supplemented with a 'shimmy' dance that seems a bit broad for vaudeville, but which can readily be tempered down for the better type of houses. Opening with a 'vamp' medley, Miss West reels off a French dialect number, comedy Indian song and a rag, in order . . . Miss West was an unqualified hit and on form can repeat anywhere. Two costumes are worn, the first a black and white combination, very tasteful, and the second a silver jet, that looks like a million dollars. A male accompanist is utilized for the songs and a jazz cornettist fills in, while Miss West is making a costume change. Miss West shows a marked improvement in method and delivery since last appearing in vaudeville.

No record has come down to us of the identity of the male accompanist or the cornet player. The 'shimmy', now Mae's signature, was already under sentence of death: in December 1918, it had already been 'given a solar plexus by the New York police', who informed all dancing places in New York – including restaurants – that 'if the shoulder and body movements are permitted during dancing, their dancing license may be revoked'. Despite this, in July 1919, New York's moral guardians noted that there were 'more than 114 specific spots in New York' where the dance has been viewed 'within the past several weeks'. Patrons of cabarets and restaurants were also bringing small bottles of whisky with them to dunk in their soft drinks while it was still legal. Managers now wanted to eliminate intermissions in vaudeville shows because they were only used by patrons to drink. Ice-cream parlours and orange-juice booths were springing up outside theatres. The shimmy and the booze were to be banished together, and soda pop was to reign supreme.

But the band played on. In late October 1919, Mae had what amounted to a one-night stand at a new Ned Wayburn show, the 'Demi Tasse Revue', which was part of the gala opening of New York's new luxury movie palace, the 5,000 seat Capitol, 'the last word in theatre construction'. The show ran for four hours, of which only one was the featured movie, Douglas Fairbanks in *His Majesty the American*. The 'Demi Tasse Revue' showcased Wayburn's latest 'automaton' girls in lush numbers such as 'The Story Book Ball', 'Old Fashioned Belles' and a chorus of Cowboys and Cowgirls. Mae West 'also scored as a single with a burlesque "shimmy" number'. The audience was suitably exhausted by the time Douglas Fairbanks leapt onto the screen. The show ran on into November, but Mae had returned to her single act once again.

The period from 1920 into spring 1921 ground on for Mae, who was back in the vaudeville groove. It may be underlining the obvious to point out that people who live through periods that are later perceived as historically distinctive do not necessarily notice the great changes of their era as more than blips on an everyday curve. When, at the stroke of New Year 1920, the US went formally 'dry', most revellers would only have experienced the dull ache of their hangovers. It was only as time went by that the realization sunk in of how profoundly Prohibition had altered American life. It would be 1925 before *Variety* would note that Times Square – between 34th and 52nd streets – boasted 2,500 speakeasies, where before Prohibition there had been only 300 saloons. In the entire country, in 1925, there were estimated to be three million 'booze joints', where 'pre-Prohibition cafés numbered 177,000'. In other words, a nation of moderate drinkers was turned into a nation of obsessive alcoholics, paying for criminals to build up an immense black market that would affect the nation's economy for decades (and continues to do so in the drug age). There would be fun, gaiety, abandon, dancing, hot-cha-cha, cheers and laughter, and buzzing joints like the Cotton Club and Texas Guinan's cabarets, but also killings, sickness, fraud, repression and the corruption of states and city halls.

Mae West, never more than a moderate drinker, was well able to avoid the worst personal perils, while the people surrounding her, like James Timony, built up connections to the folks with the dough and the power, legitimate or not – Prohibition blurred all the distinctions. She met gangsters, and at least one, Owney Madden, was said to be her lover. But all this would come later. As the 1920s opened for business, Mae still stood, feet unmoving, on the stage boards and shook her shoulders and torso to the tinkle of piano keys and the wail of cornets.

The moral guardians, however, continued their march, moving in, as King Booze leered over the city, on 'suggestive' performances and sexual innuendo. In February 1921, the Music Publishers' Protective Association began a 'housecleaning' campaign aimed at banishing 'all "blue" and double-meaning lyrics' from the market. All 'indecent material, or songs that are capable of indecent construction' should be banned. Keith-booked vaudeville shows were to be vigorously cleaned up too, 'the latitude allowed shimmy and jazz dancers' was to be curtailed. Even Lew Dockstader's Minstrels, the most old-fashioned show in town, was censured. Current slang, like 'Hot Dog', 'The Cat's Meow', 'Cat's Pajamas' and 'Hot Cat', was also on the proscribed list.

All this pressure on public jollity had its expected effect on show business – a slump both in 'legit' theatre and the business itself. The Shubert brothers, however, clearly had a fondness for Mae, and in March 1921, Mae West turned up again in a legitimate Broadway show, initially titled *The Whirl of the Town* but later changed to *The Mimic World of 1921*. In its original form it previewed in Washington and Philadelphia before settling down at Poli's, billed as 'A Huge, Gigantic Whizz-Bang in Two Acts and 25 scenes.'

Once again, courtesy of the Shubert Archive, we have a surviving script, with three sketches featuring Mae in different guises. In the longest, 'The Shimmy Trial', Mae admits in court her crime of killing the Shimmy in a somewhat surreal scene featuring several 'Shimmy cops'. The prosecutor whirls and twirls in jazz dance, declaiming:

'Chief – the kid's a wonder / Chief – chief – you've made a blunder /
You ought to set her free / Give her her liberty / Let her out – turn her
loose / Shut your mouth – get the moose [*or should it have been
'noose'? – ed.*] / Who'd you kill? / Oh Jimmie – Well if you must
know, I killed the Shimmie . . .' And Mae sings: 'Shim, shim, shim / I
was shimmying when the cops broke in / And you can bet I did my
best / I killed the shimmie in the west . . .'

In a second sketch, not listed in the tryout, Mae played La Belle, a
Paris damsel who 'speak a little one English' but does a big number
on shoulder-waggling 'Oo-la-la-la-la's. She wears watches that tell
the time in different cities all the way up her leg. Joke book dialogue
follows: 'Are you married?' 'Zat is my business!' 'How's business?'
But the most elaborate sketch is of most interest, a scene of 'Any
Night On Broadway', in which a Policeman, a Citizen, Broker, Card
Sharp, Gunman and Girl represent the denizens of midnight. The Girl
appears to fleece the gunman, pretending to be 'Lost! Lost in this big
city!' But a Salvation Army Man turns up to recognize her as 'Shifty
Liz', who 'was in Salvation Army headquarters yesterday . . . And she
stole our bass drum.' 'Well, there's one born every minute,' says the
damosel. The sketch looks forward to the mainstay of Mae's future
stage smash, *Diamond Lil*, which would segue into the movie *She
Done Him Wrong*, with Cary Grant in the Salvation Army uniform.

When the show was revamped and renamed, in August, as *The
Mimic World of 1921*, it included jazzed-up Shakespeare, with a
modern-day Hamlet, Ophelia, Romeo and Juliet, and an extended
'Café De Paris' story. The dialogue was on the level of 'In Paris all the
decent people try to look wicked and in New York all the bad people
try to look good.' Nevertheless, *Variety*'s reviewer (not 'Sime') noted,
at the opening: 'Mae West left nothing undone. She wore skin tight
clothes and cooched and wriggled and took falls and vamped. She
was pretty snappy. Her special song, though it seemed to have comedy merit, did not ring the bell. In the finale, however, her Fatima
work demanded a couple of curtains. In a tent it would have been a
riot.' It was 'good roof stuff', wrote the critic, and 'the girls were of
the usual Shubert peach type, and in several numbers wore daring
clothes and in some what never dared to be clothes'.

The *New York World* described Mae's shimmy as 'as if it were an
attempt to get out of a strait-jacket without the use of the hands'.
Another critic thought Mae's act was 'strenuous if unconvincing.

However, it made Jack Dempsey laugh.' The champ was obliging enough to come up from the audience and referee a mock match on the stage. The Shuberts pulled out all the stops in the production, including projections of close-ups of the girls in the ensemble 'upon a motion-picture screen'. The whole affair, wrote the *New York Sun*, 'employed a species of theatric TNT' with which the patrons were smitten 'into the desired state of unconsciousness and then administered liberal, if at times somewhat mediocre, doses of entertainment'. These explosive attempts were not ultimately effective, as the show only lasted for twenty-seven performances.

Broadway and Mae's desperation still was not paying off. By summer 1922 she was back on the circuit, playing the Riverside theatre with a new repertoire, which included, according to the notices, material written by Neville Fleeson, then already a popular songwriter, with 'I'll Be with You in Apple Blossom Time' and 'Alabamy Mammy' to his name. The act showed her portraying a 'French prima donna of temperament', with a series of impersonations of 'how different types of vamps put the bee on their heavy Johns'. By this time, she had acquired a new on-stage partner, pianist Harry Richman.

But this modest step, in fact, marked a watershed in Mae's development towards the revolutionary change of direction she was to take in coming years. For as she continued to tread the boards in pursuit of her livelihood, she was also pursuing a parallel project: in March 1921, Mae sent to the recorders of the Library of Congress her first known playscript – a twenty-page extended sketch entitled *The Ruby Ring*. In 1922, she added a full-length play, *The Hussy*, co-written with one Adeline Leitzbach. Mae was getting ready to spread her wings.

To a Rag and a Bone and a Hank of Hair . . .

The Ruby Ring is the first example we have of Mae West the writer, the role by which she would seek to define herself throughout the next decade. But there are clues to earlier efforts. Swinging back to one of her early reviews, in *The Player* of March 1912, we may note the comment about her sketch with the 'Girard Boys' that 'she herself wrote the lines and some of the music', as well as staging the piece. This may have been typical bragging, as performers often wanted the audience to think they were making up their own material, when they were, in fact, employing gag writers or stealing material off other acts. Mae was known to have used Thomas Grey, a *Variety* writer, who also provided some of her songs, including 'Good Night Nurse'. There is no evidence that she could write music, at this time or later. But we do have, from the new archive of Mae's own personal papers, a hitherto unknown hoard of evidence about the sheer extent of her writing, and in particular about the sources of her most well-known attribute – the famous Mae West quips.

'Come up and see me some time,' 'A hard man is good to find,' 'It ain't the men in my life, it's the life in my men that counts,' 'Some women pick men to marry, others pick 'em to pieces,' 'A man in the house is worth two in the street,' 'Between two evils, I always pick the one I never tried before,' 'If your man's dynamite to you, it's up to you to be his match,' 'Love isn't an emotion or an instinct – it's an art' and so many else besides can be heard from the lips of people who never saw a Mae West movie, let alone know about her self-authored plays. But nothing comes from nothing.

Like the Marx Brothers, W. C. Fields or any performer famous for their lines and wisecracks, Mae West never made anything up on the spur of the moment nor ever uttered an ad-lib. Everything came from hard graft: whittling down possibilities, picking and choosing, sometimes appropriating *bons mots* and jokes that were in general circulation. Even silent comedians like 'Fatty' Arbuckle were known to have amassed a library of comic material, gags and jokes. Speaking comedians, from time immemorial, have done the same.

Mae West's development as a comedienne was slow and painstaking. A careful reading of the material in her personal archive shows that her collection of quips mostly post-dates the plays that made her famous and notorious on Broadway from 1926 to 1930. After that, a cornucopia of notes pours out: roughly two thousand pages of 'gags', comprising jokes and quips copied out methodically from joke books. These are preserved in over forty folders, containing around twenty thousand jokes. Much of the material is typewritten, probably by assistants and secretaries, but over five hundred pages are handwritten in Mae's inimitable scrawl. This Herculean labour continued over the next four decades, as she was still jotting down gags and quips on notepaper up to and including the time she was preparing her last movie, *Sextette*, in the later 1970s.

This was – in essence – when one peers behind the mask of glamour, hype, publicity and subterfuge, Mae West's great secret: that she went home to her apartment or hotel room at night and wrote, turning out, from the mid-1920s, plays, skits, drafts, rewrites, versions, treatments and synopses. Most of our evidence, given the loss of early material, dates from Mae's movie period, but one can safely infer that the obsessive note-taking, drafting and stockpiling of raw material would have begun in stage and vaudeville days. Eventually, this would include a vast private library of aphorisms, one-liners and jokes: jokes about love, jokes about men and women, jokes about marriage and the eternal battle of the sexes, jokes about all the aggravations and snags of modern life, jokes on appliances, traffic cops, doctors, soldiers, Irishmen, Jews, jazz, politics, money, lawyers, athletes, prison, elevators, burglars and health fads. Many of these originated from stock publications such as *McNally's Bulletin* of 'Acts, Monologues, Sidewalk Patter, Parodies, Etc,' which appeared from 1914 through to 1940, and the even earlier *Madison's Budget*, a compendium of comedians' patter which appeared from 1898 to 1928. These jokes ranged from the mundane to the awful, by way of the ephemerally topical:

The smallest cast in the world was found in Hollywood. Ben Turpin had it in his eye.

'Interested in art, sir?' 'No, just can't afford the Follies this year.'
HOUSEWIFE: We are getting an electric washer, and so we won't need you any more.
LAUNDRESS: All right, lady, but an electric washer don't give out no gossip.'

Like a magpie, Mae would collect every piece of verbal bric-a-brac, often ticking off 'gags' for possible use: 'Honey, will yo'all marry me? – Why, this is all so southern!' 'Hello Jim, how's the pursuit of happiness? – I can't keep up the pace.' And so forth. 'She: It's better to be looked over than overlooked,' for instance, found its way unchanged into the pantheon. Another entry: 'I just shot a dog – Was he mad? – Well, he wasn't very pleased,' turns up in Mae's own version ('I had to shoot a lion once . . .') in her 1933 movie *I'm No Angel*. Others seem tailor-made as embryonic Mae West-style quips:

'They say that love is blind.'
'Yes, but he has a wonderful sense of touch.'

'You can trust me.'
'I'm not looking for a man I can trust.'

'How did you ever come to fall for him?'
'I guess his line was just low enough to trip.'

'Do you prefer men who are a trifle wicked?'
'Wicked, but not trifling.'

A girl may love you from the bottom of her heart, but there's always room for some other guy at the top.

What good is alimony on a cold night?

Lady Godiva was the greatest gambler – she put everything she had on a horse.

'I'll give you three thousand dollars for this joke.'
'I was thinking of writing a musical comedy around it.'

As indeed she was. These quips were to provide ideas, phrases or notions that could slosh around in the creative attic, fermenting and maturing. As one diligently copied quip aptly put it: 'Sex didn't begin in Hollywood – it just went there to get in the movies.'

In 1921, however, Mae was a long way from Hollywood, and her early models of play-writing were still the archetypes of the standard stage sketch and the 'legitimate' revue. Although there are already signs of the aphoristic style which would later characterize her writings,

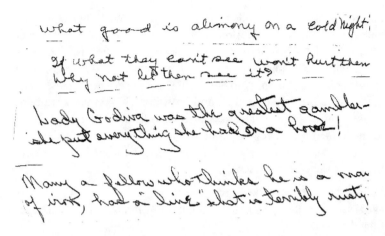

what good is alimony on a cold night?

If what they can't see won't hurt them
why not let them see it?

Lady Godiva was the greatest gambler—
she put everything she had on a horse!

Many a fellow who thinks he is a man
of iron, had a "line" that is terribly rusty

Sample handwritten letter from Mae's joke files

from the opening page of *The Ruby Ring* the world of Mae West's first available text is the familiar one of Broadway's flimflam upper classes:

SCENE I – *The scene represents an ante-room off the ballroom with conservatory with potted palms, fountain, marble bench with high back facing up-stage at back, wide archway leading to ballroom at R. Archway to hall about L.3. Dress set with good taste. Settee obliqued D.L.C. Other chairs etc.*
AT RISE – (*Handsome man in flashy foreign officer's uniform is talking to two very pretty and handsomely gowned women, one of them a brunette, the other auburn haired . . .*)
ALICE (*the auburn-haired girl. She is gushingly vivacious*): Oh *do* Captain, tell us more about your La Belle France!

Two girls, Alice and Irene, are commiserating over the fact that their men are always stolen by their third companion, Gloria, who enters, surrounded by a 'babbling circle' of men, exclaiming: 'Boys, boys, boys! You must give me a little rest. I'm only human after all.'

The entire sketch is an illustration by Gloria to her friends of how a woman who knows 'the right method' can snare any man she wants. As a demonstration, she makes a bet with Irene that she can make five men propose to her 'in less than five minutes each'. If she succeeds, she wins Irene's ruby ring.

This is, in fact, the sketch performed in Mae's 1922 act – 'how different types of vamps put the bee on their heavy Johns'. The marks are Reggie, a clean-cut college boy, John Broad Wall, 'business man, financial king and thirty', Alonzo Mesquite, a 'story-book' westerner ('I can see you – so noble in your shape, with a lariat round your neck . . .'), Schuyler Madison, 'the typical "old sport"' ('You're going on as if I were an old man.' 'No – not old – just experienced and experience is always interesting . . . ') and Professor Thinktank, 'a studious bookworm with his hair parted in the middle and wearing owl-like horn-rimmed spectacles'. Of course, Gloria eventually wins the ring.

Mae's tit-for-tat dialogue, which will become honed as time goes by, is already clearly present:

GLORIA: Do I look so wicked – so immoral?
PROFESSOR: My dear young lady – morality is merely a question of distance from the equator.
GLORIA: Whose equator?
PROFESSOR: Young lady – you're a paradox.
GLORIA: Maybe I'm the gateway to paradise.
PROFESSOR: You merely play with words.
GLORIA: In love, it is not words that count, but feelings.

This play, however, is not about love but power, the new-style war of the sexes in which woman can be triumphant at what is usually the male game: seduction purely to satisfy her own ego and to prove a point to the world. Professor Thinktank, the eminent Freudian psychologist, is a mere child beside the Circian wiles of Mae. With Mesquite, Gloria plays on masculine delusions: 'I insist that you save me from something . . . rattlesnakes or Greasers or tangerines [*note the racial* faux pas – *ed.*] . . . a great big strong man like you!' The businessman Wall is vanquished by flattery for his intellectual qualities: 'Your power – your force – your ability to *do* things – *big* things! I can see it in the keen, steel-gray of your eyes . . . The only thing that makes life hard for you is that you are not appreciated. You *should* have someone to appreciate you!'

The college boy, Reggie, in contrast, is literally a walk in the park: 'I *am* going to let you dance with me – lots and lots and take me for a walk in the park – just for a little while . . .' To him, Gloria 'confesses' that 'lately I've grown ever so much more modern – and daring'. The men are no contest for her, as she muses: 'Whew – you've got to work fast with those fellows! And here comes another. Alonzo Mesquite of the wild and wooly West. He's middle-aged and according to "How to Vamp in Ten Lessons," and all the rules of The Amalgamated Vamp's Union Number One I must be romantic. Here goes!'

This Many Faces of Mae provides an early template of the character that would endure much later, a persona more akin to the movie Mae of the 1930s than to her other 1920s plays. Mae was constructing herself as the traditional vamp, closely based on the prototype played in the movies by Theda Bara (born Theodosia Goodman). In her first starring role, in 1915, in *A Fool There Was*, Bara had played 'the woman who did not care' of Rudyard Kipling's 1897 poem 'The Vampire', a notorious seductress who ruins and robs a succession of wretched men, including a happily married Wall Street lawyer, the fool of the title. The anagram of Miss Goodman's peculiar screen name – 'Arab Death' – conjured Hollywood's early obsession with the imaginary harem woman, the abandoned hussy of the louche Orient. Further roles in *The Serpent*, *The Eternal Sappho*, *The Vixen*, *The Tiger Woman* and *The She Devil*, all made for William Fox between 1916 and 1918, as well as the more traditional *Carmen*, *Camille* and *Madame Dubarry*, established her as the epitome of the elemental force of woman's unbridled sexual powers. Theda Bara was, David Thomson writes, 'the first woman offered commercially, in movies, as an object of sexual fantasy', a far cry from the chaste beauty of Mack Sennett's 'splash-me girls'.

Kipling's misogynous 'Vampire' ode – 'A fool there was and he made his prayer / (Even as you or I!) / To a rag and a bone and a hank of hair, / (We called her the woman who did not care), / But the fool he called her his lady fair – / (Even as you or I!)' – lent its title, via Theda Bara, to an entire cycle of members of Mae West's imaginary Vamps' Union. In her own version, Mae inverted the pejorative concept, adopting the vamp with positive relish and delivering a well-deserved comeuppance to the foolish males who become enmeshed in her web.

Mae had already compared herself to a Theda Bara vamp in her song as Mayme in *Sometime*. Other models would turn up later: in 1921, the future vamp Pola Negri was still making German movies with Ernst Lubitsch in Europe, although an English version of *Madame Du Barry* was shown in the US in 1920, and English versions of *Carmen* and *Sumurun* in 1921. Clara Bow, the quintessential 'it' girl of the 1920s, was only sixteen years old in 1921, when she won Brewster Publications' Fame and Fortune contest. Thus, while Mae West shimmied towards Prohibition, the blessed Theodosia reigned alone.

Kevin Brownlow, in his book about lost and forgotten social-issue films of the silent era, *Behind the Mask of Innocence*, writes of a 1918 film, *Men Who Have Made Love to Me*, based on and starring a real life 'vamp', Mary McLane, whose book of sexual confessions (*The Story of Mary McLane*) was published in 1902. The film was, Brownlow writes, 'an episodic picture, an account of six affairs: a callow youth (Ralph Graves), who quickly bores Mary; a self-obsessed literary man (R. Paul Harvey); a depraved gentleman (Cliff Worman); a cave man (Alador Prince) she is forced to give up; a bank clerk (Clarence Derwent) who wants a baby and a cottage but loathes her smoking and drinking. The sixth is "the husband of another (Fred Tiden) who gave her a thrill one night by breaking down the bedroom door, but spoiled the ecstasy by having bad liquor on his breath."' These early films depicting the less salubrious aspects of real life were, Brownlow's archaeology reveals, more prevalent than standard movie histories would have us believe, and the similarity of the above structure to Mae's own, much more playful script is more than just superficial.

Mae's early interest in pictures has already been shown by her purchase of William Lewis Gordon's 1915 manual of 'moving picture play' writing, found in her archive. But Gordon's advice about subject matter in screenplays would not have encouraged her greatly, as he sternly urged the prospective writer to 'avoid scenes of murder, robbery, kidnapping, harrowing deathbeds . . . violent fights showing strangling, shooting or stabbing, staggering drunkards, depraved or wayward women, rioting strikers, funerals, and all such scenes of a depressing or unpleasant nature'. This did not seem to leave much of interest to anyone who wished to represent the world as it was, in all its shades and shadows. But there were obviously echoes, in Mae's first playlet, of her more serious feminist intent.

The agitation for women's suffrage was only the most visible part of a much wider prolonged struggle by women's groups and fervent women like birth-control pioneer Margaret Sanger to effect a radical change in the way male society treated and perceived women and the way women perceived themselves. In New York, as throughout the US, information on contraception was illegal, and it remained so in many states for decades. These prohibitions, as ever, affected the poor rather than the rich. Censorship of such matters was ubiquitous for both the printed word and films and was spearheaded by post-office special agent Anthony Comstock, whose self-proclaimed mission was to stand 'at the sewer mouth of society'. Vaudeville's shimmies, double entendres and slang were just the dribble of this flowing pipe.

The censorship of movies, continually strengthened and then armour-plated by ex-Postmaster General Will Hays after the Fatty Arbuckle scandal of late 1921, was to lie in wait for Mae West a decade later, when she was to become Hollywood's censorship *cause célèbre*. In the theatre, while there was no Hays-like control, state laws governed the limits of what could or could not be said or represented on the stage. Agitation against 'dirty plays' continued throughout the 1920s and stretched back as far as stage records go: in the month of Mae's birth, August 1893, the local *Brooklyn Eagle* was already grouching that 'the stage is given over to kicking and brazen faced soubrettes, to yelling song and dance men, banjo players, women who fling somersaults, youths dressed as frogs and monkeys . . . girls who march up the stage and down again in tights . . .'

Mae West, in 1921 and 1922, was not yet prepared to face this full blast of social and authoritarian censure. Both her early texts show a quite cautious approach towards her underlying feminine rebellion. While *The Ruby Ring* was performed – most probably in a truncated form – in her 1922 act, her second play, *The Hussy*, completed in the same year, remained an unperformed piece.

The script of *The Hussy* deposited with the Library of Congress is subtitled 'A Serio-Comedy Drama' and credited as 'Dramatized by Adeline Leitzbach, From Materials Supplied by Mae West.' The phrase 'Materials Supplied by' is crossed out by hand and replaced by 'and Mae West', with the 'e' of Mae oddly crossed out and replaced by a 'y'. Perhaps Mae wished to be a slightly different person in the writing, just as she presented her seminal 1926 *Sex* (and other subsequent scripts) as written by 'Jane Mast'.

Adeline Leitzbach was a playwright who had a moderately successful play – *Success* – produced in 1918. This was the story of a drunk actor who hits the skids, makes a comeback and tries to help his estranged daughter. The play was made into a movie in 1923, with the very young Mary Astor as the daughter. Leitzbach was to write several more plays and at least one more movie, a horror film, *House of Secrets*, made in 1929.

Most of *The Hussy* is a fairly standard drama set in a 'handsome suburban home' with a small conservatory and a veranda furnished with 'willow, chintz covered furniture'. The house belongs to a Mrs Clinton Somerville, who has a daughter, Jean, a son, Clinton, a ward, Nancy Baynes, and two more young people resident, Thomas Ramsey and his sister Nona, the hussy of the title – to be played by Mae West. Conversations revolve around marriage plans with rich suitors, namely one Robert Van Sturdevant, 'millionaire and then some more', whom Jean loves but who clearly fancies Nona. Mrs Somerville is a *bona fide* snob, exclaiming, about Nona:

MRS SOMERVILLE: That Hussy! All she cares for is herself. I tell you she would marry Clinton tomorrow just to get a social footing – and she'd divorce him as soon as she found someone with more money – she'd use him as a footstool . . .

The co-authorship of the play makes it difficult to detach the contributions of Miss Leitzbach from those of Mae West, but one can clearly discern references to Mae's own home life in the dialogue, distorted in a semi-Dickensian mode, as Mrs Somerville pours scorn on Nona's background:

MRS SOMERVILLE: She's a disgrace . . . and her mother's no better than she is! Took in boarders and did sewing till that hussy got started on her career . . . The shack they used to live in! Look at it now! Painted – repaired – the truck garden turned into flower beds – Nona's money – and WHERE DID SHE GET IT!

Later in the script, when Nona speaks of her own upbringing, she confronts both her mother and her brother with recollections of the 'old days' – all 'the raking and scraping and penny pinching – not half enough to eat half the time, nothing but cheap little rags to wear, and not enough of them – you working yourself into an old woman – and – dad always betting on the wrong horse!' And, speaking of her own 'vamping' of men:

NONA: Do you suppose I like this game I'm playing – like the devil I do!
TOM (*her brother*): Well, what do you do it for!
MRS RAMSEY (*her mother*): Children . . .
NONA : Because I wanted money – I want money – money to get the things these fine folks around here have – maybe if the swell bunch had never

blown into this town – I'd have been satisfied with the rags and the hash –
and ended my days behind some counter selling gloves or – but they gave me
an education . . . The old man would never let me learn a trade or a profession – what did he want me to do – scrub floors – you wouldn't even let me
finish high school – if I'd had a voice, or could have danced – or played the
piano or painted, or something – but I got just about as much talent as the
old man has – none! . . . Only difference between him and me – is I picked
the right horse once in a while!

At heart, Nona only yearns for the benefits of the prosperous middle classes – a way out of poverty and true love with a husband – but
she is misunderstood by all as the hussy. As the plot progresses, Mrs
Somerville, alarmed that Nona could be stealing the affections of the
millionaire Sturdevant from her own daughter, hires a detective,
Farron, to pose as a well-off married man looking for a good time
with Nona for financial gain, but she rejects him. To prove a point to
Jean Somerville and her girlfriends, Nona then re-enacts the serial
seduction of *The Ruby Ring*, culminating with Van Sturdevant, who
seems at first not to be the millionaire the family think he is but then,
in a *volte-face*, turns out to be the *bona fide* owner of an ancestral
estate. Nona, who wouldn't marry him as a millionaire but loves him
as a commoner, has got her diamond man after all.

The entire piece is an extended – very extended, at over a hundred
pages – play at having one's moral cake and eating it, and it is not surprising that it did not win any backers. There are even less Westian
quips than in *The Ruby Ring* and too much laboured exposition. In the
end, we are left with an apprentice work notable mainly for the parental
confrontations that will be expressed in a future, more mature play,
1927's *The Wicked Age*. But when Nona bursts out against her father,
one feels that something more than fiction may be at stake:

MRS RAMSEY (*mother*): It might be better if you did get married, Nona – and
settled down –

RAMSEY (*father*): And stop this damned running around – you'll see who's
boss in this house – from tonight – you stay in . . . do you know what the
neighbours call you – you – my daughter –

NONA: You cared a whole lot what the neighbours said when you let your
wife work herself old before her time – didn't you? . . . You didn't think it a
disgrace that you didn't give your children a decent start in life . . .

RAMSEY: I kept a roof over your head, haven't I?

NONA: A mighty leaky one, and you wouldn't have done that if your poor father hadn't had your number – You'd a sold this place a long time ago and bet the money on the wrong horse, if your father hadn't willed it to his grandchildren! You kept a roof over our head – why, you'd have told mom to go out and cook grass and serve it for spinach before you'd have exerted yourself for a day's work!

RAMSEY: You ain't overstuck on work yourself!

NONA: Don't blame me for a family trait – I take after – my father!

Imbued with the fighting spirit of Battlin' Jack, Mae was not prepared, despite her setbacks, to hang up her gloves and opt for a quiet life. Not yet accepted as a writer, she bided her time, returning, once again, to her vaudeville roots.

You've Gotta Have a Certain Something

In 1922, finally, we have a leading witness, apart from our heroine's own testimony, to Mae West in late vaudeville. The witness is Harry Richman, *bon vivant*, musician, songwriter and 'man-about-town' entertainer, with his signature top hat or straw boater and cane. Born in 1895 in Cincinnati, Ohio, he had been on stage since the age of twelve, then, at eighteen, changed his name from Reichman and launched a song-and-dance act. Richman has left us his reminiscences of his somewhat short period as Mae West's accompanying pianist in a 1966 autobiography, *A Hell of a Life*, co-written with Richard Gehman.

Richman's recollections are vivid and colourful, but his 1966 account of his meeting with Mae West clashes profoundly with another account he gave of his first encounter with her, published in a Hollywood magazine in October 1934. (The source is dated but unnamed in the clippings in Mae's personal archive.) In 1934, Richman related how, in 1915, returning from a gig in San Francisco as part of the 'Jewel City Trio', he received a call from the Keith booking office to contact a Mr James 'Timoney', then a 'New York theatrical attorney', to meet a client who was seeking a vaudeville partner. Richman continues:

It is hard to believe how like the Mae West of today the Mae West of 1915 appeared when I met her then. The same curves, bustles, curly blonde hair, floppy picture hat and all. To see Miss West today one who knew her then might imagine that here was a present-day-female Rip Van Winkle, fresh from a twenty year nap.

Her acknowledgment of Timoney's introduction was typical, and I must admit left me slightly ill at ease. She did not speak; did not even smile. Instead, her eyes swept me from head to foot, a long, appraising stare. I felt an attack of fidgets coming on. Then she spoke.

'Are you versatile?' she demanded in a low, crooning monotone, with a trace of what seemed to be skepticism in her intonation.

By this time my case of fidgets had passed the incipient stage. I felt like a schoolboy in the principal's office. But I did want that job! I replied with all the savoir-faire . . . that I could summon.

'That all depends on what you mean by versatile.'

'Well, I need a piano player good enough to do specialty numbers while I change my clothes, and keep the suckers on the jump,' she explained. 'You've gotta be able to put over a song. You've gotta be a swell actor – able to feed lines and take 'em. You've gotta look like a million bucks on the stage, even on an empty stomach, and you've gotta be able to wear clothes.

'But above all,' she concluded, 'you've gotta have a certain something.'

In his autobiography, Richman alters both the date and the spelling:

One day in 1922 in New York, James Timmony, a man I knew only slightly, Mae West's manager, called me up. I couldn't imagine what he wanted. I was a nonentity. But he said, 'How would you like to be Mae West's accompanist?'

. . . He was known in our business as a no-nonsense guy, and he came straight to the point.

'I'm going to introduce you to Mae, and she'll audition you, but don't get any ideas,' he said. 'If you ever have a romance in any way with Mae West, you're finished. Falling in love with Mae, if you're working with her, always breaks up the act. There's got to be no romance – it's strictly business.'

It is beyond the ken of the researcher to figure out why Richman of 1934 dated his meeting with Mae to seven years before history hitherto set it. In 1966, aged seventy-one, his memory might have dimmed, but logic suggests the second account is the right one. Richman, circa 1966, continues:

Timmony set up an audition. He brought Mae West to a theater, and I sat down under an electric light bulb hanging from the ceiling on a cord and talked my way through some songs. At the time I lisped a little; I always had, since boyhood . . . I was terribly nervous in that audition, and told Mae West that I was.

'Don't worry about it, big boy,' she said. 'That lisp could be the making of you. It's distinctive.'

As later proved to be the case. Richman's earlier account, which related a disagreement as to whether the act should be called Mae West & Co. or Mae West & Harry Richman, with the honours going to the latter, does not fit 1915 at all. Perhaps, in 1934, Richman baulked at the confession that until meeting Mae he had been 'a nonentity', which would have brought his obscurity, in 1922, much nearer his 1934 fame. Yet another cautionary tale of the reliability of personal memoirs.

Mae also, Richman wrote in 1966, wanted him to participate in her sketches: 'In one of them she played a queen, or an empress, lying on a settee, with a huge picture of a gladiator on a backdrop just over her shoulder. She was wearing nothing but a squirrel skin.' Harry was to play the new gladiator Mae was intent on hiring. He would come on in modern street clothes, she would explain the necessary attire, he would protest: '"Me . . . undress like that? Never. Nothing doing." This was where she would begin giving me those sly looks, and those sexy remarks, and . . . before long I was down on my knees in front of her, saying, "O.K., I'll be your gladiator."' At which point the men in the audience would stand up and applaud and 'carry on the way the people did when I saw Caruso at the Metropolitan Opera House'.

Timony's warning to Richman was left out of his 1934 version. We can assume, reading it today, that young Harry was being clearly warned off by the diva's patron, though he seems to have taken the caution at face value. Richman's reputation already as a ladies' man might well have preceded him. In later years he would nail the scalps of Jean Harlow, Clara Bow and Barbara La Marr, among others, to his totem pole. Maybe it was the lisp that did it.

Variety raved, for a change, at the new act's opening at the Riverside Theater in June 1922: 'Mae West, once known to vaudeville fans as a girl who shook a wicked shoulder, will prove a revelation to her former acquaintances . . . She rises to heights undreamed of for her and reveals unsuspected depths as a delineator of character songs, a dramatic reader of ability and a girl with a flare for farce that will some day land her on the legitimate Olympus. In her new turn she is assisted by Harry Richman, who is an ideal opposite. Richman has the appearance of a musical comedy juvenile coupled with an ability to read lines and a pleasant singing voice and delivery.' This was written not by 'Sime' but by 'Con', alias Jack Conway, who was destined to be a long-term fan.

The finish of the act, according to Richman, was the ever-transgressive 'Frankie and Johnny', which included an old blues-song line: 'If you don't like my peaches, don't you shake my tree.' The men in the audience became so boisterous that one manager complained to

the vaudeville mogul Edward Albee. This led to a special performance at the famous Palace Theater for an audience consisting only
of Albee and his secretary. Albee's response: 'A *priest* could never be
offended by that.' And the irate manager had to stand down.

Both Richman's accounts, the '1915' and the '1922' stories, agree
that Mae constantly held out for more money, demanding $750 a
week when Albee would concede at most $500. 'If she couldn't get
what she wanted,' Richman wrote, 'she remained idle, even though
her telephone, electricity, and everything else were turned off and the
bill collectors were pounding at her door.' Her stubbornness,
Richman recalled, taught him a good lesson about the business end of
show business.

The whole thing came to a precipitate end, Richman relates, due to
a curious semi-romantic moment. During out-of-town tours,
Richman wrote, he would always make sure to book a room on a different floor from Mae's, so as not to be tempted to fall foul of
Timony's *fatwa*. On one occasion, at Hartford, Connecticut, Mae's
maid called Richman in his room at 1 a.m., claiming Mae needed
help as she was 'desperately ill'. Slapping on his robe, he took the elevator down to her floor. Mae was:

. . . lying on the bed, a cold towel on her forehead. The maid was nowhere
in sight. There was a very dim light over the bed, and I could just make out
Mae's form there. To make matters worse, she was moaning. Now I really
was frantic.

'I'll call a doctor,' I said . . . In the dim light she was pale as death. 'I'll just
call the desk,' I said. Another moan. I reached for the telephone. As I did she
gently reached out a trembling hand. I took it and kissed it. I never found out
how sick she really was. All I did was kiss her hand. But the next day I learned
that the great act of Mae West and Harry Richman was finished forever.

In some of her last interviews, Mae opened her closet a crack to
allow some intriguing aspects of her relationship with James Timony
to escape. She told *Playboy* magazine in 1971: 'For years, my manager was wild about me and he was very possessive and jealous of my
other romances. He taught me that you've gotta conserve your sex
energy in order to *do* things. This is the way you store up power for
your creative work, he says.' And keep out of Harry Richman *et al.*'s
pants, one might assume. In another account, Mae confided (to her
1960s agent Stanley Musgrove) that Timony actually forbade her sex

while she was writing, on the same grounds. Perhaps he had been boning up on Freud's theories of sublimation. The elder Mae told *Playboy*: 'It was through this knowledge that I started to really write, and when I started a picture, I'd stop all my sex activities and put that energy into my work.' But this may well have been a test run for her 'theoretical' writings on sex that would soon be vented in *Mae West on Sex, Health and ESP*, her eccentric 1973 book. Mae West's reinventions always affected her remaking of herself in retrospect, continually altering her own story. The truth about Mae's sexual affairs is folded behind multiple layers of her many 'tease-and-not-quite-tell' tales. Heavyweight champion Jack Dempsey was, according to lore, an early 'come up and see me' stalwart from the period of the *Mimic World*. Tales of his interest in involving Mae not only in romance but in a motion picture starring himself turned out to be yet another unfulfilled tease.

Harry Richman was said to have boasted, despite his version above, of his access to the lady's chamber, according to a tale told to Stanley Musgrove by director–choreographer Charlie O'Curran. 'He knew Mae wanted to make it with him,' Richman was supposed to have told O'Curran, but he stalled her because of the dire warnings. 'The show deteriorated . . . she took out her frustration on him while they were onstage. So finally Harry decided he didn't give a shit and would go up and bang her. That night he did, and the next day the performance was fantastic.'

Whatever the truth of this tale, Richman's own tale of his parting with Mae is not borne out by the facts. On 8 September 1922, *Variety* reported:

MAE WEST, AUTHOR, LOSES HER PIANIST

With four weeks laid out for her over the Keith time, starting last week at the Davis, Pittsburgh, Mae West was unable to start the engagement through Harry Richman, her pianist, suddenly accepting an engagement with Nora Bayes for Miss Bayes' new show.

Since Richman left her, Miss West has been looking for another ivory player and will take to the vaudeville route while securing one.

Meanwhile the comedienne, in collaboration, is writing a farce comedy she intends shall star herself, but be produced by managerial forces.

This last reference was clearly to *The Hussy*, which would have been drafted by then. Nora Bayes was still, at that time, one of vaudeville's hottest tickets, and a post by her side at the piano keys was a major coup for Richman. His precipitate departure was probably also due to another abortive attempt by Mae to launch herself – with Richman in the act – in a 'legit' Broadway show. This was another Shubert extravaganza-to-be called *The Ginger Box Revue*, intended for the Greenwich Village Theatre. A role for Mae, written by Paul Dupont, built on her 'many faces of Mae' sketch *à la The Ruby Ring* and extended Mae's personas to include the mythological seductress Circe and a traditional vamp, who belts out 'I Want a Cave Man' to a reluctant Harry Richman. Another sketch lampooned Eugene O'Neill's recent theatrical sensation, *The Hairy Ape*, featuring Yank Smith, O'Neill's brutish everyman, echoes of whom will turn up in Mae's work as far ahead as Victor Mature's sea captain in 1936's *Klondike Annie*.

This show, alas, did not get past its previews, as, after a brief tryout in Connecticut with inadequate sets and décor, the producer, Edward Perkins, bolted, leaving the press to reveal his many aliases – 'Roy Dixon', 'Fred Carroll' and the aforementioned 'Paul Dupont'. The actors and managers had been taken in by a charlatan who had promised to 'out-Ziegfeld Ziegfeld' but who, in fact, did not even own the shoestring on which the revue was put together. The *Sunday News* dubbed him 'the Prince de Bunk of impresarios'. The electric sign promoting the show was put up over the Greenwich Village Theater in New York but was never lit. On 23 August, the *New York Clipper* noted:

Mae West, who was with 'The Ginger Box,' which opened and closed rather suddenly has returned to vaudeville, and opened at Proctor's Fifth Avenue on Monday.

Soon after, as we saw, Richman, too, bolted, although – despite the fluffy tales of his sexual contretemps – he was back some months later, reappearing with Mae in their vaudeville act, with the *Clipper* reporting their opening at the Colonial Theater in April 1923, alongside the screening of Harold Lloyd's movie *Safety Last*:

Mae West and Harry Richman also stopped the show. Miss West didn't do quite as well as far as getting laughs are concerned as she has done when they did the act before. This may be due to the fact that they hadn't done the act in so long, for she had developed into a dandy performer. Richman is class from start to finish, both from appearance and ability viewpoints. His piano work, even though most of it is accompaniment, makes an audience cry for more, and his singing is sure-fire. He's an artist in everything he does.

The duo were nevertheless hardly top of the bill, as, apart from the Lloyd masterpiece, one Thomas J. Ryan, of 'the old-time Ryan and Kelly', offered a playlet by Edgar Allan Woolf, and Montana, 'a wizard of the banjo, wowed them on number two'. Opening the show was Sultan, a trained pony, introduced by 'an attractive young lady', the moke performing 'arithmetic' stunts and 'a few comedy bits' which 'drew very good applause at the finish'.

Harry Richman went on to a distinguished career on Broadway and a somewhat less dazzling one in films, appearing in *Putting on the Ritz* (1930, director Edward Sloman, title song by Irving Berlin). But despite the many women he claimed to have conquered – and whether or not he had bedded Mae West in the teeth of James Timony's prohibition – it was not, in the end, sex that ruled his alliance with Mae but good old-fashioned business affairs.

The reality at this stage was that while Harry Richman was on the way up, Mae West was on a downward spiral. Despite 'Con''s prophecy in *Variety* that her flare would 'some day land her on the legitimate Olympus', that day was most reluctant to dawn. Mae appeared to be treading water, yoked to the vaudeville millstone as it churned its eternal circle, steadily but surely left behind by the hegemony of motion pictures. What stage comedian could compete with the antics of Harold Lloyd as he scrabbled up his Los Angeles building pretending to be a human fly, hanging perilously over the busy traffic clutching the protruding hands of time? What dramatist could compete with Cecil B. DeMille's mighty *The Ten Commandments*, bringing the Bible's saga to life? What monologuist or rhetorician could match the irony, charm, adventure and visual portraiture of the frontier West in John Ford's *The Iron Horse*?

More frustrating for Mae was the continuing dominance of the old-time vaudeville greats: Eva Tanguay, opening yet again in January 1924 with a new set of songs. 'The Dynamic Force of Vaudeville, Resistless as the Torrential Tide That Tosses Madly Over the Teeming Cataract of Niagara,' as her publicity burbled, 'As Easy to Check the Rush of Waters Over the Falls as the Oncoming Multitudes of Pleasure Seekers to the Theatres Where the World's Most Popular Comedienne Appears.' Sophie Tucker, 'Last of the Red

Hot Mamas', was still wowing them with her white versions of the blues. Fay Templeton, who had starred in George M. Cohan's *Forty-Five Minutes from Broadway* in 1906, was still headlining at the Palace in 1925 – aged sixty!

Mae would need all her reserves of self-confidence and self-belief to keep the faith in her own star. In March 1924, *Variety* noted a new act upon the boards: Beverly West and Co., Piano and Singing. This was the act that became written up later as Beverly West's child act aged sixteen (to accommodate Mae's fictitious 1900 birth date), whereas Beverly was, in fact, twenty-six years old and had been married to a Russian industrial designer, Serge Treshatny, a specialist in air-cooled engines, since 1917. Beverly herself was most reticent in her later comments on her own act, presenting it as a minor enterprise on her way to becoming her sister Mae's understudy for the 1926 play *Sex*. *Variety* did not seem to note, at the time, that she was Mae West's sister and stated only that 'she puts over her numbers acceptably'.

By now, however, Mae herself was sliding further and further down the vaudeville scale. In the same week of Beverly West's début at Proctor's 58th Street theater in Manhattan, Mae was playing the San Antonio Majestic, way out west in Texas, on the provincial Interstate circuit. This was not necessarily disgrace or exile, as in the same week of 19 March 1924 Eva Tanguay herself was in Dallas. Tanguay, however, soon sashayed back east, while Mae remained in the Big Country for at least some weeks. In Houston, she seemed to have a new *amour*, a local *Variety* stringer named Bud Burmester or Burmeister. Bud and Mae, according to author Maurice Leonard, who found the document, took out a marriage licence in Harris County, Texas, on 22 March 1924, in which Burmester's age is given as thirty-four and Mae's as the fictitious twenty-four. The licence, however, was not validated – no marriage was performed. In light of the Vanished Husband, Frank Wallace, it would clearly have been bigamous. Little is known of Burmester, who may or may not have been the same man celebrated by jockey clubs in the 1950s as 'the prominent Texas breeder'. He merits no mention in Mae's autobiography but might well have been the prodigal remembered in her song in the 1933 movie *I'm No Angel* – 'No One Loves Me Like That Dallas Man'.

By April, Mae had moved to Oklahoma to play the Tulsa Orpheum on the ninth. In late June, however, she was back in New York, play-ing Keith's Riverside Theater once again:

Her next to shut impression copped all the applause honors of the night, the blonde character artist giving them both barrels of her startling personality and making them forget the heat. Mae did 18 fast minutes, equaling the track record at the house. Opening with her vampire number, which sported a new gown, and big league head dress of aigrats [*sic?*], she followed with the French prima donna, 'You'll Be Sorry,' sung as a chorus girl would yodle it, a dramatic actress and a cabaret singer. She's one of the cleverest single women in vaudeville.

Yet again, a push from her in-house *Variety* fan 'Con'. But still the same old routine. Around the city other variety stars were breaking new ground: W. C. Fields had opened in May in his star role as the Great Eustace McGargle in *Poppy*, and the Marx Brothers opened on Broadway with *I'll Say She Is* at the Casino theater, both shows that would be massive hits. Even Roscoe 'Fatty' Arbuckle, disgraced in movies, was opening in vaudeville, in comic gags and monologues, at the Pantages San Francisco.

In late July, the Motion Picture Producers unveiled the latest pack-age by Will Hays to 'clean up on films'. Mae's old alleged suitor, Joseph M. Schenck, endorsed the 'Czar of Pictures – Says Only Man He Ever Called "Chief" – 30,000,000 People Behind Hays' Refinement of Pictures Movement,' as quoth *Variety*. At the same time, pressure continued to clean up 'dirty plays', shows and bur-lesque: 'Vulgarity of Words and Action is Out Forever on Columbia Wheel,' the circuit managers pledged.

Replacing burlesque, cabarets were now big business, hostess with the mostest Texas Guinan hugging and kissing her clients at the El Fay Club on West 45th Street. Stage and screen celebrities were fre-quent guests and Mae West was said to have featured informally, no doubt imbibing innocent sarsaparilla.

In September 1924, Mae was gracing Columbus, Ohio, with her act at Keith's Theater, followed by Detroit. This appears to be the last sighting in the lists of Mae West's vaudeville act. For the rest of the year, and through all of 1925, she drops completely out of sight. Previous chroniclers of her life have been reduced to speculation: she had returned home to Brooklyn, spent time in New York with Timony, had her affair with the gangster Owney Madden, prepared her next project, frequented more African-American nightspots. Biographer Jill Watts speculated that Mae and Timony had been involved in the financing of a hotel in New York, the Harding, a 'popular hangout for boxers, show people, and some of New York's most notorious gangsters'. Watts claims that Matilda West, using the alias of Tillie Landauer, was 'almost certainly acting as a front for one of New York's most powerful crime bosses, Owney Madden'. New technologies to search the *New York Times* in depth reveal, however, that Mrs Landauer was not Mrs West at all but rather the loyal wife of one Max Landauer (the real lessee of the Harding) and good mother of Joseph and Irving T. Landauer. Wishful thinking once again intruding.

The gossip about Mae's affair with Owney 'The Killer' Madden has persisted in all accounts of Mae in this period, along with a less common rumour linking her at some point with Al Capone. An article in the *Los Angeles Times* on 23 December 1984, by Kevin Thomas, recalled Madden's ownership of the famous Cotton Club during the 1920s. Veteran Hollywood director Allan Dwan had borne witness that 'West and Owney had a "hot romance."' Another close West friend, Herbert Kenwith, a TV director who had been stage manager of a revival of Mae's *Diamond Lil* in 1949, recalled to Thomas a warm welcome given by Mae to the gangster, then retired, whom she described as 'one of the few gangsters she knew who truly was a gentleman – and she knew them all'.

Madden's résumé hardly bears out this judgement, though he was without doubt one of the primary 'Godfathers' of New York's Prohibition era. Born in Liverpool, England, Madden had migrated to New York and become a small-time runner – or 'Gopher' – on the East Side docks. Rising to lead his own gang, the Hell's Kitchen Gophers, he was convicted in 1914 of the 'second degree murder' of another gangster, William Moore, alias 'Little Patsy Doyle', and sentenced to twenty years to life in Sing Sing. He was released on parole in 1923, which is the earliest date that Mae West could have met him, unless he was in the audience of her 1916 prison benefit. Pretty soon, Madden was in charge of the streets again, in alliance with such bootleg barons as Dutch Schultz, Legs Diamond, Vannie Higgins, Chink Sherman, the delightfully named Big Frenchy Le Mange and Larry Fay, an ex-taxicab mogul with a fondness for nightclubs who was a regular host at Texas Guinan's establishments. For almost a decade,

New York police reckoned that Madden's beer flowed freely in New York and they nicknamed him 'Clay Pidgeon' because of the many bullets he stopped from competitors. He had personally racked up six killings, the police said, but only the first charge had stuck.

Though he, too, like Larry Fay, wanted to be seen as a gentleman, a Robin Hood rather than just a hood, he was clearly a thug who survived by dint of political influence to die in bed in Hot Springs, Arkansas, in 1965 at the age of seventy-three. He was even granted citizenship in 1943, despite his long criminal career. His place in the mythic American pantheon may have been due in part to his good relationship with Walter Winchell, New York's premier columnist, who once accepted the protection of a Madden gunman during one twist of the 1930s liquor wars.

Did Mae West bed Madden? Or did he bed her? It is impossible to prove a negative. Madden's closeness to Mae is suggested not only by gossip but by a press photograph showing him by her side at the time of her mother's funeral in 1930. But the pattern of Mae's *amours*, both to date and subsequent, suggest that, Timony apart, she preferred unknown, physically suitable partners for short-term use to famous or notorious lovers, let alone so powerful a figure as Madden, whom she could neither easily set aside nor control. On the other hand, her attraction to men of violence is evident in much of her later writing, and her penchant for the more controlled aggression of boxers was to become widely known. In short, we chalk up a verdict of 'Not Proven' – another speculative ghost flapping amid the familiar Westian hints and teasing.

Because Madden was the owner or one of the syndicate of owners of the Cotton Club, he was said to be the conduit for Mae's encounter with its band leader, Duke Ellington. A decade later, Mae would feature Ellington in 1934's *Belle of the Nineties*, against studio opposition. Mae would, however, have been familiar with the Cotton Club in any case. The club, conceived as a venue for upscale white folk to enjoy black entertainment, showcased Lena Horne, Cab Calloway, Bill 'Bojangles' Robinson and the rapidly rising Louis Armstrong, among many others.

Mae's interest in black music continued to be evident, as was the case with most of her vaudeville peers. Both Sophie Tucker and Nora Bayes openly acknowledged their debt to 'negro' music and the by now ubiquitous blues. By 1922, Mamie Smith and her Jazz Hounds had recorded some of her greatest numbers, from 'Don't Care Blues' through 'Don't Mess With Me', Perry Bradford's 'That Thing Called Love' and the wonderfully titled 'You Can Have Him, I Don't Want Him, Didn't Love Him Anyhow Blues'. By 1925, Bessie Smith had recorded 'Easy Come Easy Go Blues', W. C. Handy's 'Careless Love Blues' and many more, and Gertrude 'Ma' Rainey had belted out the 'Shave 'Em Dry Blues' and much else. One need only listen to Mae's later renditions of her own movie numbers to realize her debt to these singers.

Two black songwriters, Andrea 'Andy' Razaf and Perry Bradford, bore witness to her interest in black music, as she frequented the 'black Gaiety Building publishing offices throughout the Twenties in search of fresh bawdy song material for her repertoire'. Perry Bradford, in *Born with the Blues*, wrote about one foray conducted on her behalf by her later-to-be-famous maid Bea Jackson. Perry relates the scene as Bea arrived to interrupt a 3 a.m. bootleg-fuelled party:

'What brings you here so early?' I asked. 'Miss West told me to drop by here and get a copy of some man song that you published before I left the theatre last night.'

I don't know what man song she wanted, because we had three man songs: 'He Used to Be Your Man, But Now He Belongs to Me,' 'He's a Mean Man – But He's So Good to Me,' and 'He May Be Your Man But He Comes to See Me Sometimes.'

Jimmy Johnson played 'He Used to Be Your Man' until it soaked in good, but when he played 'He May Be Your Man But He Comes to See Me Sometimes,' Bea folded up the two songs and said, 'That'll get it,' because she remembered the last song from a phrase that Miss West made famous in later years . . . Jim Burris, a great party story-teller himself, poured Bea a drink and after a few slugs under her belt she started telling some underworld stories about the 'French Guillotine.' Then Fats Waller, who had been stomping out some hot piano rags, cried out, 'The party is just beginning to get good, so let's all go uptown to Dad Brooks' apartment and let the good times keep on rolling . . .'

Note the presence in this tale of the black maid Bea, not Mae herself, who could hardly have crashed this party. Mae's recourse to black songs, music and methods, including the jazz dances taught by choreographers like Willie Covan and Buddy Bradley, was common among many white performers. Covan later professionally coached the stars in Hollywood, and, as well as Mae West, Buddy Bradley counted among his pupils Ed Wynn, Ann Pennington, Eddie Foy, Ruby Keeler, Jack Donahue, Lucille Ball and, of course, Fred and Adele Astaire. Mae was never a first-class dancer, despite her Ned Wayburn training, but black mentors continued to transform her style.

Perry Bradford described the mood of the times as 'We Never Let Monkey Business Interfere With Our Pleasure.' Soon, the new fad dance was the Charleston, shaking the speakeasies and the dance halls. 'Negro actors' were 'flooding burlesque', according to *Variety*, with 75 per cent of the Columbia Wheel's shows featuring 'colored specialties'. New York's night life, *Variety* reported in August, was 'of a daring and brilliance not approached in the halcyon days of Rector's, Shaley's and Delmonico's, when everything was wide open . . . It all sums up as the aftermath of Prohibition. "Throwing a party" means but one thing these days – booze with consistent and thorough saturation . . .' The flapper, said *Variety*, was holding sway:

Broadway has little to hold. There is more adventure and color in 'mixing' at some of the cheap dance halls, where the romance of youth at least commands a certain charm, than there is in sitting back formally at the cabarets which draw nouveau-riche trade that brags of each bottle of wine it opens . . .

The speak-easies speak dramas for themselves. Nothing hypocritical there. Everything is open and above board. You come to drink. You recline pacifically and irrigate the tonsils as thoroughly as the mental and physical pace permits . . . The common garden variety type of speak-easy has lately given way to elaborate drinking clubs, appointed with sleeping accommodation for the pass-outs or other inefficients with also other uses . . .

The upper west side apartment rendezvous of semi-public nature is another oasis of distinctive character. A dimly lit interior with anterooms adjacent, a muffled piano and a couple or three 'hostesses' are the attractions in addition to the liquor. The tariff depends on the visitor and the hostess.

Another exceptionally sordid phase of night life that seems particularly appealing to the Times square 'wise mob,' which hangs on to the fringes of show business, being not actually of the profesh, but catering in commercial or other respects to the native of Broadway, revolving on what a prominent play broker calls 'the third sex' for entertainment. These girlish boys and manly women feature a style of comedy that is as distinctive as the native negro's when he is playing to his own people and not adulterating his stuff for the whites . . . Greenwich Village was alleged to be notorious for such entertainment, but the side streets of the 40's and 50's between Fifth avenue and Broadway seem the favorite stamping grounds.

But it was precisely to these stamping grounds, the lower depths of the city, that Mae was about to turn for material to prepare her next enterprise, the play that was to catapult her into the headlines and for ever brand the name of Mae West with its provocative and ultimately scandalous title: *Sex*.

PART THREE

Sex, Drag and Rocky Roads

Mae West and suitor in 'Sex'

13

Never Has Disgrace Fallen So Heavily . . .

'I got started in plays because in 1926 I was in musicals and in revues for the Shuberts and they recognized my dramatic abilities and they wanted me to star in a drama. But I thought the plays they picked weren't right for me. And my mother had watched me changing around my vaudeville routines . . . and she told me you can write your own play. I said, "That's a lot of work, I wouldn't want to bother with it."' Such was Mae's own version of the process which lead to the writing of *Sex*, in this case as told to *Life* magazine's Richard Meryman in 1969:

Two or three months went by and still no play I liked. I was in New York one day and the traffic was so terrible and my driver got me over on the waterfront and we're just crawling along on those big cobblestones. All there was were boats and trucks and then I saw this blonde and she had two sailors and she had her arms linked in theirs. They must have been telling her a dirty story 'cause she'd laugh, throwing her head back. She had very bleached hair burnt with a curling iron, all frizzy – two big blotches of paint on her face – her lipstick was like she put it on 10 times and never washed it off – yet she had a good-looking face. Her stockings were all runs and she had on this black satin coat and it was a mass of wrinkles – like she'd slept in it and did everything else in it.

And she had on this black satin cloche, and right on back of it there was 10 fingerprints from powder. And then coming round across the front she had these two big bird-of-paradise wings . . . I had guests in the car and one of them said, 'Oh, one of those sailors smuggled it in for her. She gets 50 cents. A dollar, two at the most.' Then I knew she was a . . . 'cause I had never actually seen a prostitute.

We can believe what we wish to believe. In her own book of 1959, Mae recounted the same tale slightly differently but left out the claim about her first sight of 'chippies', as she calls them there. 'My opening situation was set,' Mae relates. 'The play would be about a girl

113

who ensnared a sailor who brought her a bird of paradise.'

Previous researches into the origins of *Sex* have turned up a somewhat different story. In 1924, according to subsequent court testimony, James Timony obtained for possible use by Mae a one-act play by one J. J. Byrne of New Jersey, entitled *Following the Fleet*. This was then expanded by Mae, working again with Adeline Leitzbach of *The Hussy*, into a full-length work called *The Albatross*. When *Sex* became successful, in the summer of 1926, Byrne sued Timony and Mae for plagiarism, claiming that they had turned his moral piece into a salacious work. The suit was eventually dismissed by Federal Judge Charles W. Goddard, who said both texts, Byrne's and Mae's, were 'designed for salacious appeal', and that 'no author of a work of this nature can expect a court of equity to support him'.

However, Mae's newly opened private archive shows yet another process at work in reaching the performed text. Although it is often impossible to date various folders, there are many script fragments and treatments of prototype plays and early versions of the 1920s plays. There is no text of Byrne's original, but a full version of *The Albatross* can be found in the archive.

The play opens in 'the San Pedro harbour district of Los Angeles'. (*Sex* was eventually set in Montreal to distance it somewhat from US soil.) This version opens with three pimps, Blackie, Gordon and Mott, seated at a table, Mott checking from a list in his hand:

MOTT: That makes five B-girls we got workin' over at Tony's place, five at the Golden Rod Cocktail Lounge, and six downstairs. Not bad, huh?

BLACKIE: Yeah, but I'd like to know who is workin' where and how they're doing so we can keep a check on their 'take.' Otherwise they'll chisel on us. It aint business-like not to know.

MOTT: Well, I got 'em all here, like you asked me, Blackie. At Tony's there's Dot and Bella, Ruthie, Frances and Camilla. They're all goin' strong. Tony says its go so now, guys come in askin' for 'em by name and spendin' their dough like water. He says he wishes we could send him five more girls now the fleet's getting in . . .

They discuss the girls, getting to the Mae West character, Margie:

BLACKIE: Margie's getting very exclusive lately. I don't know exactly what's on her mind.

MOTT: Oh, and by the way. That guy Daly was in again. Says if we don't pay-off he's gonna squawk to headquarters that the girls is rollin' the customers.

Later, when Margie faces the corrupt policeman:

Margie faces the cop, Daly, flicking her cigarette ash into his hat.
DALY (*looks in hat and shakes out ashes*): What do you think this is, an ash-can? Don't try to pull that wise stuff on me. You've been getting away with murder.
MARGIE: I don't see why anyone should have to pay for the privilege of doing business. You got about all you've ever goin' to get out of me.
DALY: Well if that's the way you feel about it we'll see how far you get.

Another scene, which has been revised in the *Sex* version, has Margie and Blackie 'at home':

MARGIE: This neighborhood is one of the lousiest holes in the world and it's getting worse and worse every day.
BLACKIE: Where are my collars? . . . Come and find them for me.
MARGIE: Find them yourself, they're your collars.
BLACKIE: Why don't you leave things where I put them? . . . You didn't even put buttons on my shirt.
MARGIE: What do you think I am, your wife? The trouble with you – you've been spoiled. Too many dames been waiting on you. Here's one baby don't fall for that stuff.
BLACKIE: Is that so?
MARGIE: If there's any waiting on around here, I'm going to get it. I'm a dame that craves service.
BLACKIE: Ain't you funny?
MARGIE: Don't wise crack at me, because I'm about ready to give you the air . . . I'm going someplace where I can play around with the folding money and see life, and get something out of it, instead of messin' around with your cheap racket.
BLACKIE: Getting highbrow. Want to play rich. You're all right where you are.
MARGIE: Think so?
BLACKIE: Getting some fool ideas about goin' straight, eh?
MARGIE: Suppose I am?
BLACKIE (*removes slippers and puts on dress shoes*): Baby, you'll never be anything but what you are. So that's that.

This does not seem to be the voice of Adeline Leitzbach, Mae's collaborator: there is a quantum leap between the standard melodrama dialogue and settings of *The Hussy* and the stark realism of the dockside lower depths that leaps off *The Albatross*'s pages. The developing plot line may well be Leitzbach, but the voice in the dialogue is clearly Mae. In the performed version, apart from the defection to Montreal harbour, the dialogue between the pimps is toned down, and the conversation between Margy (changed spelling) and her man Rocky runs:

MARGY: I'm getting tired of you and this dump.

ROCKY: Not good enough for you, eh?

MARGY: Oh, I'm going somewhere where I can play around with the heavy sugar daddies and see life and get something for it, instead of sitting here night after night waiting for your cheap bunch.

ROCKY: Gee, getting highbrow. Want to play it rich. You're alright where you are.

(*Continues as above*)

The evidence is that Mae is always pushing for a more vivid, less compromising vision, as we shall see in later cases. As revealed in her archive, there are often dry runs or abortive versions of her plays, though because they are undated figuring which version came first is often guesswork. An eight-page treatment, filed under a later play title, *Pleasure Man* (there are often scripts and papers in the archive found in folders wrongly labelled), appears to be of a possibly embryonic idea for *Sex*, set in New York City's garment district and featuring a poor girl, Jenny, who meets 'Bilge', a marine Sergeant:

. . . as they stand talking, two Jewish characters with long beards (which cover the signs slung around their necks) pass – Jenny enquires about them. 'Bilge' thinks they are from Feine's dress shop. Jenny looks up at the window next door. An enormous sign greets her eye – 'Feine's Dresses – Help Yourself – Self Service.' On the second floor is an ample window, six scrawny models pass in review, displaying dresses destined to awe some poor deluded boob. All of the latest styles in cheap robes and gowns – and even a spring suit of wide trousers. The models look like a broken down ostrich feather . . .

Inside Mr Feine's office, a great controversy is going on, amid much waving of arms. All of the models are present and the head cutter, an arrogant Russian, is fighting the usual battle for more pay and fewer hours. Feine is stalling for time. The workmen are going on strike unless he meets their demands – the phoney looking models threaten to walk out as they are afraid the union will throw bricks at the window in which they are parading. They deliver their ultimatum – unless Feine meets the demands of the union they will walk out . . .

This story then fans out into a totally different environment, as Jenny is taken on as a model, helps to settle the strike and rises 'up the ladder of success until she has reached the smartest establishment on Fifth Avenue'. She finds a new lover, Jacque, goes off to Monte Carlo, discovers Jacque is a rogue and returns to 'Bilge'. This mirrors the ending of *Sex*, in which Mae goes off with her honest sailor friend rather than with the rich boy she has been accused of ensnaring.

What is amply clear from the new archive is how far Mae's actual mode of working differed from the image she presented to the press as an impulsive gal who wrote plays off the top of her head, as she told the *San Francisco Examiner* in 1929 – 'I write my plays in rehearsal. I'm too nervous to put my thoughts on paper.' In a world of boozers, gamblers and wild nightclub crawlers, Mae was obviously loath to be a party-pooper by telling the truth about the long days and nights spent alone, painstakingly writing the notes, treatments and ideas which fed into *Sex*, *The Drag*, *Pleasure Man* and *The Wicked Age*, before she relocated her concerns to the 1890s and hit the jackpot with *Diamond Lil* in 1928. One of the versions of *Sex*, a seventy-seven-page text entitled *Love for Sale*, is a movie treatment, most probably written after the play as it renames all the characters in an attempt to disguise the story's scandalous origin.

The plot of *Sex*, branching out from its setting of dockland prostitution, involves Margy's attempts to help her colleague, Agnes, her relationship with the sailor, Gregg, and a scam by her pimp, Rocky, to compromise a 'society dame', Clara, who is slumming at the docks and whom Margy saves after she is drugged. Margy escapes to Trinidad to evade her pimp and a corrupt cop, Dawson. Both Agnes and Gregg are there, but she meets an innocent youth, Jimmy Stanton, who turns out, coincidentally, to be Clara's son. Back home, at Jimmy's house, a confrontation with Clara leads Margy to confess her background to Jimmy. He still loves her, but she realizes that she prefers the honesty of her relationship with Gregg to the hypocrisy of the Stanton lifestyle:

MARGY: Mrs Stanton, I'm giving you back your boy. I'm sure you'll teach him to forget me.

CLARA: But you are not going back to that life?

(*Gregg appeals to her mutely to remember his feeling for her. She looks at him and smiles.*)

MARGY : No, I'm going straight – to Australia. (*Holds out hand to Gregg.*)
FINAL CURTAIN

It was not the plot line or the antipodean redemption, however, that caused *Sex* to become the scandal of the New York theatre world in 1926. The title, of course, proclaimed its clear rebellion, although this was not decided on until the latest possible moment, for up until 10 March 1926, when the project is first mentioned in *Variety*, it was still titled *Following the Fleet*. *Variety*'s item referred to the resumption of rehearsals, which had been 'suspended two weeks ago at the instigation of Equity, when no bond was posted'. By 31 March, when rehearsals were mentioned once more in *Variety*, the play's title had become *Sex*.

The financing and production of the play also became controversial. Gossip about the role played by Owney Madden and bootleg money in funding *Sex*, as well as Mae's other plays, permeates the record. By the nature of such transactions, this can neither be proven nor discounted. Hocking the play around the theatrical producers, Mae had omitted her own name and used the pseudonym of 'Jane Mast' – Jane for her dropped middle name and Mast for the first two and last two letters of Mae West.

Eventually a director named Edward Elsner agreed to take on the play. Mae described him as 'something out of an Edgar Allan Poe story dusted off. He had his black overcoat draped over his shoulders like a cape . . . very thin lips like surgical scars, and these he drew back over his dry teeth in a smile which he turned on and off. It was a quick smile and you could miss it if you winked.' Elsner allegedly responded to the play much like the director in Mel Brooks's *The Producers*, shouting, 'By God! You've done it! You've got it! This is it!'

Edward Elsner, in fact, was a conventionally reputable director who had worked with the Barrymores, Gaby Deslys, Maud Adams and other luminaries. Having him on board enabled Timony to recruit a Pittsburgh producer, C. W. Morganstern, who was eager to break into the New York scene. According to Stanley Musgrove, there were two 'angels' to finance the show: businessmen Max Kolmes and Harry Cohen. Together they formed a company oddly, or perhaps satirically, named 'The Morals Production Company'.

Rehearsals began, 'the slow, hard work, the days and nights in a cold empty theatre, the dust, work lights, confusion, run-throughs and the agonies of preparing a play', not to speak of the difficulties of raising money to post the standard Equity bond. This was, the text apart, a major departure for Mae. She was well versed in the opportunities and hazards of revues, the grand Shubert sagas, the lavish – or hopefully lavish – sets, props and costumes, the Wayburn-like machines of the chorus. But this was the down-to-earth theatre, the world of risk and insecurity, the entire weight of the enterprise resting on her own dramatic talent. It was Elsner, she wrote, who kept highlighting the sexual element of Mae's persona, 'gay and unrepressed' as she quoted him, until she decided that the ideal title for the play would be that one word: *Sex*.

This did not, of course, make it any easier to find a venue for the play. The issue of 'Dirt Plays' continued to occupy both moral guardians and the professional critics, reaching into the halls of Congress. In February 1925, Representative Frederick Dallinger, a Republican from Massachusetts, introduced a resolution 'asking for an investigation as to what action was being taken by the District Commissioners to prevent the presentation of "improper" plays'. One suggestion involved setting up a panel of 300 jurors 'qualified to pass judgement upon what is and what is not objectionable in the theatre', a kind of early focus group. Reformers and church workers were said to be jubilant over Dallinger's intervention, claiming that 'show business was given enough rope, with the natural result that they have hung themselves'. Show business did not seem, however, to be deterred, for, by the time-worn principle of the bottom line, as *Variety* wrote, 'the current dirt shows are reaping a harvest through the sensational publicity given the move to curtail them'. The spotlight fell upon such minor encrustations as W. A. Brady's *A Good Bad Woman*, as well as impresario David Belasco's *The Harem* and *Ladies of the Evening* and Eugene O'Neill's *Desire Under the Elms*.

In 1925, Broadway was said to be enjoying a 'superfluity of hits', featuring the usual big-budget revues, though a visitor from Memphis, finance commissioner Charles R. Shannon, complained that 'the shows in New York are reeking with immorality, vice and a lavish display of nude women. They would be closed in Memphis at the very first showing . . . The jokes are funny, but they are indecent, and the women were beautiful, but the way they were dressed or rather undressed – it was awful.'

On 23 December, *Variety* reviewed the out-of-town début of the play *The Shanghai Gesture*, by John Colton, 'the most sensational drama ever played here' – here being Newark, New Jersey – with spectacular scenes set in a Chinese brothel run by one Mother Go-Dam, 'a Manchu princess of high attainments, who holds Shanghai in the hollow of her hand because of her intimate knowledge of the lives of the prominent people in the natives [*sic*] and foreign quarters'. The play featured miscegenation, prostitution and pimping, with Prince Oshima, a 'Japanese libertine', enjoying an evening with Poppy, 'an English girl of noble family but a nympho-maniac'. An auction of the white girl as a slave to Chinese junk men prompts a narrative by the brothel madame of 'her life on the junk where she had lived chained to the deck, tortured horribly to give her liveliness, and forced to suffer as many as 50 filthy men of all colors in one night'. The reviewer termed this 'one of the most terrific narratives ever heard on the American stage'.

We might keep this in mind, as it impacts on the development of a later Mae West playscript, *Frisco Kate*, as well as yet another version of *Sex*-as-*Love for Sale*, which opens in a Chinaman's brothel. But in the meanwhile it is worth noting that 'sex' was not a new commodity in the American theatre (nor anti-Chinese racism, as we shall also note in due course). This show was a massive hit, going into the New Year of 1926, while Mae and her company rehearsed in the dust.

Plays apart, this was also the era of 'immoral magazines', with titles such as *Hijinks*, *Hot Dog*, *Artists and Models*, *Art Lovers' Magazine*, *I Confess*, *Snappy Stories* and *La Vie Parisienne*, whose publishers were sued in Kansas. In Chicago, they were still pursuing the 'cooch dances', while in Los Angeles O'Neill's *Desire Under the Elms* was actually closed and its players arrested for 'appearing in an indecent play'.

The 'Morals Production Company' opened *Sex* in Stamford, Connecticut, in April, to a cool house, then poked its toe into Waterbury and New London, a port town where sailors on leave packed the theatre. Harry Cort, manager of New York's Daly Theatre, now came on board, and the play was booked into Daly's, on 63rd Street.

The show opened in New York at the end of April, and on the 28th *Variety* delivered its verdict, a landmark notice, perhaps the most outraged and apoplectic review in the entire history of the journal:

Never has disgrace fallen so heavily upon the 63rd street theater as it did Monday night, when a nasty red-light district show – which would be toler

ated in but few of the stock burlesque houses in America, opened and called itself 'Sex.' Miss West, under the nom-de-plume of Jane Mast, is credited with the script . . . The star Monday evening, according to the billboards, is the vaudeville singer Mae West, who has broken the fetters and does as she pleases here. After three hours of this play's nasty, infantile, amateurish and vicious dialog, after watching its various actors do their stuff badly, one really has a feeling of gratefulness for any repression that may have toned down her vaudeville songs in the past.

. . . Although New York isn't the nicest town in the world, it is impossible to believe that it will ever offer profitable business to such an atrocious bit of 'entertainment.'

Many people walked out on it before its first act – the nastiest thing ever disclosed on a New York stage . . . was over. The second act saw more withdrawals, and the third act played to lots of empty seats. The audience was strictly mug, there being two other good openings at the Guild and the Mansfield, so this one got what was left over . . .

Mae West plays the rough gal, and in the first act does it well. But she goes to pieces after that, because she doesn't change when the play calls for it, and, although the script has her speaking the lines of a good gal, she's still slouching and showing the figure just as if she were drumming up business as a bad one . . .

A police pinch or a flood of publicity on its dirtiness is the sole salvation of 'Sex.' Three of the daily reviewers who covered the opening agreed not to mention its filth, but just to kid it as a rotten show, being wise enough to know that those behind the piece would welcome every denunciatory notice which commented on its obscenity . . .

The whole production looked like a stock performance by an 85c top company in Dubuque, whereas it was playing a $3.30 house.

Sisk

The Scarlet Sisterhood for Life

There were no prizes for guessing the reason why Mae West's *Sex* turned into *the* scandal of the New York stage in 1926, despite the trail of so many other so-called 'dirt shows'. It was explicit in 'Sisk''s review: 'Because she doesn't change when the play calls for it.' Even when the words and the plot allowed Margy Lamont to show a remorseful and redeemed woman, Mae played it on stage as if her behaviour called for no redemption at all: 'Still slouching and show-ing the figure just as if she were drumming up business as a bad one.' Mae portrayed a woman who had nothing to apologize for, and, in a play about prostitution, this was a social sin too far. In a society that blamed sexual transgression on women, Margy turns the heat on her pursuers:

MARGY: Why ever since I've been old enough to know Sex I've looked at men as hunters. They're filled with Sex. In the past few years I've been a chattel to that Sex. All the bad that's in me has been put there by men. I began to hate every one of them, hated them, used them for what I could get out of them, and then laughed at them, and then – then he came.

Referring to the lover, Stanton, who will later be rejected. But when challenged by Stanton's mother, the society lady Clara, Mae fights back:

MARGY: I'm going to dig under the veneer of your supposed respectability and show you what you are . . . You've got the kind of stuff in you that makes women of my type. If our positions were changed – you in my place, and I in yours – I'd be willing to bet that I'd make a better wife and mother than you are. Yeah, and I'll bet without this beautiful home, without money, and without any restrictions, you'd be worse than I have ever been . . . It's just a matter of circumstances.

Mae was playing a character that had developed out of the primal material of 'Nona', as portrayed in *The Hussy*. But this time the scene

is raw and bloody. Exploitation and hypocrisy are laid bare. Not that
Mae did not have her supporters among the critics, for on 5 May, a
week after 'Sisk', her favourite *Variety* fan 'Con', writing under his
full name Jack Conway, weighed in slugging and slanging in the
'Vaudeville' section:

MAE WEST, 3-STAR SPECIAL IN 'SEX' PLAY
'The Babe Ruth of the Stage "Prosties"' – New Show Realistic.

New York, May 1.

Dear Chick,

My three-star special is Mae West in 'Sex,' at Daly's 63rd Street. Get a
load of it. If you don't agree with me that Mae would heat up Dawson City
and is the Babe Ruth of the stage 'prosties' I'll turn square . . . Chick, Mae
is hot. In the second act, a cabaret scene in Trinidad, she turns in 'Sweet Man,'
very Harlem, and with a jazz dance right out of the off-sharp department.
Some of her lines knock the peasants into the aisles.

She sure saxes sex and how that blonde baby knows her stuff . . . It's realistic and realism all the way. Mae's conception of Margie La Mont will sentence
her to the scarlet sisterhood for life . . . What a break if the fleet were only in.

Grab a look, see and don't forget to bring along your sweat shirt. You'll
need it.

Conway's plug was most welcome, as his colleague's sour predic-
tion came close to the truth when Police Commissioner McLaughlin
called the producers of *Sex* and 'talked with them concerning taming
down the show's lines and business'. Attendant publicity and cut-rate
seats boosted the box office accordingly. *Sex* was spared the fate of
another play which was soon to close after one night only: *Beyond
Evil*, at the Cort Theatre – featuring 'a married woman, who had a
month's affair with a mulatto and then called herself a prostie' – was
booed off the stage on opening night and marked by *Variety* with the
poignant headline: 'World's Worst Play Quits.' At the end of May the
police visited *Sex* at the theatre and 'persons connected with the management were requested to call at District Attorney Banton's office'.
This appeared to follow a diatribe against the play by the local *New
York Graphic*. The volunteer citizen's jury, however, already in action
over 'dirt shows', did not censure Mae's play. Another transgressive
play, *Lulu Belle*, produced by David Belasco and featuring a racially
mixed cast, also escaped censure. But it was *Sex* that really took off.

For the first time in her 'legit' theatrical career, Mae West had lucked out. By happenstance, she had opened a scandalous play at the time of a commercial slump on Broadway. The 17 March headlines had read: 'B'WAY IS ALLEY OF DESPAIR FOR LEGIT SHOWS RIGHT NOW. Business Still Dropping – Some Shows Played to Under $1,500 Last Week . . . Plenty of Dark Houses by Easter.' The perennial *Abie's Irish Rose* was still playing, and *The Jazz Singer*, 1925's hit, which was destined to be the silent cinema's Waterloo when filmed in 1927, was only just declining. But, in a slow post-Easter season, astonishingly, *Sex* was hot!

It is tempting to find straightforward reasons, in hindsight, for this success, which to some analysts appears to have been preordained once Mae had fixed on her specific appeal to 'working-class' audiences in a middle-class world. But, given Mae's previous track record in 'legit', it could equally have been one more flop. There was, of course, a tremendous risk involved in putting on another 'dirty play' at a time of heavy pressure to 'clean up' the New York theatre, as the fate of *Beyond Evil* showed. *Sex* was not, as one can see from the published text, a bad play, but it was brilliant neither in plot nor dialogue; it was still, for Mae, an apprentice work. The ace in the hole was not text but performance, the all-stops-out Mae on stage.

It is always a puzzle to moral reformers that their efforts encourage the very object of their condemnations. It never occurred to the zealots of Prohibition that they were fostering all the evils – excessive drinking, crime, corruption, moral degradation, disease and premature death – that they were so eager to eradicate. When moral reformers force laws on a society that considers them either unjust or frankly ludicrous, contempt for the law in general is the outcome. This can only be properly squashed in a tyranny. In a democracy, social bonds are weakened. Everything is up for grabs. Questions abound about other transgressions, sex being the most obvious.

Mae's character – Nona/Margy – expressed an exploited woman's dilemmas. But the audience for her first transgressive play, at the beginning, was mostly composed of men, who came to enjoy her sassy antics. Mae was, paradoxically, the heterosexual man's dream – an available dame, shaking her protuberances, egging them on from the stage. No wonder sailors, soldiers and students lined around the block for tickets.

These were the 'mugs' whom 'Sisk' noted in his diatribe about her première at Daly's. Soon, women, too, began paying attention to this new theatrical voice, even though Mae's choice of subjects was condemned as far too risky. This would be magnified in the choice of subject for her second play – homosexuals, hardly the stuff of working-class theatre.

Mae had found her niche, and she would press the concept further, on stage and screen, as the Great Dissimulator. She would use sexuality to project a whole series of contradictory images: the old Eva Tanguay I Don't Care Girl; the sexual reformer and educator; the dame who is up for it – come up and see me some time; every son's mother's scourge, and every boy's secret dream; every woman's dream of absolute freedom; the woman who knew how to get her man, who can get whom she wants and also send him packing; the woman who can take it or leave it, but prefers to take; and, most bold of all, the friend of those on the utmost margins.

This last was Mae's most authentic face and the object of her most spectacular paradox: embracing those stranded at the bottom of society's ladder while constructing an image of ultimate glamour which raised her to the very top rung. This was a magical feat, worthy of Houdini himself, and like Houdini's tricks, it might have appeared easy to the onlooker, but was the outcome of a great deal of toil and sweat.

In time, Mae would construct a seamless persona that could glide between these contradictory fields, strutting her stuff with diamonds and jewels while presenting life in brothels, drug dives, hooch parlours, bathing-beach contests and circuses. This was, in fact, an old tradition of variety – topsy-turvydom, the world turned upside down.

The success of *Sex* provided Mae, for the first time, with a war chest she could use to fund her next move. On 9 June, for example, the play was taking $16,500 at the box office, amazing for an off-Broadway house like Daly's, competing with the mass-appeal *Earl Carroll's Vanities* at $17,000, though still falling short of *The Shanghai Gesture*, grossing $23,000 at the Shubert in the same week. The show was doing so well that it merited an out-of-town tour, arranged by mainstream producer Gus Hill in a 'sterilized' form – Hill had jazzed up the settings of the play at Daly's, contributing a set of 'a millionaire's home in Westchester' that had previously graced his 'Mutt and Jeff' show. July saw 'Broadway's Worst Week for Legits,' with terrible business hitting even the Marx Brothers' *TheCocoanuts*, while *Sex* was holding steady. Timony successfully beat back a new lawsuit by backers Harry Cohen and Max Kolmes, who now wanted a greater share of the profits but were refused a receivership of the company.

Mae could now turn her attention to a follow-up. Rehearsals began in the autumn for *The Drag*, the play that would make *Sex* look like a summer romp in the park.

Given what we now know about Mae's working habits – and the lie of her making the show up in rehearsal or after a few intensive nights scribbling in a hotel room – it must be clear that *The Drag* pre-existed by the time *Sex* was being performed, if not in final shape then in some draft. The archive does not contain working drafts of *The Drag*, being top-heavy with later versions of an unfilmed, probably unfilmable movie script. But Mae was a slow rather than a fast writer in reality, as opposed to the myth.

The Drag is not a great text. To our eyes it is a somewhat laboured, very tentative and dated attempt to present homosexuality to a rabidly heterosexual eye. It opens in a doctor's office, in which, after some dialogue between the physician and his middle-aged sister, two young men are ushered in, one, David, in a state of great agitation, begging for help and confessing his 'perversion':

DAVID: Always, from the earliest childhood, I was born a male, but my mind has been that of a female. Why, as a child I played with dolls – I even cried when they cut off my curls. As I grew older the natural desires of a youth were unknown to me. I could not understand why women never interested me. I was attracted by my own sex. How was I to know it was wrong, when it seemed perfectly natural to me.

The taboo on discussion of homosexuality in the 1920s was predominant, despite the fact that a vibrant gay subculture existed, as *Variety* had pointed out, alongside the speakeasies in Times Square and Greenwich Village, with parties and shows often attended by 'straight' slummers. But Mae wrote, in her article 'Sex in the Theatre' in *The Parade* in 1929:

I admit that in my play 'Drag' I was a little bit premature. The public is still too childlike to face like grownups the problem of homo-sexuality. How few are the people who even know what the word means? . . .

Many of our famous lawyers, doctors, bankers and judges are homo-sexualists. Thousands of others suffer because they are starving for love both in body and soul, and they become mental prostitutes. Five thousand perverts applied for only fifty parts when we were casting for 'Drag.' One vice-president of a large bank begged me to let him secretly act in 'Drag' because there only could he do what he was starving for – act like a woman and wear expensive, beautiful gowns . . .

It was nigh impossible for Mae, even in her violation of the taboo, to avoid presenting homosexuality as a pathological condition, an 'inversion' or the 'third sex', which was the muttered term in use. *The Drag* proceeds with a long turgid scene in which the doctor and a judge discuss the ethics of the laws that have 'forced this vice into a corner, just as it has forced prostitution into shady byways', in order to protect 'normal' society. Unbeknownst to these two worthies, however, the doctor's daughter, Clare, is married to Rolly Kingsbury, the judge's son, who is secretly gay and consorts wildly with his fellow 'inverts'. When Rolly is shot, murdered, the terrible secret is revealed, but when the homosexual David confesses to the killing 'because I loved him', the police, protecting the judge's reputation, proclaim the case as suicide.

In 1959, when Mae wrote about *The Drag* in her own book *Goodness Had Nothing to Do with It*, she wrote that she had always hated 'the two-faced, the smoother-over folk', who preach in public the opposite of what they do in private. But she added – oddly for those who celebrated her many years later as a gay icon – that 'in many ways homosexuality is a danger to the entire social system of western civilization'. The bisexual habits of Greece and Rome, Mae wrote, drawing on some cod historical nonsense, broke down the family unit, allowing the virility of their 'breeding lines' to decay 'under attacks from more virile and child-breeding savage tribal orders'. Not that Mae contributed anything to the breeding lines herself. In the 1950s, however, homosexuality was still a fearsome taboo, and Hollywood was plagued by the vicious gossip magazine *Hollywood Confidential*, which traded on the exposure of homosexuals – as long as they lacked the backing of powerful studio moguls, as in the case of Rock Hudson. Liberace was 'outed' in 1957 but never admitted being gay until his dying day. Mae herself had been attacked in 1955 over her alleged yen for 'tan' boxers and would have been doubly on her guard.

After this pressure had eased in the late 1960s, Mae recalled in later interviews that her play 'glorified homosexuals. The big scene is a dance, with about 40 of 'em in drag – I even had a taxicab and truck-driver types in drag. I directed it but didn't appear in it. They never used the word sex, but I had screamin' gay great-lookin' guys flauntin' it out all over the place. There were at least a dozen curtain calls after each of the three acts and it took an hour to empty the theater – everyone wanted to visit the actors, even though a great percentage of the audience were women.'

This last point is borne out by contemporary accounts of the opening of the play in the staid locality of Bridgeport, Connecticut, as reported on 1 February 1927 in an article describing the somewhat surprising response by the local 'straight' audience:

WENT TO BE SHOCKED – FOUND 'THE DRAG' CLEAN

All Bridgeport turned out last night to see the first showing of the latest play by Jane Mast called 'The Drag,' billed as a 'homosexual' comedy drama, exploiting sixty – count 'em, sixty – of those strange individuals that pathologists call 'the third sex.'

Many people came to be shocked . . . from New Rochelle and up the line as far as Hartford. And in the gathering were all the sewing circle censors, set with a fringe of police officials ready to clamp on the law as soon as moral turpitude was bent . . . The censors had refused the play a hearing at Stamford, and the report was that it would be about as clean as the Augean stables.

The Park Theater, where 'The Drag' had its première, is known as the 'coldest house in the coldest theatrical town in all Connecticut.' It has never held in twenty years the throng it had last night, and the great percentage were women . . .

There were gasps as the curtain rose, showing the debauchees and rake-hells in a terpsichorean stunt. It was their high spot in glorifying the 'Girls of All Nations.' How the big audience, embracing the literati, the illuminati, the cognoscenti and the et ceteri, leaned forward!

It might have depicted the 'qualities of enjoyment' of the heart and mind of the dissipated life that arose in Paris after the Reign of Terror – or the cold, gay life of the Barbary Coast, out Golden Gate way. But it was life, if even not your life or mine . . . The expected effluvium and stench were absent. It is true that it featured the 'culls and scraps' of a cross-section of humanity, but it did not debase, or degrade.

There is not a ribald line in the whole play, unless one can construe this: 'You must come over some time, dearie, and I'll bake you a pan of biscuits.' And staid Bridgeport rocked in laughter! . . .

'The Drag' hopes to secure a New York home, commencing February 7 or 8.

It's exceptionally well handled, and certainly comes well under 'the licence of the times.'

By Staff Correspondent

Variety, for its part, responded with another sour tirade (this time from 'Rush'), calling *The Drag* 'the dramatization of a wild party given by a rich pervert to his group of painted and bedizened friends . . . all hands are rouged, lip-sticked and liquid-whited to the last degree. During the whole scene a jazz orchestra plays "hot" music in the background . . . The whole venture is without justification and merits the unqualified condemnation of the public, the theatre and the authorities, not to speak of calling for the prompt intervention of the police.' The atmosphere of debauchery, it was suggested in a *Variety* gossip column, had spread to the after-show party, at which Mae's sister Beverly was arrested for 'disorderly conduct' in director Elsner's room at the Arcade Hotel – an event which would figure in a divorce suit being brought against her by her by-now estranged husband, Serge Treshatny. She claimed to be in Elsner's room at 5 a.m. looking over the playscript, although she had no part in the play.

The reviews of *The Drag* demonstrate the danger in interpreting Mae West's plays strictly in the light of their texts, even when we do have more than one version. Many bits and pieces of business, stunts and entire numbers were clearly developed in rehearsal, as the 'terpsichorean stunt' reveals. The dry legal discussion of 'inversion' would, of course, look different coming after a mass drag 'Girls of All Nations'. As with *Sex*, the juice was in the performance, the very presentation of the forbidden subject. Once again, reformers were wrong-footed by a wider than expected interest in society's outer fringes. Why not drink? Why not take a frank look at prostitution? Why not talk of taboo sex?

This Mae West thing was clearly going too far. The New York authorities finally clamped down, targeting the still-running *Sex* before *The Drag* could find its own New York venue. On 9 February, after Mayor Jimmy Walker – whose views on New York's sins were relatively liberal – had departed on a long vacation to Florida, Acting Mayor Joseph V. McKee (nicknamed 'Holy Joe') sent the cops in to raid three New York plays, *The Virgin Man*, *The Captive* and *Sex*. The shows were stopped and the cast and producers arrested. C. W. Morganstern, Mae West and the rest of the actors, Barry O'Neill, Warren Sterling *et al.*, were booked and fingerprinted and released on bail of $1,000. James Timony and the director Edward Elsner were arrested a little later.

It seems clear that the reformers preferred to take Mae West demonstrably off the stage in person, despite, and perhaps because of, her commercial success. In effect, their move against *Sex* also impacted on *The Drag*, which was swiftly taken off by the producers. Mae wrote in *The Parade* in 1929 that she 'voluntarily removed' the play, but it was clear that fighting the *Sex* bust would consume both time and money. On 15 February, in the West Side court, Mae and her producers were offered the possibility of an 'implied immunity' in return for pulling the show. They turned it down and the play continued running. But Mae, Timony, Morganstern, Cort of Daly's, the actors and the Morals Production Company itself were indicted by a grand jury, charged with 'producing an immoral show and maintaining a public nuisance'.

"THE DRAG" DRAGGED OFF BOARDS IN BAYONNE; MORE N. Y. RAIDS COMING

Hundreds of these would-be patrons of "The Drag" were disappointed when the Bayonne, N. J., officials barred it. It's amusing to all those lined up under this huge sign, "Headquarters League to Redeem Our City," isn't it? Mae West, of "Sex," sponsors "The Drag," also. At the same time it was announced that New York police would strike tonight at the nude revues. Cabarets and night clubs are also threatened. Story on Page 3

'Every One in the Police Force is not a Dancer'

Few actors have embraced martyrdom with such relish as Mae West in 1927. The Night Court arraignment of the cast and producers of *Sex* on 9 February at 54th Street was already a circus, with Mae, dressed in furs, and Helen Menken, star of the lesbian drama *The Captive*, jammed up together in a scrum of bondsmen, and the casts ferried to the court in a convoy of taxicabs from the theatres. 'I enjoyed the courtroom as just another stage,' Mae wrote, 'but not so amusing as Broadway.' Mae did not think much of *The Captive*, since lesbianism always appeared to her as wholly 'unnatural', and was said to have kept her distance from La Menken: 'After considerable of a squabble, Mae is reported to have gathered her ermines about her and carried the night with the succinct remark: "Well, anyhow, we're normal!"'

Acting Mayor McKee, however, reassured the press: 'This is not an attempt to provide a lot of free advertising for these shows. It is a definite attempt to wipe filth off Broadway. The actors and actresses in these shows will be arrested every night they try to go on with these plays.'

The US seemed to be experiencing what *Variety* called a 'Censorship Epidemic', with 'improper motion pictures' being closed in Iowa, art models being arrested in Milwaukee and censorship bills proposed in several states, including a 'padlock bill' in New York which would close for a year any theatre convicted of showing a 'dirt play'. Texas Guinan's '300 Club' was raided and threatened with immediate closure. Madam Guinan was held in a cell for nine hours.

Despite McKee's warning, a court injunction kept the raided plays running while the court proceedings got under way. The hearing of charges against *Sex* in the Magistrate's Court on 15 February continued the farcical atmosphere: Inspector A. Bolan, who 'had taken copious notes' on the play, read them out in detail, as the *New York*

Times reported: 'He . . . searched his mind for chaste circomlocutions in which to convey to the court some of the things which had shocked him. The Inspector chose his words so meticulously as to disappoint a crowded court room, and before he had testified for an hour scores had left in indignation at the tameness of the show. Two or three others who came to blush remained to sleep. One vigilant attendant shook a man into consciousness three times.'

Discussion about the difference between 'sugar dandy' and 'sugar daddy' injected some titters into the proceedings, the judge riposting firmly that 'this is not a show. It's a trial. If there is any one here who sees any mirth in this testimony, this is not the place for him.'

On 19 February, the moral guardians of New York were strengthened by a visit from the nation's most famous evangelist, Mrs Aimee Semple McPherson, who told an overflowing crowd at the Glad Tidings Tabernacle on West 33rd Street that she had come to conquer the city and purge it of sin. Her goals included supporting Prohibition, stopping suicides in schools by preventing the teaching of evolution, and promoting prayer and Bible reading. To examine sin more closely, she toured the nightclubs and even entered Texas Guinan's condemned premises, being introduced from the dance floor to remind the revellers of the scripture 'What doth it profit a man if he gain the whole world and lose his soul?' Madam Guinan, fresh from her overnight sojourn in jail, then declared: 'This is a woman I admire. She has the courage of her convictions. Give this little lady a good hand.' Her guests obligingly, if warily, complied.

Mayor Walker, meanwhile, stayed on in Florida, enjoying a dinner dance in his honour while the Bible thumping and purging proceeded at home. Acting Mayor McKee proved more than able to hold the fort, raving on, at a dinner of the Grand Street Boys at the Commodore Hotel, about 'outsiders' and 'visitors' polluting the city's culture, 'who believe they will find here an opportunity to prey upon their fellow men'. He exhorted his fellow diners to 'go forth and preach the gospel of the native New Yorker', this mythical beast being presumably lily-white and Christian to the marrow.

Bowing to the pressure, the producers of *The Captive* voluntarily shut down their play, avoiding prosecution. *Sex* continued to run, but after an initial box-office surge, attendance began to fall. In March, the cast rebelled when a 25 per cent pay cut was imposed by the management, and most of the actors decided to quit. On 21 March, the show was closed, having grossed $6,000 when it needed $7,000 a week to break even.

The agitation over censorship was matched by a wave of patriotic fervour erupting over a crisis in China. Battles between two warlords, Chiang Kai-shek and Wu Pei-fu, had spilled over into attacks on western foreigners, and, familiarly, British and American troops were now engaged in military action overseas. The Grand Jury indictment of Mae West's *Sex* played to a background of headlines such as: REDS INCITE MOBS TO ATTACK SHANGHAI; AMERICAN AND BRITISH KILLED IN ATTACKS AT NANKING (as well as MARINES REPEL LIBERALS' ATTACK IN NICARAGUA – the *New York Herald Tribune*, 29 March.)

By 30 March a jury in the *Sex* trial had been selected, twelve stout and true citizens, all male. The prosecution's chief witness was Sergeant Patrick Keneally of the Midtown Vice Squad, who read out the entire lines of the play from memory in a thick Irish brogue, 'frequently, under the instructions of the Prosecutor, assuming poses to demonstrate the manner in which the members of the cast delivered their lines'. The prosecution, unable to find profane language in the text, claimed that it was Mae West's 'personality, look, walk, mannerism and gestures [that] made the lines and the situations suggestive'. Mae's curvy dance was once again in the spotlight, with Sergeant Keneally testifying that 'Miss West moved her navel up and down and from right to left'. 'Did you actually see her navel?' Mae's lawyer queried. 'No, but I saw something in her middle that moved from east to west.' The Sergeant declined defence attorney Norman Schloss's request that he demonstrate in the courtroom, as prosecuting counsel Wallace primly observed: '"Every one in the police force is not a dancer." "Nor an actor," retorted Mr. Schloss, while Miss West and her confrères tittered at the embarrassed Sergeant. The dance was not staged.'

Insults flew between defence and prosecution counsel and were summarily cut short by Judge George L. Donnellan. The defence produced various witnesses who said they had found nothing offensive in the play and that the dance movements that so shocked Sergeant Keneally were no more than 'jazz, or "shimmie" dances' – Mae's old staple coming back to haunt her again. One customer, Harry M. Geiss, a manufacturer of pyjamas, 'volunteered that he had seen "Sex" twice and found nothing obscene about it'. Even the Bible was invoked in defence of the play, as Timony's own attorney, Mr Harold

Spielberg, 'addressing the jury, delved into Genesis, also, for precedents for frank language', adding: 'If your morals have not already been corrupted I am afraid they will be before I finish reading from this Bible.'

The prosecution, of course, swatted all this away. In summing up, the District Attorney called on the jury to 'protect the youth of the city' from the influence of those who depicted 'scandalous "red light" conditions' for monetary gain. After a great deal of legal wrangling, the judge instructed the jury that, if they only found certain lines and scenes in the play that 'tended to corrupt the morals of youth and others' rather than the entire play, they still had to convict.

On 5 April, the jury found the twenty-two defendants guilty and reserved sentencing for 19 April. On that day, District Attorney Joab Banton asked for jail sentences for the three principal defendants, Mae West, Morganstern and Timony. 'These people were given sufficient notice,' he declared, 'at least two weeks before the police interfered with the show, but they continued to produce it. They could have closed it any time, but they insisted upon offending the community . . . The failure to close this play was an outrage on public decency, and those who are responsible for its production should be shown no mercy.'

The jurors, unusually, presented a petition for clemency, signed by eight out of twelve, stating that the play had been passed by the play jury, the actors were bound by contract to perform and the play had now closed. But Judge Donnellan was not swayed at all.

'The Jury,' he said, 'has rendered a just verdict, based on the moral standards of today . . . Obscenity and immorality pervaded this show from beginning to end. Since Mayor Gaynor's time a certain form of vice had been driven from our streets. The producers of "Sex" paraded this vice upon the stage. The play was part of a wave of immorality that was demoralizing the stage.'

Mae, Timony and Clarence Morganstern were sentenced to serve ten days apiece in the workhouse, Mae on Welfare Island and the two men in the Manhattan Tombs. Mae and Timony were also fined $500 each. Before being taken into the Black Maria, Mae made her own statement, assailing District Attorney Banton for his 'small and petty attitude'. Then she told reporters: 'I never expected to be sent to jail . . . Closing "Sex" has cost me many thousands of dollars, and Mr. Banton should be satisfied with this instead of pleading that I, a woman, be sent to prison.'

The *New York Times* added: 'Asked if she might write a play while she was on the island based on her experience there, Miss West said that she probably would and added: "It would probably have to be approved of by the learned District Attorney." . . . Miss West also issued a vague warning about parasites, warning the public to beware of them.' She then entered the prison van and was whisked away.

CELL MOPS FOR 3 IN 'SEX' thundered the tabloid *Daily News*. 'Because they wouldn't help the police clean up Broadway, Mae West, James A. Timoney and Clarence William Morganstern for the next ten days will clean up the city's prisons with mops and pails of water.' Mae's eight days on Welfare Island, a former hospital and insane asylum (she got two days off for good behaviour), became an essential part of her legend. During her stay, Mae maintained contact with *Daily News* reporter Nick Kenny, who published a daily report on her progress. On Thursday, 21 April:

'Give my regards to Broadway!'

That was the message sent to a reporter for THE NEWS by Mae West yesterday as she began her first day on Welfare island . . . The star and author of 'Sex' was awakened at 7 a.m., an unholy hour for an actress. She was bundled into a Black Maria with two colored women and three white women prisoners, and taken to Welfare island.

There she was searched and bathed – her bath being minus the perfumes and lilac water to which she is accustomed – and then exchanged her clothing for the prison clothing.

'Ugh' she said, as she pulled cotton stockings over the legs that helped to make 'Sex' infamous. 'Can't I even keep my silk stockings?' Her request refused she flamed up and declared:

'I'm going to be a woman and show them. I'm going to make believe I am acting before an audience and forget that I am doing ten days in the hoosegow.'

In August 1927, Mae described her experience in detail for *Liberty* magazine, beginning her account of her descent into the world of the condemned with the scene in the courthouse itself:

I was ushered into a waiting room. There was a colored woman, with a gold badge, in charge.

She was intelligent, and during my half-hour wait I talked to her, asking her various questions about Welfare Island. I like to know something about a place I intend to visit.

Later, five women were brought into the room: the first a woman who appeared to be about sixty-five years of age. Later I learned she was only forty-one. She claimed she had lived alone for twenty years, without relatives or friends, and was homeless and penniless. Her clothes were old and torn.

Number Two was a colored woman wearing a black-knitted cap. She had a very deep voice and a comedy personality, with Bert Williams' speech and delivery. I learned later that she was a drug addict.

Number Three was a tall, thin woman with gray hair, a spinster type, with a long scar on the side of her face and her neck that looked like a burn. She spoke with an Irish accent. She had been sentenced to ten days for stealing a $3.89 pair of shoes at a sale.

Number Four was another colored woman – rather young and healthy looking. I was surprised to learn that she too was a drug addict.

Number Five was the most pitiful of all: a woman about five feet five, weighing not more than seventy pounds. Her eyes were sunken; her face long and narrow – just skin and bones. A drug addict in the last stages of tuberculosis; a mental and physical wreck.

At her first port of call, the city jail, she had 'a very small room with bars in front and an iron cot with springs only. But the matrons were quite nice to me. They gave me new sheets, a pillow, and a few blankets.' The other inmates were 'elated over my being there . . . they continued to shout my name, asked me how I liked the place, and repeated different lines from my show, Sex, in order to let me know they had seen it'.

The next day, going over the Queensborough Bridge at 59th Street, the black wagon was lowered down to the prison island on a huge elevator. Mae stepped out to find 'this marvellous, gorgeous stone structure most attractively decorated with big sheet-iron doors and plenty of bar-work. The doors opened and I made my grand entrance.'

Upon entering the reception-room, I saw several matrons. Number One took my purse, my valuables, and my pedigree.

I was met by the second matron, who said, 'Strip!'

I said, 'What? I thought this was a respectable place.'

She smiled and said, 'I am sorry, Miss West, but I will have to divest you of all your civilian attire.'

Mae was then given 'a piece of blue-and-white-checked material that looked like two aprons sewed together . . . I didn't like it at all; no lines to it.' Coarse underwear, those cotton stockings and flat outsize slippers – 'Oh, those terrible shoes!'

Assigned to a room with six girls, three of them coloured, Mae was discovering for the very first time the real impact of racial sharing. One of the black women, 'Lulu', was a 'stick-up' woman, which gained Mae's instant respect. One of the other white girls, Adele, was a professional shoplifter; some pointers on the trade were passed on. On her second day in jail, Mae was asked to visit the sick bay and ran a gauntlet of wild shouts and greetings: 'Here comes Mae! . . . How do you like the dress, Mae? How do you like the shoes?' Mae visited the wards, which housed women suffering from venereal disease and drug problems. Matters that had been theoretical before now became very real and present. For her own part, it was more revelation than trauma, and she admitted to interviewer Charlotte Chandler, decades later, that despite her dolour over the prison clothes, 'I wore my silk underwear the whole time.'

The *Daily News*, at the time, had reported on offers of knock-on jobs that Mae was turning down: 'A night club wants her to mop up the floor in prison costume for a few weeks at a fat salary . . . But, Miss West . . . told the warden she is writing a new play in the intervals between dusting and making beds – "a play that will do people some good and keep them out of jail – though I still don't admit there was any harm in 'Sex.'"' The *News* just loved the opportunity to repeat that three-letter word as much as possible, and preferably in the headline.

Poor Timony and Morganstern's ordeal in the Tombs, on the other hand, made few headlines. One small item reported that Timony's 'initiative and ambition' got him made the 'boss of the mop and broom squad'. Aimee Semple McPherson might well have rejoiced at such an enterprising outcome to the humbling of the profane.

The Wicked Age

When she came out of jail, Mae wrote in 1959, she 'looked around and thought of Hollywood and films'. Once again, as in 1915, she peeked out towards the west, realizing that both vaudeville and the theatre were being overtaken by the movies. The problem, of course, which the Marx Brothers faced too, was that the movies were still silent, no medium for the verbal comedian. By mid-1927, however, some 'talkie' experiments had already been made, and Mae could have read in her weekly *Variety*, in May, that two-reel talking pictures with comedian George Jessel and Cantor Josef Rosenblatt were being planned. In the event it would be Al Jolson who would warble a more modern liturgy in *The Jazz Singer*, in October, changing the motion picture for ever.

An intriguing item in Mae's archive points to a possible earlier lead, which was abandoned: in a folder, misleadingly – and enticingly – labelled 'Vaudeville, by Jane Mast', there is a full hundred-page silent-film script, which at first deceived your author into believing it to be a hitherto unknown Mae West work. The script lacks first and last pages and is therefore untitled itself, but it turns out to be that of an existing movie called *Flame of the Yukon*, directed in 1926 by George Melford, itself a remake of a 1917 film of that title, produced by Thomas Ince and starring Dorothy Dalton as 'The Flame'. The part was played in 1926 by Seena Owen.

It is possible that this script was swept up into Mae's collection later, when source materials that might pertain to her 1936 film *Klondike Annie* were being obtained by Paramount studios to safeguard copyright problems – though it seems far-fetched that an old silent script would be included, and there is no sign of it in the Paramount studio files. Mae's own files include some fragments relating to a character called 'La Flame', which turn out to belong to a much later version of one of her post-war plays.

The film is about a saloon dancer, The Flame, who entertains the rough prospectors in Alaska during the Yukon gold rush, the same setting for Chaplin's 1925 movie. The 'Midas Saloon and Dance Hall' in Hope City features a 'motley crowd of gold seekers, adventurers, birds of prey and dance hall girls', presided over by 'Black Jack Hobey, the suave, brutal, unscrupulous proprietor of the Midas'. The Flame is 'a gay siren of the Arctic Portals', dancing on the tables and climbing on the saloon piano to sing to the crowd. A young miner, Fowler, falls for her, but when a destitute woman with a baby comes to town looking for her missing husband, also named Fowler, The Flame is desolate. In the end, she discovers the two Fowlers are different men and battles Black Jack's attempt to divest her young beau of his earnings.

The story was said to be roughly based on the real-life history of Klondike Kate, a.k.a. Kathleen Eloisa Rockwell, whose speciality in the saloons was her 'flame dance', which earned her the name Flame of the Yukon. In the 1920s she was very much alive; she lived, in fact, till 1957.

Doubts over the date at which Mae acquired this script still linger, but her expressed interest in movies in the silent era suggests it might well have been a role she would have liked to portray on the screen. Like everything else that came Mae's way, it went into the cooking pot of her many influences. Certain intertitles in the film appear to look forward to future characters that Mae would create, most of all her seminal Diamond Lil: 'You paid to see me go bad,' says The Flame, 'who's going to pay to see me go straight?' 'Your kind can't go straight,' scoffs Black Jack, 'you'll be back – flaming fiercer than ever!' – echoes of the line spoken to *Sex*'s Margy Lamont: 'Baby, you'll never be anything but what you are.' *Klondike Annie* would come some years in the future, following the contours of Mae's unperformed 1930 play *Frisco Kate*.

In 1927, however, 'The Flame' had already been screened, and Mae turned her thoughts and plans back to the stage. Her next play, *The Wicked Age*, was on the boards within six weeks of the appearance of her *Liberty* essay. The play opened once again out of town, in New Haven, but this time survived to its New York opening at Daly's Theatre in November.

With *The Wicked Age* we can finally nail the fib that Mae wrote her plays quickly, off the cuff. The new archive contains numerous versions of the play, including some with copious notes, deletions, additions and changes in Mae's own hand, showing the work in progress. Mae claimed this was the play she had mulled over in prison, but, once again, it must have been in progress far earlier. The play was to be, she wrote, 'an exposé of the bathing beauty contests of the 1920's – the Miss Americas, crooked contests and fixed winners'.

Unlike *Sex*, *The Drag* and *The Pleasure Man*, which have been published, *The Wicked Age* is known only to a handful of researchers, which is a great pity, as it is the most sassy of Mae's dozen known plays. (There are several more hitherto unknown 1930s plays in the new archive, which we shall reach in due course. A thirteenth play, *Chick*, included in the Library of Congress set, is not a play by Mae West at all.)

The Wicked Age opens in a living room at the house of a prominent citizen of the small seaside town of Bridgeport, New Jersey, Robert Carson. Another town worthy, Ferguson, is proposing to put the town on the map by holding a bathing-beauty contest:

FERGUSON: The basis of any industry that needs immediate attention of the public for success today is based on the exploitation of the female form . . . Look at the musical comedies, with their beautiful curtains of living beauties . . . everything is an excuse for a horde of almost naked women to parade up and down the stage, to give the out of town buyers a kick . . .

Carson is reluctant, but his granddaughter, Evelyn 'Babe' Carson, is all hot to enter the contest. She is, it is clear, a hot kinda gal, as she calls her friends on the telephone:

BABE: Hello Bob – this is Babe Carson – come on over, I'm giving a party – I'm wrecking the old homestead – Bring over your uke – and bring some gin – a lot of gin – and Bob, bring a girl.

The young folk gather, as Babe ushers them in – 'come in boys – father's out and we have no dog . . .' Mae was obviously pushing things a bit, playing a late-teenager at the not so pristine age of thirty-four. But Grandad walks in on the party, frothing: 'Fine example to bring into the world another generation – The fall of every great nation in the past has been preceded by the immodesty of its womanhood – and it requires no prophet to tell that America is drifting to the very lowest . . .'

In memory of her own teenage years, Mae brought into the cast to play her grandfather none other than Hal Clarendon, leader of the Stock Company which launched her acting life proper. The argument Babe has with Grandad mirrors the dispute between Nona and her parents in *The Hussy*:

CARSON: This is filthy, low – wicked – bad –
BABE: Bad – I want to be bad – I'm sick and tired of trying to live the life you want me to live – I don't want to be good – I want to be rotten – I want to be filthy low – vile – call it anything you please – but God I want to live my own life . . .

Babe enters the beauty contest, which provides the requisite under-dressed girls – Babe's aunt: 'This is terrible, each girl wears less, I've never seen such immodesty in my life.' The men pass various comments on the contestants:

'Look at that one, she's built like a Mack truck.'
'She must weigh 200 pounds . . .'
'Look at that one with the big ankles.'
'I guess her ankles are big to keep her knees from running into her shoes.'

And so forth. Babe wins this sleazy contest and is set for greater things. She becomes well-known, goes from show to show, managed by John Ferguson, and is wooed both by a rich businessman, Stratford, and a seedy French count. Another plot line intrudes, as her cousin Gloria, another beauty contestant, is found murdered and suspicion falls on a retarded young man, Willie, who is devoted to Babe. This is an interesting pointer to the influence of the aforementioned movie script, *Flame of the Yukon*, which also features a retarded youth, Solo Jim, who is devoted to the saloon girl, The Flame. Babe, by this time, has become a minor starlet, arguing with manager Ferguson over endorsements at Atlantic City contests:

FERGUSON: I'm getting sick of this job. Nothing I do suits you. Nothing anyone does suits you. Anyone would think you're the Queen of Sheba.

BABE: That piker. She was only Queen over some Polacks or something while I am queen of all the bathing beauties . . .

JEANETTE (*the maid*): There's a man waiting for you. He says it's very urgent. He's been waiting since ten o'clock.

BABE: Serves him right. Disturbing me at this time in the afternoon. Let him wait.

JEANETTE: But he wants to give you a thousand dollars, and go.

BABE: Well, take the thousand and TELL him to go.

JEANETTE: He gave me this letter. His firm wants you to endorse something. Wants a testimonial.

BABE: Is that all he wants? (*reads letter*) Tell him to make it two thousand, that's the lowest price for endorsing chewing tobacco.

FERGUSON: You got twenty-five hundred for letting them use your name for that evaporated milk from contented cows.

BABE: I should have gotten a million, everyone thought I was the cow. I was the laugh of New York when the posters came out, 'drink Babe Carson's milk, it never runs dry.'

Another version of the same scene tries variant dialogue and then brings in the featured jazz band, bringing its black players onto the stage and into the narrative, racially mixing the cast, with Mae guying her own frenetic off-stage life:

FERGUSON (*walking up and down room*): You certainly are the most temperamental dame I ever handled, while you're alive Sarah Bernhardt ain't dead.

BABE: Don't compare me to dead ones. Why, Sarah Bernhardt never got half the headlines I do.

FERGUSON: She was a great actress.

BABE: Only on the stage, I'm a greater actress off.

Ferguson urges her to rehearse her new song with the black band he has brought 'all the way from Harlem'. Babe's maid, Bea, enters:

BEA: There's no scandal in the paper about you today. The first time in weeks.

BABE (*upset*): What, nothing about me in the paper? What sort of a manager are you? Nothing about me in the paper, I'll sue all the editors, I'll horsewhip them.

FERGUSON: They only took you out for the afternoon edition, someone committed a murder.

BABE: Why didn't you keep me in, what am I paying you for, why didn't you think up something, have me married, divorced, or kidnapped, or all three, why?

FERGUSON: I'm getting damn sick of this job . . . (*to the players*) If she sings this song, boys, you have to give her a thousand dollars down and sign over to her the mechanical rights, the publishing rights, the radio rights.

BABE: The only thing he can have is the Scandinavian rights, but if you're very good, boys, I might let you have the Lenox Avenue rights.

FERGUSON : Lets hear the song, Jazzbo.

(*One boy sits at piano and strikes about one or two notes*)

BABE : That piano, that piano, I can't stand it, it's awful, throw it out the window.

FERGUSON: I had it tuned yesterday.

BABE: Go and get yourself tuned, I don't care when you had that piano tuned, it's awful and when I say it's awful, it is awful, how can I hear a song on that piano, I can't stand it, I'll go crazy, get me a gold piano. (*goes around room in a tantrum*) Everything you do is wrong, everything (*takes sheet of music and tears it up*).

FERGUSON: You're tearing up the song, the song they wrote for you.

BABE (*tearing it into bits*): What do I care, I'll tear it into little bits and bits and make you eat them. (*stuffs them in his mouth*) They can write me another song, a hundred songs, a thousand songs, if they don't I'll shoot them (*goes for boys, boys get scared and start to run from her*).

BABE: Don't you dare go until I tell you, how dare you leave my royal presence, don't you know who I am, Babe Carson, the bathing queen, the great Babe Carson, the only Babe Carson, the girl with the most perfect toes in the world.

FERGUSON: Babe don't get excited, remember your indigestion.

BABE: Don't be vulgar, a bathing beauty never has indigestion, only mal de mar.

BEA (*enters with pile of letters*): Here is some of your mail Miss Carson, your secretary is opening the rest.

BABE: What a bore, what a bore, I should ruin my beautiful eyes reading such piffle. Here you boys have nothing to do, read my letters to me (*throws letters at them*) while I recline, and Bea, fan me, fan me gently with my most beautiful fan.

But as Babe proceeds from flapper tantrums to the darker shores of a cocaine habit she is visited by an older show-woman, Lottie, who relates to her the flip side of fame:

LOTTIE: The ravages of time, dear, the ravages of time. My picture like yours adorned the front page of every newspaper. Yes, I was a beauty, not a bathing model but an artist's model . . . then I became a famous stage beauty, but success was too much for me, I was feted, yes, wined and dined. In those days they didn't have automobiles but I had carriages with handsome horses . . . But that isn't the way to keep your beauty, I know, I've been over the road, when you start to lose your youth and beauty, no one wants to wine and dine you, then, there is always someone there to take your place, younger, more beautiful, so the thing is to guard it, treasure it, hold on to it as long as you can . . . I'm not preaching, I'm talking from bitter experience. Goodbye, Miss Carson, try and keep me before you as a picture of what that thing can bring you to.

(*She exits, leaving Babe on stage. Babe has an illusion and imagines she sees herself, an old broken down woman, she takes the cocaine and throws it away . . .*)

We cannot, of course, tell which version of the paper texts was performed on the stage, though 'Drink Babe Carson's milk, it never runs dry!' is mentioned in *Variety*'s review of 9 November. The review, true to form, dismissed the play as 'theatrical tripe', though 'it possesses enough in the star and theme to develop into a money-maker'. Interestingly enough, cocaine is not mentioned by the critic, though whether this is out of deference to his readers or because it was excised from the play, one cannot tell. This is the first time Mae brought the drug issue into her scripts, most likely as a result of her time in jail, and the theme would return some time later in *The Constant Sinner*.

Note, too, the first appearance of the black maid Bea as a Mae sidekick, clearly based on the true-life Bea Jackson, something that would be a feature of more than one of her films. In the movies, her real-life maid in Hollywood, Libby Taylor, played the role twice, in *I'm No Angel* and *Belle of the Nineties*, though she was not the Beulah who is told 'Peel me a grape!' in the former (that was a role for Gertrude Howard). Miss Taylor was said to have met Mae on the stage, and though she does not figure in any play's credits, this does not mean she was not there. In a 'Mae West's Personal Maid Tells All' article in *Hollywood Magazine* (January 1934), Libby is given the standard dialect that a maid must have in the argot of the age, discoursing of 'muh mistress', 'dat woman ain't got no spah time. If she ain't makin' a pitchah, she's writin' huh next one, and if she ain't writin' a pitchah, she's writin' a story or a book of some dialogue or somethin'.'

The maids may have a role, but separation both of race and class is paramount: 'Before Mae is going out, she permits Libby to help her dress and then gives her the entire evening off. Mae always selects the clothes she wishes to wear, "She doan need no hep from me on that!" Libby laughs. Before Libby leaves, she turns down the covers on the bed, but, "Muh Madam doan need no hep to get to bed. No, Muh Madam doan care for pajamas; she's partial to nightgowns, an' the prettier they ah the bettah she sleeps, yes suh!"'

Babe Carson was destined to go a long way . . . But in the play, she has to overcome her attraction to the French count, her pusher and, it turns out, the killer of the retarded Willy, so as to plight her troth with the fairy-white all-American Jack Stratford. The transgressions may only be a long diversion, after all. *Variety* added:

Miss West is well fortified with masculine support. None is less than six feet and a couple are above the 6–3 mark.

No one will believe that Babe is exactly a lily of the valley. She knows too many fly comebacks. Even hoyden flappers don't ad lib that 'while he was a quarterback at Notre Dame, he's now fullback for this dame;' or, in response to an equally demure flapper's inquiry, 'I was up in the Count's room alone last night – did I do wrong!' with Babe responding, 'How do I know? Don't you remember?'

'The Wicked Age' thus resolves itself into a dialog of sidewalk wisecracks for its brighter moments.

Thus, knowingly or inadvertently, the critic outed Mae as already a voracious copier of *McNally's Bulletin*'s 'sidewalk patter'. In the last act, the critics reported, in her New York apartment, 'Babe Carson waxes temperamental to jazz obligato, firmly condescending to rehearse a few numbers with her colored jazzhounds at the piano and trumpet. Five songs, credited to Miss West, Jack Murray and Charles Pierce for authorship, are reeled off to cooch accompaniment.'

Despite her best efforts, Mae could not coax another 'Sex' bonanza out of *The Wicked Age*, which the police wisely ignored. Box office was not spectacular. By 16 November the play was reported to be in financial difficulties. The show was not performed one Monday due officially to Mae West's indigestion, but in fact, as *Variety* reported, 'failure to pay salaries appears to have been the problem'. When the play reopened, the journal reported in the regular gossip column 'Inside Legit' a blatant example of what we today call 'product placement': 'Mae West paid off her shoes and costumes with freak exploitation credits during the presentation of "The Wicked Age." For her Sam Mayo costumes she boldly tells the maid . . . she will don her Mayo creation, and the Cammermeyer shoes are plugged via post cards distributed between acts, showing Miss West in full length pose on the mailing card with the caption that "Cammermeyer shoe creations (capitalized) have a leading role in my wardrobe."' By this date, 23 November, *The Wicked Age* was counted out, closing for good after only three weeks.

But Mae was already well advanced in the planning of the play which would transform both her image and her fortune. Within five months of closing one play, she was ready with another: the all-singing, all-dancing, all wisecracking *Diamond Lil*.

'Diamond Lil' – the cast, 1928

I Want to Be Bad!

From the *San Francisco Examiner*, 17 November 1929:

Interview by Edgar Waite

ME: Miss West, as the most persistent sensationalist in the theatre today –

MAE *gratefully*: So sweet of you.

ME: So tell me frankly. Is it your purpose to reflect life as it is lived, or are you trying to elevate the stage?

MAE: Don't kid me. I've had one dominating purpose in writing such plays as 'Diamond Lil,' 'Drag,' 'Sex,' 'The Wicked Age' and 'Pleasure Man.'

ME: Moral uplift?

MAE: Box-office uplift.

ME: What luck?

MAE: Assorted. Last Monday at the Curran we took in $300 more than Ethel Barrymore on her opening night last summer. On the other hand, if the district attorney of New York hadn't closed 'Sex' because the curbstone bidding for tickets took too many cops off their regular beats, I'd have owned my own theater by now.

ME: Do you consider your plays quite moral?

MAE: I consider them a theatrical representation of those phases of life which interest the public more than anything else, and have since the days of Sappho, Aspasia and Delilah.

ME (*scribbling*): And when was that?

MAE: Forever.

ME: Isn't 'Diamond Lil' just a bit offensive to decent people?

MAE: Pooh! There aren't enough offended people to count.

ME: You mean, not enough decent people?

MAE (*sparring*): Didn't say so. Decent people are just regular people under the surface. Everybody's either human, or a hypocrite.

ME: Do you object to hypocrites?

MAE: They're a menace to civilization. The only play I ever saw that was repulsive to me dealt with organized immorality in the hands of a hypocrite. This is an age of frankness. People should be frank with one another. Pretended virtue is the worst vice . . .

Unrepentant, Mae flung down the gauntlet yet again. Once more, there was controversy over the source material. The Morals Production Company having been shut down by the morals police, Mae needed an untainted front for her production now that Timony and Morganstern were jailbirds. While Timony remained her mentor, personal manager, perhaps still lover and certainly friend, she contracted an alliance with a mainstream theatrical producer, Jack Linder, a former top vaudeville agent. Jack's brother Mark had written a play called *Chatham Square*, set in the New York Bowery in the 1890s, which Jack wanted to propose for Mae. Mae always claimed to have written her own version of *Diamond Lil* before the Linders came on board. Linder's play, she said, was 'tired in construction, banal in plotting, characterless'. Still, Jack was a major player, raring to go as a fully fledged Broadway producer, and Mae's own ideas would need serious money to be realized on the stage.

Stanley Musgrove and George Eels, in their biography of Mae, claimed that gangster Owney Madden once again stepped in, providing 50 per cent of the cash. Whatever the truth of all this, the credits of *Diamond Lil* would, when produced, read 'period and locale by Mark Linder'. Mae wrote in her own book that a passing conversation with a night porter at her hotel, who was admiring her diamonds and asking her about her next play, brought out his recollections of his own time as a police captain many years before: 'It's still wild and crazy and full of misfits and monsters,' he said, recalling, 'you remind me of a sweetheart I had then . . . She had a lot of diamonds, just like you. And how the men did run after her!'

So Mae conjured up Diamond Lil. Or her memories of her own mother's reputation as 'Champagne Tillie' might have had something to do with it. Or, others have speculated, it was the current staging of Somerset Maugham's *Rain*, the tale of a missionary's clash and then affair with a prostitute, that gave her the play's central love interest. (*Rain* was first performed in New York as far back as 1922, and by 1928 a film was being made, *Sadie Thompson*, directed by Raoul Walsh.) Or she may well have recalled the encounter between 'Shifty Liz' and the Salvation Army officer in 1921's *The Whirl of the Town*.

The movie *Flame of the Yukon*'s period setting could have been another spur. As ever, Mae picked and chose from her variety of sources and came up with something which became uniquely her own.

The alliance with Jack and Mark Linder would eventually come to grief amid the familiar recriminations and their legal attempts to claim copyright and a bigger piece of Mae's action – 'The Linders got a break when they hooked up with me. I'm the one who brings people to this theatre,' Mae would later tell the press, which reported: 'As for the Linders' assertion that they paid for her meals and board, Mae said that when she had first walked in to their office she had $20,000 worth of bracelets on her arms.'

The jewellery taken care of, Mae proceeded with gusto to recreate the Bowery saloons of old New York on the stage. Among her many sources, the stage veteran Chuck Connors II, who played a small role in the play but a more prominent one in the subsequent *Pleasure Man*, provided her with tales of his father, Chuck Connors I, a vivid Bowery character who had been known as the 'Mayor of Chinatown' at the turn of the century. Chuck Connors' annual Chinatown Ball had been renowned for its transgressive revelry; in the words of a contemporary 1903 *New York Times* account: 'There were Chinamen dancing with white girls, negro women waltzing with white men in evening dress, pugilists from the Bowery, well-known theatrical folks from the up-town theatres, society men and women who had come in their carriages just to look on, and a raft of humanity from the Chinese quarter . . .' An earlier 1898 account gave the names of less salubrious luminaries attending: 'Paddy the Fake, Cherrynose Jack, Stew Johnson, Blizzard, The Cable Car, Billy Shagnassy, Plug Kelly, Baldie Carroll, Rats and the Terrier.' In the event, Mae's own version was more tame.

Press reports detailed later how the Royale Theater's property man had gone down to junk shops and 'found a beautiful bar . . . he was assured that it actually graced no less famous a resort than that run by Steve Brodie . . . In the same junk shop the Royale property man found a half dozen wooden-top tables, faded and inelegant, which seemed to blend nicely with the architecture of the bar . . . in another junk shop he purchased the heavy glasses and mugs.'

A whole cast of veteran performers was assembled to add character and experience to the reconstruction, particularly to play the singing waiters who delivered a medley of authentic old-time songs: 'Big Jack Howard, who sings "More to be Pitied Than Censured" in the style which brought down the house three decades ago and who gets a sure-fire laugh at every performance when he ambles across the stage with a barrel of beer balanced on his shoulder; Frank Wallace, also a tenor, small and frail looking by contrast with Howard . . . Pat Whalen, who thumps the queer-looking, upright piano with its tinny tones . . . knows all the old songs and can play them on demand.'

This Frank Wallace would cause endless confusion when Mae's unknown 1911 marriage was revealed in 1935. No one could figure out if he had been the alleged husband or not. In photographs they certainly looked similar, but the Frank Wallace of *Diamond Lil* was said to have died soon after and so could not have turned up in 1935.

Another recruit for the 1890s show was one Jo-Jo Lee, a.k.a. Joseph Levy, who 'actually was a singing waiter in the days before that profession turned sour and caused him to turn vaudevillian. Irving Berlin can testify to this, for Jo-Jo was one of the entertainers and beer-slingers at the famous Nigger Mike Salter's place when Berlin, then Izzy Baline, a frail youth unknown to fame, came there at . . . the beginning of his career.

'Jo-Jo and Irving Berlin sang a number together, "If I were King," and Jo-Jo declares that the lyrics were written by the now distinguished composer of light music . . . At any rate, Jo-Jo reports that it was a "hop" song; that is, it purported to be the ecstatic dream of the smoker of opium . . . Jo-Jo, who is a few years older than Irving Berlin, worked on the Bowery during the actual period of the play, and remembers well the principle joints . . . Steve Brodie's saloon, at 123 Bowery, was perhaps the outstanding resort, for Steve was a famous person, widely publicized as a result of his plunge from the Brooklyn Bridge, an exploit which has made his name immortal in the English language. Jo-Jo slung beer and warbled ballads there and in a dozen other joints. There was no lack of a place to go to work when one job folded up, for a saloon stood on almost every corner of the Bowery . . .

'Jo-Jo, who ought to know, declares that the atmosphere of "Diamond Lil" is quite authentic. The schooners of beer, which sold in that blessed era for a nickel . . . the coins that were flung on the floor as a just reward for talent, the oldtime songs like "A Bird in a Gilded Cage" – all these have a genuine ring in the ears.'

Jo-Jo claimed, in recollections quoted by veteran songwriter Ray Walker, that he had taught Mae West the words of 'Frankie and

Johnny', which also featured in the show, 'one night in a room in the old Harding Hotel'. Jo-Jo had been a singing clown at the turn of the century and got his name from guiding 'Jo-Jo, the Dog Faced Boy, a blind freak, from one freak show to another. "Those days," said Jo-Jo, "a singing waiter toted as many as sixty beers on one trip, three trays, one on top of the other. Tumble and you'd drown the customers, which would have been a good idea . . ."'

Mae was taking her penchant for realism into new realms. Reading the script of *Diamond Lil* gives only a partial idea of the atmosphere that the production conjured up on the stage, with the old songs vigorously setting the tone for the story, as is evident from the singing waiters' rendition of 'She Is More to Be Pitied than Censured':

> *At an old concert hall on the Bowery,*
> *Round the table were seated one night,*
> *A crowd of young fellows carousing,*
> *With them life seemed cheerful and bright,*
> *At the very next table was seated*
> *A girl who had fallen to shame,*
> *All the young fellows jeered at her weakness,*
> *Till they heard an old woman exclaim:*

Chorus:

> *She is more to be pitied than censured,*
> *She is more to be helped than despised,*
> *She is only a lassie who ventured*
> *On life's stormy paths ill-advised*
> *Do not scorn her with words harsh and bitter*
> *Do not laugh at her shame and downfall,*
> *For a moment just stop and consider,*
> *That a man was the cause of it all.*

Mae's method of adding and altering material, as a result of casting, also affected the show. 'Not only does she build up scenes which in manuscript are fragmentary,' noted the *New York Herald Tribune*, 'she writes in new ones':

In the early stages of 'Diamond Lil' one of her assistants dismissed applicants for positions with the word that all the jobs were filled. Miss West noticed one of the rejected applicants, a woman, ambling across the stage towards the exit. She was impressed by the woman's appearance.

'Where are you going?' she called.

'Home,' the woman said, 'The stage manager said there was nothing for me.' That was eighty-two year old Ida Burt, who every night now at the Royale contributes one of the most entertaining bits in the last act. Miss Burt used to be a dancer and proves now in the play that she hasn't forgotten the art of the hoofer, despite her years.

Diamond Lil previewed in Brooklyn at Shubert's Teller Theatre and then began its run at the Royale Theatre on 9 April 1928. This time the reviews waxed ecstatic, with even the highbrows, like Charles Brackett in *The New Yorker*, forced to admit that 'pure trash, or even impure trash though it is, I wouldn't miss *Diamond Lil* if I were you', while a former detractor, critic Percy Hammond, weighed in with 'It is one of the "hits" of the waning season and vies in money-making values with the most prosperous output of dramatists who have never been in jail.'

Robert Garland of the *New York Evening Telegram* wrote that Mae West was 'so blonde, so beautiful, so buxom . . . that she makes Miss Ethel Barrymore look like the late lamented Bert Savoy', a noted female impersonator. Mae's own archive, diligently clipping all the notices, includes cultural writer Stark Young's adoration in *The New Republic* of 27 June, with her own pencil underlining the first sentence:

'Glamor Miss West undoubtedly has, a kind of far-offness, a foot-lighted dif-
ference, an unpredictable something about her that we watch as we do animals in a cage . . . If the play is largely bosh, it is not essentially more so than
many others. It uses every tried and trusted trick, hokum, motive and stage
expectation, but always shrewdly . . . Two thirds of the last act consist of a
dancing, singing character scene, in which up-town society visits the saloon
and sees a sort of vaudeville exhibition – for which the ensemble playing is
the best in New York . . . I have no idea what is in her head or what she
thinks of the whole occasion she promotes, just as I have no idea, standing
before the bars of circus cages, what is going on in the eyes looking out at
me. I gather, however, that the performance is more or less on the level, that
she sees herself seriously enough . . . She may, for all I know, even think the
play itself she has written is a great drama . . . Where there is no delicacy of
mind there may be a kind of animal subtlety and astuteness. An intuition of
theater technique, a past in vaudeville to test and clinch it, and a cynical perception of its results – and you have Miss West's stage method.

And nobody, seeing her play, can fail to wonder at that audacity of leisure,
motion which becomes an intensity of movement by its continuity, but is
almost stillness because it is so slow. The whole body – not a beautiful one – is
supple, flowing, coolly insinuating, the voice and enunciation only more so.

From such a quality and aim ensues the quality of the whole performance . . .

My notion is that 'Diamond Lil' is the popular theater's joke on our theater
of culture; and that Mae West is a part of the secret of Pan before the footlights.

Mr Young's accolade was important, as he had denounced *Sex* as dull
and Mae's performance in it as 'crude, ugly and idle'. Mae was finally
being noticed by those intellectuals who had pulled vaudevillians like W.
C. Fields and the Marx Brothers up the social ladder of success. It was
no longer the prurient or the 'mugs' alone who were allowed to enjoy
Mae's theatrical outrages. For the middle classes, Mae West had arrived.

The key, of course, was in displacing Mae's wildcat social criticism
from the uncomfortable present, with its visible irritants to the moral
reformers' fantasy world – the three 'p's: prostitution, 'perversion'
and pleasure – to the safety of the past. This did not make the reformers any better disposed to her work, but it found a way around the
obstacles they had scattered in her path.

The earliest extant text of *Diamond Lil* remains the one registered
with the Library of Congress. The date of registration is 6 February
1928, and the manuscript has been sent by Mae West from the
Harding Hotel, West 54th Street, New York:

DIAMOND LIL
A drama of the New York underworld in 1900

ACT I: *Dance-hall run by Gus Jordan. (Curtain lowered two minutes to denote lapse of six hours)*
The dance-hall of Gus Jordan, on the East Side in New York at three o'clock in the afternoon.
Full stage set – piano at left down stage – tables and chairs – swinging doors at back center. Stairs at right, going up to small balcony. Door of Lil's room opens on this. Walls of room covered in disorderly arrangement with old-time posters, programs, framed things etc. Typical of Suicide Hall, once famous in the New York Bowery, in the 15th precinct.
AT RISE: *Jim, the piano player, sits idly before the instrument reading a paper. He is dressed à la Chuck Connors: Bright blue flannel shirt covered with white buttons, a white tie, and a brown derby hat in which is a blue quill feather. Hat tilted forward – cigarette cast down.*
Two or three groups sit around listlessly at the tables. A waiter brings in beers. The waiter wears a long white apron from the waist – no coat – and has a towel over left arm.

Enter Flynn, a rival of Gus Jordan, who has ambitions to take over Jordan's joint. Flynn tells another barfly, Kane, that a well-known procuress, Rita Christina, has brought her new boyfriend, a Latino hunk, to town and that he plans to use this man to make trouble between Jordan and his moll, Diamond Lil:

FLYNN: You know what a blazing ice-box Diamond Lil is. Straight with Gus Jordan, in spite of the fact that she drives men wild. Wait until she gets a look at this here Wop.

KANE: You're crazy! That dame wouldn't fall for John the Baptist. She knows her little book too well. Anyway, what good would it do to you if she did?

FLYNN: I'm coming to that! Listen *(looks around suspiciously)* – you know and I know that Jordan is all sewed up in this traffic business. This place don't pay nothin' big; and the coin which has put him in soft, has been got off these here fallen angels shipped down to Rio.

KANE: I get what you're drivin' at; but where does this greaser come in to help?

FLYNN: Well, if Lil falls for him, and I think she will for she ain't seen nothin' like him in the States, he can get the drop on the whole game.

KANE: Why are you so sure that Lil will fall for him?

FLYNN: I know women, Kane. The wisest jane in the business will give the shirt offen her back, to the guy what makes her blood steam up a bit.

Mae's use of slang, like her collection of quips, was built up as much by picking words and phrases from written sources as any oral memory of underworld phrases. One clipping in her personal archive, dating from April 1929, a year after the opening of *Diamond Lil*, gives a clue to her ongoing magpie tendencies: an article by one Colonel Givens, ex-Chicago reporter, in the *Saturday Evening Post* sets out the different slang words used by crooks in particular cities and notes the origin of much slang from 'the old cant language of England' as well as 'carnival and doper slang'; old English terms such as 'cadge . . . patter, filch, moonshine, booze', or the prison argot: 'death house, hot seat . . . slug, blackjack, heat, rod, gat', et cetera.

Back at Diamond Lil's, we hear that Chick Clark, notorious Chicago gunman and Lil's ex-flame, has made a getaway from the State Penitentiary and is on his way to reclaim his old girlfriend. Jordan enters, exchanging banter with Flynn, and then a woman in distress, Sally, enters and is taken within, followed by Rita, with her hunk, Juarez. As they converse, a man at a table suddenly cries out: 'My God! I've been robbed!'

(*Diamond Lil enters through the swinging doors; and all eyes are focused on her.*)

DIAMOND LIL: What a hell of a greeting!

MAN (*hopelessly groping through clothes*): I've been robbed, I tell you, just plain robbed!

DIAMOND LIL: How lucky! Most men lose everything they've got before they land here. Hello, Gus. Who's the town crier?

JORDAN: Just one of the men a girl turned the trick on.

MAN: Help! Police! Get the police! I've been robbed!

DIAMOND LIL: What a big voice for such a little man! He should be in Congress.

(*Waiter enters and goes to man.*)

DIAMOND LIL: Greetings, Rita, glad to see you back. Hello there, Flynn, where have you been hiding? For what, and from what?

FLYNN: I've been traveling, Lil, just traveling.

DIAMOND LIL: Ah, a salesman! I always thought you pretty deep.

MAN: But I won't get out I tell you, until I get my money back.

DIAMOND LIL: His money back! Bill, (*to waiter*) give the guy his carfare, and tell him how lucky he is!

(*Waiter drags man off protesting loudly.*)

FLYNN (*so earnestly it does not escape Lil's notice*): This is Mr Juarez, Lil, a man from Brazil.

DIAMOND LIL: Glad to meet you.

JUAREZ (*bowing low*): The pleasure is mine, I am sure!

RITA: Mr Juarez is my assistant, Lil.

DIAMOND LIL: Your assistant! Day or night work, Rita?

RITA (*defiantly*): Both! Pablo is very, well, sort of.

All laugh.

DIAMOND LIL: I know what you mean. Jack of all trades.

(*Pablo is very much smitten on Lil, which fact does not escape the notice of Flynn, although Jordan beams unconsciously on the situation.*)

The background plot of *Diamond Lil* involves the rivalry between Jordan and Flynn and the shady business done in Suicide Hall, tricking young women into being sent to Rio by Rita for obvious purposes, though Lil, by the necessity of the plot, believes they are going to be hired as dancers. Diamond Lil convinces Sally to go to South America, as she has obviously been left high and dry – and pregnant – by a married man:

SALLY: South America? But, but I haven't any money!

DIAMOND LIL: Listen, dummy, a woman don't need money, if she has any sense.

SALLY: I do not quite understand you.

DIAMOND LIL: You will. I speak a language which all women can understand in the due course of time. Now listen, you probably left the old folks on the farm flat. I know the story, it is old and should have been set to music long ago.

SALLY (*bursting into tears*): You – you are so horrible!

DIAMOND LIL: No I ain't! I'm just human. And I don't kid myself or nobody else either. For you to get out of the country would help, now wouldn't it. Oh, you don't have to stay there, but you can leave the son and heir in the tropics; come back, and who would be the wiser?

SALLY: I could, couldn't I? . . . but I have not the money! And I look so awful!

DIAMOND LIL: Well, you don't look any too spry, but that's easy enough. Fine feathers make fine birds. You've got a nice face, if the lily was painted becomingly . . . Listen kid, don't be fool enough to throw your life away for any man. It flatters them too much. Women have been pulling that stunt for ages. Get yourself together and see this thing through . . . Men is all alike. Married or single, it's the same game. *Their game.* I happen to be wise enough to play it their own way. You'll come to it . . .

The departure of Sally sets the scene for the second element of the plot, the involvement of a Salvation Army officer, Captain Cummings, who comes searching for the missing girl. This role was played on stage in 1928 by Curtis Cooksey and was to be transformed four years later on the screen by the young Cary Grant. For the first time, Mae was setting out her stall in a text by means of a proper dialogue of ideas rather than a scene between the put-upon woman and a series of somewhat dummy-like male villains:

(*Cummings calls, Lil sees him in her boudoir.*)

CAPTAIN (*desperately*): Put some clothes on and I will explain my business.

DIAMOND LIL: What has my clothes got to do with your business?

CAPTAIN : I prefer to talk to women when they are dressed.

DIAMOND LIL: Oh, is that so? I prefer to talk to men when I am not dressed. It's merely a slight difference in our business . . .

Cummings tells Lil he has come to enquire about the missing Sally on behalf of her parents, declaring to Lil: 'I know that somewhere inside of you there must be a heart.' Lil suspects initially that he may even be the girl's boyfriend, 'the father of her unborn kid'.

CAPTAIN: You dare say such a thing as that to me?

DIAMOND LIL: Why not? You're human, ain't you? And you're certainly damned interested in the whereabouts of this here girl.

CAPTAIN: It is my duty!

DIAMOND LIL: Duty! Jiminy crickets, that's a high powered word with you people. Why the devil don't you start trying to save people before they need it. It would be more to your credit.

CAPTAIN: If we only could. Come now, what kind of sport are you? Do one decent thing in your life. Tell me, where was this girl sent?

DIAMOND LIL: You think I COULD do one decent thing?

Nevertheless, she tells Cummings the girl was sent to Rio.

CAPTAIN: Who paid her passage?

DIAMOND LIL: None of your damned business. Say, if you've come here to trick me into somethin' you're on the wrong ball field.

CAPTAIN: I am not trying to implicate you in anything, Lillian.

DIAMOND LIL: Lillian?

CAPTAIN: That is your name, is it not?

DIAMOND LIL: It's a long time since I was called Lillian. (*Stares at him a moment.*) Why don't you call me Diamond Lil, same as all the rest?

CAPTAIN: You are not Diamond Lil to me. (*then, sorry that he has said this*) Thank you, I must be going.

DIAMOND LIL: Oh, now you've got what you want out of me, you're going to beat it?

CAPTAIN: What more is there to be said?

DIAMOND LIL: Can't yer – can't yer loosen up a bit and give us a kiss?

CAPTAIN: That sort of thing just isn't in me.

DIAMOND LIL: Oh, ain't it now. I'll bet you've got a past that could draw rings round this here Bowery.

CAPTAIN: If I have, I know nothing about it.

DIAMOND LIL: Mean to say you've never made love to a woman?

CAPTAIN: I have never been in love with any woman.

DIAMOND LIL: You know what I mean – ain't you never wanted to hold a woman close to you (*moves nearer to him*) – very close.

CAPTAIN: Perhaps I may have wanted to, but –

DIAMOND LIL: Come now, YOU be a sport; you ain't no virgin are you?

CAPTAIN: Really now, I must be on my way. I thank you for your information about Sally.

DIAMOND LIL: Gee! You're the most peculiar cuss I ever seen, out of a ZOO.

Loath to let this cuss go and with a thunderstorm breaking outside, she lights up a cigarette, prompting an exchange about women smoking, and fingers her diamonds – 'So this is why they call you Diamond Lil?' He kids her about flashing the diamonds around; perhaps even he, Cummings, might 'be just the one to take them all . . .' Lil chides him about his courage: 'You ain't got guts enough to pull off that kind of a game . . . All you goody-goodies are cowards at heart. That's why you are out to reform folks who have the nerve to do the things you'd like to do, and dare not.'

This shades into a dialogue about morality and the excitement of a life of sin, as she flashes her diamonds at him again:

DIAMOND LIL: Ain't they grand!

CAPTAIN: Very dazzling! You look like a glittering palace of ice!

DIAMOND LIL: I ain't ice!

CAPTAIN: I did not mean to infer that YOU are. Diamonds always seem cold to me – they have no warmth, no soul.

DIAMOND LIL: Gawd you're a queer piece of machinery. Why diamonds are the most valuable thing a body can have.

CAPTAIN: A body, yes – but not the soul.

DIAMOND LIL: Maybe I ain't got no soul.

CAPTAIN: Yes you have but you keep it hidden under a mask of gee-gaws.

There follows a rather curious discussion about God – 'a pretty good scout, ain't he?' Lil queries. She tries to dig out of Cummings whether his God would 'masquerade behind a devil, to do a good turn':

CAPTAIN: Every really good deed is inspired by God.

DIAMOND LIL: And He gets all the credit?

CAPTAIN: That is a strange question – but HE should.

DIAMOND LIL: Well, I'll be damned!

CAPTAIN: What do you mean?

DIAMOND LIL: Oh, nothin'!

CAPTAIN: Good-bye Lillian.

DIAMOND LIL (*standing between him and the door*): Not until you kiss me of your own free will.

CAPTAIN (*kisses her on the forehead*) There, that's the pass-word. Bye-Bye. (*Exits.*)

DIAMOND LIL (*coming down stage*): Gawd! Ter think I'd stand for a kiss on the brow – and like it. I must be going daffy. (*goes over to mirror and looks herself over*) Gee! Them are beauts! No soul to diamonds. He would say somethin' as crazy as that!

The background plot returns as Chick Clark comes in, eager to reclaim Lil, but he ends up shooting Rita by mistake. In later versions and in the film, *She Done Him Wrong*, it is Lil herself who kills Rita in a struggle. The body is taken away. But Jordan's 'white-slavery' business unravels, as Captain Cummings is revealed to be, in fact, a cop, Detective Drummond of the 5th precinct. In the final scene, Lil offers herself to him as his prisoner, ready for handcuffs, prompting the closing lines:

CUMMINGS: Yes, I want you – as a prisoner – but not with bracelets. My idea is a plain gold ring.

DIAMOND LIL: Then I DO appeal to you.

CUMMINGS: Of course, I am human.

DIAMOND LIL: My Gawd! I never thought you had brains enough to admit it.

And curtain, to tumultuous applause.

Miss Don't Give a Damn

W. C. Fields, as another ex-vaudevillian, once told an interviewer:

The first thing I remember figuring out for myself was that I wanted to be a definite personality. I had heard a man say he liked a certain fellow because he always was the same dirty damn so and so. You know, like Larsen in Jack London's 'Sea Wolf.' He was detestable, yet you admired him because he remained true to type. Well, I thought that was a swell idea so I developed a philosophy of my own, *be your type*! I determined that whatever I was, I'd *be* that, I wouldn't teeter on the fence.

And so William Claude Dukenfield became W. C. Fields, and stayed that way, a much easier course for men, who expect to define themselves, than for women, who find their image more often refracted through the expectations of others. Mary Jane West, who swiftly became Mae West, in fact teetered a great deal on the fence before finding, in Diamond Lil, a mask she could inhabit with comfort. There was always a problem with Nona, of *The Hussy*, or with Margy Lamont, of *Sex*, who were presented, in text and on stage, as, in the end, victims of a male world. With Babe Carson, Mae found a character who made her own way, regardless of conventions, but in *The Wicked Age* Babe escaped victimhood only by the time-honoured method of hooking up with the richest man in the cast. Diamond Lil, however, was different. She may have occasional doubts, she may even have morals, of a kind, but she defines herself as she pleases and ploughs ruthlessly through the field. Her choice at the finale of the fake Salvationist Cummings, a.k.a. 'The Hawk', is due not to his moral stance, since he turns out himself to be an impostor, but to his physical charms – as she would exclaim in the later novelization of the play: 'I always knew you could be had!'

In the age of the flapper, Mae had transformed the modern, sexually liberated young woman into a gawdy 1890s spectacle, without losing her independence. As she told the *Chicago Evening American* in February 1929:

The wicked women of old days were more fascinating because there was real get-up and glamour to her. Nowadays the flappers take the edge off it for everyone else. Even if the flappers aren't 'mean,' they look it. They don't conceal a thing, either of their feelings or otherwise . . . A girl might as well be nice, or at least nice looking, because the nice ones are so tough looking. That explains why I set 'Diamond Lil' back in the old Bowery days to make it more distinctive. Get me? . . . Nowadays all the girls look alike – same build, slim and sexy, short skirts, same kind of stockings, same kind of paint, same kind of hairdress, and same kind of thoughts, if they'd only admit it. So it's just like seein' the chorus of a show go down the street. That's why I say that the dames of the old Bowery days had it all over the women of today for originality, and looks too, for that matter. Am I right?

No one would dare to contradict Mae at this point. Where *Sex* had gained her notoriety, *Diamond Lil* provided real stardom. Interviewers and press hacks clustered round her like moths, and her local *Brooklyn Daily Eagle* newspaper proclaimed her 'the most unusual, most curious, most baffling and, at the same time, most diverting phenomena in the American theater today'. In his article, *Eagle* writer George Halasz ejaculated a great geyser of extravagant praise: 'Future historians,' he wrote, 'will classify her with Jesse James, Buffalo Bill, Old Man Barnum, John L. Sullivan . . . William Jennings Bryan . . .' Oddly, no famous women were included in this list. 'A year ago,' Halasz continued, 'she "did a stretch" of ten days at Welfare Island . . . a few weeks ago motorcycle policemen raced before her auto, as if she had been a conquering general or a transatlantic flier. As a matter of fact, both Mae West and the transatlantic fliers were presented with keys. The latter with keys to the city – Miss West with a huge, nicely carved, handsomely painted key to the prison.'

Not only was Mae 'one of the biggest box-office attractions Broadway has ever known', but also, the *Eagle* noted, 'the only woman today in America who writes her own plays, casts, stages and directs them and also plays the star roles'. Mr Halasz was sorely smitten: 'She lives with her mother and sister in Kew Gardens, Long Island. She is a buxom creature, with rich flaxen hair, sparkling eyes and strong muscles. She is barely twenty-seven years old. Sometimes she looks like Lillian Russell . . . She has a natural intelligence, an inborn shrewdness, an innate sense of the theater.'

In fact, of course, Mae was thirty-five years old in 1928, but she was certainly not counting. She fired her producer, Jack Linder, who vainly filed charges with Equity. Timony, who for years had been her mentor and rock-steady backer, now became in effect her subordinate, as her 'business representative' and attorney. She remained, however, strongly grounded in the theatrical troupe that helped her to power: when the stage doorman at the Royale, Joseph Schloss, died on duty during the run of the show, Mae staged a special midnight benefit for his family, attended by legions of Masons, Redmen and the Order of Eastern Star, all of whom counted Schloss as their member. Pleasing these orders was solid-gold business, too.

On 10 September the *New York World* reported that tickets for *Diamond Lil* were being sold as far ahead as New Year's Eve. But Mae did not rest on her laurels. She was still smarting over the ignominious fate of *The Drag*, and though she could not revive the play directly, she had another script ready, also involving homosexual characters. Some have seen this as in effect a rewrite of *The Drag*, but it appears to derive from another set of ideas, initially entitled 'Vaudeville', to which the gay themes have been added. Another interim title seems to have been 'Back Stage', but the final title of the piece was *The Pleasure Man*.

It seems astonishing that Mae would not be content with the accolades that had crowned her, after so many years of effort, with public respectability. But apart from the natural intelligence and inborn shrewdness deduced by the admiring Halasz, she also retained the stubbornness that had demanded just *that* doll among the hundred and had sustained her in vaudeville. As Mae's legend would eventually read – see our prologue – she would never 'walk when I can sit, or sit when I can recline. I believe in saving my energy – for important things'. And the important thing was, as ever, the play.

Rehearsals for *The Pleasure Man* commenced while Mae was still in the heat of the initial run of *Diamond Lil* at the Royale: in Mae's own account, rushing over after the evening's show to attend the night rehearsals of *The Pleasure Man* at the Biltmore Theatre on 47th street. At the same time, Mae wrote in *Goodness Had Nothing to Do with It*, she was conducting another of her affairs, with a Frenchman she named as 'Dinjo', who had 'bedroom eyes, the body of a duelist and the charm of the French Ambassador'. He never had much to say, she related, but 'he didn't need to say anything'. Mae's intellectual life was busy enough; *l'amour* proceeded on the run. 'The results were like a high speed film – blurred but exciting.' At some point, as they were rushing around town in a taxi a woman ran towards them shouting, in true melodramatic fashion: 'So, Dinjo . . . This is why you don't come home nights. Why I sit home alone with our child.' Mae had inadvertently violated one of her sacred 'Things I'll Never Do' – cavorting with a married man. Dinjo was sent packing. Or so Mae tells the tale. Later, when the play went on tour in Chicago, according to another titbit, this time in Mae's 1973 special *Mae West on Sex, Health and ESP*, she enjoyed another brief fling, this time with a bodyguard hired by Timony to guard her collection of diamonds. One night, when Timony was away in New York, the new hunk was hustled up to the bedroom. 'I carried twelve protectors in my trunk,' Mae tells us, with the indiscretion only a lady of eighty can muster. 'We made love, starting at one in the morning, and around three hours later I noticed that all twelve were gone . . . Well, if I had known he was coming to tea, I would have gotten a baker's dozen.' This paragon, we are told, clocked up a total of twenty-six bouts that day, though we are not informed whether room service came up with the shortfall.

The pressures of a high-speed life were, however, already leading Mae into another field which would later consume much of her private passion: the pursuit of spiritualist and occult gurus. Actor Jean Hersholt (among whose many great performances counted his Marcus in Erich von Stroheim's *Greed*) bore vivid witness to such an involvement when he was invited to attend a séance in the smoking room of the Royale Theater after one night's show of *Diamond Lil*, relating in *Variety* of 11 July:

'We all sat round a big table in a darkened room,' said Hersholt, 'I sat next to Mae West and held her hand for four hours, some kind of a record. The medium told us we were going to talk to Caruso and Valentino. The medium kept asking us if we could not hear Caruso singing? We could not, but I was waiting to hear from Valentino, who was a friend of mine.

'Suddenly a voice said, "Jean." I answered, "Yes Rudy. Where are you and how are you?" Ruddy [*sic*] then proceeded to tell me that he was happy and that Natacha Rambova had lied when she said that he had ever talked to her after his death . . .

'Then Rudy called upon Mae. Mae was all aquiver and said, "Yes, Rudy, I am right here." Rudy said, "Mae, you have a lot of enemies and don't trust any of them." Mae was quick to promise, "No, I won't, Ruddy."

'A mysterious character named Bill wanted to talk. Nobody knew Bill, but

Mae piped up and said, "How are you, Bill?" Bill said he had killed himself and Mae answered, "Yes, I know, Bill. I hope everything is all right now."

'Mae and Bill had a rather lengthy conversation and Mae was very serious about it. Then Mae and I, who were called on most of the evening, were told to come up to the altar to be blessed. We went up hand in hand, and someone threw a glass of water over us, only most of it hit my wife, who was sitting at the end of the table. She guessed she had gotten most of the blessing.'

Mae herself claimed her first encounter with unseen forces took place at a slightly later date, while on tour with *Diamond Lil* in Chicago. In *Goodness Had Nothing to Do with It* she relates that, while in her hotel room one night, she suffered unexplained abdominal pains which did not abate until Timony delivered to her room a 'lean, dark man' named as Sri Deva Ram Sukul, who was 'President and Director of the Yoga Institute of America'. This eastern magus took her hands in his, and after what appeared to be 'some Houdini-designed mumbo jumbo', cured her on the spot. 'I knew that in some marvellous way,' Mae wrote, 'I had touched the hemline of the unknown. And being me, I wanted to lift that hemline a little bit more.'

For the moment, however, the hemline that Mae was lifting more immediately was that of the familiar robes of New York's morality forces, chaffing over the triumphal return of the wicked witch from her cotton-knickered correction. As per tradition, her new play opened off-Manhattan: a week at the Bronx Opera House from 16 September, then a short run in Queens at the Boulevard Theatre. The show was booked to open at the Biltmore on the night of 1 October 1928.

Mae's most consistent fan, Jack Conway of *Variety*, gave her an unexpected boost on 19 September with a veritably camp review:

OH, MY DEAR, HERE'S MAE WEST'S NEW SHOW –
GET A LOAD OF IT AND WEEP

Oh, my dear, you must throw on a shawl and over to the Biltmore in two weeks to see Mae West's 'Pleasure Man.' Monday night at the Bronx Opera House it opened cold and was adorable.

It's the queerest show you've ever seen. All of the Queens are in it.

Lester Sheehan will kill you in drag in the last act.

You haven't seen anything like it since the gendarmes put the 'curse of the seven witches' on 'The Drag' . . .

The whole thing is backstage stuff and surefire. Those Queens will sell the show if nothing else does . . . The thing ran two hours and a half. It needs plenty of cutting and rewriting, but will it get the pennies? . . . That West girl knows her box office, and this one is in right now. It can't miss, and if you think it can, hope you get henna in your tooth brush.

But don't miss it, because you must see it to appreciate the strides we girls are making. You can't possibly imagine it.

And go early, for some of the lines can't last.

Quite what the two-and-a-half-hour version of *The Pleasure Man* offered is lost to us, as all the versions extant in the archive mirror, more or less, the somewhat short text published by Lillian Schlissel in *The Three Plays of Mae West* (*Sex*, *The Drag* and *The Pleasure Man*), as deposited at the Library of Congress. It is indeed a very different affair from the somewhat clunky special pleading of *The Drag*. Gone is the pseudo-scientific discussion on 'inverted sexual desires' and the plot highlighting the tragedy of homosexuality denied. Instead the gay characters have been placed almost as a Greek chorus in the cast of vaudeville players, preparing to perform their standard repertoire of acts, along with the straight leads, chorus girls and the 'Otto Brothers', a German acrobatic team. The main plot has a heterosexual betrayal theme: Rodney Terrill, leading man and complete shit, is a 'voluptuary', seducing women whether they are single and unattached or married, like Dolores, a dancer whose husband, Randall, is her on-stage partner. Around 'The Pleasure Man' swirls the cast of scrubwomen, small-time vaudevillians and the female impersonators 'Peaches' and 'Bunny'. As one thing leads to another, Rodney is murdered off stage, and though Randall is suspected, the killer turns out to be another player, Ted Arnold, whose sister Rodney had seduced and whose revenge has been to castrate The Pleasure Man – a 'surgical operation' that has gone wrong. The 'c' word is not used but deduced from on-stage talk: 'death due to an operation performed by someone who had a knowledge of surgery . . .'

In a bloody irony, The Pleasure Man has been punished for pursuing a sexual freedom that the writer, Mae, claimed as her right, though his seductions are portrayed as predatory and malicious, deriving from his obsession with male power over women. His pleasures are the women's downfall, abandoned as they are to shame and ridicule. The gruesome outcome, however, comes after a cascade of quick-fire comedy scenes between the players, the tit-for-tat of vaud veterans' repartee:

EDGAR: You know, a stage hand hung himself in my dressing room last week. You can imagine how I felt when I came in and found him hanging to the pipes.

LEADER: Did you cut him down?

EDGAR: Well, not right away. He wasn't dead yet. Now, after we sing this song –

STANLEY: You go straight to your dressing room.

EDGAR: No, we take a lot of bows.

STANLEY: You take 'em – where do you get 'em from? Say, how did you get on the stage?

EDGAR: I fell out of the balcony.

STANLEY: Why don't you get on to yourself and get back to your trade?

EDGAR: I'm at my trade. My father was an actor and my grandfather was an actor.

STANLEY: I suppose if your father and grandfather were bums – you'd be a bum?

EDGAR: No – I'd be a stage hand.

To make this text work, Mae cast a slew of authentic vaudeville old-timers, led by Stan Stanley, a comedian, tumbler and all-round show-man who had been a staple of vaudeville routes for the last two decades. His comical ads were a familiar feature of the stage magazines, an early sample from 1910 showing 'Stan Stanley and Brother' cavorting on car-toon trampolines, claiming both were adept at 'doubles, full and half twisters . . . Stan, the comedian, has an odd delivery of talking, looks ungainly and gawky with his six feet of height . . . but then he's a nut.' Chuck Connors II, son of the 'Mayor of Chinatown' and advisor on *Diamond Lil*, was also in the cast. He had been one of the 'singing wait-ers' who, with Jo-Jo Lee, were said by Ray Walker to have taught Mae West the vaudeville ropes. Another golden oldie, Ed Hearn, played 'Toto', a retired performer who hosts a great drag ball in the Third Act, as Mae's collection of quips comes into its own in gay banter:

(*The Drawing room of Toto's apartment. At rise of curtain, all the guests are dancing to a jazz orchestra . . .*)

FIRST BOY: I hear you're working in a millinery shop.

SECOND BOY: Yes, I trim rough sailors.

THIRD BOY: My, what a low-cut gown you've got!

FOURTH BOY: Why, Beulah, a woman with a back like mine can be as low as she wants to be.

FIRST BOY: I hear you're studying to be an opera singer.

THIRD BOY: Oh, yes, and I know so many songs.

FIRST BOY: You must have a large repertoire.

THIRD BOY: Must I have that too?

FOURTH BOY: Oh, look, I can almost do the split.

SECOND BOY: Be careful, dearie, you'll wear out your welcome.

And so forth. It seems clear that Mae was baiting her opponents in the morals police – rather than tone down the outrage, she was turning up the dial, albeit in a format which at least one critic agreed came within the legal stage remit. After all, the drag ball was technically incidental, and the main theme demonstrated immorality censored with the most painful cut of all. Perhaps Mae thought she could get away with it.

Opening night at the Biltmore Theater proved otherwise. As the headlines told the next day, 2 October:

MAE WEST SHOW RAIDED –
SEIZE 56 AT OPENING –
POLICE ARREST ENTIRE CAST OF 'PLEASURE MAN'
AFTER LAST ACT AT BILTMORE

The *New York Herald Tribune* told the tale in detail:

Before the performance began five patrolmen and a sergeant from the West Forty-seventh street station stood guard at the curb in front of the theater to prevent swarming of friends of persons in the cast. These were ordered inside to their seats as soon as they appeared. Between the first and second acts it became known that the raid would take place, and it was expected that the third act would not be presented. Police did not interfere, however, until half-way between the second and last acts when two stage exits were locked and all auditorium exits guarded to prevent escape by members of the cast. These were told at the close of the performance to remove make-up and gowns and prepare to go to the station house . . .

Lead actors, bit players, female impersonators in full regalia packed into the patrol wagons. As the *Daily News* declared: 'The police raid on The Pleasure Man was even more sensational than the last act.' The *Evening Post* reported:

MAE WEST RAID OPENS CRUSADE TO PURIFY STAGE
MAYOR WALKER ALLEGED SPONSOR OF DRIVE TO
REFORM BROADWAY

. . . persons close to the Mayor said that he had told Police Commissioner Warren that any custardy dramas even slightly odorous were not to be tolerated on Broadway this season. New York must be good in Presidential years . . . The frail young gentlemen who had been powdered, rouged and mascaraed for the last act of the play were greeted with cheers, hoots and catcalls as they were paraded from the Biltmore's stage door and jammed into patrol wagons and commandeered taxicabs.

Some of them tittered their amusement at the vast crowd which had gathered, despite the night stocks of a corps of patrolmen, to watch the triumph of righteousness. Others were dejected and downcast.

Several young girls of the cast wept into their opening night bouquets, desolated by the thought that the play, after weary weeks of rehearsal, might be closed.

As in the case of *Sex*, the producers and managers of the Biltmore secured an injunction to allow the play to continue while charges were being considered. On 2 October, the show went on again, for a matinee, with some lines and a song 'expurgated'. The house was packed. The show, however, was raided again and the entire cast rearrested before the play could run its course. It had lasted for one and a half performances on Broadway.

Apart from the loyal 'Con' of *Variety*, only one other critic dared to suggest *The Pleasure Man* had merits – Thyra Samter Winslow, who had interviewed Mae for *The New Yorker*, writing in the *Jewish Tribune* that the play was 'full of a curious native wit and some rather keen observation'. Most – male – critics denounced it as an 'abomination', 'filth and degeneracy' and 'the kind of Harlem "drag" that the police peremptorily raid'. The men were at one with Gilbert W. Gabriel of the *New York Sun*, who wrote about LAST NIGHT'S FIRST NIGHT:

'PLEASURE MAN' – SOMETHING OF A DESCRIPTION OF THE
SOMEWHAT INDESCRIBABLE –

On a night when two worthy repertory companies were beginning their seasons downtown with reminiscences of Dickens and Molière, here was a new play by Mae West. I had never seen a play by Mae West. I hadn't seen 'Sex' or 'Diamond Lil.' I had not travelled out to the quaint places where they acted 'The Drag,' the play once forbidden to enter New York alive. But so many chirrupy columnists and highbrow weeklies and fellow playwrights had gone Mae West, I fell for the tosh and went, too . . . went as far as the Biltmore, anyhow, and got what I doubtless deserved.

Firstly, I saw a ham-greased imitation of 'Burlesque' and about every other behind the scenes bunkum since 'Zaza' was a centenarian. Secondly, I saw some heavily splayed melodrama concerning a small-time headliner who, for his sins among the ladies is murdered in a manner too surgical for celebration in anything except the musical comedy just across the street from the Biltmore . . . But seeing was only half the sickening. The – shall we call them female impersonators? – were many, and were made to go through all sorts of perverted antics and Harlem bacchanales in various stages of robe and disrobe. What they had to speak was worse.

Perhaps they enjoyed it. The fouler phases of exhibitionism may be interesting to pathologists – but they make for pathetic playgoing, to say the least . . . But now I hear of the author under bail and fifty-five performers arrested. You can't kick fifty-six non-descripts when they're down. But the next time there's a Mae West play I shall rush to all the repertory theaters in town.

The Constant Sinner

One year and three weeks after Mae West's show was raided, American capitalism suffered its most dangerous blow when, on 24 October 1929, the Wall Street stock market 'laid an egg'. This was to have a disastrous effect on Broadway in the ensuing two years, shutting off the lights and closing down many theatres. Mae West was not financially damaged, as she had not, by then, amassed any kind of fortune and certainly no appreciable nest egg in stocks.

The intervening year between the Biltmore Theatre raids and the Wall Street Crash saw the continuing run of *Diamond Lil*, lasting six months in Chicago after its full year on Broadway. All this time, Mae and her fellow accused waited for the other shoe to drop from the District Attorney's office. D.A. Banton, chaffing at his failure to clip Mae's wings with her ten-day sentence for *Sex* offences, was held back by various motions put forward by Mae's new counsel, Nathan Burkan. The indictment had been presented promptly by a Grand Jury in October 1928, charging Mae West and fifty-eight others with unlawfully preparing, advertising, giving, presenting and participating in 'an obscene, indecent, immoral and impure drama' depicting and dealing with 'the subject of sex degeneracy and sex perversion', and with 'contriving and wickedly intending . . . to debauch and corrupt the morals of youth and of other persons and to raise and create in their minds inordinate and lustful desires, unlawfully, wickedly and scandalously' et cetera, et cetera.

The trial did not, in fact, take place until March 1930. But apart from appearing in *Diamond Lil*, Mae was by no means treading water, as, once again, she prepared further outrages against the moral order of the state. Two major projects, one which came to fruition late in 1930 and the other written but never staged, must have taken up a great deal of her time during 1929. *Babe Gordon*, an original novel published in November 1930, was hardly, despite the usual blather, completed in a week or two, and another play, *Frisco Kate*, went through the usual try-out-and-abandoned drafts. *Babe Gordon* would be renamed *The Constant Sinner* after a publicity competition judged by columnist Walter Winchell and the publisher, Macaulay, to find a more peppy title from the public. (A lady, Effi Mattison, of New York City won the somewhat meagre $100 prize.) This became, *ipso facto*, the title of the play Mae had by then written based on the book. Mae's second book, *Diamond Lil*, a 'novelization' of the play, followed in 1932. (This has been republished in our era using the film title *She Done Him Wrong*. Mae's third novel, *Pleasure Man*, was an afterthought brought out in 1975. Another novel, the unpublished *Margy Lamont*, based on *Sex*, can be found in the new archive, most probably deriving from the same later period.

Mae's adaptation, or alleged pilfering, of material from other sources for her plays inevitably raised the issue of ghostwriting. In the case of *Babe Gordon*, Mae wrote in her autobiography that the idea of writing a book about black–white relations originated with an actor, Howard Merling, who had played Eben in Eugene O'Neill's *Desire Under the Elms*. Merling, though white, lived on the fringe of Harlem and claimed familiarity with its vibrant night life. Mae writes: 'Negroes had become the rage of society. Artists and Critics like Covarrubias and Van Vechten had taken them on. Their vices charmed thrill seekers. The newspapers were printing a so-called exposé of Harlem night life. I hadn't paid much attention to it.'

As ever with Mae's own account of matters, one has to look at the angle of presentation of a particular fact at a particular time. In 1958, when Mae was writing her life story, she was much more defensive about cross-racial relationships than she had felt the need to be a quarter of a century earlier, most probably due to *Hollywood Confidential*'s outing of her affair with the 'bronze boxer' Chalky White. Contemporary witnesses place her in much closer proximity to Harlem's night life than she later let on. Jazzman Andy Razaf recalled her frequent presence along 'Jungle Alley', 133rd Street between Fifth and Seventh Avenues, where white trade was welcomed at The Nest, owned by her local friend Johnny Carey, and no one cared much 'with whom he mingles, or why or how'. Gossip about Mae's black lovers has always abounded, and it is unlikely that the steamy black–white love scenes portrayed in *Babe Gordon* were wholly imagined fantasies.

There is no reason to doubt that Howard Merling's notes and research on the 'high life and low down on Harlem . . . the speaks, the numbers rackets, the clip joints, night clubs; the fly characters' provided important background. But the voice is unmistakably Mae from page one:

Babe Gordon leaned against the crumbling red brick wall of the Marathon Athletic Club in Harlem, at 135th Street off Fifth Avenue, and pulled at a cigarette. The Saturday night fight crowd picked its way under the glaring arc lamp in front of the main entrance like a slow moving black beetle. Babe scanned the humans with an eye to business. Babe was eighteen and a prizefighters' tart, picking up a living on their hard earned winnings. Her acquaintances numbered trollops, murderers, bootleggers and gambling-den keepers. Two well-modelled bare legs were crossed at the ankles; her waist pressed to the wall rose to voluptuous breasts that almost protruded from the negligible neck of her black dress. Babe waited for Cokey Jenny.

More than the 'ghostwriting' it might be intriguing to know about the literary influences that lay behind Mae's incursion into the world of the pulp thriller, already a well-established genre. The most prominent writer we know of this period was Dashiell Hammett, already successful with his 'Continental Op' stories based on his own years as a Pinkerton detective. Hammett's novel of city-wide corruption and gangsters, *Red Harvest*, was published in 1929. (*The Maltese Falcon* dates from 1930 and *The Thin Man* followed later.) But Hammett's first short story was published in 1923 by *Black Mask*, a magazine founded in 1920 by no less than H. L. Mencken and George Jean Nathan, though it soon passed into other hands. *Black Mask*, which pioneered the American private-detective story, also featured lurid covers, one fifteen-cent issue showing an enraged blonde cradling an armful of gats and a tommy gun. *Babe Gordon*'s cover featured an outstretched blonde, armed only with her natural charms. A more obscure possible model was a Jewish writer, Octavus Roy Cohen, who published in the *Saturday Evening Post* and whose stories were set in Birmingham, Alabama, with a variety of sleazy black characters talking the usual 'Negro' patter.

Mae would have done well to learn structure and construction from Hammett, but, as ever, her concern was with dynamic characters and lurid scenes. Babe Gordon latches onto an up-and-coming boxer, Bearcat Delaney, despite his manager Charlie Yates' disapproval of mixing dames with training. Against her normal procedure, she falls in love with The Bearcat and marries him, but his sexual obsession with her ruins his chances of boxing success. His career goes into decline, he becomes a taxi driver, and they drift apart. Babe takes up with a black gangster, Money Johnson, who uses her to sell morphine to addicts, but she is betrayed by her rival, Cokey Jenny. Inevitably for a Mae West tale, there is an external character, a rich playboy, Wayne Baldwin, who owns the dime store she uses as cover to push drugs. Wayne's own obsession with Babe ends in a shoot-out with Johnson, but Babe persuades the cab-driving Bearcat, who's still besotted with her, to take the rap and plead the case of a white man confronted with a black raping his wife. The Bearcat is acquitted after a virulent speech by a defence attorney invoking the 'unwritten law': 'Think what passed through his [the husband's] mind, when he burst into that room to find the wife he loved and adored, naked and helpless in the cage of that black gorilla . . . He was mad with anger that bordered on insanity. He had his gun with him and he fired three times at the black demon in defence of his own life and to save the woman he loved.'

Mae's treatment of her black characters, her use of shock expectations and out-and-out exploitation of the 'vice' milieu of Harlem has caused conniptions among her latter-day interpreters battling to square Mae's status as the iconic pioneer feminist with her stereotyped portrayals of blacks. In fact, it does not require jargon-rich scholarship to state the obvious banal fact that, by and large, white people in the 1920s and 1930s, whatever their progressive or transgressive views on sexual and racial matters, did not view black people or gays the way many liberal white people profess to do today. I.e., there is a belief, defined by some as 'political correctness', that applying a different, non-pejorative language denotes a full discernment of equal status, of freedom from racial perspectives. Another argument, however, would point out that equal status – such as has been won or is still being contested – derives from constant struggle and social pressure by black people to achieve equal rights in social, economic and political fields, from which cultural changes arise.

The era that Mae West lived in was in any case awash with images of blacks that have long since been banished to the warehouses of antique collectors – a plethora of grotesque representations, such as

Aunt Jemima jugs, golliwogs, 'coon' postcards with outrageous racial jokes, toy crocodiles devouring 'piccaninnies', minstrel blackface, Jim Crow dancing dolls and endless popular characterizations of blacks as semi-humans.

It is of little use, in my view, to either praise Mae West for her perspicacity in raising the issues of sex between black men and white women, or vice versa, to lambast her for presenting these issues in exploitative lurid terms. The problem is in trying to shoehorn our heroine into a preconceived, convenient size. If the shoe doesn't fit, don't make the lady wear it. She has walked her own path up till now.

Once again, as a showgirl, Mae twists and winds in her manifold contradictions. Often it's anything to get an effect:

Yes, hell had broken loose at the Harlem Breakfast Club! The coloured band was playing with its soul in every note. It had to play at fever pitch to bring out the cry of passion and debauch.

The bodies of almost naked coloured women, wriggling and squirming, moved about the dance floor; brown skinned busts shook frenziedly, hips swayed, abdomens protruded. The music excited, irritated, inflamed the animal instincts . . .

What was and remains particularly distinctive about *Babe Gordon* (*The Constant Sinner*) is the tone of the central character and her indefatigable pursuit of self-gratified sexual pleasure above all else: 'Babe was the type that thrived on men. She neeeded them. She enjoyed them and she had to have them.' Some women, Mae tells us, 'have no desire for men and therefore become old maids, or enter nunneries'. Others 'live a normal, conventional sex life and enter into marriage and motherhood. And then there are women so formed in body and mind that they are predestined to be daughters of joy. These women, whom the French call "*femme amoureuses*", are found not alone among women of the streets, but in every stratum of society.' By implication, Mae was including herself among the category to which Babe Gordon 'by nature' belonged. It was a peculiar, pre-Freudian idea, more old-fashioned than it might seem. 'Babe was non moral,' Mae adds. 'If she had tried to rationalize her attitude, she would have said that the whole world is selling something: goods, ability, personality. Just as a salesman would sell his goods with every ounce of energy and then sit back and enjoy his success, so Babe would enjoy selling herself and her personality. The manner in which she would walk by a crowd of men, or even one man – the toss of her head, the flash of her eye, the light of her smile, all were calculated to win patronage and the consumer's dollar.'

And so, one assumes, Mae West's use of her thespian talents, her way of telling a story, her manner of walking across her stage, the flash of her diamonds, the swish of her hip-swirled gowns and stunning hats were as calculated to sell her personality for the box-office take. Outing herself as The Naked Capitalist, Mae disarmed and outflanked her detractors. It is no wonder, and no aberration, that Mae appeared in one of her tableaux presented in her 1934 movie *Belle of the Nineties* wrapped in the stripes of the flag, with spiked crown and flaming torch in the pose of the Statue of Liberty. Mae West was as American as Wall Street, if better built not to crash.

Mae's racialization of sex in *Babe Gordon* remains disturbingly ambivalent, with her talk of 'yellow' girls and other varieties of skin tone deriving from minstrel-era definitions. Money Johnson craves white women – 'he wanted the whitest and most beautiful, and so he fell for Babe Gordon'. And later: 'He loved Babe with all his deep-rooted primitive passion. In that great mirrored room in Striver's Row Money Johnson appeared like an army by reflection and she was like a shimmering white quicksand ready to consume those black battalions.' And at the end, even when Babe has been removed to Paris by her rich white lover, Wayne Baldwin, from Harlem, the 'pool of sex, where all colours are blended, all bloods mingled', Baldwin still 'cannot avoid thinking of Babe's white body and Johnson's black body, darkness dating with dawn. It is terrible, and yet it gives him a sensual thrill like the one he received when he first saw Babe and the black man in the Harlem Breakfast Club . . .' Black is still the colour of the forbidden, and it is the forbidden, not any sense of individual worth, that remains the enticement and the sexual rush.

Mae's second project of late 1929 spilling into 1930 in fact deepened her problematic incursions into the world of inter-racial sex. The Library of Congress typescript of *Frisco Kate*, registered in December 1930 and hitherto the only known version, restricts the story to the voyage of the 'hell ship *Java Maid*', whose brutal Captain, Bull Brackett, presides over a motley crew which is 'an animalistic collection of the dregs of the waterfronts'. Act 1, Scene

I tells us that 'among those who have been taken aboard the ship through the shanghai method is Frisco Kate, a former character of the Barbary Coast. The CREW is ignorant of her presence.' When the crew discover there is a 'naked woman' on board, all hell threatens to break loose. The Captain, meanwhile, is besotted with Kate because she is like the white doll in his cabin rather than the 'tar-babies' down in the Indies, who 'come aboard without no underclothes . . . they look so pretty with white silk on their yellow bodies and I always dress 'em up. But them bodies is yellow, not like my statue. And you're going to look like my statue right now.' Once again there is a white boy, Stanton, who is going to rescue the heroine.

The play derived more than a little from the 1925 hit *The Shanghai Gesture*, and Mae's personal archive contains an earlier version of *Frisco Kate* which includes an entire deleted prologue set in the 'Lounge Room of the Celestial Casino' in Singapore. The setting is similar to the Chinese brothel location of one of the many (earlier or later?) versions of *Sex*, though much more exotic: the room 'is done in the height of Oriental splendor, and epitomizes the lure and mystery of the exotic East'. A group of white diplomats are guests at the casino of the Chinese owner, Chan Lo, who is keeping a white woman, White Lotus, in his gilded cage. The dialogue is racially charged:

CHAN LO: Pearl of pearls, you are so tired.

WHITE LOTUS: Now don't give me that oil, Chink. I'm not blind. This place is crawling with your yellow snakes, their lemon-skinned faces staring out at me when they think I'm not looking . . . Sure I'm tired. Tired of seeing your stupid mug, tired of you tagging at my heels like a yellow puppy – I've had a year of this and I'm fed up – sick of it – washed up.

CHAN LO: You are consuming me with unjust words.

WHITE LOTUS: And you're consuming me by wanting to own me body and soul. . . I'm nothing but a prisoner here, and you know it.

In the event, Mae excised the entire Singapore section from the play she hoped the Shuberts would eventually open in their theatres, omitting such lines as 'Chinese know many ways to curb the mate of one's couch,' though, as we shall see, it crops up in a truncated format in the movie that eventually morphed out of the playscript, 1936's *Klondike Annie*. What survives (more or less) into the registered version, though not in the movie, is Mae's passionate speech to the Captain on board the *Java Maid*, which mirrors the narrative of Mother Go-Dam in *The Shanghai Gesture*, who confessed an equally horrific degradation in her past:

There ain't been nothing so awful or terrible I ain't lived out here . . . I've been in the black hole of Calcutta – in the rotten dirty alleys of Flag Street – callin men from straw huts – I been in the lowest dives of Siam and in the Portuguese houses of Penang, and saw everything that was until *nothing* was new to me. I'm Frisco Kate. I've seen all the races of the earth in the houses I've been. I'm the last step down in the dirt. But I ain't apologizing to nobody. And I ain't begging your respect neither. For a year I've been trying to get away from the rotten sinks of the East. I come aboard this ship to get away from a Chinaman, and the only way I could do it was to kill him. Yes – goddam it – I killed him. I stuck a knife into his yellow guts. And what the hell do I care what you or anybody else thinks of me? If this ship doesn't get out, it means I'll be caught by Chinamen or I'll have to hang. And with only one thing on this ship to save me, what do you expect me to do? . . .

In another early version Frisco Kate, pursued by the crew after having killed the lecherous Captain and promising them her body if they do her bidding, cries out, in her most abandoned manner:

FRISCO: In an hour's time, we're going to have the engines spinning and we're going singing out of harbor like a torpedo out of hell. We ain't going to meet up with no police. That ain't my idea of fun and it ain't my idea of living. While there's joy to be had, we're going to have it. And if there's any yellow bastard in this crew that hasn't got the guts to carry out this sporting venture then he ain't never deserved to know Frisco Kate, and he ain't going to know her now. I don't want your money. I don't want anything you could think of buying me with. I got a hankering to be out at sea when the sky turns gold in the morning and I'm offering for the spin of those engines. Get them racing . . . What do you say?

THE CREW OMNES: Yes – Yes!

(*Music of accordion and shouts of crew as curtain descends.*)

But this anarchic ending was dropped for the more familiar rescue by the true lover, the only honest man in this nautical Sodom: the ship goes down, and only Frisco and Stanton are left on a raft – 'a shaft of sunlight pierces the clouds. [Liner] whistle sounds nearer and stronger. Stanton takes Frisco in his arms as the CURTAIN slowly falls.'

These fond dreams, or nightmares, however, were never destined to be staged, for, in the early months of 1930, Mae was distracted by two interlinking events which took up all her attention: the looming *Pleasure Man* trial and the death by cancer of her mother Tillie West.

'Song's Words Don't Offend, But Tune Does'

Mae's mother died on Sunday 26 January 1930 in Brooklyn. Mae wrote: 'her death was the greatest shock and deepest sorrow of my life. I had always managed to remain calm in the many emergencies and crises in my own life. This was the most crushing blow, and I was frantic with grief. I dramatized my sorrow and became widly hysterical and frenzied. Father and another man had to hold me as I howled for self-destruction.'

Mae purchased a family vault in Cypress Hills Abbey, bordering Jamaica, Queens and Brooklyn. Correspondence from 1933 shows that Mae and Beverly later paid for five crypts to be prepared for the rest of the family to be laid beside Tillie. The run of *Diamond Lil* continued, though after the Saturday night show at the beginning of February Mae was reported to have 'collapsed in her dressing room at the Shubert Riviera Theater . . . and had to be carried to her home by members of her company'. Her attorney, Nathan Burkan, denied rumours that her collapse was due to the imminence of the *Pleasure Man* trial. Miss West, Burkan said, 'is not in the least worried about the outcome of her impending trial'. The trial, nevertheless, was postponed from its scheduled 4 February start and got under way, finally, on 16 March.

The *Pleasure Man* trial was a delayed-action repeat of the *Sex* trial three years before, although, as Mae was more famous now, it was covered by the press in greater detail. Even warm-ups involving jury selection were described blow-by-blow:

'Do you have any prejudice to a play in which female impersonators appear, Mr Chandler?'

'No, I attend one of those every year. A college play.'

'Oh, a college play, eh?' asked the lawyer. 'The college boys play the parts of women?'

'Yes,' that's it, replied the talesman.

Miss West, during this long, and to her dull process, sighed, looked at the ceiling, inspected her manicure . . . Mr Chandler was accepted. Juror No. 1.

Eventually, the first four 'baldish, yet domestic-looking jurors' had been chosen, and eight more, all men, followed. Mae, wearing a 'small hat and a long coat and billowing fox fur . . . took her seat to hear Mr. Wallace (the Assistant D.A.) object to the absence of the majority of the fifty-seven indicted with her . . . "I have learned," said Mr. Wallace, "that some of those defendants have enlisted in the Navy. What right had they to enlist while an indictment was pending against them?"'

Defence Attorney Burkan tried but failed to get a motion to dismiss the case on the grounds of 'insufficient allegations'. To which Mr Wallace riposted that Mr Burkan had in the past year and a half 'made more motions than the defendants made on the stage'.

Motions, manners and gestures were to become prime prosecution matters, as old veterans like Patrick Kenneally – now Acting Lieutenant – and Lieutenant James McCoy, as well as Detectives Harvey and Kane, were on hand to describe the abominations on the stage. 'At the request of the prosecutor,' McCoy acted out several of the roles, using the copious notes he had taken at the time. To Mr Burkan's questions, McCoy answered that he had in his past been a bit-part actor, as well as 'in a circus for a while, doing hard manual labour, putting up tents and things like that'. Concerning one of the songs, 'Queen of the Beaches', Burkan demanded that McCoy demonstrate how it was sung: 'Go ahead, captain. You're a pretty good imitator – yesterday you gave a good imitation of how they said "Whoops."' But the prosecution objected: 'This officer is not a singer and not qualified to demonstrate.' Objection sustained. The prosecution, however, was getting into trouble over the argument that even if the words and lyrics were of themselves innocent, it was the way they were delivered that constituted the offence. As the *New York American* put it: 'SONG'S WORDS DON'T OFFEND, BUT TUNE DOES.' Burkan made much play with McCoy's faulty memory, goading him over whether he had heard the word 'chronic' or 'platonic love affair'. The defence called the cast members to testify that the play consisted of 'vaudeville tricks – done in a spirit of fun'. The veteran Stan Stanley went over the 'lines that the police found quite blue, and made them, in a husky, male voice, sweet and pink':

The police reported that one of the characters was sewing on a fancy lamp-shade and talking like a seamstress as well. Stanley gave his version of the scene and dialogue in the manner of a traffic cop relieving his mind.

'Those lines,' he said, leaning back in his chair on the witness stand, 'were between Chuck Connors the Second and his dancing partner, a man. Chuck comes up to me and says, "I don't like me dancing partner. He don't seem regular. In his spare time he makes lamp shades." So I asks the fella will he make me one – a green one – for my bedroom and he says yes, and takes my name down in his book . . . It gets a big laugh.'

Chuck Connors II came on and sang, which caused Judge Bertini to clear the courtroom when 'his accent and mannerisms drew from the spectators a ripple of laughter'. The two German tumblers who had played the 'Otto Brothers', Herman Lenzen and William Selig, put on their act: '"Oops!" said Lenzen, the taller of the pair. "Oops!" said Selig, a half pinter. Then he rested his head on his partner's chest, his legs were flung into the air, and down the pair came . . . Lenzen was asked to display his pants to the jury, and he walked along the rail of the jury box, exhibiting his tremendous breeches. He said that when he performed on the stage, he wore four pairs of trousers, a coat and a vest. Never, he testified, had he heard any of the words policemen swore female impersonators used.'

Beyond the obvious ribaldry, Burkan's defence was quite sly: he was turning the case away from the concepts of immoral words, behaviour and obscenity to the simple demonstration of the fact that actors acted and that what was presented on the stage was a perfor-mance, not an incitement to audiences to behave as the players did. Mae herself had already presented an affidavit describing the process and motive of writing and producing the play, denying any indecen-cy and stating that it was 'good, clean, wholesome dramatic enter-tainment'. She also, within her statement, revealed that she had written the play 'within a period of about 2 or 3 months', which gave the lie again to the old saw about her cobbling her texts together on the rush.

Mae did not take the stand, as she had not herself been on the stage in the performance of *The Pleasure Man*. In his summing up, attor-ney Burkan minced no words, proclaiming he was going to prove 'that the police who testified here were vicious perjurers – that the courtroom has been defiled by their perjury. They went out there to get Mae West and the others.' It was no crime, he reminded the jury, 'for female impersonators to appear on the public stage' or for them to speak in 'high-pitched voices . . . swinging and swaying themselves like women . . . Look at these people themselves and see if there is anything wrong with them.' Mr Burkan 'swept the room with his glance, and his eyes rested on the blonde Miss West, dressed in black, looking demure and solemn'.

The Assistant D.A. was, this time, wrong-footed. He complained that none of the female impersonators, who might have presented quite a different image to the court than the bullish Connors and Stanley, had been called; but they were out of reach, on US vessels upon the high seas. This meant that the case against thirty-four of the original fifty-eight defendants had to be dismissed before it went to the jury.

In his own summation, the judge, as in the case against *Sex*, tried to narrow the grounds for the defence's objections by telling the jurors that 'the play is not to be judged as a whole. Under the law, it is only necessary for the people to show that parts or portions of the play were obscene, indecent, immoral or impure.' But, on 3 April, the jury had to inform Judge Bertini that they could not agree a verdict. Their final vote was seven to five for acquittal, with 'no chance for unanimity'. The District Attorney's office threw in the towel. Assistant D.A. Wallace declared that 'in view of the fact the raid was made as far back as October 1, 1928, and the offense was not likely to be repeated, it might be undesirable to put the county to the expense of another trial'. In the words of *Variety*:

MAE WEST BEAT IT
Mae West beat the 'rap' on 'The Pleasure Man.'
Jury disagreed.

The best show in town was over.

The issue of censorship, however, continued to fester, with the *Pleasure Man* jurors sending a letter to Governor Franklin D. Roosevelt, requesting that some form of play censorship should be introduced to avoid the kind of farce upon which they had just in vain sat in judgement. This was not, of course, an issue limited to the US. In Britain, the regular stage censor barred the Pulitzer-winning all-black Bible play *Green Pastures* for 'presenting the Deity on stage', and in Germany, in the Nazi-dominated state of Thuringia, Erich Maria Remarque's pacifist book *All Quiet on the Western*

Front was banned, anticipating the Nazi ban from 1933 of all Jewish and 'unpatriotic' material.

Still mourning for her mother, Mae returned nevertheless to her works. Much of the summer and autumn of 1930 was taken up with the continuation of efforts to find a stage for *Frisco Kate*, while *Babe Gordon* was being prepared for publication by Macaulays. The Shuberts were eager and willing to follow up the hit of *Diamond Lil*, but the Wall Street Crash continued to echo. As Mae noted in *Goodness*: 'Shows closed, backers blew out their brains, almost everybody's face was green and drawn . . . The theatres were so empty that a vaudeville actor coined the famous line: "The place was so empty you could shoot elk in the balcony."' The wags said that Hubert's Flea Circus had to lay off its performers. Dance halls and ballrooms were 'Starving', Broadway gold-diggers staying home, 'to Hang on to Papa'. Models took jobs singing in department stores 'to Lull Buyers Into Buying Dresses'. On 29 October 1930, *Variety* reported '25,000 IDLE STAGE ACTORS', with all branches, vaud, burlesque, legit, hit. The only things in show business still making money were motion pictures, which had been boosted by the massive shift in investment from silent film to the talkies.

The writing was on the wall: Go To Hollywood. But Mae had not yet given up her belief, as stated in her *Parade* article of 1929, that the theatre was the best medium for her subject matter. However onerous the guardians of the stage, she would have been well aware that the more rigorous motion-picture censorship would rule out most of her themes. There remained, of course, the potential of *Diamond Lil*, but that time had not yet come.

Instead of *Frisco Kate*, the Shuberts decided to revive *Sex*, playing first in Chicago and then moving on through the Midwest during November of 1930. This provided a minor boost to the sales of *Babe Gordon*, which, according to Mae, went through five editions, topping 90,000 copies. Mae could now contemplate a stage version of the renamed *Constant Sinner*, and this duly opened as a Shubert production in September 1931.

The Constant Sinner was Mae West's last Broadway show before her *hegira* to California. There would be later plays and revivals of *Diamond Lil* in the late 1940s, but this was the true swansong of Mae's 1920s transgressions. In all respects, it was a straightforward adaptation of the novel, with the same Harlem settings and the same set of characters. The quadrangular affair between Babe, the 'Bearcat', the black Money Johnson and the rich white Wayne Baldwin forms the centrepiece around which the small fry swirl. Mae recruited black actors from the cast of the recent hit *Green Pastures* – Harry Owen, Henry Matthews, Florence Lee and Allen Cohen moved from the celestial fantasy fish-fry to Mae's Harlem dive. Three other actors, Ollie Burgoyne, Trixie Smith and Marie Remson, had been in another hit, *Show Boat*. Others were well-known Harlemites: Paul Meeres, R. C. Rains, Jimmy Dunmore and Lorenzo Tucker.

Mixed casts were no longer a novelty on Broadway, though the presence of so many African-Americans in a white show was still unusual – up to thirty at any one performance. The real pitfall for Mae was the portrayal on stage of her sex affair with the black gangster. In the event, she had to give in to her managers, and Money Johnson was played by a blacked-up white actor, George Givot. Lorenzo Tucker, who was said to be her first choice for the role, turned up in the cast as 'Headwaiter'. Many years later, at a tribute dinner for Mae West in 1982, Tucker did not mention this problem but only recalled an incident in which, after a first-night celebration, he turned up rather the worse for wear and was reprimanded by the theatre: 'I went to Miss West's dressing room and told her. She says, "Listen, I'm not going to tell you not to worry, but are you going to do anything about that drinking?" I said, "Yes, I'll never drink again as long as I live." She said, "Don't tell me a lie . . . Just say you won't drink before a performance." I said, "I will never." I kissed her and she said, "Don't worry." They gave me the runaround for about two weeks from the Shubert office, but I wasn't fired. I shall never forget the lesson that I learned.

'Practically all her shows,' Tucker praised West, 'she had Negroes in them. The NAACP didn't have to bother her. I would like to tip my hat and say, "This is one of the greatest ladies of the theatre."'

Biographer Stanley Musgrove reports that Mae had always intended Lorenzo Tucker eventually to take on the role of Money Johnson, beginning with a projected week's run in late November at the Belasco Theatre in Washington D.C. Biographer Jill Watts appears to believe that this indeed took place and was the cause of the subsequent local outrage. There is no evidence for this. Indeed, it would have been bizarre for Mae to avoid casting Tucker as Johnson in 'sin city' New York only to attempt such a provocation in what was after all a conservative, segregated city, for all that it was the nation's capital. The black weekly the *Pittsburgh Courier*, which followed all such events, had noted appreciatively on 17 October that 'Mae West Employs 30 Race Artists In Her Latest Production', writer Floyd G. Snelson Jr calling it 'about the cleverest piece of artistry to be expected from a woman of the Caucasian race . . . It openly discloses the coherent lust and sensual greed that has long existed between the black and white races, with both thrilling and bewildering effect.' But when the show opened in Washington there was no hint in the *Courier* of Tucker's alleged elevation, the journal noting only that 'the whole story came as a great shock to white Washingtonians'. The *Washington Herald* wrote clearly in its review on 24 November about 'George Givot's Money Johnson' giving off 'the aroma of Mae West's hybrid dialogue', but bemoaned that 'their very good performances are but further occasion for true theater-lovers to bow their heads in grief'. The *Washington Evening Star* found the whole affair 'tawdry and . . . lacking in even the mildest demands of every day conventionality,' while the *Washington Post* found that 'the intermixture of race in this play is not a pleasant quality'.

The upshot was that the the local District Attorney, Leo K. Rover, threatened 'to arrest the entire company of fifty-one if another performance were given', although the manager of the Belasco, L. Stoddard Taylor, had assured the authorities that 'the performance last night had been deleted considerably, much profanity and dances by Negro members of the cast having been eliminated'. But, faced with the option of a year's imprisonment and a $500 fine, the manager closed the show, and the entire company prepared to return to New York. Following events of the day in the *Pittsburgh Courier* and elsewhere, one can note that this was a time of high racial tension over the trials of the Scottsboro Boys, nine black teenagers accused of raping two white women in Alabama. Their first trial, held in April 1931, had resulted in eight death sentences. In Washington itself, black and white hunger marchers were about to descend en masse upon the Capitol, where armed police stood on nervous guard. Mae, as ever, had chosen a tough moment for her provocation.

But even in 'liberal' New York, *The Constant Sinner* was regarded with the usual sniffiness accorded to a Mae West play. The *New York Times* was particularly scathing: 'The play settles into a slough of boredom from which its generally inexpert writing and its disinclination to face most of its dramatic climaxes never permit it to rise . . . [it] is also, as might be expected vile as to speech, and generally something that is nicht fur kinder. Seldom, come to think of it, has fouler talk been heard on the Broadway stage, even in these frank and forward times. But this is a matter which, if the gendarmerie insists, can easily be remedied; the dullness that is inherent in the writing of what might be a cheaply exciting melodrama is something else again . . . In a curtain speech Miss West confided to her public that she was not really a Babe Gordon offstage at all, but was more the home girl type. She did not, however, confirm reports that she would act next year for the Children's Theatre in "Snow White and the Seven Dwarfs."'

The *New York American* weighed in, calling the theme and the manner of its presentation 'the final word in vicious vulgarity', while the *Sun*'s Stephen Rathbun called it 'a low-grade play', adding, 'It is only fair to say that Mae West received many curtain calls at the end of the play and was called on to make a curtain speech. Miss West even was given a few cheers. But what the cheering was about I could not discover.' Howard Barnes, in the *Tribune*, was less harsh, pointing out that Mae had 'mastered the trick of complete restraint on the stage . . . That she is an atrocious playwright and appears in her own dramas is her only failing as an actress.'

This was, from so eminent a critic, an unexpectedly dim understanding of the whole point of a Mae West production. The contradiction inherent in Mae's wish to square the circle of breaking social, sexual and racial taboos for an avowedly educational purpose in the form of dynamic, popular-pulp melodrama was never more pointed than in this play of her book. The other inherent problem, fashioning a dramatic text out of what was originally a different type of prose, rather than thinking from the outset in dialogue, which was Mae's particular strength, affected the critics' perception that the play was tedious. But this was more of an excuse, since it was clear those elements that attracted an audience of ordinary paying Joes and Janes – the lowerdepths milieu, the wisecracking and slangy language, the downright losers, both black and white – merely bored the intellectual élites. Perhaps, as the liberal impulse still dictates today, they expected that issues of race, crime and morals should be presented in a balanced fashion, so as to avoid stigmatizing the very subjects that good liberals wish to save from their iniquitous surroundings, rather than being faced with such amoral stuff as:

HARRY: We're fixin' to go into a store up there with these.

BABE (*takes out a gold plated rouge compact from the carton and opens it*): Four capsules. Coke? Heroin?

HARRY: Morphine.

BABE : What's my rake off?

HARRY: One third of everything, morphine, heroin and coke.

BABE: It'll be the first time I ever peddled that kind of a thrill.

LOU: Babe, you won't turn us down?

BABE: I never turn down anything but the bed-covers.

Even worse, at the end, as in the book, crime is not punished: the rich man who shot Money Johnson gets off scot-free while the working-class stiff, the Bearcat, is also let off due to Babe's playing of the outraged white female rape gambit and the avowed racialism of the jury. As the defence counsel perorates: 'I appeal to your sense of honor – your pride in the women of your race – to your intelligence – to your love of justice – and in so doing I repose in you the trust and faith of the defendant . . . and the undying gratitude of his good and [crossed out "beautiful"] faithful wife.'

If Mae thought she was going to get another rise out of her constant enemies – the police, District Attorney Banton, Lieutenants Kenneally, McCoy and all – she was mistaken, as it was the economic climate and the critics that put paid to her production this time. The influential Percy Hammond, in the *New York Herald Tribune*, mocked her in a vitriolic piece headed 'Is There No Flit?':

There has been a change in the attitude of government toward Miss West. No longer do her impudences affront the forces that made for good. Where they were once hostile they are now acquiescent. In 'The Constant Sinner,' at the Royale, she is free to go as far as she likes, an artiste liberated. This she does, a little wistfully, perhaps regretful of the good old days when an actress could be arrested for public misbehavior . . .

Since Miss West is established in the Theater as one of its most competent sorceresses, I may have the right to ask 'Why?' . . . As I see this petted favorite she has few of the endearing attributes of a successful star. Heaven forbid that I should say that any actress is not beautiful, and I shall refrain from objecting to Miss West's over-conspicuous charms. She is a large, soft, flabby and billowing superblonde who talks through her nostrils and whose laborious ambulations suggest that she has sore feet . . . She is so different from anything you have seen outside a zoo that you decide that her impersonation is deliberately outlandish. When her various heroes ply her with

jewels and admiration you suspect that they should be feeding her peanuts
. . . She is a menace to art, if not to morals, and she is entitled to an investigation. I suppose the easiest thing to do is to put the blame on Hoover.

There were, nevertheless, still loyal fans. A kinder scribe, Arthur
Pollock, wrote in the *Brooklyn Eagle*, before the play opened:

The woman has got something. It is difficult to say just what. She doesn't
drink, they say. I'm not sure if she smokes or not. Probably she swears.
Maybe not. But she can put something into plays, crude as those plays are,
that is unlike the things other dramatists can get into theirs. Something raw
and vigorous. Perhaps it is merely crudity, an original, flavorous crudity, that
has the quality of iron ore, a crudity that is vitality.

There is no grace in the things she does, no taste, of course, no art . . . just
a virile kind of artlessness.

And there is a tang, somehow a great tang. She throws raw color on a can-
vas in splotches and lets it go at that. It doesn't look like anything, but nevertheless it does . . .

She is a natural. Whatever you may say of her skill, of her quality, of her
character itself, there is something definitely there and it marks her off from
the rest . . . make[s] her a novelty, makes the things she does marketable.

Mae West had become her own commodity, a unique brand, a set
image that she could no longer escape. The constructed character
that was to become so familiar was already moulded out of her own
self-knowledge of her limitations as of her strengths. She was indeed,
as Percy Hammond noticed, not 'beautiful' in the traditional or fashionable sense of her day. She had her 'over-conspicuous charms', i.e.,
a large bosom and a manner of moving which suggested a most languid, I-don't-care come-on. She overdressed in the manner made necessary by Eva Tanguay and Lillian Russell, her white models, but also
by the voluptuous, 'heavy-hipped, heavy-voiced' black mentor of her
developing moves and sounds, blues queen Mamie Smith. She had
achieved a very clear knowledge of how to project this image and
what effect she wanted to have on her audience. To the men: Here I
am, boys, come up an' see me, but be prepared – I'm in charge. To the
women: You can do it, girls, you can have it all, but you need the confidence to carry it off. Inside this mask, Mary Jane West, the little girl
who had always craved the spotlight, finally felt truly at home.

To another columnist, Robert Grannis of the *Evening Graphic*, she
revealed the 'strange fan letters' she got from people 'who take it for

WORDS DON'T OFFEND SONGS

WORDS DON'T OFFEND SONGS

Mae West's Play Disrupts Stage Censorship Body

The Conference Board of the Theatre, which was organized to control stage smut in an effort to forestall state censorship, has been split by the withdrawal of its playwright members—and Mae West's "Constant Sinner" is reported to be the immediate cause of the split.

The board consisted of Edward Childs Carpenter, Elmer Rice and Marc C o n n e l l y, for the playwrights; Lawrence Langner, Brock Pemberton and Rowland Stebbins, for the producers, and Frank Gill-

Mae West   Elmer Rice

more, Katherine Emmett and Arthur Byron, for Actors' Equity. Dr. Henry Moskowitz was honorary secretary.

A Break for Mae.

According to yesterday's information, the dramatists resigned after an afternoon newspaper had suggested to Dr. Moskowitz that the conference board form a play-reviewing committee and send it to the West melodrama.

Moskowitz is understood to have favored the suggestion, but his board was broken up before he could act.

New Equity Plan.

In resigning, however, the playwrights are understood not to have mentioned any one production. They quit because they feared the conference board would establish just as strict a censorship of plays as a legislative organization would.

By quitting the censorship organization, the Dramatists' Guild has placed new emphasis on its stand that it will not support a system for regulating the writing of its members.

Equity, it is understood, will shortly arrange for a new reviewing organization—for Equity still fears an attempt by the legislature to control the stage.

granted that she is like the characters she plays. "I have to expect that, I suppose," she said, "just the same as I have to expect a crowd wherever I go. I don't dare go anywhere alone. Always manage to be in a group, where I won't be bothered. At least," she wisecracked, "people seldom offer to reform me by mail."'

'Don't believe,' Mae told Grannis, 'that in my search for realism in the plays I write I invite police interference. My last trouble with the police cost me a small fortune in litigation and a lot of headaches.'

The Constant Sinner ran for sixty-four performances, over eight weeks, in New York before its truncated out-of-town tour. Apart from *Frisco Kate*, at this point there were no more stock-piled playscripts in finished form. An untitled script in Mae's archive, which may or may not have dated from this period, is set in a familiar lower-depths setting, this time composed of white 'goombah' gangsters, in which a Babe Gordon type, 'Mavis', gets engaged to a socialite, 'Tremont', as she tells her previous lover, the ungainly 'Duke': 'When a woman gives herself to a man he feels he owns her. Unless it's just a money proposition. He's not satisfied with her body. He wants her soul, too – whatever good that is to him . . .' And to her gay friend 'Francis' she confides: 'All most men want is a woman's body . . . my only true friends have been fagots [crossed out and replaced by "pansys"] . . . They understand women, all they want is our friendship and they are always laughing and happy . . .'

But Mae had run out of takers for her exploration of society's rejects at a time when more and more people were falling over the edge to join their ranks. And there were fewer and fewer theatres available in the straitened circumstances that now had a new name: the Depression. Mae retreated to her quarters to try her hand at her new novel, rearranging *Diamond Lil*. A strict potboiler, it was a way to raise much-needed finance from her best-known tale, though the book was not published until the autumn of 1932, when Mae was already in Los Angeles.

Opportunities on the New York stage were shrinking fast. Even on the other side of the continent, economic woes were mounting, unemployment rising, movie attendances dropping. Hollywood studios were looking for new ideas, novelties, sensations that could revive sagging fortunes. Now that the movies could talk, sing and babble, new voices were wanted, and the more sassy the better.

Out of the west, fingers beckoned. Mae was now ready to respond to the call.

PART FOUR

Belle of the Thirties

Being Bad in a Nice Town

Let us flash forward forty-two years to the autumn of 1974: two young interviewers are making their way down Hollywood's Vine Street in the direction of North Rossmore Avenue, heading for the Rossmore Apartment Building at No. 570, a little way up from the Wilshire Country Club. Their names are Anjelica Huston and Peter Lester and they are pursuing an assignment from *Interview*, a celebrity magazine founded at Andy Warhol's 'factory', to speak to Hollywood's pre-eminent sex goddess for the last four decades, Miss Mae West. They are about to enter the star's sanctum, her central place of residence since she arrived in the city to begin her screen career. In their published article, they set the scene:

(The Rossmore Apartment Building)
ATMOSPHERE: *Misty with climate control. Cream venetian blinds drawn down. Air conditioner humming lazily. The scene seems to be shrouded in the mists of dry ice.*
SETTING: *Small room, cluttered with carefully arranged memorabilia. An eye that glanced at Versailles and then squinted at Southern California. Cream, white, cream, white. Ormolu for days.*
IMPRESSIONS: *Grandeur squat on voluptuous legs, heavily embossed surfaces in mirrored gold. Photographs from the past, teasing in sepia furs, Miss West as she was. Photographs everywhere, some standing proudly atop a Dresden baby grand; alabaster nudes, variations on hand to hip, hand to hair, amidst extravagant arrays of artificial foribunda.*
 We're dying for a cigarette, but the absence of ashtrays alerts us. Mr. Grayson, Miss West's personal secretary indulges his habit out in the hall-way. The only visitor ever permitted to smoke had been Bette Davis, and she didn't overdo it . . .
 Drawn to us as if by a magnetic force concealed beneath the floor, Mae West enters, gliding almost mechanically to her chair . . . Silence as she allows herself to be scrutinised – freshly painted, hair waving softly champagne to her shoulders, shoulders draped in lace. Her eyelids droop shyly as she lifts

her gaze, deeply shaded by mink lashes. The pupil of one eye overflowing in
its iris; she smiles behind a coral cupid's bow as she adjusts a lurex cushion
to the small of her back; tidies the folds of the shocking pink negligee about
her bosom and crosses her legs.

The interviewers are awed, 'completely stunned by the legend' in
the flesh, though Miss Huston would have had her own entry into
this world – her famous father, John Huston, had co-starred with
Miss West in her most recent, controversial and sensational movie

comeback, *Myra Breckinridge*. But they can only stammer out their first stock question – 'To what do you attribute your looks?' – prompting a familiar response:

Mae West (*Tapping her teeth*): See – they're mine . . . I have no face lifts . . . it's all mine. There's no change in me. I wrote this book about it. It's called Sex, Health and ESP, you know. I eat the right foods, exercise, take care of myself . . .

The young tyros indulge her ESP fixation for a short while, then ask:

Do you entertain here?
Off and on. Friends stay sometimes, but mostly at my beachhouse. It's got twenty-two rooms, eight bedrooms with bathrooms, you know, so there is more space. Then there is a ranch I have in Sepulveda. So you see this is just one place I live in. I wasn't looking for a home in this apartment, so I just had it fixed up and started to live here.

For how long? ·
Since 1932.

Do you feel that people working then in Hollywood were more talented than now?
Talent . . . no. But then you see there was so much of an outlet for it. Every studio made a hundred or so movies a year . . . now they're down to ten or twelve.

They were always testing . . . there were talent scouts everywhere. All over the country going to small towns, looking for girls for movies. They never had enough talent then. Now you see, it is all television. Small scale. We had great artists . . . great writers working here. It's not the way it used to be . . .

In 1932, when Mae West immigrated to Hollywood from the Broadway stage, the city of Los Angeles had certainly grown from the lazy, orange-grove town of the early 1910s to become the commercial hub we know, mutating along its radial spokes, though still a city of clattering streetcars rather than the freeway monster of later years. Veterans who recalled getting off the 'Chief', the train that thundered into its downtown station, remembered still the citrus scent that lingered in the clear air. On 19 June, when Mae arrived, alighting from the train at Pasadena, the press, rousted out by her new employers at Paramount Studios, was on hand to record the moment: '"DIAMOND LIL" IN TOWN FOR FIRST TALKING PICTURE,' headlined the *Illustrated*

News, showing a waving Mae West – 'svelte and blonde . . . tired, not cranky, but peeved at the Great American desert for providing her with weather that was too torrid for even Mae to work in . . .' The journalists' first observations were hardly flattering: '"Boy, have you reduced!" . . . "Reduced – whatcha mean – reduced?"' ripostes the diva. '"Don't get me wrong – I'm not that large and never was – when I played Diamond Lil, the role called for overstuffing and I was fixed up like one of those comfy chairs you have in your swell movie drawing rooms . . ."' The hacks noted that Mae was 'sartorially' rigged up, with 'a black chiffon travelling dress . . . a black turban, trimmed with black and white . . . a white brocaded jacket . . . sleeves trimmed with black fox bands . . . black satin slippers and sheer hose. She said she guessed she brought the heat with her, as it has been this way since she left the Big Town . . .'

Mae's ascent had been literally heralded, by the *Los Angeles Herald*, a week before her arrival, with the news that:

Mae West, according to the dispatches, has signed a contract with Paramount to appear in the filmization of Louis Bromfield's story, 'Number 55.' Mae has much, aside from her literary talent, to recommend her. She must be about 40 years old, but, to see her, you wouldn't suspect that she is a day over 39.

Mae began her professional career as a blues-warbler many years ago . . . Mae is better known, however, as a playwright . . . 'I don't really write plays,' she says, 'I just make them up out of my head. That is, I have an idea, and I work it out, from scene to scene, as the players are rehearsing. You see, most of my characters are, well – very human – and I find it helps to have real people before my very eyes.'

Of Mae, it has, in all truth, been said: 'When the curtain rolls up on one of her plays, you know you're going to see a show.'

You ain't kiddin'. The usual gossip and fuzzy memories surround the circumstances of Mae's *hegira*. Paramount executive B. P. Schulberg recalled that she was hired hurriedly and bundled off from the east coast, with a quick stop-over in Chicago to cancel the run of *The Constant Sinner* that had been scheduled there. The *Los Angeles Herald* story suggests, however, that Mae's contract was hardly a rush job. As we have seen, Mae was flirting with the idea of pictures from 1915, but her verbal skills had no place in the silents. Once the talkies were launched, she had another problem, as the censorship issues she so relished challenging had given her a reputation more likely to deter Hollywood's cautious moguls than to produce a breathless charge with desperately waving contracts. Sex in Hollywood had always been rigorously policed, even before the 1921 Fatty Arbuckle scandal, which prompted the industry to appoint its own morals czar, ex-postmaster Will Hays.

The Hays formula was supposed to protect the studios from the various State Censor Boards, sometimes openly called Political Censor Boards, which could decree ruinously expensive different cuts in each state. The appositely named Colonel Jason Joy was appointed to oversee a set of over thirty proscriptions that were recommended to the studios: thou shalt nots included Profanity, Nudity, Drug Trafficking, Sex Perversion, Miscegenation, White Slavery, Sex Hygiene, Venereal Diseases, as well as such non-sexual matters as ridiculing the clergy or offending other nations, races or creeds – prohibitions that would today be approved of in the quest for social harmony. These prohibitions did not stop Hollywood finding a way around these subjects by insinuation, allusion and suggestion, or the on-screen attributes of Erich von Stroheim's anti-heroes, or 'It Girl' Clara Bow's sassy antics, or the pale-going-on-scorching aura of Greta Garbo, although her 1929 movie *A Woman of Affairs,* based on Michael Arlen's *The Green Hat,* bowdlerized its plot aspects – the heroine is infected by her husband with a venereal disease – so thoroughly that one could not figure out what was driving the characters in the movie into such a fearful bate. The old 'vampires', Theda Bara and Pola Negri, had long gone, but the new sophistication of Marlene Dietrich – whose American début, *The Blue Angel,* was rehearsed in 1930 – was yet to set her own challenge to the proprieties in *Shanghai Express* and *Blonde Venus,* both released in 1932.

An intriguing item in the new Mae West archive is a four-page synopsis of the unperformed *Frisco Kate,* undated but most probably written in 1931: an 'Introductory Note' states that 'it was my intention to appear in my play version of it next season'. This appears to be a movie proposal Mae was suggesting as a vehicle for Dietrich rather than for herself. Parenthetical notes in the synopsis make this clear as she describes the heroine, White Lotus, a.k.a. Kate: 'NOTE: Of course, for Miss Dietrich, the early background may be changed in this manner: She is a Viennese of good family; in the starvation days after the World War she is left alone in the world. To keep body and soul together she is forced to become a woman of the demi-monde, and of course, keeps her body but loses her soul.' In a later paragraph: 'Dialogue will necessarily be altered to fit Miss Dietrich's characterization.' Mae had altered the title of her piece to 'Desired Woman (Frisco Kate)' and toned down the moral anarchy of the original to accommodate movie rules: 'Dialogue, naturally, will have to be moderated,' she writes in her preamble.

Such a proposal flies in the face of the accepted image of Mae West ever out for her own glory. Later movie-magazine puffs show her indulging in a friendly rivalry with La Dietrich, as we shall see, but there has been scant evidence of any close relationship, despite the fact that both served the same studio – Paramount.

As ever, stray jigsaw pieces can blur the picture or suggest unexplored sidetracks. It does appear that Mae's desire to see her texts in action overrode her age-old ache for the spotlight. But if the play was the thing, it made even more acute the dilemma of which, if any, of Mae's performed texts could possibly be adapted for the screen. As noted, Mae did write a movie treatment for *Sex*, calling it *Love for Sale*, with locale and character names altered, if not the plot. Colonel Joy's prohibitions, however, definitely excluded *Sex*, *The Drag*, *Pleasure Man*, *The Wicked Age* and *The Constant Sinner*. This only left, most obviously, *Diamond Lil*, which the guardians of Hollywood's moral vessel were already girding up to repel as soon as it approached the gangplank.

In fact, the censor files reveal that the Hays Office was debating and rejecting Mae West's plays as early as January 1930, strong evidence that Mae's entry into pictures was no sudden leap into the pool: as Colonel Joy wrote in his résumé of 11 January 1930:

Universal is considering the purchase of Mae West's play, '*Diamond Lil*,' and Junior Laemmle has asked me to see the legitimate production, with Mae West in the title role, which is the current attraction at the Biltmore Theatre. I have advised Mr Laemmle that because of the vulgar dramatic situations and the highly censorable dialogue, in my opinion, an acceptable picture could not be made of the material suggested in the play. The possibility of employing Mae West as a member of Universal's writing staff was brought to my attention. Of course, I discouraged the idea.

A 22 April 1930 memo from Will Hays to Colonel Joy set out the general principles:

To exercise every possible care to the end that only books or plays which are of the right type are used for screen presentation; to avoid the picturization of books or plays which can be produced only after such changes as to leave the producer open to a charge of deception; to avoid using titles which are indicative of a kind of picture which could not be produced . . . and further to endeavour to establish and maintain the highest possible moral and artistic standards of motion picture producers . . .

Another memo listed titles the Association of Motion Pictures Producers and Distributors declined to produce: 'Virtue's Bed', 'Dishonoured Lady', 'Love, Honor and Betray', 'Pleasure Man', 'Diamond Lil', 'Sex' and 'Bad Girl'. The reference to 'Junior Laemmle' (a.k.a. Carl Laemmle Jr), Universal's heir-executive, suggests he was Mae's long-term fan at that studio, though his passion appeared to be that of a browser rather than a shopper.

The tale told so far of Mae's relocation to Hollywood names her friend, actor George Raft, as the main conduit of her transfer. Raft, born to German immigrants Conrad and Eva Ranft, had grown up as a streetwise kid in New York's Hell's Kitchen neighbourhood and dabbled in boxing before moving on to the less bruising world of ballroom dancing. Adept at winning competitions, the young man graduated to New York's 'tea rooms' – 'dark, well-appointed cafés which women frequented in the afternoons', according to his biographer, Lewis Yablonsky. 'Idle housewives, high-class prostitutes, and wealthy dowagers were the main clientele . . . the female patron would be seated at a table, place her order for tea or coffee, and then at her leisure select one of the tea-room gigolos seated conspicuously at one end of the room.'

Before Prohibition, these affairs were evidently more genteel. But Prohibition brought George, propelled from obscurity to Texas Guinan's El Fey club, into direct contact with the gangs of New York. He became, as the tale goes, a confidant of and runner for Owney Madden, 'regularly picking up the receipts of Diamond Lil'. His personal connection to Mae was said to have begun at that point, leading him to become her 'second string' lover at the time of 'Dinjo' and the Chicago paragon. In 1929, he was already in Hollywood, appearing in a movie based on Guinan's high life, Queen of the Night Clubs.

Possessing no acting experience, Raft had nevertheless parlayed a close observation of gangsters' moves and gestures, their combination of thuggery and the pretence of the suave man-about-town, into a convincing character that became his bread-and-butter on the screen. Four films later, in 1932, he was co-starring with Paul Muni in Howard Hawks's breakthrough *Scarface*, in which Hawks gave him his trademark mannerism of continually flipping a coin. Paramount now recognized him as hot box-office material, and the Louis Bromfield tale, 'Number 55', was procured for him to star in its movie version, *Night After Night*. The character of Maudie, a flippant ex-girlfriend, struck him, so the tale continues, as an ideal role for Mae West, and thus she was plucked forth from Broadway.

Raft's nudges may well have played a part in Mae's casting for the movie, but she already had a much more powerful mentor at Paramount. This was William LeBaron, one time playwright-producer, in whose short-lived piece, *A La Broadway*, she had appeared back in the autumn of 1911. LeBaron had joined the Famous Players-Lasky-Paramount team in 1924 as an associate producer at their Long Island studio. He had gained more production credits with other companies, including RKO, and then returned to Paramount in 1932. If Mae was signed up quickly in June that year, it was most probably LeBaron who recruited her, just as he swept up her 'opposite number', W. C. Fields, whose many classics he was to oversee and produce.

Paramount was undergoing seismic changes. Despite the talkies boom that had carried the studio through the Wall Street Crash and its immediate aftermath, by late 1931 it was experiencing the full weight of the Depression. The banks, which had poured money into the conversion to sound, began demanding blood, and in May 1932 Jesse Lasky, co-founder of the studio, and B. P. Schulberg, its famous chief of production, were kicked out. Schulberg's replacement was a short, ugly, feisty man-of-action, Emanuel Cohen, who came into office promising new box-office profits with movies highlighting not art but 'showmanship'. The age-old dictum of 'giving the people what they want' was to be the new commandment at Paramount. And what Cohen instinctively knew the people wanted at a moment of stark economic crisis and gloom was Comedy, Sex, Violence and Wisecracking, whether Will Hays liked it or not.

Paramount's little Napoleon, Adolph Zukor, was not particularly keen on the Sex angle and no fan of Mae West. But he was a number-one fan of making money and gave his new executives the authority to press forward as best they thought. Emanuel Cohen was to become, as we shall see, the unsung hero of Mae West's career surge at Paramount, her backer through thick and thin, her ungainly knight, armour-plated against the barbs of the Hays Office; he would even support her as an independent producer to make her last two golden-age movies, *Go West, Young Man*, in 1936, and *Every Day's a Holiday*, in 1937. He had, oddly enough, little experience of drama, as he had cut his teeth on newsreels, but he had a talent to see around commercial corners and to fight the censors with a cunning and guile that gained the grudging respect even of Hays' chief enforcer, the new missionary of 'clean' movies, Joseph Breen.

Mae's first appearance in a movie, however, did not cause the censors much concern. *Night After Night* was conceived and presented as a vehicle for George Raft, highlighting both his thuggish credentials and their contradictions, his vulnerability and lack of guile. As a speakeasy owner, Joe Anton, Raft engages a middle-aged college teacher, Miss Jellyman, played by the full-bodied Alison Skipworth, to teach him how to speak properly and pontificate on the important issues of the day. He falls for the fey Miss Healey – Constance Cummings – whose lone vigil at one of his tables intrigues him till he discovers she was born in the house the speakeasy is set in and that her attraction to him is due precisely to his underlying illiterate violence.

Mae appears in only two scenes, turning up almost forty minutes into the movie as Maudie, an ex-girlfriend who breezes into Joe Anton's joint and upsets him with her boisterous tales of the good times they had when they were both drunk and rowdy and when it took twelve waiters to throw them out of a club and five cops to toss them in jail. Her entrance into motion pictures resembles a whirlwind coasting up the shore, as her voice is first heard outside the speakeasy door, behind the backs of three young louts:

YOUNG MEN: We're going in with you, Maudie.
MAUDIE: Aw, you know my father's very strict and he doesn't let me see boys after nine o'clock.
YOUNG MEN: Oh cut the kidding, Maudie!
MAUDIE: Why don't you guys be good and go back to your wives?
MAN BEHIND SPEAKEASY WINDOW: Who is it?
MAUDIE: The fairy princess, you mug!
MAN: Maudie!

She slides in, brushing the young men aside – 'Say, don't let these guys in, they'll wreck the joint' – hip-swirling with her great white fur and glistening accoutrements, as she hands her wrap to the hat girl, leading to her first immortal line:

HAT CHECK GIRL: Goodness, what beautiful diamonds!
MAUDIE: Goodness had nothing to do with it, dearie!

For the first time, Mae's diligent work copying out endless quips from joke books can be seen bearing its fruit. The 'original' patter, scrawled in Mae's handwriting (Gag Books, Folder No. 1) and ticked by her for reference, goes simply:

'There's a certain reason I love you.'
'My goodness!'
'Don't be absurd.'

The hundreds of pages of copied gags apart, Mae's archive also includes several pages of her original notes for the film, building the dialogue she hoped to insert into the script. First come assorted one-liners that might or might not be of use, such as:

'I've never loved but once – that is, the same man.'
'I may be a bad woman but I'm a good actress.'
'I do my best acting on a couch.'
'The meaner you treat 'em, the sweeter they act.'
'An old maid is a girl who has failed in the school of experience.'
'Most fellows that try to find the way into a girl's heart have a darned poor sense of direction.'
'Many a girl climbs the ladder of success wrong by wrong.'
'The only thing that guy ever made was cigarette ashes.'

Then there are exchanges meant for specific movie scenes but which failed to make it into the film:

REPORTER: Your second husband was your first husband's brother, wasn't he?
MAUDIE: Yes; you see I hated to break in a new mother-in-law.
REPORTER: Can you tell us what your next play is going to be?
MAUDIE: I'm gonna play the love interest in a big Bible play all about Cain and Mabel.
MISS JELLYMAN: You've been married several times, haven't you?
MAUDIE: Say, I've been married so often, dearie, wedding bells sound like an alarm clock to me.
MISS JELLYMAN: I understand, my dear, that foreign men are charming. How did you find the men in Paris?
MAUDIE: I didn't have to find them, they were out looking for me.

The scene has Maudie gate-crashing the dinner Joe Anton is giving Miss Healey, accompanied by his 'social tutor' Miss Jellyman. She rushes up, throwing her bare arms around his tuxedo, embarrassing him with the cry of 'Joey, Joey, well come here and kiss me, you dawg

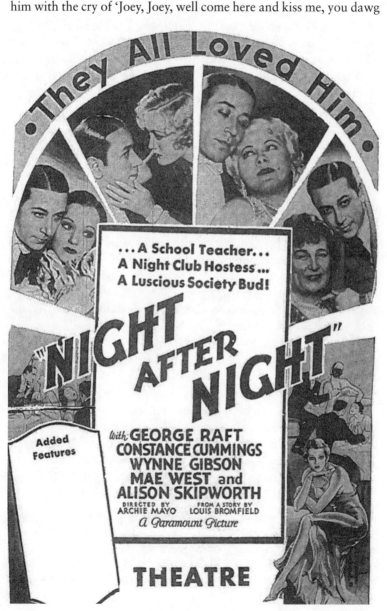

– let's take a look at yer! Well, yer lookin' great! Who's yer tailor now? Who's the dames?'

Introducing herself as 'Maudie Triplett, one of the blue bloods of Kentucky, and if you don't like the color, honey, we'll change it,' she plonks herself down, seizing the champagne bottle and riffing with Miss Jellyman as Joe and Miss Healey slink off to 'look at the house'. Mae regales the prim and proper teacher with booze and non-stop repartee about life and her old boyfriend: 'When I met him he was a third rate pug!'

MISS JELLYMAN: Maudie, do you believe in love at first sight?

MAUDIE: I don't know, but it saves an awful lot of time.

MISS JELLYMAN: Do you really think I can get rid of my inhibitions?

MAUDIE: Why sure, I got an old trunk you can put 'em in.

A lot of Hollywood inhibitions were being stuffed in an old trunk with Mae's commando raid of a début. Hollywood had seen it-girls, vampires and sassy broads, as well as the diffusion-lit, unreachable stars, but not this bejewelled girl-at-the-next-barstool, both sexy and available, back-slapping and loud, able to blow off any man she didn't fancy and pleased to be a good pal to a lady friend in dire need of a liquid top-up and some hearty advice. That long training on the stage pays off with an immediate confidence and whiplash delivery, and the 'gag books' are looted for their best lines. What seems limp on the page is transformed when delivered by Mae in her unique drawl and wiggle. 'It ain't what I say but the way that I say it' was yet another Mae axiom.

In her second scene, Mae is waking up in one bed with Miss Jellyman, who is groaning under an ice pack after her night on the tiles – 'Oh – the price of pleasure . . .' – Mae still determinedly upbeat and dismissive of her distress at missing her 'political science' class – 'A gal with your poise and class, why you'd make thousands in my business!' Prompting an exchange that would be unlikely to survive the more rigorous Hays Code that was still two years off:

MISS JELLYMAN (*flustered at the suggestion*): Why, of course, I recognize that your business has been a great factor in the building of civilization, and of course it helps to protect our good women – and thereby preserve the sanctity of the home – and there were such women as Cleopatra – and of course France owes a great deal to Du Barry – but me, dear? Don't you think I'm just a little old?

MAUDIE: Say, what kind of a business do yer think I'm in? . . . Listen, dearie – you got me all wrong – why, I got a chain of beauty parlours!

MISS JELLYMAN (*vastly relieved*): Oh, I see . . . a cosmetician . . .

MAUDIE: You'd make a swell hostess. I'm openin' a new place here in Noo Yawk – the Institute de Byoot – not bad, huh? What I gotta have is someone that looks distinguished, like you . . . I'll give you a hundred dollars a week . . . You stick with me, dearie, an' I'll make you a platinum blonde!

Paramount's press releases pushed George Raft for all he was worth. 'Suggested ad lines for your lobby program' included such nuggets as 'they all loved him . . . a school teacher – a night club hostess – a luscious society bud'. Quotes from *Screenland* magazine were proudly reissued: 'I believe Raft will be the greatest male personality draw in motion pictures if he is given the right stories – a male Garbo!' Mae was relegated to the bottom of an inner page: 'Mae West has been a well-known stage figure since she was five years old . . . Born in Brooklyn of a theatrical family, Miss West made her professional début in her parents' vaudeville act. Even as a child, she had a great talent for mimicry and her most successful vaudeville acts took that form. "Sex" was her first play, and her most recent one, "The Constant Sinner," ran for six months last season on Broadway.'

More lies, damn lies and publicity. There would be plenty more of this as Mae continued her charge up from the also-ran department of Hollywood towards the major headlines.

Coming Soon: The Street of Scarlet Memories . . .

Night After Night was directed by a reliable craftsman, Archie Mayo. He had been directing films since 1926 and one of his last films would be the somewhat lacklustre *A Night in Casablanca*, made in 1946 with the Marx Brothers. Mae described him as 'ball-bearing shaped, a bundle of energy and bounce. He had a Hollywood sense of humor and loved gags, like the hot foot, the pulled-back chair, the lace panties in a husband's pocket . . . He was amusing to work with – but not at first.'

Mae took time to adjust to the pace of Hollywood, having been frustrated from the start at the delay in being called into work. Settling down at the Rossmore Apartments, Mae claimed she found doing nothing for $5,000 a week somewhat unnerving, and the part written for her in the script she was eventually sent by Paramount appeared banal and unrewarding, at least until she could rewrite the lines. We now know that Mae was never doing nothing, her spare time being spent in continuous production of her notes, gag folders and quips. But as she was to write in her autobiography: 'It was a new medium, a technique I had to learn, bend to my will, and forget, in order to give a natural performance.' The studios, Mae soon discovered, were 'giant factories turning out the same length of scented tripe, dressed up with the same rubber stamp features of large cow-like heads, mammary glands, and ten-foot high closeups of nostrils you could drive a cadillac into'.

Mae could well have been worried by these great close-ups disclosing the fact that, as some shrewd journalists had surmised, she was about to breast the forty-years-old tape rather than the official thirty-three marker, wondering how she could re-enact the trick that the distance of the stage and theatrical make-up enabled her to carry off. She need not have worried, as Hollywood had been playing this game since before a thirty-one-year-old Mabel Normand had to be a teenage sprite. Nevertheless, the working practices of the studio were unsettling. Natural movements were cut up by the shots, actors didn't know their lines, directors seemed to lack all direction, and avoidable mistakes appeared to be wasting money like water. But Jim Timony, ever by her side, consoled her: 'Mae, it's not real money to them. It melts like snowflakes.'

The impact of those two short sequences in *Night After Night*, however, exceeded all expectations. George Raft would later say of the picture: 'Mae West stole everything but the cameras.' Mae had noted, while shooting, that everything in the movie was slow: the actors moved languidly, they spoke deliberately, and the technique both of Raft and of Alison Skipworth was slowed down to Mae's taste. Her two scenes, although she is sitting still or standing (swaying) most of the time, suddenly erupt due to the speed of the delivery of her lines. Both the form and content of these scenes pleased audiences no end. Box office was firm. Executives Emanuel Cohen and William LeBaron saw that it was good and girded themselves up for the real battle.

Night After Night was formally released on 29 October 1932, having been shot from late August through mid-September. But the war over Mae West's next picture had already begun, eleven days earlier. On 18 October, Will Hays had written directly to the studio's boss, Adolph Zukor: 'In re "Diamond Lady," "Diamonds," pursuant to the action of the Board of Directors at the meeting of December 10, 1930, it is suggested that the above titles not be registered.' Lest Zukor misunderstand, another letter sent the same day added: 'These titles are not offensive per se, but the question runs to the production of the play, *Diamond Lil*, under any title.'

In Hollywood, the village of ever-beating tom-toms, news of a prohibition resounded as a concealed licence. On 19 October rival studio head Harry Warner cabled Will Hays at the producers' association in New York:

Please wire immediately whether I can believe my ears that Paramount has arranged to make Diamond Lil with Mae West and Metro The Painted Veil. Recollect that it was absolutely definite that Diamond Lil and Painted Veil were not to be produced stop I am not sending this wire as a protest but I want to know how to run our business in the future.

Hays wired back the same day explaining to Warner that *The*

Painted Veil (which would be – but not till 1934 – a Greta Garbo vehicle based on a Somerset Maugham story about an unfaithful wife) had been approved by the Board but that he had 'communicated with Mister Zukor explaining situation stop On October seventh Paramount withdrew suggestion of making Diamond Lil . . . Believe situation plainly understood by Paramount and that there is no danger of their violation of the agreement.'

In order to understand the determination of LeBaron and Cohen to bust this prohibition by hook or by crook it is useful to look at the context, Hollywood in 1932. The period between 1929 and 1934 is often referred to, inaccurately, as 'Pre-Code Hollywood'. Although the Hays Code was revised for talkies in 1930, there was a certain laxity in its observation by the studios, due to a combination of factors. When the talkies began, the studios had to recruit a new breed of writers who could deal with dialogue rather than demonstrate the peculiar skill required to write a non-speech picture. Some of these recruits were playwrights, but many had cut their teeth in the hardboiled world of reporting – Gene Fowler, Ben Hecht, Charles MacArthur and Charles Lederer, to mention but a few. They were perfectly attuned to quick deadlines, sharp observation and good repartee but not to being told by a bunch of sanctimonious Presbyterian or Catholic reformers what to write and what to omit. Schooled in the Prohibition years, they had much to say about the corruption, hypocrisy and sheer anarchy of contemporary life and proceeded to produce scripts that reflected this and the degradation of the Depression. Tales like Gene Fowler's *Union Depot*, directed by Alfred Green, or Frank Capra's *American Madness*, a satire on banks whose title speaks for itself, were both shot in 1932. Hecht and MacArthur's *The Front Page*, originally a play (and later remade by Howard Hawks as the madcap *His Girl Friday*), ripped into the ruthlessness of newspaper hacks in 1931. Capra's 1931 *The Miracle Woman* starred Barbara Stanwyck in a coruscating satire on the reforming evangelist Aimee Semple McPherson. The gangster-movie cycle had been well and truly launched with *Little Caesar* and *The Public Enemy*, both in 1931, and *Scarface* in 1932. In the 'sex' department, titles like *Call Her Savage*, *Love Is a Racket* and *Unashamed*, all made in 1932, expressed no great obeisance to the Hays Code, while Marlene Dietrich weighed in with *Shanghai Express* and *Blonde Venus*, her characters selling themselves in a dog-eat-dog world for as much as they were worth.

Then, as now, the audience was willing to pay for sin, violence and lust on the screen, albeit within the parameters of the time. It was not that the studio heads were in any way inclined to radical ideas or stories, but if Warner Brothers and Columbia could up the ante with the hot stuff and make money, why should MGM and Paramount lag behind?

There was, nevertheless, a political dimension too, as the spring and summer of 1932 saw the rolling bandwagon of Franklin D. Roosevelt's election campaign for the Democrats, leading up to his overwhelming victory at the polls in November. The Hays Office, formed in the heyday of Republican administrations, was, albeit for a brief period, on the defensive. On 5 November, an internal cable, returning to the problem of Mae West and Paramount, was sent to Hays enforcer Colonel Joy, relaying a message given 'in confidence' by Maurice Pivar, another Paramount executive, to wit that

Zukor and Hertz promised that they will abandon 'Diamond Lil' and will make an announcement to that effect tonight. They have also notified Emanuel Cohen on the coast to that effect. This does not prevent Mae West, however (who is under contract) from writing another story and having it presented.

But Cohen and LeBaron already had a subterfuge in progress which would get round this problem, having prepared a script with a new title: 'Ruby Red'. Both this and the original 'Diamond Lady' treatment dated 18 October were written by John Bright, working off Mae's stage script. Bright, a twenty-four-year-old spark, had co-written William Wellman's *The Public Enemy*, as well as another Jimmy Cagney–Joan Blondell movie, *Blonde Crazy*, and the aforementioned *Union Depot*. No better collaborator for Mae could have been found.

LeBaron's note to his production staff on the first treatment stated: 'It is taken for granted that you are familiar with the play and practically all the principal scenes will be used as they were in the stage version. In this outline they are only suggested.' The 'Ruby Red' script, dated 8 November, is credited as a 'screenplay by Mae West and John Bright. Dialogue by Mae West.'

Continuing their revolutionary disobedience, Cohen and LeBaron were preparing to rush this script into production by 14 November.

It is difficult for us, in an age when movie projects stagger through lengthy pre-production periods, to envisage this kind of schedule. Clearly crew, studio space and cast would have been ready well before the script was finished. The executives of this golden age of the studios had real power to get things done, and quickly. Armies of typists were on hand to produce new versions of the script on a daily basis, faster even than a speeding PC. No wonder the internal Hays Office memos reflected a rapid response: on 11 November – 'The basic story of Ruby Red is Diamond Lil . . . If the picture went through this way it would be recognised as the old story and looked upon as a subterfuge and a violation of the agreement of the companies amongst themselves. There is no objection to Mae West writing any story she wants, but they must stay away from basic plot of Diamond Lil . . .'

On 9 November, Paramount's Harold Hurley had written an 'Inter-Office Communication' to LeBaron outlining a series of changes required to get the story past the censors. These included changing the Hispanic characters of Rita and Juarez to Americans and Rio de Janeiro to San Francisco to avoid ethnic and national offence. Lines that should be cut included:

'I ain't runnin' no Sunday School.'
'Diamond Lil was his woman.'
'Diamond Lil would do anything for diamonds, eh?'
'For God's sake, don't!'
'I gotta have you, Lil. I must have you.'
'Enter a convent.'
'Your whole reforming crowd.'
'Gawd! You got to give a man more than clothes.'
'I always knew you could be had!'

The project was still 'Diamond Lil' at Paramount, despite the title change. On 16 November, Will Hays wrote again directly to Zukor demanding that 'this story of Diamond Lil be abandoned or steps taken to endeavor to clear it through the Board of Directors under the terms of the company's agreement'.

On 21 November, the story had been 'considerably cleaned up but still essentially Diamond Lil'. At this point, Zukor made his move to clear things up with his fellow studio bosses, who were peeved that Paramount might get away with defiance while they played ball with

Hays. 28 November: 'It was decided that Paramount might make a picture to be entitled "Ruby Red," written by Mae West and others, utilizing the suitable material in "Diamond Lil" . . . in strict conformity with the Code.'

Another script was forwarded, and by 30 November it had a completely new name: *She Done Him Wrong*. The day before, James Wingate of the Hays Office wrote Harold Hurley at Paramount another letter of censorial guidance:

We have three basic suggestions to offer as to the treatment which we have just read, all of which are important in carrying out the expressed intention of the studio to make the picture in every way satisfactory. These are:

1. In order to remove even the slightest suspicion of white slavery, we suggest that you include inserts of the photographs of the girls indicated in Sequence A-14, in order to show the audience that these girls are dancers, singers, etc . . .
2. In order to counteract as much as possible what may be considered the rather low general level of the backgrounds in this story, as well as of the type of women portrayed by the principal character, it should be definitely established that neither Chick Clark, nor Flynn, nor any other man before Gus, has ever kept her.
3. You will, of course, not want to use a regulation Salvation Army uniform on Cummings. However, it seems to me that you might safely put him into a nondescript uniform of a mission worker, if you so desire, since it is clearly stated that he is not a minister, and later is shown to be a police officer in disguise.

There follow bullet points on the already noted phrases like 'For God's sake', 'Gawd', 'last guy she *had*', and so forth. Paramount appeared to fall in with this, as on 2 December a further Hays memo noted Paramount's 'major contribution . . . in changing the original elements of the traffic in girls to counterfeiting, thereby removing any possible suggestion of white slavery . . . so far they certainly seem to be doing their best to avoid the difficulties inherent in this subject'. The Board also approved several proposed songs for Mae West: 'Easy Rider', 'Haven't Got No Peace of Mind', 'Mazie', 'A Guy What Takes His Time' and 'Frankie and Johnny' – apart from 'Lord Gawd' in the second line. The film, however, had already gone into production the week before. It wrapped in December, well in time for a good Christmas break for its cast and crew. The 'negative cost' was around $200,000. It was released in February 1933 and grossed $2.2 million.

This was Paramount's biggest gross of the year, until Mae West's next film, *I'm No Angel*, topped it with $2.3 million.

Mae West was now the queen of the lot.

Cary Grant, Mae West, closing on success

'If He Swallows It, I'll Buy It' – The Legend Begins

Aside from work, Mae was settling in to live the life expected in Hollywood. Setting aside the misgivings she would write about many years later, she smoothed the press with suitable olive oil:

MAE WEST SEES HOLLYWOOD AS ALL SWEETNESS
Mae West, the gal who has done so much to brighten the Great White Way, has discovered that in Hollywood all is sweetness and light. New York, she says, is a city of constant wrangling, intense and unceasing in its effort to take away a living from others . . .
'I always thought Western hospitality was a myth,' she says. 'I was in New York for eight solid years without leaving it. The struggle for a living was terrific. You have to outfight everyone else to succeed.
'But Hollywood is different. I hardly could believe it when people helped me and advised me and did favors for me . . .'

And all this in July 1932, while she was still fuming over Paramount's delay in sending her first script along. By October, while the studio was wrangling with the Hays Office over the next, she was basking in the trivia of gossip columns. The purchase of a pet monkey, nicknamed 'Bad Boy', provided a good excuse for some flimflam, as the *Los Angeles Times* had it:

GEM MISSING – MONKEY HAS IT
MAE WEST'S PET CHEWS ON DIAMOND

'Bad Boy' had, it appeared, accompanied Mae as she sat in her automobile outside her apartment with a diamond dealer, Isaac Licht, and his 'heavily-armed guard, Frank E. (Turkey) Roberts, a former police officer, and another man, a friend of Miss West's'. Licht had $100,000 worth of diamonds with him, including a four-carat gem, which mysteriously and suddenly disappeared:

Licht goes frantic. He yells and a crowd gathers. They shake down the automobile, but still no diamond.

'Bad Boy' is nonchalant. He is munching on something. Roberts, the guard, spots the munching monk.

'What's that monkey eating?' he asks.

'Whee, he's got the diamond,' screams Miss West. 'But don't get excited,' she spluttered, 'if he swallows it, I'll buy it.'

Miss West grabs the monk. Her fingers go around his neck. With the other hand she searches his mouth. Out pops the diamond. Miss West gives a sigh of relief. Monk gets a spank.

And business is called off for the day. Licht packs up his stock and is told to return another day when 'Bad Boy' isn't around.

This story was the prelude to another, three days later, relating a hold-up which had taken place two weeks earlier, on 28 September, in which 'bandits' robbed Mae at gunpoint of '$16,000 in jewels and $3,400 in cash'. The police figured it as an 'inside job . . . someone "fingered" her for a "heist,"' they declared. Two days later, as the tale was told, a man called Mae at her home and 'described the location of a vacant lot in the heart of Hollywood and informed Miss West that her purse could be found there'. The purse, keys and 'a string of beads' were duly found, but not the major haul. This event would fuel the interest of the Los Angeles police, the FBI and the newspapers for several years to come.

The public now knew Mae West was in town and was 'Diamond Lil' in fact as well as fiction. In December, the *Los Angeles Times* gossip columnist Grace Kingsley reported further on her proclivities: 'The majority of Mae West's evenings are spent at prize fights . . . [she] has ring-side seats at the Olympic Auditorium every Tuesday, at Santa Monica's pavilion Wednesday, in Pasadena Thursday, and at the American Legion Stadium Friday.'

This would not have left Mae much time in the studio to shoot *She Done Him Wrong*, one might have thought, but Miss Kingsley wrote that despite her passion for the fights, 'her days are spent in arduous work. Before starting her task for Paramount in the morning, she works on her next novel.' (The novelization of *Diamond Lil*, which would be published the same year, 1932.) 'This means rising at 6 o'clock. Reporting to the studio at 8 she prepares for the day's scenes. When not actually in front of the cameras she works in her dressing room on her new play . . .' After watching rushes, rehearsing the next day's scenes and working with the composer on music and songs, 'it seems as though she must have three or four hours to herself before 5 and 6 in the morning!'

Throughout the period when Paramount were jousting with Will Hays, the press were given the cover story that Mae's new film was entitled 'Honky Tonk'. Through January, when the film was already shot and being cut, suggestions for rewriting lines were still being sent to Paramount by Hays man James Wingate, such as '[suggest] you rewrite Cummings' speech . . . to read somewhat as follows: "You're still my prisoner and *as soon as you are clear with the law* I'm going to be your jailer for a long long time."' After the film was released, the files disclose a letter sent to Will Hays from one Sidney Kent:

I went last night to see the Mae West picture, *She Done Him Wrong*. In my opinion it was the worst picture I have seen. It was the real story of Diamond Lil and they got away with it. They promised that the story would not be made . . . I cannot understand how your people on the Coast could let this by. There is very little that any of us can do now.

Not that they stopped trying – on 2 March, Paramount warranted that they had cut 100 feet out of the song called 'A Man Who Takes His Time'.

The film that attracted such fire and brimstone comes down to us, in our age of 'anything goes', as a vintage piece of Hollywood charm, particularly as today's audience cannot compare *She Done Him Wrong* with the original *Diamond Lil* play. A lengthy and clumsily worded title over the opening shot of a period Bowery street proclaims, mangling the words of an old song:

The Gay Nineties –
When they did such things and they said such things
on the Bowery, A lusty, brawling florid decade when
there were handlebars on lip and wheel –
and legs were confidential!

What sort of things precisely were done and said on the Bowery remains vague by design. There follows a sequence of street scenes – a horse-drawn streetcar passing by the sign of 'Gus Jordan's Place', a performing monkey, women and men on bicycles, and a 'bicycle made for two' on image and soundtrack, a man sighing as he clears his horse's dung, a Jewish street-trader, women with large hats, the brass band and the swinging doors of the saloon. A close-up of the sign 'Lager Beer – 5c' is followed by a hand wiping the foam off a row of glasses. Then

The star in reclining mode at home

we are at the bar, and Tammany Young (who would later specialize in being a W. C. Fields straight man), playing, according to the credits, Chuck Connors, is regaling a bar-stool friend with gossip about 'the fight last night'. Everybody's glances go to an immense nude portrait – with a foreground head always tastefully hiding the midriff – of the famous 'Lady Lou': 'A guy don't need any breakfast when he can look at her.' 'She sure is beautiful . . .' The entrance of Dan Flynn, crooked ward boss and rival of the saloon's owner, Gus Jordan, Lou's present lover, sparks off the exposition of the plot. When we cut to the street, Mae swoops in aboard a horse-drawn carriage, dressed to the nines, with hat to match, as the men tip their hats, and she halts to pat a poor small boy on the head. His mother's adoring 'Oh, Lady Lou, you're a fine woman' extracts another famous Mae quip: 'One of the finest women ever walked the streets!'

Before Mae's entrance we have been already introduced to her co-star, Cary Grant. The tale Mae always told of casting Grant for the picture was that she had seen him walking along the lot one day when leaving the Paramount office with William LeBaron and another executive, Al Kaufman: '"Who's that, I asked?" Kaufman recognised him. "Cary Grant," he said. "He'll do for my leading man," I said. "But," Kaufman protested, "he hasn't made a picture yet. Only tests."'

Much as one does not wish to accuse a lady of misleading us so shamelessly, again, this was not true. Grant had been playing a variety of bit parts through 1932 and had a leading role with Marlene Dietrich in *Blonde Venus*. And, as we have related, Mae had met him before, even if only as a child stilt-walker in LeBaron's *A La Broadway* revue.

The plot line of *She Done Him Wrong* follows *Diamond Lil* quite closely, though all the recommendations of the script censors were taken into account. Gus Jordan's raucous saloon has replaced the seedy 'Suicide Hall'. Rita and her beau are no longer Hispanic but Russian, with Juarez becoming Serge Stanieff, although the character is played by the most Hispanic Gilbert Roland, while Rafaella Ottiano, who played Spanish Rita in the play, now plays her as a Slav on the screen. The 'white slavery' aspect of their prostitution ring has become a counterfeiting scam, and the exploitation of the seduced girl, Sally (played by Rochelle Hudson), is now a private scheme between Gus Jordan and Rita to supply her 'gin joints' on the Barbary Coast (no trace of Rio de Janeiro). Most of the offending dialogue has gone, apart from a playful 'You can be had!' to Cary Grant on the steps to Lou's boudoir.

Grant is perfectly cast as Cummings, the apparent mission officer whose ideas of reforming 'Lady Lou' are overcome by his increasing attraction to her, while he is, in fact, a police spy, 'The Hawk', who gets both the crooks and the lady in the end. Or rather, he has been got, as the subtext of the body language between Mae and Cary projects clearly underneath their dialogue. Mae was discovering that the camera's predeliction to record and magnify small things – those 'ten-foot high closeups of nostrils' – could enable her to suggest things that she was prevented from expressing in words. She could move her hips and shoulders just so, and tip her head ever so slightly, and move her eyelashes, and mutter 'umm' and 'oohh' and 'aahh', and ooze out a languid glance, and allow ideas and promises to hang in a pause, reflecting her entire stage repertoire of transgressive, bawdy, assertive and mischievous women in a manner no stage audience could have appreciated, even through steamed-up opera glasses. These accretions, combined with her outrageous overdressing, would come to be described as 'camp', but they derived from practical challenges and solutions to the direct problem of censorship, right up to the extraordinary weight attached to the most simple phrases: 'Why doncha come up and see me?' or 'Do you get me?' More quips culled from the years of joke-book copying, old chestnuts like 'When women go wrong, men go right after them,' took on a new lease of life when uttered by Mae West, just so.

Cary Grant showed that he could hold his own in all this, even without the long experience Mae had enjoyed in delivering to an audience. The combination of light and shadow that would characterize his performances, the double-sided sense of integrity and concealment, attractiveness and arrogance that would make him so intriguing to movie-goers is already present. The effortless ease and calm, even in neurosis, which deepened this ambiguity would come later. But Grant did not require the long dialogue, quoted earlier from the stage play, to express the contradiction inherent in 'Missionary' Cummings' conversations with Lil/Lou about her diamonds and her soul. Some of this is displaced to the last scene, set in the carriage in which he is taking her away from the saloon after Jordan and his accomplices have been arrested:

CUMMINGS: You remind me of a glittering palace of ice.

LOU: I ain't ice.

CUMMINGS: I didn't say you were, but your diamonds are all going to the storehouse.

LOU: You said I had a soul – I looked for it but I didn't find it.

CUMMINGS: You will.

LOU: Where, in jail?

CUMMINGS: No, that's not the place for you.

LOU: You got me, aincha?

CUMMINGS: Yes, I got you. You're my prisoner and I'm gonna be your jailer for a long, long time.

LOU: Oh yeah?

CUMMINGS: Yeah. You can start doing that stretch right now. (*Puts glittering ring on her finger.*)
LOU: Where d'you get that? Dark and handsome . . .
CUMMINGS: Mm, you bad girl . . .
LOU: Mmm, you'll find out . . .
(*Clinch and fade-out.*)

The rest of it, the subsidiary characters – the chunky saloon enforcer Spider (Dewey Robinson), Flynn (David Landau), Noah Beery Sr's Gus Jordan and Owen Moore's psychopathic escaped convict and ex-lover Chick Clark – pass smoothly in Lowell Sherman's workmanlike direction. (Sherman was a silent-film actor who first appeared in Griffith's *Way Down East* and played either smooth lovers or lecherous villains; he would die while filming Hollywood's first three-strip Technicolor feature, *Becky Sharp*, in 1934.) Louise Beavers plays the first in a long line of black personal maids, Pearl, dresser and confidante: 'Oh, Miss Lou, you's so rich.' Lou: 'I wasn't always rich . . . I was once so poor I didn't know where my next husband was comin' from.' One bizarre scene, to portray a visit by Mae to Chick Clark in prison, features a succession of desperate convicts calling out to Mae from behind their iron bars, like the damned supplicating a reluctant angel. But in the main the movie keeps to the original stage setting of the Bowery saloon, omitting the air of the brothel.

A couple of the old songs remain in the movie: a moustached warbler rendering a tearful 'Silver Threads Among the Gold' that makes hardened men weep into their beer, and a verse of 'She Should Rather Be Pitied than Censured', as in the original play. Mae gets to sing three songs, the first two in her most magnificent costumes – designed by then-beginner Edith Head – first black, then white, with giant hats to match. When Mae sashays on to belt out 'I Wonder Where My Easy Rider's Gone' – ostensibly a song about a jockey – the lust and lasciviousness of the triple meanings shimmers in the air. For the first time in a mainstream front-rank Hollywood movie, the authentic sound of black blues *à la* Mamie Smith wails out, but from a white face. Mae's second song, 'A Guy What Takes His Time – I'll Go for Anytime', has lost the 100 feet chopped out by Hays' command, and the third, her old staple 'Frankie and Johnny', provides the film's title line with 'He Was Her Man – and He Was Doing Her Wrong' before being cut short by a pistol shot – Chick Clark shooting the treacherous Dan Flynn – that ushers in the last scenes of the film.

The press book for the film made every effort to hide the film's derivation from *Diamond Lil* by listing instead Mae's other stage exploits and highlighting the period reconstruction of the 'Glitter and Squalor of [the] Street of Scarlet Memories': 'Truth Is Too Strange! Mae West Tones it Down to Make it Believable,' runs one reassuring item among the articles inserted by the publicists in the knowledge that lazy newspaper editors would print them verbatim. 'So lurid and melodramatic were the events upon which her plays and novels were based that she couldn't use them without toning them down. Miss West, a spectacular figure along New York's white way for the past decade, makes her début as a screen star in "She Done Him Wrong," which she herself wrote . . .'

Reviews were cautious, *Variety* stating that 'Mae West in pictures should stand out as she did in legit – as a distinct personality,' but warning that 'she needs extreme care in the literary department. Also some nursing. This premature shove into the foreground could retard her progress.' The advisory *Harrison's Reports* wrote that 'for a picture of its type it is entertaining; but it certainly is not for the family circle or for squeamish adults . . . Not suitable for children or for Sunday showing.' The *New York Herald Tribune*, however, praised a 'hearty, hilarious and handsomely rowdy motion picture . . . the film is filled with excellent types and Cary Grant, the best of the oncoming juveniles, is excellent as what passes for the hero . . . The film should be a complete delight for any one annoyed by the frequent slyness of the films' adventures into the Rabelaisian. Then, too, as Miss West says, "I ain't ice," and, as another *Herald Tribune* reviewer added, "she's right, she ain't."'

The public agreed with that, lining up round the block, and not only in the big cities. As a later letter from a somewhat smitten Hays Office official, Kirk L. Russell, to a Miss Mildred Martin at the *Philadelphia Inquirer*, defending the film, if under the heading: 'PERSONAL, NOT FOR PRINT', put it:

Let's . . . make some reference to the millions of small town people who have made possible 6,000 'repeats' of SHE DONE HIM WRONG – the greatest record of 'repeats' since THE BIRTH OF A NATION – and then the question concluding your comment of July 23 would properly read –

'As long as these perfectly respectable people do not mind but actually express a decided liking for 'hussy' or 'loose lady' films, who is going to complain?'

' . . . Rahab, the loose-living lady of ancient Jericho possessed a heart of gold in not only sheltering the men sent by Joshua, but saved their lives,' points out Len G. Shaw of the Detroit Free Press to those who want more rigid police censorship of 'wicked' films to save the children.

Shaw further points out that women sinners have held their place in the spotlight in all ages and that this is 'an explanation rather than an apology for the presence on the screen of so many bad girls.'

Mae had shown what she was capable of and packed 'em in. Just as she had presented on stage a woman who misbehaved as a matter of choice and got away with it, so she managed to present on screen, despite the obstacle course of the Production Code, a woman who defined her own life and her own morality, who went from man to man as she chose, who initiated action, treated the men the way men in movies were expected to treat 'their' women, redefining the concept of a 'woman's picture' and, most of all, refusing to be a victim.

As 'Lady Lou' tells the seduced Sally, relaunching her lines from the stage: 'Men's all alike, married or single. It's their game. I happen to be smart enough to play it their way.'

24

'Beulah – Peel Me a Grape!'

From standing on the Pasadena railway platform, fending off questions from a handful of hacks asking her whether she had lost weight, Mae West, in 1933, found herself catapulted onto the celebrity track. Now everybody wanted to know what she thought, how she lived her life, whom she loved or disliked, and any tidbit that might serve the fans' feeding frenzy. Any nonsense would do. Bad Boy the monkey (a.k.a. Boogie) soon paled. The jewel-robbery story was ongoing and would be revisited regularly, just to show our heroine did not venture naked into the streets. 'Mae West Sued Over Bill for Silken Scanties' by a New York store was short-lived. One of the earliest and most peculiar pieces appeared in the *New York World-Telegram* on 15 February, during the red heat of *She Done Him Wrong*'s opening run. This involved Mae's declaration, on a promotional visit to New York, that the only man she had really wanted to meet in Hollywood when she arrived was a local eccentric – Peter the Hermit:

HERMIT PETE SCOFFED AT MAE WEST'S HIGH HEELS;
MADE HER PROMISE TO IGNORE TROUSERS STYLE
The star of 'She Done Him Wrong' walked down the hall and entered her dressing room – moving slowly like a sea wave on a summer beach. She sat down and ceremoniously crossed her legs. She pulled nine heavy bracelets off her arms and piled them on the table. The she unhitched two incredible ear-rings.

'Let me pull some of my harness off,' she said, adding the earrings to the pile of bracelets, 'and I'll give you a few words of wisdom. Oh yes, I feel good today. The snow and all. And getting back home and all. I been in Hollywood. I guess you know. I had a lot of adventures out there. I met a hermit . . . He was the only man out there that interested me. His name was Peter the Hermit. I called him Pete. Everybody in Hollywood knows him. He lives up in the mountains and trains donkeys and raises dogs. He thinks Hollywood is the place the preachers talk about when they tell people where they're going when they die. Well, he told some friends of his that he wanted to meet me. I was excited on account of I never met a hermit and I wanted to see how one acted.

'So one day I got into my automobile and went up in the mountains to visit him. He was 70 years old and as strong as an ox. I guess it was a love affair that turned him into a hermit. Well, I thought he was going to lecture me like he does the other movie women, but no, he just said I shouldn't wear high-heeled shoes. He said I should go bare-footed and I should fill my lungs full of fresh air every morning. He said I should come up in the mountains and stay for a month or so.'

'He wasn't a backward hermit, was he?'

'Oh no, not at all. He seemed to get a kick out of me. He had me feel his muscle. Oh, he had a good muscle, and he got on one of his donkeys and jumped over some hurdles he had there in the front yard. He said it took a lot of training to make a donkey jump a hurdle. And he gave me one of his photographs and wrote across it, "From Peter to Mae." He had a beard a yard long and I told him the next time I went to see him I was going to bring him a present. He said, "What kind of a present, Mae?" And I said, "A nice safety razor, Pete."

'And he said I should promise him not to wear pants like the other movie women. And I said, "Don't you worry . . . not only would I look a fool in pants, what with my figure and all, but it also wouldn't help my career."'

Mae announced to *Variety* on 31 January that 'you never hear about good women in history. The only good girl to make history was Betsy Ross, and she had to sew up a flag to do it.' (Mae would repeat this line again and again in interviews right up to *Playboy* in 1971.) 'People are more curious about something not good . . . My realization of this universal human tendency put me over in the drama . . . I built up a loyal public in the theatre and I'm going to keep faith with my public in pictures.'

The New York press were not yet ready to glorify Mae, however, the *Daily News* returning to the weight issue with the snide remark that 'Hollywood has thinned Mae. She no longer looks like a member of the Beef Trust . . . This is the same Mae West, by the way, who when a kid was always dressed in Little Lord Fauntleroy clothing.'

For New York, Mae was still a local broad from Bushwick Avenyah, whose airs and graces no one could take seriously. Although one local scribe, William Gaines of the *Citizen-News*, extracted a promise from her that 'I'll never try to go sweet and simple in the movies,' Gaines noted that, behind the razzle-dazzle, Mae had been helping many of the women she had met on Welfare Island 'when she served 10 days there several years ago for offending the censors of the drama in this most free and liberal New York . . . She has become deeply interested in the work of rehabilitating such human beings – has helped men as well as women.' Gaines went on: 'She doesn't go about this business with any of the hocus-pocus of social service: just boosts them along in her hail-fellow-well-met way.'

Los Angeles was generally more inclined to take her as she came and print the legend, though Mae let slip to columnist Alma Whitaker that, contrary to her usual version of her self-education by theatre, '"I'm well educated. I went to private schools and had tutors – I learned both French and German."' Mae further surprised her interlocutor by stating, '"I go to church every day of my life, but I don't go around telling it. I go to the Catholic church, but I'm not a Catholic. It just does me good to begin the day that way. My manager's a Catholic," she added, with seeming irrelevance.' Miss Whitaker noted that 'Mae likes to be sensationally shocking – strictly professionally. I'd say she was a good business woman first, last and all the time,' adding: 'In the meantime, her big "Irish" manager limps around behind her wherever she goes, as would a devoted police dog. I'll wager he doesn't know who is being managed half the time.'

But Timony was not so ignorant, by now, of who was calling the shots. Although he was no longer sharing her bed, Mae would no more think of dispensing with her most loyal mentor as she would chopping off her leg. Legs, by the way, being a sore point with Timony, whose limp caused LA's jaded journos to speculate that his own limb was wooden, till he had to bare his pants to show the genuine white east coast flesh. Against the stereotype of Timony as a gangster-affiliated hard-boiled fixer, he began soon after his arrival in the west to dabble in his own theatrical projects, leading to some hitherto unknown contributions by Mae recently found in her archive (of which more anon).

Mae had one advantage, however, over some of her equally famous cohabitants in the movie capital. According to her second most important mentor, William LeBaron, interviewed in 1935 by *Motion Picture*, 'she takes long drives in her car, goes to prize fights now and then and either dines at obscure cafés or goes to popular ones early before the crowd arrives. She is seldom recognized because the publicly accepted picture of the actress doesn't resemble the real woman at all.'

This had been the case since the 1920s, when newspaper photographs of Mae at her court hearings and trials revealed a somewhat dumpy, short and almost nondescript figure, at complete odds with the glamorous and sinful image. 'She is one of the greatest show people ever to invade Hollywood,' said LeBaron, 'but the real Mae West will never be seen on the screen, and in Hollywood life is rapidly becoming as legendary as Garbo . . . Mae's whole life is wrapped in her screen personality. Every gesture she makes – every line that she speaks – every move that she takes – during the shooting of a picture is the result of almost agonizing study and concentration.'

From the choice of dresses taken at the sketch stage to unpicking the storylines and deciding that this or that might be a good story but 'it's not my type', Mae made crucial decisions: 'I can't play that role. But I'll bet Colbert or Dietrich can – and do a swell job. Go and tell it to them.' When anyone at a story conference went off the tracks in a direction Mae didn't favour, LeBaron recounted, 'she starts humming to herself. "Stop it, Mae," I tell her. "What am I doin'?" she asks. "You know," I advise her. But by this time the spell of the story has been broken and as far as she is concerned, the day is over.'

Mae West, LeBaron said, 'is a very easy person to work with . . . We're like the proverbial ham and eggs. We've never bickered, never had a misunderstanding' – which may have been gilding the lily, but LeBaron clearly knew a good thing when he saw it, and Mae knew which side her bread was buttered.

Within weeks of the release of *She Done Him Wrong*, Mae's second starring movie was being touted. Another period piece was proposed: 'Her next picture will be "The Golden Soubrette," dated in the nineties, about the time of the big Fitzgibbons–Corbett fight,' reported the *Los Angeles Times* on 9 April. Another possibility was a Claude Binyon and Frank Butler story called 'Rings on Her Fingers'. A week later, the *New York Herald Tribune* wrote that 'Mae West's next Paramount production will be "Don't Call Me Madame," a story written by herself . . . the star's original story was written under the title of "Montana Belle."'

In the event, Mae's next picture was *I'm No Angel*, which began filming in July and wrapped in September 1933. Acquiring a circus story by Lowell Brentano, Mae fashioned it into a proper vehicle for a character as close to the 'real Mae West' as any of her films or plays would be. The on-screen credits would lead with the unusual 'By Mae West' and specify: 'Story, Screenplay and All Dialogue by Mae West; Story Suggestions by Lowell Brentano; Continuity by Harlan Thompson.'

Once again, Cary Grant co-starred, as the suave and rich Jack Clayton, who is, conveniently, Mae's true love. Other young and not so young men form a ladder which Mae's circus dancer Tira climbs, from the freak show up, to a luxury four-maid boudoir. And yet the men alone are not the only means of Tira's success, for her real talent, we are shown, lies in the ultimate act of show-business courage – sticking her head into a lion's mouth.

I'm No Angel was and remains Mae West's best film, perhaps for the simple reason that it was the one least affected by the moral battalions of Will Hays. Most of the Hays Office's energies appear to have been expended on trying to censor the songs, in particular the suggestive 'No One Loves Me Like That Dallas Man' by Gladys Dubois, Ben Ellison and Harvey Brooks, which nevertheless survives on the screen, though we have lost the stanza:

> *Why brother – he's a wild horse trainer*
> *With a special whip –*
> *Gals you'll go insaner*
> *When he gets you in his grip . . .*

Strangely, 'They Call Me Sister Honky Tonk' raised no objections, even to the verses:

> *I'm free and easy, my life's my own,*
> *I come and go as I choose . . .*
> *Just look me over, say! I'm plenty known,*
> *I take what I want or refuse.*
> *I've got the face of a Saint,*
> *On the level it's paint,*
> *So beware of these eyes,*
> *I'm a devil in disguise,*
> *And they call me sister Honky Tonk!*

Other intense blues numbers, the 'bluest' in all of Mae's repertoire, slipped through the net, like 'I can make it heaven when the shades are drawn / I'm no angel – believe me . . .' and 'I Found a New Way to Go to Town', 'I'm high – I'm low / Takes a good man to make me / No man can shake me / Until I let him go . . .' (although 'make' did get changed to 'break'). The Dallas man with his 'special whip' became 'He's a cowboy wooer / Roaming on the hills / Just a big lassooer / With a stirrup full of thrills,' which suggests the good Catholics of the Board just didn't get that last line. Other objections, from James Wingate to Paramount executive Botsford, were relatively mild:

July 11 1933

The underlined words 'If you've watched me dance *you can tell*' should be deleted under the Code.

We believe the line of dialogue 'We're going on the same as ever' may prove censorable.

From the standpoint of censorship we suggest care with this action of

Tira crossing her legs, and the subsequent reaction shown by the jurors. We also believe it will be advisable not to show the Judge craning his head to look, but to play him throughout as perfectly straight.

The underlined words 'Make 'em wait for it' should be deleted under the Code.

It is possible that the line 'Take a lot and give as little as possible' may be censorable.

We believe the line 'one man at a time' should be modified under the Code.

Page D-7 – Care will be needed with this scene of Slick coming out of the bedroom, not to have him in pajamas, but preferably fully clothed, perhaps wearing a dressing gown instead of a coat.

We believe the line 'You didn't lose your honor' is too suggestive to be permissible under the Code.

The best decision made over *I'm No Angel* was to adopt an original story instead of trying to adapt one of Mae's plays. This put the censors off their guard and enabled Mae to write freely, without trying to tie herself and her co-writers in knots as they tried to find inoffensive substitutes for brassy dialogue or hard-hitting scenes. This also enabled Mae to scour her joke folders for a cornucopia of gags and quips, with several pages of loose repartee clearly meant for this project, as the character names are included among the rough-draft suggestions, along with standard joke-book material:

ALICIA (*cattily*): I don't suppose that in your profession you've had much time for self-cultivation.

TIRA: Well, I have cultivated my natural assets.

'My love will last forever.'
'How about your money?'

'Oh, come on, let's do it for better or worse.'
'You mean for more or less.' (*This one ticked by Mae but not used.*)

'What a beautiful leg.'
'Yeah, some men get a big kick out of it.'

'So you're fooling around with other men.'
'Not me, I don't fool with them.' (*Ticked.*)

'Where are you stopping during your visit here?'
'Stopping at nothing.' (*Unticked but used in the film.*)

TIRA to Alicia: The only difference between you and me – we break different commandments.

TIRA: Listen, Beulah, when Mr Lawrence comes up, kick a few guys out of the doorway and let him in.

TIRA to Slick: All right, mustard plaster, I guess I'm stuck with you. *(takes out some money)* Here's some dough – now let me hear your heels broadcastin' 'Good-bye Forever'.

As William LeBaron noted, Mae worked methodically, leaving nothing to chance or ad-libs – the characteristic of all stage-trained comedians, from W. C. Fields to the Marx Brothers. The old joke about shooting a dog can be revamped to fit the lion:

TIRA: I had to shoot a lion once.

SOCIALITE: Really? Was he mad?

TIRA: Well, he wasn't exactly pleased about it.

As the curtain comes up, or rather the credits roll, the circus music blares over the Big Top scene. In this production, Mae had a new director, comedy specialist Wesley Ruggles, who had reputedly started life as a 1914 Keystone Cop, appeared in Chaplin shorts, and began directing in 1918, churning out titles such as *Uncharted Seas*, *Slippy McGee*, *Broadway Lady*, *Beware of Widows*, *Silk Stockings*, *The Fourflusher*, *Condemned* and *Girl Overboard*, all in the 1920s. In 1930, he had directed the Oscar-winning western *Cimarron*, with Richard Dix and Irene Dunne. He knew how to handle comics and he certainly knew how to move the camera, as the somewhat static compositions of *She Done Him Wrong* give way to a more fluid style, exemplified when the crowds surge towards the gatling-gun patter of the circus barker, Flea Madigan, who cries the wonders of 'Joe the turtle boy . . . half man, half turtle . . . he plays the zither . . . Tira, the beautiful Tira, the dancing singing marvel of the age – supreme power of feminine pulchritude – the girl who discovered you don't have to have feet to be a dancer!'

From a tent bearing the sign TIRA THE INCOMPARABLE a curtain rolls out, and Mae, attired in the burlesque not-quite-see-through costume of the old-time cooch dancer, emerges, wiggling her hips and shoulders in a close approximation to the murdered shimmy, as she cajoles the crowd: 'No wisecracks . . . mmm . . . penny for your thoughts . . .' The barker barks on: 'Next to her a wiggling worm looks paralyzed . . .!' After a brief rendition of 'They Call Me Sister Honky Tonk', Tira slinks back into her tent, muttering, 'Am ah makin' myself clear, boys?' and, under her breath, 'Suckers!' while Flea Madigan is still in full stream: 'The only show in town where the tickets are made of asbestos!'

In its parodic way, *I'm No Angel* follows the trajectory of Mae's own rise, from the rough and ready platforms of burlesque towards the white and satin boudoirs of show-business stardom. An ogling fan, flashing his big diamond ring, has little trouble arranging to come up an' see her at a hotel room in town, a rendezvous for which she has to dodge both her boss, Big Bill Barton, and her rat-like familiar, pickpocket Slick Wiley. Wiley, however, turns up as she is sweet-talking the diamond-bearing 'Mr. Brown', the 'Dallas man', who confesses he has been married five times, thus enabling Mae to recycle a joke she had earmarked for Maudie in *Night After Night* but not used: 'Wedding bells must sound like an alarm clock to you.' Wiley barges in to try a crude shakedown which results in the mark stretched out on the carpet, beaned over his head with a bottle by Slick. Leaving him for dead in the corridor, minus his ring, Tira and Slick rush off but the mark recovers, and Slick is caught by the cops. Tira now needs to get money from Big Bill to pay for her New York shyster lawyer, Benny Pinkowitz (played by the most shystersome Gregory Ratoff). In return, she promises to pep up her second-string lion-taming act by putting her head in the lion's mouth, a trick which Flea Madigan enthuses will put her among the big-time acts.

Before the shakedown, we are treated to a sly reference to Mae's own occult predelictions in a scene with 'Rajah', the show's tur-banned fortune-teller (played by Nigel de Brulier): 'You just tell me about my future; you see, I know all about my past.' The seer hands her her personal horoscope, after foreseeing 'a man in your life'. Mae: 'Only one?' The seer peers into the crystal ball: 'I see a change in position . . .' 'Sittin' or reclinin'?'

Tira's ambitions for change remain fixated on finding a rich sucker: 'Somewhere there's a guy with a million waiting for a dame like me . . .' Nevertheless, her climb to fortune has to be earned by her courageous stunt with the lion. Mae told John Kobal many years later: 'I only ever wanted to be a lion tamer. As a child I was always being told that the lion was the king of the animals and the most beautiful and ferocious beast, and my father took me to them and told me how they were the greatest. So years later I wrote myself a part in *I'm No Angel* in which

I played a lion tamer. When I went into that cage, I felt at home because I had wanted to do this so much since I was a child.'

As Mae told the tale in her autobiography, she was eager to get into the cage to gratify her old urge, but the director objected, and the head trainer, in this account, 'had his arm almost torn off' that morning by one of the lions. William LeBaron and executive Al Kaufman were called for, as Mae insisted that 'This lion scene is the main reason I'm doing this picture.' In the event, Mae wrote, she entered the cage of ten lions with men standing by with loaded guns.

In reality Hollywood had a surfeit of well-trained lions, as well as the elephant which Mae rode triumphantly into the ring before sliding down nicely on its trunk. Most of the shots in which Mae is in the cage with the lions are process shots, such as those in which she cracks the whip while a lion yawns: 'Where were you last night? . . . Come on, get up . . . Speak up for yourself . . . Oh yeah . . . you'll end up as a rug!' There are a couple of long shots in the cage which could either be Mae or a stand-in. When the lone lion enters, there are two authentic shots in which Mae approaches the lion and strokes its head, preparatory to the 'face-in-the-mouth', another process shot. These would have been enough to earn Mae the crew's applause, even if, as rumoured, the lion was heavily sedated.

Mae's encounter with the lions can be seen as her most metaphorical image of the heroine vanquishing the ultimate male, red in tooth and claw. This is the only male in her oeuvre who could truly be said to be no pushover. The others are easy, particularly the swell, Kirk Lawrence, played by Kent Taylor, who snubs his snooty fiancée, Alicia (Gertrude Michael), to become the supposed 'dark man' of her horoscope as well as her most lucrative bank account. A montage of cheques ripping out of cheque books, jewellers' counters and expensive dresses pulled out of gift boxes leads into the razzy scene of Mae's luxury boudoir, with Mae's own pet monkey Boogie in a gilded cage and miniature portraits of all her amours on a table set beside a variety of suitable china animals – Big Bill Barton meriting a skunk while Slick Wiley gets the coiled snake.

In the scene, Tira is being dressed and pampered by her quartet of black maids. These include the iconic Beulah, played by Gertrude Howard, Hattie McDaniel, six years before her performance in *Gone with the Wind*, and Libby Taylor, Mae's real-life personal maid. Mae is flouncing about doing her number 'I Found a New Way to Go to

Town' – crooning 'I'm high – I'm low . . .' – as the maids gather giggling around her.

Mae's parade of the black maids has been interpreted kindly as her self-depiction as an 'honorary' black person, jazzing it up, an African-American in all but colour. But it is quite evident that Mae and her maids, joke and banter as they may over men and husbands, are very far from any equality, for all Mae's portrayal of a sassy working girl who has made good: 'What kind o' men do you like, Libby?' 'I'm jest crazy 'bout dark men.' 'You want to have a big time in Africa.' Not quite stuff that stands the test of time. 'You know, Miss Tira, I has the impression that you is a one man woman.' 'I am – one man at a time.' Mistress and maids might cackle together, but when the man comes in, whether Kirk Lawrence or his later business partner, Jack Clayton, the mantra is 'I wanted to see you alone.' The black maid has become invisible, even if

clearly present in the scene; as Mae greets Beulah, in a later scene, on the witness stand: 'Listen, Shadow, what are you doin' here?'

The times, once again, trip us up into wishful thinking. The dilemma for the black actresses was obvious: in 1930s Hollywood it was only roles such as these that African-Americans could hope to be employed in, with very rare exceptions. Hattie McDaniel herself, answering criticisms of her roles, stated that she could have either earned $7,000 a week acting a black maid or $7 a week being a black maid. On the screen, the stereotyped Jim Crow style of speech was *de rigueur*, to the extent that the 1930s most successful black actor, 'Stepin Fetchit' (born Lincoln Theodore Monroe Andrew Perry, four presidents recruited for good luck), made a fortune pushing his shuffling caricature to its most absurd degree. The bottom line, to use that phrase, was that, however friendly the patter, it was the black maids who were on their knees fixing Mae's dress, not the other way around.

The scene with the maids is interrupted by the snooty Alicia, who enters to try and buy Tira off her alliance with Kirk, only to be roughly shoved out the door. As Mae swings back in, all regal in her blonde coiffure and black trailing dress, she delivers her most famous line of all:

'Oh, Beulah!'

'Yes, mam?'

'Peel me a grape!'

This derived, Mae wrote, from Boogie, who 'was an expert' at this delicate feat.

It is not until this point, well past the halfway mark in the film, that Mae introduces her main romantic interest, dashing, ultra-suave Cary Grant. Now no longer a sharp cop masquerading as a moral crusader but a millionaire in good standing, as Jack Clayton, Kirk Lawrence's business partner, he tries to buy the circus woman off, only to fall for her himself and offer marriage. At last, the Hays Office could not cavil at true love with an upright member of society being the final destination for Mae West. But this only comes after another classic sequence: the breach-of-promise trial launched by Tira when Jack breaks off the engagement after being fooled by a dirty trick pulled by Mae's spurned former partners, Big Bill Barton and Slick Wiley. Barton arranges the sabotage of Tira's chauffeur-driven car, while Slick, newly released from jail, confronts Clayton in her rooms in a dressing gown, pretending to be her lover.

The trial section is reminiscent of another famous Hollywood flim-flam court scene, in William Wellman's 1942 *Roxie Hart*, based on the 1927 silent movie *Chicago* – which would become the present-day musical of the same title. Gregory Ratoff is the defence lawyer, with the prosecution calling a row of previous men in Tira's life to deprive her case of any merit. One by one she demolishes them on the stand, while exchanging smiles and simpering nods with the judge, cuddly bald old Walter Walker. A lady reporter's query to Tira at the end – 'Why did you admit to knowing so many men?' – prompts a repeat of another famous line: 'It's not the men in my life that count, it's the life in my men.'

Grant and Mae are reunited after Grant concedes the case, when Slick Wiley's deception is revealed to him on the stand. Monogamy, however, may not quite be imminent, as Mae is seen flirting in her room with the judge, as well as taking a phone call from 'Juror number four . . . you were the one with the kind face . . . come up and see me some time . . .' The maids slink away, leaving Cary and Mae to clinch as she croons: 'I can make it happen when the shades are drawn . . . mmm . . . I'm no angel . . .'

In the film's press book, a lavish, many-paged affair compared with *She Done Him Wrong*'s relatively meagre package, the synopsis of the film has a different ending, which was either shot and discarded or scripted without being shot, as there appears to be no other record of it:

Clayton agrees to settle in full. But still Barton hasn't won his point, for Tira insists on quitting the circus. To collect the insurance money, Barton and Slick plot to kill her, substituting a vicious lion for the trained animal . . . In the ring, Tira discovers the deception, bravely resists the charging beast. Just before he leaps, she sees Barton's leering face outside the ring, pulls her gun and fires three shots. Two kill the lion, the third, diverted slightly, kills Barton.

In this version, Clayton rushes to the hospital where Tira is lying injured 'to beg her forgiveness – and Tira's record of always getting her man is intact'.

It is curious to find so different an ending in publicity intended to be sent out just before a movie's release, though it does show how quickly these studio films were rushed through the assembly line: unlike our day, cutting proceeded as the film was being shot – the director rarely being involved in this phase – and the film previewed

I'm No Angel – Tira wooing the jury

and premièred within weeks. Perhaps the incident with the lions mentioned in Mae's account made mad-lion scenes an unattractive idea or perhaps – as might well be the case if one thinks about it – such a coda was seen to be structurally redundant. In any case, it ain't there.

The publicity campaign went to town promoting the movie, including some vintage flimflam in the Paramount press book, ostensibly by Mae herself, about the lion's-mouth moment:

I must confess that it gave me a real Biblical feeling. Now I know how Jonah felt when he slipped down the gullet of that whale, and how Daniel felt when he entered the lion's den. 'Jezebel in the lion's mouth,' I heard one of the electricians on the set mutter, as I explored the inner regions of the king of beasts. But I guess if I really were a Jezebel, the lion would have clamped down his jaws in punishment for my wickedness.

My exploration of the lion's roaring canyon enabled me to learn one vital olfactory fact . . . Lions surely do have halitosis! However, I don't believe many other persons are going to get close enough to be annoyed by it . . .

An old lion tamer told me, 'Lions are just like men, Miss West. Treat 'em the same way, and you won't have any trouble.'

So that's just what I did. I treated them very sweetly, then I cracked the whip, and we had no trouble.

On the other hand, it was 'Woman's Duty to Be Beautiful, Mae West, Film Charmer Says' – so went another heading, just beneath the above. 'Curved Figure Back In Favor' warbled another puff. The Sales Analysis for theatres showing the movie, the press book proposed, was simple: 'Let nature take her course . . . When you sell curvacious, gold mine Mae West, keep the copy short and quotable. People like to tell each other what Mae West said; and the whole nation is making love with Mae West nifties. Soon sweethearts will replace "You can be had" with "You fascinate me – you do," and the box-office will give them its blessing.'

This was the strength of Mae's joke-book quips – they were so easy to slip into the language, in the quick and slick Hollywood style: 'When I'm good I'm very good, but when I'm bad I'm better.' Or her motto to her circus colleague Thelma, played by newcomer Dorothy Peterson: 'Get all you can get, and give as little as possible: Find 'em, fool 'em and forget 'em.' Given the success of her first starring film, it was no surprise that the second, which surpassed it, topped all box-office records, even if Mae did not, as legend has it, single-handedly save Paramount from bankruptcy, since the Paramount company went technically bankrupt anyway, only to rise again from its own ashes. Nevertheless, Sid Grauman, owner and founder of the famous Chinese Theater on Hollywood Boulevard, published a full-page, super-gushing encomium to Mae in *Variety*:

Mae West – 'the lady who was known as Lou' – Of Thee We Sing . . . the most amazing personality on the screen . . . the woman who upset theater precedent . . . broke every box office record . . . changed the fashion modes of the world – the despair of all women . . . the delight of all men – the hottest front page newspaper copy of the day – Mae West we salute you . . . congratulate you . . . we thank you for 'I'm No Angel' and we are proud to present your picture in our Chinese Theater, the most distinctive playhouse in all the world.'

Mae knew, however, that it was not enough, whether on Broadway or in Hollywood, to make a smash, or even two. Once you had reached that peak you had to go on. By February of 1934, Paramount was presenting to the Hays Office the third of Mae West's special challenges to the proprieties of the reformers' dreamtime Hollywood. The script was, at first, provocatively titled 'It Ain't No Sin'.

But by the time the crucial battle over the screenplay came to be fought, the Hays Office had undergone its major renovation and acquired a reinforced mandate, sharper teeth and a fresh new enforcer, Board member Joseph Breen. This was to be Mae's Valley Forge, Trafalgar and potential Waterloo all in one, the test case for the new Production Code against the freedom and licence of Hollywood to answer to its audiences and, above all else, the talent of its crew and performers.

It was time to decide whether 'It' was a sin or not.

A Diversion – The Secret Life of Mae West

What are A Woman's Secrets, especially one as famous as Mae West, newly deified as the Sex Goddess of Hollywood, pursued by the world's most rapacious 'paparazzi' long before the word itself became commonplace, her every utterance rapturously received by gossip columnists who, nevertheless, found it difficult to penetrate her shimmering magic shield? Even after seventy years of Mae West watching and analysis, and repetition of rumour and innuendo, the picture is soft with diffusion, the make-up thick and multilayered, the gleam in the eyes more likely to be the shafts of inky-dinky spotlights, the epitome of cinema illusions.

On sex, Mae always wrote that it ruled her life and proclaimed herself the world's greatest expert on the subject, long before the gimlet gaze of Mr Kinsey stripped many of its mysteries away, at least as far as Americans were concerned. In her 1973 book *Mae West on Sex, Health and ESP*, Mae wrote that 'the basic secret of sex is glamour – and it's far more than skin deep . . . I've always been aware of sex, and it's always been aware of me . . .' A range of fairly banal homilies then follow – about knowing your partner, finding what's right for you, and so forth. Mae, like Tira, who was No Angel, believed in doing what came naturally and casting off inhibitions, as long as the object of the enquiry was validated by astrology. This gave her the opportunity to indulge, in her old age, in much befuddled reminiscence:

CAPRICORN – The symbol of this sign is the goat, and there have been lots of Capricorns I've liked locking horns with . . . A Capricorn guy can hear a girl say, 'No!' but he has good enough sense not to listen . . . AQUARIUS – One of the first men in my life was an Aquarius – I don't recall his name, but I never forget a body! . . . PISCES – The Pisces guy may come on a bit shy at first – but take it from me, he's worth getting to know . . . ARIES – When it

comes to men – and it usually does with me – Aries is one of the strongest
sex signs in the heavens . . . they don't call the guys born under this sign the
Rams for nothing . . .

And so forth. But Mae's broad-mindedness, as can be gauged by a
careful reading of all this frivolity, was subject to various limitations.
Her views on the acceptable aggression of men would hardly be considered 'correct' nowadays, and her fascination with male homosexuality was not matched by her view on lesbians: 'I've always been a
bit put off by lesbians,' she confesses, relating an uncomfortable
encounter with 'a glamour girl I met when I first came to Hollywood'
who came into her dressing room when she was washing her hair and
placed a towel round her head, commenting, 'I've always been an
admirer of yours.' Some have seen a reference here to Marlene
Dietrich, who might well have been the only person eligible at the
time to walk into Mae West's dressing room ready for same-sex
action.

Despite the barrage of names of lovers true or false, famous or
obscure, few emerge properly verified, aside from long-term mentor
James Timony, the accordionist Deiro, the husband Frank Wallace
and much later liaisons with body-builders, most prominently

Mae's second long-term partner, Paul Novak, a.k.a. Chuck Krauser. It might be tempting to compile an encyclopaedia of names of men who would enthusiastically compete to be included. What Mae West was like in bed was a question many would wish to have answered, with one witness testifying to biographer Emily Wortis Leider that she was more mechanical than passionate. Mae herself let it be known that while so many men had indeed come up and seen her some time, none were allowed to stay the entire night, as she required the full length and width of her great bed to stretch out properly when sleeping. Of her lustful techniques, Mae kept her counsel, apart from a sex scene in her unpublished novelization of Sex, Margy Lamont, still under embargo by her Estate. Suffice to say her methods involved a muscular control of the vulva, which 'gave great voluptuous pleasure' to the male recipient of the moment. But fiction apart, some have suggested that Mae's love life might, despite the legend, have been somewhat loveless; that the 'oohs' and 'ahhs' and 'mmms' emitted as she massages the biceps of putative lovers – as she does with the circus strongman and the sucker 'Mr Brown' in *I'm No Angel* – mask a deep malaise, a great insecurity, a fear of a long-term relationship of true rather than bogus intimacy. This easy psychiatry might be belied by the much more obvious fact, often candidly admitted, that the main, supreme object of the adoration and love of Mae West was herself. But unlike other narcissists – a condition practically compulsory for stars and even for less famous performers – there were many other shades and aspects to her private, off-screen persona apart from her penchant for sex with throwaway men. Her kindness and concern for other actors, particularly women, and for working staff and crew was evident during the years on Broadway. Her involvement with prison reform, which would result in a somewhat entertaining sidebar later on in 1941 at San Quentin, was ongoing. Close collaborators like William LeBaron testified, as we have seen, to her highly professional attitude to her work. And above all, we can return to her mainstay, the deep passion that ruled her life for so long: the stubborn struggle of Mae West, the writer.

The script of *I'm No Angel*, in itself, testifies to Mae's continued development as a creator of dynamic characters and witty dialogue. The centre of the piece, of course, was the Mae West character, armed with her arsenal of put-downs and quips, mottoes and slogans for the liberated woman on the make. The underlying social reality is similar to that of her stage plays: the world of Men is one of arrogance, corruption, double-dealing, lies and a wanton pursuit of money and power. The smart gal plays it 'their way', beating them at their own game. Behind the power play there are new ground rules: fair play for a pal, a recognition of the rare buds of honesty and only steal another woman's man if she deserves it, particularly if she is a card-carrying member of the snobbish upper classes. Cheating a little on a lover is, nevertheless, acceptable, as there are so many delectable goods on the market you can't blame a gal who wants to sample.

The morals and immorals of the age-old battle of the sexes continued to imbue Mae's writing. In 1933, various newspaper reports suggested that she was still writing plays. This has been taken to mean some reference either to *Frisco Kate* or the polishing up of performed texts such as *Diamond Lil*, which would indeed be resurrected. Mae's personal archive, however, reveals that she did indeed write a number of new plays, hitherto unrecorded.

Many of these survive as 'unidentified fragments', untitled and undated, which could derive from any point from the late 1920s through the next three decades. An early unproduced treatment for a 'Mae West Talking Picture' is dated 31 January 1933 but credited as a 'Synopsis by Elsie Janis' – a fellow vaudevillian – 'from a suggestion by Al Kaufman', one of Mae's Paramount backers. This has Mae as 'Kate Regan – the All-American Champion Blues Singer', sailing aboard the SS *Olympic* to London for a foreign adventure. This was clearly set aside as unsuitable. Another fragmented script is titled 'Too Many Husbands' and involves 'Della Roscoe, beautiful but crude, intelligent but on the lower rung of Society's ladder', who is going steady with poor songwriter Jack Thurston, while keeping a stable of other lovers, such as aircraft mogul Hamilton J. Power. (The story looks vaguely similar to Warner Brothers' *Gold Diggers of 1933*.) The partial text exists mainly in handwritten sheaves, the unusually broad strokes of Mae's pen suggesting that it was, as she often claimed was her habit, written in bed.

The earliest dated complete work in the files, hitherto unknown, is entitled, in its first version, LOOSE WOMEN. The manuscript is marked 12 December 1933, 'Property of J. A. Timony, Knights Club,

8th Avenue and 50th Street, New York.' This is the first of a number of plays staged by Jim Timony as an independent producer, who would soon transfer to California and open the Hollytown Theatre. When the play was presented in Los Angeles in 1935, it was entitled *Ladies by Request* and credited to one Tom Kavin, although a local paper, the Ontario, California, *Outlook*, called it 'the naughtiest show that has hit town for years . . . Tom Kavin is credited with writing the piece, but at least a score of witnesses whispered during the showing, "it was really written by Mae West, you know."' Another of the plays Mae wrote, presumably gratis, for Timony, *Havana Cruise*, bears the credit 'Jane Mast', Mae's old pseudonym for her transgressive Broadway shows.

Loose Women is a play about 'two husbands who fear their wives have gigolos, and so, in order to trick their mates, they hire two female impersonators to pose as their girl-friends'. The anti-heroes are three businessmen, Marston, Foster and Carter, who are perturbed to find that:

MARSTON: My trusted wife and your truthful wives [have been] entertaining three couch-spiders right here in my home tonight . . . It seems to be quite the thing.

FOSTER: What do you mean?

MARSTON: Wives being entertained. Expressing themselves . . .

FOSTER: Something has got to be done!

The men think about divorce, then decide on their crazy scheme, recruiting three college boys, who will dress up as Betty, Grace and Edna to fool the wives. The reason for the subterfuge is the legal problem that if the men try to fool around with real women, their wives will be able to claim alimony.

The trick descends to farce, as the wives' three muscle-bound gigolos turn up and go for the 'broads', eventually departing in a huff when the fake girls don't respond. The wives then come home and decide that the 'girls' will sleep with them tonight, so as to remove temptation from the men. Much running about between bedrooms and bathrooms ensues, till the men admit their trick and reconcile, introducing the male impersonators as they really are.

The whole project appears to be an attempt by Mae to rework her old theme of toleration of gender-bending as a harmless act, although the issue of homosexuality is fudged because the 'college boys' are only dressing up. There are no great Westian quips and the piece is more akin to the kind of 'wife-swapping' stories that local amateur or stock groups might find playable. The irony is, however, that when Timony staged *Ladies by Request* in 1935, he and the cast of fourteen players were arrested, in a strange echo of Mae and Jim's New York adventures, and charged with 'conducting an illegal theatrical performance', as well as 'failure to obtain a fire license'. The real crime, it seemed, was that the Hollytown Theatre, at 1743 North New Hampshire Avenue, was next door to a church.

Another new-found play is titled 'The Way to Love or Hold That Man or Love 'Em and Leave 'Em, an adaptation by Mae West of "The Cradle Snatchers"' and probably derives from a much later date, as one of its versions is marked 1954. The plot is an inversion of the theme of *Loose Women*: two women think their businessman husbands are cheating, pretending to go out hunting when they are, in fact, out with young girls.

A more contemporary Hollytown playscript, *Clean Beds*, is dated 1936 and marked 'a play in three acts by Youga G. Satovsky (??)'. The tale is set in a men's flophouse during the Depression years and has been recorded in legend as the premier appearance of a very young Anthony Quinn, who was said in one of his obits (*St Petersburg Times*, 4 June 2001) to have 'made his acting début . . . in Mae West's Clean Beds'. The text, however, reads more like cut-down John Steinbeck than Mae West and contains none of her tell-tale dialogue.

The other new Hollytown text, *Havana Cruise*, is unmistakably Mae's. This, too, is undated, but its setting – a yacht cruise to Cuba, with dialogue references to Mussolini but not to World War II – places its writing in the mid-to-late 1930s. A disparate group, including the yacht owner and his wife, two other couples, the owner's young daughter and her college-student fiancée, and an older friend of the owner, are on board, along with an Italian singing teacher, Antonio, who is trying to make love to the ladies. One of the wives, the beautiful Irene, is flirting with the young college student, Roy Brent, lecturing him on the iniquities of marriage:

IRENE: You're awfully old-fashioned, Roy. You should know that slavery is abolished.

BRENT: But marriage isn't slavery.

IRENE: No, but it's the most immoral practice of today.

BRENT: Immoral?

IRENE: Of course. Suppose I would attempt to sell my child to slavery today. What would happen? They'd commit me to an insane asylum. And when I sell myself, my own body, to some man in exchange for food and clothing, and contract myself to the most atrocious form of slavery, for the rest of my life – they call it holy matrimony. Do you follow me? . . .

BRENT: Don't you believe in fidelity, Irene?

IRENE: Fidelity is nothing but a mental state. As long as a husband doesn't know of his wife's infidelity – he's not losing anything. In fact he gains a great deal. His wife becomes more experienced in the art of love.

BRENT: You're awfully straightforward, Irene.

IRENE: Truthful, Roy, truthful. Why should we conceal the facts – from ourselves? If I like the man, if his proximity thrills me, why should I shrink from it? After all, we live but once! (*Presses her almost naked body against his.*)

Caught out by his fiancée kissing the older woman, the depressed student jumps overboard, with other couples slipping into the wrong spouses' embrace, prompting dour thoughts from the men about women: 'Nature meant women to be bad . . . Since the memorable day when Eve ate that apple in the garden of Eden the women were doing nothing but consuming tons of apples daily . . .' Irene is also making out with the yacht's owner, Walker, who denounces her refusal to leave her husband for him: 'Women are made of lies of every possible sort . . . but you are the monstrous example of your monstrous sex!' Irene answers with her own outburst: 'Only a few minutes ago, when you thought I would submit to your wishes, you were ready to crawl at my feet . . . and now – when you see that my duty of a faithful wife would not allow me to do what you wanted – you're branding me a prostitute. Very logical and very manly . . . I hate you men, every one of you. Because you're all so alike and all so stupid – low depraved animals!' Nevertheless, they reconcile, but as a hurricane hits the boat, Irene is lost overboard too. The implication is that Walker has pushed her over, but the yacht's captain, his friend, pretends not to have seen it. 'Shall I enter the accident into the ship's log and notify harbor authorities?' The sinful woman has been suitably punished.

This is the only text (of those I have seen – there might be even more hidden in old shoeboxes!) of Mae West in full rhetorical flight, minus jokes. It is intriguing that she chose to present this 'heavy' mode only anonymously, through Timony's theatre. It provides a window into the darkest side of Mae's feminism, the side that saw the eternal push and pull between men and women as a struggle ever on the brink of breaking into open warfare, with an immense residue of hate on either side. Male pursuit of naked power in the guise of love troubled her more deeply than she would let on, except in these bleak pages, and perhaps sheds a new light on her insistence that, in her life, these power relationships should be reversed. Sexual affection, for Mae, could only be tolerated if no man could control her. Again, since in show business, as in life, we are often enmeshed in contradictions, she had allowed one man, Timony, to turn her tap on and off, to guide her towards her 'sublimation' of the sex urge – her creative work as a writer.

There are many other sketches and texts in the archive, versions of later plays like the 1940s *Catherine Was Great* and *Embassy Row* (a.k.a. 'Come On Up', 'Come On Up, Ring Twice', 'The Magnificent Sinner', 'Perfectly Innocent', 'A Woman of Much Importance', etc.), much later TV projects, and script treatments with titles like 'Men', 'St. Louis Woman', 'The Lady with the Pen' (a.k.a. 'A Woman of Desires' or 'Madame Montmartre') or 'The Bowery Beaut', a four-page synopsis, possibly a movie proposal for a *Diamond Lil* era follow-up:

Velvet Royal is the wife of a gambler, Duke Royal, murdered in a hotel, who turns out to be broke. Spin Tabor is 'a smooth guy' who tries to latch on to her, but she rejects him. She discovers the only part of Duke's property not in hock to creditors is 'a cheap moving picture house down on the Bowery near Chatham Square, where they show two features, a newsreel, a cartoon and a "Deadwood Dick" serial for an admission price of five cents. It is patronized mostly by stumble-bums who go there to get warm and to sleep.'

As it's called the Lucretia, her real name, she takes it on, and finds a young man asleep one night, whom she helps revive. Harvard educated, she takes to him. Spin Tabor tries to put the squeeze on her but the young man ('Happy') remembers a witness to her husband's killing. 'Together, Velvet and Happy comb the joints of the Bowery and Chinatown, and after several adventures locate Spotty (the bum witness)' the killer turns out to be Spin. 'Happy ending. Velvet and Happy.'

One undated script, 'It Takes Love', is credited to 'Jane Mast,

Beverly Arden and Lee Lawrence (Larry Lee),' a drawing-room drama presumably intended for sister Beverly, who by 1933 had joined her in Hollywood, along with brother Jack. Their father joined them in March 1934, to live out his last year on a six-acre ranch in the San Fernando Valley that Mae had purchased some months earlier.

The overall picture is of a writer's workshop, full of proposals and notes, abandoned projects, entire scripts that would lie fallow in agents' offices, reworked versions, proposed films of old plays, such as *The Drag*, *Pleasure Man* and *Sex*, as well as manuscripts of the three published Mae West novels and the unpublished *Margy Lamont*.

In Hollywood, the city of bold dreams and magic tricks, of garish premières and the glittering high life, of Cocoanut Groves and pleasure palaces for the rich and famous, of manifold opportunities for alcoholic or narcotic oblivion, a woman sits, in her apartment, ranch house or office, wielding her pen or typing (despite her assurance that she would never harden her fingers on the keys) or dictating (some typescripts bear the stamp of professional typing services) a non-stop flow of ideas, stories, plots and dialogues. Her scribbled notes, folders of gags and subscribed joke annuals are always at her disposal. When all those who came up to see her have pleasured her to her content and departed, this is the secret Mae, at her labours.

The Devil's Daughter

On 16 September 1933, days after shooting was completed on *I'm No Angel*, James Wingate of the Hays Office sent an unusually warm 'Night Letter' from Los Angeles to his colleague Vincent Hart in New York:

JUST SAW ANGEL PICTURE STOP WE THINK IT IS SATISFACTORY WITH EXCEPTION VERY FEW LINES STILL UNDER DISCUSSION STOP ON THE WHOLE MUCH BETTER THAN WE EXPECTED

On 4 October, Mr Hart wrote even more enthusiastically to another colleague, McKenzie: 'It is a knockout all the way through . . . The songs have been toned down, and while many of the gags border on questionable dialogue, the fadeouts are so arranged, that most of the suggestions are left to the imagination . . . The picture, in my opinion, which may receive some objection, will be one of the biggest box offices of the season. I'm for it, irrespective!'

But despite the strange sight of Will Hays' executives suddenly turning into the Mae West fan club, this sunshine was not to last. On 23 February 1934, having read the first drafts of the screenplay for Mae's next picture, 'It Ain't No Sin', the Board officially wrote to Paramount executive A. M. Botsford that 'the general flavor of the story, in our judgement, is highly offensive, and the general story factors based, as they are, upon seduction, gambling, robbery and arson, together with the brutal treatment accorded one of the characters, which is so definitely part of the plot, suggests to us the type of picture which we, in this office, would be compelled to reject, if and when the finished picture is presented for our examination'.

What had happened between the autumn of 1933 and the deep winter of 1934 to sour the atmosphere between Hays and Mae?

In fact, the runes were cast some months earlier, not long after Paramount's 'Voluntary Petition in Bankruptcy', which marked a particularly bad tremor in the tectonic shifts of the Depression. The company itself claimed to be solvent but made the move to conserve its assets against multiple lawsuits converging from many states and foreign countries on the ailing corporation. The $4.5 million gross from the two Mae West movies in 1933 was helpful but hardly crucial to a corporation with liabilities of $55 million and assets of $153 million. Warner Brothers, Fox and Universal were under similar pressure. Paramount's petition was filed barely a week after the new Democratic President, Franklin D. Roosevelt, was sworn in, promising his famous 'New Deal'. Within three months, reforming legislation was passed in the fields of banking, agriculture, home finance and labour.

The Industrial Recovery Act, approved by Congress in June, directly affected the motion-picture industry. The act specifically called for regulatory codes for production, distribution and exhibition all to be welded together into one industry code. It was not clear whether studio and craft unions would participate in drawing up this code, and disputes over this would lead to a strike by six thousand union members in July. The National Association of Theater Owners' President, Ed Kuykendall, led the call for the industry to set down the code before the government stepped in to impose it. The basis of the Production Code had been in place, as we have noted, since 1930. The provisions regulated 'the picturization of crime, sex, vulgarity, obscenity, dances, profanity, indecent costumings, religion, national feelings, salacious titles, hangings, third degree methods, brutality, gruesomeness, branding of people or animals, cruelty to children or animals, surgical operations, and the like', to quote the *Motion Picture Herald* of 17 June. What was going to happen was that this Code would now be an integral part of the working practices of the industry; in effect, part of the Roosevelt reforms. Something which had been arranged as a voluntary mechanism for the motion-picture producers to defend themselves against individual states' often conflicting strictures and keep the werewolf of scandal from the door would now be part of the law of the land.

This provided an opportunity for the hardliners of the Hays Office to clamp down on what they believed was an unacceptable laxity in their own ranks – and particularly with regard to the films of Mae West. James Wingate, the successor to Colonel Joy, was fingered as the main culprit. He was also, apparently, suspected by some in the business to be anti-Semitic. Perhaps he was merely soft on blondes. In the event, he was kept on but replaced in the hot seat by Joseph Ignatius Breen. Where Wingate had been, in the views of the Board, an effete academic, Breen was an Irish Catholic fighter. He had been a journalist, had seen service in Europe in the Great War and was a close associate of Martin Quigley, the devout Catholic editor of the *Motion Picture Herald* and progenitor of the original Code. Motion pictures, Quigley believed, had to be conceived in moral terms, as an entertainment that could 'shape the bodies and souls of human beings'. In this he appeared to agree with Stalin, though he would have been appalled to have this pointed out. The movies should produce a 'correct' entertainment for their audiences, the American masses. The Presbyterian Will Hays agreed wholeheartedly and adopted the Code as his own.

Throughout the summer of 1933, Catholic newspapers led demands for a boycott of 'immoral motion pictures'. An Episcopal Committee on Motion Pictures was formed in November 1933, proposing that pressure be put on 'financial institutions like the Chase Bank of New York to prevent it from lending money to the producers of filthy pictures'. A 'Legion of Decency' was formed to campaign against 'salacious motion pictures which . . . are corrupting public morals and promoting a sex mania in our land'. Earlier in the year, William Randolph Hearst himself had weighed in, calling for a federal censorship to save the movies from 'degeneracy'. Addressing the argument that the public demanded what he called 'vulgar and lewd pictures', Hearst declared that 'there may be an element of the public which patronize prurience and vulgarity, but the screen should appeal to the better element of the public and endeavor by constant presentation of pictures of high quality and character and equally high entertainment value to educate the lower element of the public out of its debased tastes'. (Of course, Hearst, Quigley and Breen were not alone: throughout the world moral guardians of disparate political regimes, from the democratic British Parliament to Japanese autocrats to Soviet commissars, demanded the same thing.)

Into this maelstrom Emanuel Cohen, William LeBaron, A. M. Botsford and the other malefactors at Paramount Pictures submitted their early synopsis and script of Mae West's new film. They were well aware, of course, of the vice tightening around the movies and had their own strategy in place. They were, after all, powerful men, with the means and resources to make things happen rather than, as was the case with the Board, to stop things happening on the brink. For her next picture, Mae was given a top-rank director, Leo McCarey, an early mentor of Laurel and Hardy and veteran of the Hal Roach studios before moving to Paramount. He had just completed his bout with the Marx Brothers in *Duck Soup* and was to tangle with W. C. Fields, also in 1934, in *Six of a Kind*. As cinematographer, they engaged Karl Struss, who had received an Oscar (shared with Charles Rosher) for F. W. Murnau's *Sunrise*, to help recreate the ambience for another foray into the 'Gay Nineties' period.

As far as the censors were concerned, Cohen had a cunning strategy. He would start out with a script that was outrageous by the Board's guidelines and then grind the Board executives down by their own procedure of arguing every dot and line, eventually to emerge, so he hoped, with a version that was acceptable to them and not too distant from the one the producers wanted to achieve in the first place. Rather than be cautious with the new, fresh and furious bull, he rushed forward with red cape waving to provoke it.

The main provocation consisted of the opening scenes of the first draft, which an early treatment described thus:

IT AIN'T NO SIN

In police headquarters, three detectives are examining the records on Ruby Carter. Not only are they impressed with her picture, but, also, with her extraordinary luck in getting out of police scraps. Suspected of murder, she was not indicted for lack of evidence; arrested for possessing stolen bonds, the bank president refused to prosecute; when a millionaire disappeared from his yacht on which she was the sole guest – she inherited some of his money – and was acquitted. She was so notorious that now – years later – she is still cashing in on it. She is a star in a burlesque show in rowdy St. Louis of the middle 1890's.

It would be difficult to imagine anything more certain to make Joseph Ignatius Breen's brain explode and bile pour forth from his mouth like lava. Far from toning down the 'Diamond Lil'-like character that had caused so much ire among the reformers, this narrative was making her into a multiple fraudster, thief and actual murderess for financial gain. On and on the transgressions go: Ruby encourages a prizefighter, the Tiger Kid, to fall in love with her, telling her black maid after her show: 'Unwrap the body, Jasmine. I been modest long

THE DEVIL'S DAUGHTER

enough.' In her room, while she flirts with the Tiger, 'their kiss is interrupted by the arrival of Ruby's song writer, a scratchy, sniffy sort of fellow who twitches about until he gets into the next room "for a glass of water." He comes back a new man, full of vim and vigor with everything under control.' Tiger's coach, miffed at the attention Tiger gives Ruby, sets him up by getting one of his minions to pretend to be familiar with her. Tiger breaks off his affair and Ruby decamps to New Orleans, where she is wanted for a new show. On the boat, she is 'as usual the center of attraction to all the men aboard, and the object of disdain on the part of the women. But Ruby doesn't care, even when they say, "Five men were seen entering her stateroom and none coming out."'

We are hardly one third of the way into the picture and already multiple screaming violations of the Production Code have been marked. To top this, one of the songs proposed for the movie and sent to the Hays Office was entitled 'Creole Man (It Ain't No Sin)', with music by Harry Revel and lyrics by Mack Gordon thus:

This is where you become a King or Queen,
On a tiny puff o' reefer
Known as marihuana, you puff –
Then you puff some more . . .
Strong lovin' arms
Then holds me and turns the heat on
That's the kind of love I'd never want to cheat on
Oh – I'm talking 'bout a Creole man –
Warm, high brown skin
The kind of face to share your bread and gin with
The kind of guy it's heavenly to sin with
Oh – I'm talking 'bout a Creole man . . .

'You Don't Know What You're Doin' to Me', also by the above, included the lines: 'Cuddle up and love me like nobody can / I'll make you forget you're a married man' and 'Why do I sigh when I look at you the way you do / I can see the devil in your eyes / how can I resist you / (hum:) Mmm . . . Baby start in warmin' me / Do it, do it / start that certain stormin' me . . .' and so forth.

A. M. Botsford sent this incendiary material off to Breen on 17 February 1934, stating that, 'we are quite aware that this script contains many lines which are censorably dangerous and it is our intention to correct these danger points, which will be done in the next

253

script'. Breen responded with the 23 February letter quoted earlier in this chapter, but when Paramount sent him a revised 'white' script, on 7 March Breen responded even more ferociously:

Dear Mr Botsford,

We have read with very great care the white script (dated March 2, 1934) of your production, It Ain't No Sin, and we are gravely concerned about it. The story, as we read it, is a vulgar and highly offensive yarn which is quite patently a glorification of prostitution and violent crime without any compensating moral values of any kind. From the outset, the leading character is definitely established as a person with a long and violent criminal record who displays all the habits and practices of the prostitute, aids in the operation of a dishonest gambling house, drugs a prize-fighter, robs her employer, deliberately sets fire to his premises and, in the end, goes off scot free in company with her illicit lover who is a self-confessed criminal, a thief and a murderer.

This script suggest [sic] the kind of picture which is certain to violate the provisions of our Production Code for any one – or all – of the following reasons:

(A) Vulgarity and obscenity
(B) Glorification of crime, criminals
(C) Glorification of a prostitute
(D) The general theme of the story which is definitely 'on the side of evil and crime' and 'against goodness, decency and law'.

The treatment of this story is certain to 'throw the sympathy of the audience with sin, crime, wrong-doing and evil.'

Because of all this, we deem it our duty to say to you that a picture based upon this script is certain to be the kind of picture which we, in this office, in the dispensation of our responsibility under the provisions of the 'Resolution for Uniform Interpretation' of the Production Code will be compelled to reject in toto, if, and when, the picture is presented for our approval.

With kindest regards, I am,
Sincerely yours,
Joseph I. Breen

Breen understood the situation clearly as a declaration of war by Paramount, as an inter-office memo passed between Breen, Wingate and their colleague Geoffrey Shurlock on the same day reveals: 'The company officials, especially Mr Botsford and Mr Hammell, sought to persuade us that the reading of the script suggested a very difficult picture, but argued that deft treatment, which they proposed to give the script, and their proposal to play the whole story in a light, humorous vein would result in an inoffensive picture of high entertainment quality . . . We warned the company of the danger in the situation. They advised us that they propose to go ahead pretty much along the lines suggested in the script, although they did say that a number of details which appeared to us to be objectionable would be removed from the script.'

On 13 March, the Board objected to another song, the supposedly innocuously titled 'Pom Tiddley Om Pom', as sung in the film by the 'Beef Trust Chorus' burlesque girls. Even this was seen as subversive by Breen:

Dear Mr Botsford,
It is difficult for us to suggest our definite reaction to the lyrics of 'Pom Tiddley Om Pom' to be sung by the Beef Trust Chorus and the Comedian in your proposed production, It Ain't No Sin. Its acceptability under the provisions of our Production Code will depend almost entirely upon the manner in which the song is sung and the action accompanying the music. A critical reading of the lyrics suggests danger to us. If, in the rendition of the song, the action of the girls, or comedian, is such as to give to the lines a salacious, or otherwise unsavoury, connotation, the entire song may be adjudged a Code violation and, as such, will have to be deleted.
We respectfully suggest that you exercise very great care in staging this number in order that we may have no difficulty with it later on.

Oddly enough, Breen had already okayed another proposed song, a 'Spiritual', music and lyrics by A. Johnstone and S. Coslow, which was to provide Mae with probably the most poignant blues song in her entire canon, although Breen was later to advise Paramount that in Britain censors invariably deleted scenes of 'Negro spirituals', presumably for racial reasons. A barrage of ammendations to the various script versions fired across the lines met with continued objections. It could not have escaped the notice of the Mae-watchers on the Board that the 'Tiger Kid' plot line in the story derived from Mae's racially transgressive play The Constant Sinner, and this would have put them even more on their guard. As is the case with Board documents, the objections are detailed as to specific actions, lines and words: 'In the scene in which Scratch first makes his appearance, you will have to exercise great care lest it be suggested that Scratch is a hophead . . . Page B-7: The business of Ace testing "the bed with his hand" is censorable . . . Page B-12: Ruby's line "Yeah, give 'em all my address" is censorable . . . Page B-15: Ruby's line "Looks more like an old mistress" is highly questionable . . . Page B-28: Ruby's line "Don't try to get to heaven in one night" should be deleted . . . Page B-30: Ruby's line "It pays to be good – but it don't pay much," should be deleted . . . Page D-3: Ruby's line "I ain't the only woman who has got one of those things" should be deleted . . .' and so on and so forth.

On 28 March, Will Hays wrote to Paramount boss Adolph Zukor, warning him that his executives appeared ready to proceed with a movie that, if shot as they wished, the Board would be compelled 'to reject in toto if and when the picture is presented for our approval'. Breen added: 'I know your personal interest in the matter and the company's purpose to protect itself and the industry against the difficulties, and I am confident of your cooperation.'

Zukor appears to have declined to put a brake on his executives, as the picture had already begun shooting in the studio. Through April and May the censors continued to argue over specific scenes, objecting to a burlesque-show sequence (which is not in the finished film) in which the 'Queen' – presumably played by Mae – 'slowly raises her dress, removes her garter, and throws it towards the Lieutenant'.

Even with these agreed deletions, the picture as presented to the Board on 2 June was rejected. Under the Production Code provisions, the studio had the right of appeal to a jury of the Board's production committee, presumably the same people who had turned it down.

Emanuel Cohen now embarked on an extremely risky strategy, requesting that the Board withhold the news of its decision to reject the film and refrain from writing him an official letter of rejection on the grounds that he was making several further changes to the picture that would render it acceptable. This Breen thought most sneaky:

INTERNAL MEMO
I think you will readily see the danger to our entire machinery if such a plan is followed in all studios . . . I am considerably concerned about the turn of events in the past week or ten days. There is much 'under cover' work going on that smacks to me of a desire on the part of the studios definitely to out-smart and outwit the machinery of the Code, and to fly a lone kite in the matter of production, without any counsel, guidance or reference to New York offices.

The general attitude we have found here with regard to the public criticism which has become so widespread, is to belittle it all, to sneer at our critics and to continue to make pictures to suit ourselves. I am deeply concerned about it all.

Breen presented Paramount with twenty-three specific points on which the Board had rejected the movie on the basis of Code principles:

Section III of these General Principles states that 'Law, natural or human, shall not be ridiculed; nor shall sympathy be created for its violation' . . . under Section II . . . under the general heading of 'Sex' the Code ordains that 'Pictures shall not infer that low forms of sex relationship are the accepted or common thing;' that 'excessive and lustful kissing, lustful embraces, suggestive postures and gestures are not to be shown.' We feel that these principles are violated in numerous instances throughout the picture.'

The twenty-three points included those quoted above and then some, including more Ruby lines, such as her reply to the question 'Is fighting your favourite sport?' – 'Please don't embarrass me' – and 'My morals are all right . . . Take it easy, you'll last longer.' On 4 June, Breen cabled Adolph Zukor:

OUR JUDGEMENT IN REJECTION YOUR PRODUCTION QUOTE IT AIN'T NO SIN UNQUOTE IS FORCED UPON US BY GENERAL LOW TONE IMMORAL AND CRIMINAL THEME OF STORY AND ITS LACK OF SUFFICIENT COMPENSATING MORAL VALUES STOP.

This finally galvanized Zukor into rapid action, prompting a quick massacre in the cutting room and a prompt reappraisal, re-view and acceptance of the film on 6 June, with Breen writing to another Paramount executive:

Mr John Hammell,
Paramount Studios, Hollywood, Calif.

Dear Mr Hammell
We had the pleasure this morning of witnessing a projection room showing of your picture, It Ain't No Sin, and I am sending you this to say that it is our considered judgement that the picture conforms to the provision of our Production Code and contains little that is reasonably censorable.

Hays man McKenzie cabled Breen from New York:

I AM TRANSMITTING TO YOU MISTER ZUKOR'S EARNEST REQUEST THAT THERE BE NO PUBLICITY ON MATTER ABOUT WHICH YOU HAVE COMMUNICATED WITH HIM STOP I ASSURED HIM THAT WOULD BE ALSO YOUR OWN EARNEST DESIRE.

Paramount's 'little Napoleon' had sorted out his rebellious executives. The new Mae West picture was made safe for the good citizens of the United States, under a new title: *Belle of the Nineties*.

In all this storm and raging, Mae West played no great part. She might have been consulted on this or that line change, but although the movie bears the credit 'Story and Screenplay by Mae West,' others would have undone and retightened the nuts and bolts of Paramount's revisions.

The main battle was a strategic one, with Paramount's west-coast executives testing the ground of Breen's new satrapy at the Hays Office. Some have seen this as a skimpily hidden war of the Christians and the Jews, with the anti-Semitic forces of the legions of

Mae and her Paramount mentor, Emanuel Cohen

Mae West between the Paramount executives (John Hammell on her right)

'decency' battling the moguls who had come, at the turn of the century, out of the ghettos of Europe to shape the new movie medium. Neal Gabler, in his intriguing thesis on 'How the Jews Invented Hollywood', argues that studio bosses like Harry Cohn, William Fox, Carl Laemmle, Louis B. Mayer, Adolph Zukor and the Warner brothers, Jack and Harry, were most comfortable in presenting an assimilated melting-pot image, with a new American identity overriding the chaotic diversity of an immigrants' nation. Nativist zealots always saw this diversity as a threat and, as in Joseph 'Holy Joe' McKee's theatre-bashing rants in New York, accused outside forces of polluting a pristine America. Catholic moralizers, representing mainly Irish and Italian newcomers, were late converts to this trend, which had, in the nineteenth century, regarded Catholics themselves as the very worst offenders. But what united the religious reformers most strongly was sex. Assertive women, challenging the procreative axioms of God, were perhaps the most dangerous strangers of all in this presumed America of true believers.

First and foremost, however, the studio bosses were businessmen, tasked, in a period of economic crisis, with saving their enterprises from financial failure. In movies this meant pleasing their audiences, the old adage of 'giving the public what it wants'. And the public, not only that 'lower element' denounced by Hearst as patrons of 'prurience and vulgarity', clearly wanted Mae West.

The trailer for *Belle of the Nineties* promised 'MAE WEST AS YOU WANT TO SEE HER.' This, of course, would only be partly true, as the released film could not help but bear the scars of its last-minute cuts and deletions. But if the movie that emerged from this process was disjointed, this was largely due to Paramount's decision to use it as a battlefield in the first place. The introductory sequence in the first draft treatment, as quoted earlier, with three 1890s detectives relating Ruby Carter's explosive past, could not possibly have been written with any expectation that it would ever appear on the screen, despite some of Mae's own 'dialogue notes' for the movie, which suggest a more hard-boiled character than we now have in the film, with lines like: 'Don't ask me to follow the straight and narrow, it's too slippery,' or 'I suppose you consider yourself a great man-killer?' 'Sure, and those I don't kill I cripple.'

At the very centre of the movie, coming after her misadventures with the prizefighting Tiger Kid and the ruthless New Orleans club owner Ace Lamont, lies Mae's powerful blues lament, delivered on a balcony overlooking a black evangelical meeting and intercut with a spiritual chant designed to cast out the devil – 'Pray, chillun, and you'll be saved / You're going to weep no more / Dat's what the good book says . . .' – as she presents the most melancholy moment in the entire Mae West oeuvre:

> *I'm gonna drown down in these troubled waters,*
> *They're creepin' 'round my soul,*
> *They're way beyond control,*
> *They'll wash my sins away before the morning.*
> *They say that I'm one of the Devil's daughters,*
> *They look at me with scorn,*
> *I'll never hear that horn,*
> *I'll be underneath the water Judgement morning.*

Oh Lord, am I to blame?
Must I bow my head in shame
If people go around scandalizin' my name?

Though this appears, in hindsight, to be a direct reference to the furore surrounding the movie, not to speak of future Mae West projects, it was, as we have seen, present in the planning as early as 23 February 1934, when it was submitted to the Hays Office and accepted by Breen. This protest at being misunderstood by the moralizers, springing from the deep sediment of Mae's long history of having her name scandalized from the days of the shimmy through *Sex* and *Diamond Lil*, is consistent with the character of the free spirit that she had been constructing as her stage and screen persona for well over a decade. It does not, however, fit with the character as presented in the movie's first draft, suggesting that it was the producers rather than Mae who devised that presentation.

Other decisions, both in script and casting, made *Belle of the Nineties* less than the gem it might have been. The Tiger Kid plot itself, deriving from *The Constant Sinner*, is fairly banal, and the actor chosen to play the part, Roger Pryor, did not project the required charisma or even hunkiness to be a convincing object of Mae/Ruby's desire (though he appears to have been a minor heart-throb of the time – his début movie was entitled *Moonlight and Pretzels*). The 'Cary Grant' part, that of the rival suitor, rich New Orleans playboy Brooks Claybourne, was played by John Mack Brown. Brown had been a football player described as 'the famous All-American halfback who won the Southern Conference championship for Alabama with a play that sent fifty-thousand onlookers into tremors of excitement'. In a September 1934 puff in *Motion Picture*, entitled 'Making Love to Mae West is Like a Football Game', he couldn't contain his enthusiasm:

'It's a tingle that goes up your spine and down again, for all the world like the moment you're crouched on the one-yard line, waiting for the ball to be snapped,' Brown said, searching for a way to explain Mae's effect on the blood pressure of a healthy male specimen like himself.

'And after finishing a scene with her, you feel as if you had made a touchdown against the entire field. The only difference is you have no kick coming! After a couple of hours in a huddle before the camera with Mae West, there have been so many little shivers of excitement romping over the gridiron of your emotions that you feel positively limp!'

The piece even included a graphic 'Score Chart' showing the West–Brown encounter as a football play. *Motion Picture* couldn't get enough of these sporting metaphors: 'Mae West would get by fine as a football coach. She knows how to get teamwork out of the boys. She plans plays that will romp through opposition. She never gets her signals mixed. She never calls for a substitute. She knows how to skim the sidelines without getting out of bounds.'

Indeed. The press book for the film was full of similar hoopla, including a vintage piece of flannel headed 'Mae West's Sound Kisses Stun Sound Men':

Mae West's kisses give her studio-sound-men headaches!

The trio of expert sound technicians, who recorded Miss West's dialogue for 'Belle of the Nineties' . . . coming to the . . . Theater, found the blonde siren's voice a 'cinch' to handle. But when she started her love scenes with her leading man, Roger Pryor, their troubles began.

'Smack!' went the first kiss, and E. L. Kerr asked for a second 'take' so that he could pull the microphone back a bit and diminish the aural result of Mae's osculating.

'Smack!' went the second – and Harry Mills, the sound mixer, had too much volume sizzling through the wires into his sound booth. Director Leo McCarey cautioned Miss West to take it easy, and she agreed. But a third attempt shocked the recording apparatus again.

Miss West, a bit nonplussed, informed all present that if she kissed her leading man at all she would have to do it roundly – let the sound fall how and where it may.

Kerr and Mills finally solved the problem by wrapping a piece of silk around the microphone.

Returning to the period design of *She Done Him Wrong*, the art directors, Hans Dreier and Bernard Herzbrun, surpassed their predecessors in reconstructing the decor and props of the 'Gay Nineties'. The opening scene of the movie is one of Hollywood's finest reconstructions of an early burlesque show, complete with the overweight mighty-thighed ladies of the 'Beef Trust Chorus' and the comedian, played by Tyler Brooke, who delivers the 'Tiddley Om Pom' song with just enough winking and nudging to poke the fine gentlemen of the Hays Office in the ribs. This is followed by Mae's strangest and perhaps most memorable entrance, in a series of tableaux illustrating a male singer's warbling of 'My

American Beauty'. Shimmering in the spotlight, Mae appears first as a butterfly, then a bat, then a sparkling rose, a spider in the midst of a web, and finally, most notable of all, as the Statue of Liberty, with crown and torch and clad in the stars and stripes. This, of course, brings the house down, including the enthusiastic Tiger Kid, who has been skiving off his training to worship at Ruby Carter's all-American altar.

The best parts of the movie are, as ever, the Mae West quips and songs. Some of the quips have stubbornly survived the Breen massacre, such as Ruby commenting when shown one of Ace Lamont's 'old masters' in his plush 'Sensation House': 'Looks more like an old

mistress to me . . .'; and a barrage at the gambling saloon, surrounded by fawning men:

'Do I bother you if I look over your shoulder?'
'No, do I bother you?'
'Are you in town for good?'
'I expect to be here, but not for good.'
'May we ask what types of men you prefer?'
'Just two, domestic and foreign.'
'Where are you stopping during your visit here?'
'Stoppin' at nothin'.'

And the old saw, taken directly from the joke-book repertoire: 'It's better to be looked over than overlooked.' As well as her fine riposte to Ace Lamont's 'I must have you, your golden hair, your fascinating eyes, alluring smile and lovely arms . . .': 'Wait a minute, is this a proposal or are you just takin' inventory?'

Some of Mae's quips are reserved for her repartee with her maid, this time one lone servant, Jasmine, played by her real-life maid Libby Taylor:

'Mr Brooks sure been good to you. Wasn't you nervous when he gave you all them presents?'
'No, I was calm, and collected.'
'What kind of husband do you think I should git?'
'Why don't you take a single man an' leave the husbands alone.'

For her New Orleans numbers, Mae racked up one stubborn victory: the hiring of Duke Ellington and his band, whooping it up in a rare appearance in a mainstream picture of this era. The studio was said to have objected to the expense, saying they could cast cheap black extras and dub the music, but at least in this Mae prevailed. Thus enabled, Mae could deliver the classic blues number her New York maid Bea Jackson had brought forth from Perry Bradford's Harlem-era party back in 1923: 'He Was Her Man, But He Came to See Me Sometime'. Mae belts out the song's mischievous lines dressed all in white, with perhaps the largest feather ever seen on her hat: 'I had a good man in Memphis but the fool he laid down an' died / Because his old woman, she hung a knife in his side / now he was her man, but he came to see me sometime / I lived six flights up, and he was sure willin' to climb . . .'

Butterfly Mae ('Belle of the Nineties')

The Hays Code-busting 'Creole Man' has been dropped, but Mae's other songs imbue the film with a sense of melancholy that is unique in all of Mae's movie work: the poignant torch song – 'My old flame / I can't even think of his name . . .' – and her 'Negro Spiritual' lament. In early drafts, it is clear that Mae was supposed to deliver this in the midst of Brother Eben's evangelical prayer meeting, but the racial exigencies evidently required that she be separated from it, at least in space. McCarey solved this problem by superimposing her singing close-up on long-shots of the congregants, who have been shot against a studio curtain which reflects the rippling river as shadows behind them, their waving hands and heads bobbing in ecstasy framing her face. The scene is highly unsettling, as the chanters shake and shiver in their exorcism of the devil, projected by the optical tricks and cutting almost as if they were Mae's familiars, calling out her own demons from the very depths of her soul.

A Member in Good Standing

In 1934, Mae West became the highest-paid performer in the US, bar none, with an annual income, according to the press, of $399,166. The next female performer in line was Marlene Dietrich with a mere $145,000, while among the males, none could muster more than W. C. Fields's $155,083.33 – we may be sure he collected those 33 cents! Chaplin took in a mere $143,000, though as he owned his own business, he was paying his own salary. Cary Grant came in way down the list with a measly $39,708.

Belle of the Nineties was not as big a hit as *She Done Him Wrong* and *I'm No Angel*, both of which were to remain on the books as Paramount's highest-grossing pictures for the early years of the 1930s, thus establishing her as a major studio asset whatever the Production Board might say or do.

Mae's status as a favourite of gossip columnists and fan magazines was well established by November of 1932, when *Screen Play* magazine highlighted the 'Dynamite Lady – Mae West, the girl who brought sex to Broadway, invades Hollywood with sensational results!' Mae was already holding forth on her favourite subject – MEN: 'Clark Gable? Oh, really, he has about as much sex appeal as a dish of left-over potato salad!' Not all of Mae's pronouncements were to stand the test of time . . . 'One of the greatest compliments paid me,' she told the magazine, reversing her previous lament on the same account, 'is that to most people I am off-stage what I am on; a deep dyed hussy without a moral in the world. I am glad people think so, it is a tribute to my art but as a matter of fact I live quite a decent, quiet moral life. I am a showman and I know that the public wants sex in their entertainment and I give it to them.'

Picture Play, in April 1933, took up the same theme: 'Call her sexy, call her siren. Call her savage. Say that she's a wild woman – the last word, and Mae West will adore you. Innuendos are the grist in her mill. Being a woman they talk about is her main object in life. It's the secret of her success.'

In January 1934, *Motion Picture Classic* began its serialization of Ruth Biery's *The Private Life of Mae West*, while other magazines, like *Screen Play*, added titbits of their own, poking into her morning boudoir: 'She has a most unusual way of dressing. First she puts on her stockings and shoes. Then she combs her hair and puts on her hat. This makes a pretty picture. Come up some time and see.' Mmmm! 'All her dresses are cut very low below the neck. Mae knows how to put herself on display. Her ears are really beautiful – if you ever look up there.' To spoil the dream, *Screen Play* added: 'Her hair isn't as blonde as it appears. For many of her scenes in pictures she wears a wig.'

Libby Taylor, Mae's maid, weighed in with more personal details in *Hollywood Magazine*:

Mae West designed every bit of furniture in her bedroom. A color scheme of gold, green and a very delicate shade of pink is carried out in everything in the room, pillows, drapes, counterpane, upholstery – even the picture frames and toilet articles.

Although Miss West is tiny and dainty, she does not surround herself with dainty things. She likes big things, 'Something you can get your hands on,' she explains. She has large perfume bottles, large cream jars, large powder boxes. Her daintiness running to materials and colors only.

Mae West always has her breakfast in bed, dressed in one of her many pretty negligees, with lacy pillows behind her back.

'An' is she a pitcha foh ya eye?' Don't ask Libby, unless you really want to know, 'Yus suh!'

For breakfast Mae, according to Libby, has mostly fruits, a little toast, maybe a little egg or creamed chicken and coffee . . . After breakfast, she wiscecracks all the way to the bathroom. She prefers a tub bath with plenty of hot water, scented soap and oodles of bath salts. And Libby thinks that's all right, 'Ah likes 'em mahself 'couse they smells so good.'

Libby was not forthcoming about other matters of gossip, the only man mentioned in her piece being the chauffeur who conveyed her lady to the studio – 'the short distance between the car and Mae's dressing room requires from fifteen minutes to half an hour, not that Miss West is slow – you remember how she warbled, "I'm a fast moving gal what likes it slow," – but because everyone from the gateman to the president knows and adores her and isn't afraid to stop her long enough to say so'.

Motion Picture, in November 1933, had been more forthcoming about Mae and the male sex, headlining 'Three Men – and ALL Kissed by MAE WEST!' This was apparently the new proud boast in Hollywood, though all three samples quoted had, in fact, smooched her on the stage. *The Constant Sinner*'s Arthur Vinton recalled that on stage was not as off: 'She was generous in the extreme to other members of the cast . . . To my knowledge she never made, or even thought about making, a single pass at any man in the cast . . . I was intrigued by this, and, one day, on the train, going to Chicago or

Kissed by Mae West? With Noel Coward and Cary Grant

somewhere with the show, I said to her, just for fun, "Miss West, I'd like to know – do you like me or dislike me?" She looked at me, with a flicker of amusement in her eyes, and said, honestly, "I've never given it a thought."'

Jack La Rue, who played the Spanish lover in *Diamond Lil*, claimed he had fallen in love with her after the first rehearsal for their clinch, when Mae had drawled at him, 'Not bad – not bad.' La Rue said: 'They have said that Mae West is not a lady. Well, what is a lady but one who does considerate, unselfish things delicately and quietly? . . . I remember a girl in our company who got into trouble. She was in a bad way, afraid of her family finding out about her, out of money, out of luck. Mae fixed everything for her, saved her reputation and her very life, really. That girl, to-day, is married and living a happy, successful life and she has no one but Mae West to thank for it.'

Russell Hardie, another *Constant Sinner* smoochee recently arrived in Hollywood, claimed Mae West had taught him his most important lesson – 'never to lose my nerve'. Having 'worked in the medium of sex (a tabu subject so often) and off-color stuff' that 'might have landed her in a burlesque show', she had taken 'the defects she had and made them assets. But she was shrewd enough to make what she had one hundred per cent.'

A couple of issues later *Motion Picture* was making merry with Mae's supposed rivalry with Marlene Dietrich, although La Dietrich scoffed at the 'latest rumor that I am jealous of Mae West'. On the contrary, after the preview of *She Done Him Wrong* she was 'so thrilled by this new, arresting, dynamic personality . . . I recognized Mae West as a star before anyone else did. I met her before I left for Europe and we became friends.' Miss Dietrich, it was said, had sent 'bushels of flowers' to Mae, though no mention was made of the tale that she had slunk into Mae's dressing room to fondle her hair.

The next supposed rival for the gossip mill was Katharine Hepburn: 'Mae West take a back seat! Katharine Hepburn has you backed off the map when it comes to sex attraction!' This in June 1934, *Motion Picture* comparing 'West with her swivel-chair walk, her billowing undulation' and 'the hollow-cheeked Hepburn, tragic of mouth, firm of brow, lithe, spirit like . . . anything but a vamp'. A local psychologist, Dr Arthur Frank Payne, had it all figured out: 'The average repressed male watches a Mae West picture and reacts pleasurably. To him she is a woman who is flamboyant, unbridled.

She gratifies his sub-conscious . . . Not so with Miss Hepburn. Here is a complex personality, stern, self-disciplined. She is beautiful and apparently cold. Presto – his interest is aroused!'

'WILL I LAST? ASKS MAE WEST' in June, or rather *Motion Picture*'s Maude Latham asked provocatively in her place, only to get the tart answer: 'The popularity of Mae West will continue just as long as Mae West herself wants it to continue . . . "When I lose my stamina, when I am no longer determined to please, I will be through with pictures, and not until then!"'

For the little girl who always wanted to be in the spotlight, Hollywood was the unmovable spot upon which it seemed she could shimmy for ever, until dragged physically off her podium. Censored on screen or not, she was never long out of the news. Her pet monkey Boogie expired in September 1933, allegedly of poisoning, Mae whispered darkly, mourning the loss of the only primate who could stay overnight and share her breakfast table: 'He had his meals at his own little kitchen table, ate his food with a spoon, would obtain articles and bring them to Miss West at her command and was able to chatter responses to conversation.' As well as peel her grapes. He was buried at the Los Angeles Pet Cemetery, accompanied by 'a little group of mourners . . . A tribute to his loyalty to his mistress will be voiced.' Shades of Evelyn Waugh's funeral-home satire, *The Loved One* . . .

The 1932 jewel heist continued to be good for headlines trumpeting new developments, as a 'well-known night life character', Harry Voiler, tried to obtain $5,000 from her in return for information on the whereabouts of her stolen treasures. Voiler was arrested in December 1933 along with one Morris Cohen of Detroit and Edward 'Happy' Friedman, a gambler from the east coast. Voiler had once been a manager for Texas Guinan, and the whole affair had echoes of old gangster links. Voiler and his wife had, according to the cops, been friends of Mae West. 'I have known Voiler for a number of years,' Mae told a grand jury that, happily, was indicting someone other than herself. 'He has now turned out to be a snake in the grass.' Friedman confessed but soon repudiated his confession, accusing police of using 'the third degree'. District Attorney Burton Fitts was then accused of slapping defence attorney William J. Clark in the face. The grand jury soon indicted Friedman for another hold-up. Meanwhile, Mae made a radio plea for the poorer children of Los

Angeles, who had to be funded out of a 'community chest'. 'MAE WEST URGES CHEST AID,' proclaimed a possibly unintentional double-edged headline.

In October 1933, Mae had been made a 'Kentucky Colonel', an honorary commission vouchsafed for show-business and other luminaries by the well-named Governor Laffoon. Even Mae's sister, Beverly, was making the news, due to her engagement to 'a wealthy Parisian perfume manufacturer', Wladimir Baikoff. Beverly was not too pleased at seeing herself portrayed only as an adjunct to her famous sister but there was precious little she could do about it, and her new husband-to-be was reputed to have a long-lasting drug problem. For the time being they all lived comfortably, if not happily ever after, at Mae's new Van Nuys ranch.

In early 1934, Mae's jewel-theft saga became a real hazard when Mae had to be assigned two bodyguards after being warned off testifying against the indicted thieves. She received death threats in the mail, and ugly phone calls were made to her home, threatening to throw acid in her face. The broadening of the case across state lines brought in the FBI. The court case, which began in January, made daily headlines as Mae clashed on the stand with the defence attorney, who accused her of orchestrating the entire hold-up as a publicity stunt. Photographs of the accused, Friedman, after being 'beaten to a jelly' by the police to get his confession, were produced in court. The main accused, Harry Voiler, the 'brains' behind the robbery, was still free in Chicago pending an extradition order. Mae's appearance in court seemed to reprise in real life her scene from *I'm No Angel*, as the *Los Angeles Times* reported: 'She swayed into court on high French heels and hitched up her hips as she made ready to climb into the witness box. A mink coat made Miss West look like any other well-dressed woman from the rear but it was the front view that wowed the crowded courtroom. It may not be done on purpose but Miss West has a trick way of carrying her hands when she walks . . . and there is no question that it went over big. She wore her coat unbuttoned and placed the backs of her hands on her body just below the hips, well to the rear.'

Flanked by her husky guards, Mae was perhaps rehearsing another act she would perform, on the stage of life, albeit without the songs. Whatever the extent of the real threats to Mae from Chicago racketeers, the publicity continued to flow. The *Daily*

News reported in April that she had ordered an 'armored automobile, machine-gun and pistol proof,' to cart her around. *Movie Mirror* of July 1934, headlined 'Mae West's Life in Danger!' over a photograph of Mae firmly holding a tommy gun, having been 'given lessons in the use of an automatic rifle'. District Attorney Fitts weighed in with his praise: 'If all citizens were as public spirited and brave in the face of death threats as Mae West, there would be few gangsters left!'

No one raised the question, in public, of what had happened to Mae's old New York gangland contacts, who might have helped lift the heat that summer. After the repeal of Prohibition, the main power base of Owney Madden and his like had been weakened, and legendary figures like Legs Diamond and Larry Fay had been dispatched by 1933. Madden himself had to continually beat off attempts by the law to return him to jail for violation of his parole from the original ten-to-twenty-year sentence. He may well have had no appreciable clout to protect Mae from the new breed of rapacious thugs, who saw rich pickings among the glittering nouveau riche of Hollywood. Mae West, reported *Movie Mirror*, 'will spend her vacation in Hawaii, far from the reaching tentacles of the gangdom she has dared to defy. She isn't afraid of gangsters,' the magazine waxed courageous on her behalf, 'but the gangsters are afraid of her. And that is why Mae West is on the spot and her life, and still worse her beauty, is in danger.'

Friedman was eventually sentenced to the bizarre term of one year to life in San Quentin prison for the hold-ups, while his accomplices were still being sought. Press interest shifted briefly to reports of a rift between Mae West and Jim Timony, a 2 May item in the *Citizen-News* revealing that he was occupying a separate apartment at the Rossmore building together with Boris Petroff, an ex-Russian ballet teacher who had directed a live promotional stage show for Mae in New York during her publicity tour for *She Done Him Wrong*. As Petroff was rumoured to be her current lover, the living arrangements of the West ménage were certainly curious, with brother Jack reported to be the only live-in partner at her own apartment. Mae's official tale was that Timony was as close an advisor as ever, but her business affairs were now to be handled formally by a professional movie agent, Murray Feil.

Mae's Hawaii vacation would have been a good opportunity to

take a breath before returning to the studio floor for her next picture, due to begin shooting in December 1934. This was eventually released as *Goin' to Town* but began life as 'Now I'm a Lady'.

Unlike her three previous films, the new project was not based on Mae's own scripts and material but on 'an original story' by Marion Morgan and George B. Dowell. As Paramount's top earner, Mae now had her own production unit, with William LeBaron as producer and Emanuel Cohen standing guard over her strategic fortune. They decided to provide Mae West with a property that would produce the image and form demanded by her audience, without provoking the censors by its content. The confection thus produced is well synopsized in the official press book:

In a dance hall in the Western cattle-country, Cleo Borden, a beautiful blonde, earns an honest living and is happy, until Buck Gonzales, wealthy rancher and one of the toughest of the leaders of the cattle-rustling industry of the region, persuades her to stake her single-blessedness on a turn of the dice. Cleo agrees on condition that Buck sign over all his property to her – in advance.

Cleo loses the throw and prepares for the wedding but, just before the ceremony, the sheriff catches up with Buck and Cleo finds herself with a dead bridegroom and a fistful of Western cattle and oil country on her hands. In her new status she becomes interested in a handsome young engineer, Edward Barrington, who is testing her property for oil. He scorns her advances, however, and when the oil comes in, Barrington goes out – to Buenos Aires.

Barrington's scorn whets Cleo's interest in him. Counselled by her cultured manager, Winslow, Cleo determines to become a 'lady' and, from a society magazine, selects Mrs. Crane Brittony, who is in Buenos Aires for the races, as her pattern. Fortified by her new oil millions, she follows Barrington to South America and enters a horse in a race.

One might see the entire project as a satire on Mae's own new status in Hollywood. No longer the uncouth hussy at the bottom of the social ladder – the burlesquer-prostitute-madame with her finger on the pulse of the lower depths – she is a glorified arriviste intent on using her newly gained money to elbow her way into the élite. The problem was that this downplayed the tale's other theme, Mae climbing from man to man to achieve her ends, a tale with a distant echo of Barbara Stanwyck's Hays-Code provocation *Baby Face*, produced in 1933. But Stanwyck's character in that film, like Mae in her own

narratives, was a woman driven by harsh circumstances into utilizing her only asset, her sexuality, to get what she desired. Mae in *Goin' to Town* falls into a state of fabulous wealth by chance, and then uses it to vault into the very class that does her wrong. There is an air of terrible snobbery about the movie, with its arse-faced money-men, its bizarre coteries of Russian hunks in a Buenos Aires strictly conceived as a playground for rich idiots. As the plot progresses, Mae's Cleo marries a rich blue blood, Fletcher Colton, Mrs Brittony's nephew, a man drowning in alcohol and gambling debts who exchanges his pedigree for her money. The snooty Brittony hatches a plan with her Russian gigolo, Valadov, first to nobble Cleo's horse, and then to compromise her, back in the States, in the blue-blood colony of Southampton. Surprised in Cleo's room by Colton, Valadov shoots him in a struggle and tries to blame Cleo, but she wins through to clinch with the oil engineer, Barrington, who turns out, lo and behold, to be the Earl of Stratton.

There is some scope in the film for Mae's quips, but not many: 'What excuse has a girl like you for runnin' around single?' 'I was born that way.' Or: 'For a long time I was ashamed about the way I lived.' 'You mean to say you're reformed?' 'No, I got over bein' ashamed.'

Once in Buenos Aires, the jokes get a little more tired, if still suggestive:

'I didn't know you spoke Spanish?'
'Don't think I worked in Tijuana for nothin'!'
'I'm sorry, I didn't get your name . . .'
'It wasn't your fault, you tried hard enough.'
'Where have I seen your face before?'
'Same place you see it now.'

To Valadov, who tries to get her to marry him as a ruse: 'We're intellectual opposites – I'm intellectual and you're opposite.' And to the society lady who asks: 'Have your ancestors ever been traced?' 'Well, yes, but they were too smart, they couldn't catch 'em.'

Too much of the film, however, is taken over by the convoluted plot, interrupted only by a sequence in which Mae tries to woo society by putting on an opera – *Samson and Delilah*, with herself in the female role: 'I have a lot of respect for that dame – there's one lady barber that made good.' The scene in which Mae, already the despair of her Italian voice-trainer, flounces on, bobbing and weaving more in the manner of the football field than La Scala, is perhaps the first instance of authentic 'camp' in one of her films, as she toys with Samson's locks while belting out her aria. But the scene is cut short by the discovery of the dead body of Colton and the quick wrapping up of the tale.

Despite these complications, the film is bounced along fairly efficiently by its director, Alexander Hall, who was to make his name at the helm of many 'sophisticated' second-line Hollywood comedies, such as *This Thing Called Love* (1938) and *My Sister Eileen* (1942). The film's male cast, considered strong for its day, included as Mae's suitors Paul Cavanagh, Fred Kohler, Ivan Lebedeff and Monroe Owsley, none of them now household names. Cavanagh, playing the English Earl-cum-oil engineer, had gained a reputation on both the English stage and screen, but while considered handsome by the standards of the time, he could hardly have been described as young. Pushing forty, he was nevertheless two years younger than Mae, and that problem was already showing its contours in the face and body of the star. The rivalry with Katharine Hepburn might have been pure press puffery, but Hepburn's figure was certainly in stark contrast to the fleshy delights of Diamond Cleo Borden. Not for nothing had Mae railed against the 'flatness' of 1920s flapper types.

A Paramount press release of 1933, quoting one James Davies, 'masseur and physical culturist attached to the Paramount studio', shows the studio's concern about the unfashionable contours of their new diva. Mr Davies explained his advice to Mae not to 'try to reduce', as she was 'perfect for the camera . . . This slenderizing, boyish figure for women, which has been in vogue up to now, has been all wrong. It has been most detrimental to women's health. It is natural for women to have curves . . . Now that Miss West has revolutionized the styles from straight lines to wholesome, feminine curves, women can eat sensibly and need no diet to tear themselves down . . .' Davies described the exercises done by Mae West, 'a very strong woman – in fact, with one arm she can lift me from the floor, and I weigh 185 pounds! One exercise in particular seemed to interest her. You lie flat on your back on the floor, with your arms overhead, hands clasped to the back of the neck. Then, clamping your toes under a heavy bit of furniture, lift yourself up so that your elbows touch your knee . . . Miss West "came up" more often in this exercise than almost any man I have trained. She could "come up" a hundred times without being exhausted.'

A model for women, she did not drink or smoke – 'drinks lots of milk, however, realizing that this helps preserve her marvellous teeth' – Davies emphasizing the 'sparkling health' that gave her 'that sex appeal, magnetism, and vital appeal which are synonymous with her name'.

So far, so good for Paramount. The Hays Office raised minimal objections to *Goin' to Town*, mostly involving the two songs which bookended the plot. The first, sung in the saloon – 'He's a Bad Man, But He Treats Me Good' – prompted the censor, Breen, to suggest changing the line 'I made the bed and now you're laying in it' with 'the proper grammatical word, "lying."' (It was Breen who made the seducer Russian by insisting, yet again, that South Americans 'are particularly sensitive about being characterized as gigolos'.) The closing song of the film, 'Now I'm a Lady', Breen wrote, 'seems to us to be a definite violation of the Code. As we read it, it is the boasting of a woman of loose morals who has had any number of men in her time, and has climbed over them to the top of the ladder where she has finally married respectability.' One verse was considered particularly objectionable:

> *I used to dig for gold without any conscience,*
> *I'd go away with a lot,*
> *But now I'm a lady,*
> *I only take what they've got.*
> *There was a time I had to work for my pennies*
> *To keep my cloud silver-lined,*
> *But now I'm a lady,*
> *I get my sugar refined.*

This was transformed in the movie to:

> *I used to put my heart and soul in my dancing*
> *To keep the wolf from the door,*
> *But now I'm a lady,*
> *Don't have to dance any more . . .*

The next-but-last verse, which Mae sings to the camera before taking her fade-out bow, now reflects the movie-makers' apparent capitulation, wry as it is, to the politics of the Code:

I used to play around without any conscience
I just broke hearts left and right,
But now I'm a lady,
I've learned to be more polite . . .

After the film was released Breen wrote in an internal memo to Will Hays: 'GOIN TO TOWN: This latest Mae West picture has been handled satisfactorily, the studio having conscientiously avoided the more serious difficulties that have attended some of this star's previous pictures.' We might reflect that once Mae's character was using money rather than sex to get her way and her men, this was considered an acceptable, even all-American mode of behaviour, which did not violate the tenets and the doctrine of the Production Code.

Reviews of the film were mixed, with *Daily Variety* stating that it 'compares favorably with "She Done Him Wrong" . . . What it lacks in story it makes up in Westian wisecracks . . . West fans will revel in the work of their fave.' The weekly version of *Variety*, however, noting Paramount's change of tack with their heroine, called it 'Mae West's poorest . . . It's punchy enough on the dialog, but deficient on story . . . Secret of Miss West's previous pix has been that they stayed in character. The studio probably decided it's time to get her out of the mauve decade, and while it's a commendable attempt, it's gone astray.' The *Hollywood Reporter* was even harsher: 'Writing Is Shoddy, Direction is Slipshod . . . The audience-appeal that Madame West has always flaunted is carried out in grand style, but to this reviewer at least, what once looked like hearty bawdiness has palled to the point where it's just the handwriting on the back fence or barn door . . .'

On 5 January 1935, while Mae was still filming, her father Battlin' Jack West died of a stroke in Oakland, having suffered a previous heart attack in November 1934. In contrast with her devastation after her mother's death, Mae took only one day off filming to attend the funeral in Los Angeles, and her brother and sister took the body back east to the family vault. On the day after her father's death, the *Sunday Dispatch* had printed an article in a new series about Mae, the Hollywood legend: 'I'M AN ANGEL REALLY – MAE WEST TELLS FOR THE FIRST TIME JUST WHAT SHE IS REALLY LIKE.' Of her father, Mae had told the paper: 'Pa was the good old prize-fighter who fought a nifty battle, loved the game and made a nice little reputation for himself. Just now Pa's in California with me. He spends his time reading the sporting editions, one foot on the mantlepiece and the other tucked under him. He's always been one of my two best pals, and I'm obliged to him for the physique he gave me. As sound as a bell himself, I guess he brought me up that way . . .'

No mention of the quick-tempered bruiser whose rancid cigar smoke so repelled his little daughter. Mae was never keen on painful memories. But just as one vital figure of her past departed, another, very much alive, suddenly appeared, plunging Mae into a newspaper maelstrom that was, this time, most unwelcome. Frank Wallace, the

vanished vaudeville husband of 1911, had turned up in town, all spruced up, ready and eager to claim his dues.

Revenge of the Song-and-Dance Man

MAE WEST MYSTERY!
ONE MAE WEST WED; NOT STAR, SAYS SISTER
WEST 'HUSBAND' STORY WOWS HOLLYWOOD
MARRIAGE IN MILWAUKEE IN 1911 DENIED BY MAE WEST
RIDDLE WIDENS IN WEST CASE
FIND MAE WEST 'MATE' STILL LOVES HER
8 'MATES' CLAIMED MAE
MAE INSISTS IT'S NOT SO
MAE WEST FACES 'WEDLOCK' TEST

The story broke on 20 April 1935, in the run-up to the release of *Goin' to Town*, overshadowing Paramount's press plans. Frank Wallace had appeared in Los Angeles, agent in tow, prompting a search in Milwaukee which swiftly uncovered the marriage licence issued on 11 April 1911. Sister Beverly, as well as James Timony, sprang to Mae's defence, insisting, in Timony's words, that 'there were three Mae Wests on the stage . . . This Mae West never was married. It might have been one of the others, but not our Mae.'

The embarrassment, and the confusion, was increased by Mae's creative shift of her birth date from 1893 to 1900, enabling her, for a brief moment only, to scoff at the claims that she had been married at eleven years of age. 'I've gotten a lot of bunnies on Easter, but this is the first time I've ever received a husband,' Mae tried to laugh it all off. 'I've never heard of the fellow . . . and I never was in Milwaukee until four years ago.'

Mae's old manager, Jack Linder, weighed in with the memory of the Frank Wallace who had appeared in *Diamond Lil* on the stage and was now dead – 'he died after an operation two years ago', Linder told the *Los Angeles Herald*. But newspaper files from 1911 were soon found, chronicling Mae West and Frank Wallace's appearance in *A Florida Enchantment* in 1911. The mystery deepened when it emerged that Mae had not signed the Milwaukee marriage licence. Maybe it was a fake after all?

Mae formalized her denial in a statement to the *Los Angeles Times* on 23 April: 'I hate to spoil a good story . . . I don't believe in secret marriages. Whenever I take a husband I'll be the first one to know it. And I'll tell the world . . . I'd never hesitate to admit I had a husband – if I had one. But I haven't. And yet, by actual count, eight men have called me up since January to tell me I'm their wife . . . No, I guess somebody's just done me wrong!'

By this time Frank Wallace was telling his tale in detail to whomever might care to listen. Details of his first meeting with Mae, her early songs, the Gaiety in Milwaukee and the day of their marriage, with the poignant declaration of his love, were splashed across the pages. Intrepid reporters dug up evidence of an affidavit given by Mae in 1927 during the *Sex* trial, in which she had declared herself married, although she had given her age, at that point, as twenty-six. Jo-Jo Lee, the veteran Bowery actor who had appeared in her plays, weighed in with his opinion that the Frank Wallace of *Diamond Lil* was probably the one she had married, but that Wallace was definitely dead. In 1911, however, that particular Frank Wallace, according to his brother Lew, had only been sixteen or seventeen, and he was not in vaudeville till 1918.

Mae tried to brazen out the 1927 revelation, claiming, 'I don't believe it's in the records . . . It must be a mistake.' Meanwhile, at Gary, Indiana, a policeman, Harold Brown, who said he had played the drums for the 'Mae West Syncopaters' in 1914, recalled that she was married then to 'an accordionist named d'Arragh'. This name was so weird that no one traced it to the real lover, Deiro. The marriage licence of Mae and Bud Burmester, of Houston, Texas, on 22 March 1924, also surfaced, but Burmester turned up at Fort Worth to dismiss this, saying, 'it's the result of a distorted publicity gag'.

If newspapers seek, they find. One Trixie La May, described as Frank's dancing partner, who 'wears her hair like Mae West and does a "Mae West" dance in their act', told the *Los Angeles Herald* that Wallace was forty-two years old and Mae forty. Frank had often talked of his marriage to Mae, she said. 'He wouldn't spill it because he was still loyal to Mae West . . . But he always went to see her in her pictures and said he wished her luck and that she had improved a lot in her technique over the days when they used to work an act together.' Miss La May also wanted 'to make it clear to the general public that she had fixed her hair up that way long before Mae West ever thought of doing it'.

Soon enough, Wall Street bets were being taken as to whether Mae was married or not, at four to one, though columnist Harry Carr wrote that he believed it was all a press agent's stunt: 'By the P.A.'s contrivings, an insignificant hoofer chased Hitler, the N.R.A. and the quintuplets off the front page of every newspaper in America for the period of two weeks.'

By May 1935, Wallace was revealing more details, claiming that James Timony had approached him in 1915, suggesting to him that 'Mae is going places, you're not,' and tried to enter an uncontested divorce, which Wallace now wished to contest in court as an 'illegal divorce', citing a civil right of 'declaration of judgement'. No record of this divorce, however, surfaced. The suit, filed on 10 May, was quite dangerous for Mae, as it would require her to declare in court whether she was married or not. Her response was still to try to shrug the affair off: 'Well, I've been sued for everything else,' she said tartly, scoffing at Wallace's claim that his 'standing in the community' had been injured because of her denunciation of him as an impostor. 'Whoever heard of Frank Wallace until he broke into the newspapers over my name? . . . He'll just have to come up and see my lawyer some time.'

As *Goin' to Town* was released, Mae sat in her dressing room and took calls from twelve 'motion-picture editors or their assistants . . . on a coast-to-coast hook-up'. Mae 'arrived late for the national conference with the editors. She came bustling in from her limousine, wearing a yellow blouse, white fur, light skirt and a tam slung jauntily across her tousled very blonde hair . . .' She still tried to make merry over Wallace: 'well, years ago I met an actor named "Pansy" Wallace – not that he was effeminate, but in fact a little roughneck – who came into my dressing room with Jack LaRue . . .' This, she claimed, turned out to be the only Frank Wallace she knew – 'that Frank Wallace died two years ago. They said I buried him. I didn't even know he was sick!'

Mae's joust with Frank Wallace went on for more than two years before she had to admit the bald facts of the case. The courts worked slowly, and the newspapers moved on, for the moment. In July, the press agents were able to link Mae to a story about potatoes, which were said to be half the price per barrel they were when Mae West was on the stage, a statistic that was said to enrage the potato growers: 'With women trying to look like Ginger Rogers we're lucky to sell them for $2 a barrel, and that's just breaking even,' opined a grower, Calvert Williams.

Soon after, Mae was in the news again on a more ominous note, as once again threats to attack her with acid were allegedly made by an extortionist, George Janios, a 'Fox studio busboy' who was caught in a sting collecting money that Mae's chauffeur, 'Chalkie' Wright, had placed in a palm tree. Detectives on a 'stake-out' rushed out with submachine guns to apprehend the suspect. A picture of one of the detectives, Harry Dean, in 'feminine attire', beside Mae West appeared on 8 October, along with the extortionist's scrawled handwriting: 'MISS WEST WE TOLD YOU BEFORE $1000 OR YOU HAVE YOUR FACE LIFTED SUNDAY BY 8 OCLOCK . . . [signed] ACID BURNS.' Two more 'eastern hoodlums' were being sought for the crime. Within two days, however, the Fox busboy was released, as it turned out he could neither read nor write. FBI agent E. P. Dunn said that 'after the publicity which has been given the case it is most difficult to pick up any threads of evidence'.

At least Frank Wallace had been pushed back. Mae soon realized she had to make her own publicity or else be dragged along with the press's own obsessions. Newsmen for both the *Los Angeles Times* and the *New York Times* were invited to 'come up and see her' at her Ravenswood apartment. For the first time, the public could see photographs of that famous bed, 'made specially to conform with her Louis XV apartment . . . built very much after the pattern of the famous "Swan" bed which she had in New York, but without the swans. The hangings above the bed are pale pink brocade, edged with heavy lace, and the headboard is quilted in the same color. The bed and pillow coverings are fashioned of heavy white satin, edged in lace. Above the bed and on either side are mirrors outlined in white and gold.' The *New York Times*'s John C. Moffitt noted that 'all the coffee tables and consoles were topped with mirrors. These had gold instead of silver backing. When you stooped over to light a cigarette you caught a gilded glimpse of yourself . . . "It cheers you up," Mae said. "Every time you see yourself in one of these table mirrors you get the feeling you're in the money. Cute, isn't it?"'

The living room was 'dominated by a white and gold baby grand piano and a large white sofa. The sofa has a long white fringe fore and aft, like the mane and tail of a circus horse.' A large polar bear rug was stretched out 'in an attitude of complete exhaustion . . . "They talk about me being married," Mae snorted. "Would any woman in danger of a husband dare get furniture like that? It's lady-like and would be plain ruined if some man put his big shoes on it. I don't waste money that way."'

The builder, said Mae, had not been happy placing the mirror above her bed for fear of earthquakes. 'I told him if I saw it coming down I would be under the bed by the time it hit . . . They've anchored it to the floor of the apartment upstairs. Every time they dance they jar the object of my reflections.'

Said Mae: 'I'm just a bachelor girl and a home girl . . . Now that you've been up to see me, I hope you can see I'm just like any other woman. I like nice things and I like to keep them nice. I don't want no man knocking bric-a-brac over and leaving beer bottles on the piano. I'm not the standard model, but I guess I'm just an old maid.'

By the time Mae was showing her domestic arrangements to the nation she was already launched upon her next motion picture. Perhaps due to the lukewarm reception to her attempt to be a Polite Lady in *Goin' to Town*, or perhaps because it had been a necessary diversion, she had received the green light from Emanuel Cohen and William LeBaron at Paramount to embark upon another of her stage-play projects. This was to be another kick in the teeth of the censors and the most explosive of all her movie scandals.

The Devil's Daughter Revisited

Viewing the version we have of Mae's *Klondike Annie*, which was released in February 1936, it is difficult to square this rather innocuous if somewhat sly satire with the demonic threat to American civilization that was the subject of an internal copy of a press memo found in the movie's censorship file:

COPY TO ALL MANAGING EDITORS
The Mae West picture, *Klondike Annie*, is a filthy picture.

I think we should have editorials roasting the picture and Mae West, and the Paramount Company for producing such a picture – the producer – director and everyone concerned.

We should say it is an affront to the decency of the public and to the interests of the motion picture profession.

Will Hays must be asleep to allow such a thing to come out but it is to be hoped that the churches of the community are awake to the necessity of boycotting such a picture and demanding its [word indistinct but probably 'withdrawal'].

After you have had a couple of good editorials regarding the indecency of this picture then DO NOT MENTION MAE WEST IN OUR PAPERS AGAIN WHILE SHE IS ON SCREEN AND DO NOT ACCEPT ANY ADVERTISING OF THIS PICTURE.

This bilious missive is attributed to William Randolph Hearst in person, who was thereby committing his entire newspaper empire to a crusade against Mae West. What could she have done to provoke such ire?

The film – the extant version – opens once again in the 1890s, this time in San Francisco's Chinatown, at 'The House of Chan Lo', a gambling club frequented by a mixture of Chinese and high-society slummers. They are fascinated by the exotic atmosphere and the tale of Chan Lo's kept white woman, Rose Carlton, alias the San Francisco Doll: 'I hear he is madly jealous of her and he makes every white man keep a respectable distance,' chatters an inquisitive dowager.

Chan Lo, as played by the most un-Chinese Harold Huber, is presented as a perfect barbarian, a man of smooth manners and speech who shows his guests the latest item in his collection, a Malay kris, which has, according to its legend, 'pierced many times the hearts of beautiful ladies who were unfaithful to their lords'. We should be able to recognize the racially dubious ambience of Mae's unperformed 1930 play *Frisco Kate*, adapted from the original 'Singapore' setting of the earlier draft omitted from the Library of Congress script. The openly racist dialogue of that scene has been toned down, reduced to Mae's complaint: 'You stifle me . . . Why do you keep me from having men friends of my own race?' To which Chan Lo replies: 'Because it is written that there are two perfectly good men – one dead, the other unborn.' 'Which one are you?' asks Mae.

One can begin to appreciate the squirming discomfort of the Production Code Board. One of the strongest prohibitions of the Board was miscegenation, to quote: 'sex relationships between the white and black races is forbidden'. This raised the question of the definition of non-white Asians, such as Indians, Chinese or other far-eastern people. As in apartheid South Africa, there was a scale of acceptability. South Africa designated the economically powerful Japanese as 'honorary whites', and for the American cinema, the Chinese hovered around this grade. D. W. Griffith had tackled the issue of white–Chinese relationships in 1919 with *Broken Blossoms*, and Hollywood actors Sessue Hayakawa and Anna May Wong tested the limits of white consciousness of the 'yellow' – the combination of exotic allurement and inscrutable danger. On screen, liaisons between whites and Asians were almost invariably acceptable only if between white actors. Edward G. Robinson became an 'honorary Chinese' in 1932's *The Hatchet Man*, and Boris Karloff, of course, became the perfect Fu Manchu. The Swede Warner Oland was soon to play Charlie Chan repeatedly, and Peter Lorre moonlighted as the Japanese detective Mr Moto. Frank Capra, in *The Bitter Tea of General Yen*, showed that racism itself could be a proper subject for the movies – again, as long as the actor playing the Chinese lover was white.

In *Klondike Annie*, Mae is careful to avoid any physical contact on screen with Chan Lo. Paramount's earliest outline of the script, submitted to the Hays Office on 29 June 1935, explicitly stated, in the words of executive John Hammell: 'There is to be no implication whatsoever of an existing sex relationship between the West character

"Boys, You Sleigh Me!"

The one and only Miss West as the spell of the Yukon, the call of the wild, the bird cry of the frozen acres, the gal who kids the face off the barroom floor...

Adolph Zukor presents

Mae West

"KLONDIKE ANNIE"
with VICTOR McLAGLEN

Directed by Raoul Walsh · A Paramount Picture

4 new hit songs with Mae singing "I'm an Occidental Woman", "Mr. Deep Blue Sea" and "Little Bar Butterfly"

T H E A T R E

'An occidental woman in an oriental mood for love. . .'

and the mandarin.' We can assume the Hays Office, even if it had procured a copy of the unstaged *Frisco Kate*, would not have been aware of the excised scene presenting Mae as the Chinese boss's moll. The Board was, however, concerned about scenes in which Chan Lo's men tortured Mae's confidant, Ah Toy, to reveal Mae's plans to escape with her white paramour. The scriptwriters had added that this scene was based on authentic research on Chinese finger torture – 'See Plate X in "The Punishments of China"' – but the Board ordered all explicit shots to be cut: 'There should be no suggestion of excessive gruesomeness or brutality.' A similar scene, in which Chan Lo is about to torture Mae by burning out her eyes with lime ('See Plate XI – "The Punishments of China"' – Research Department) and the tormented Ah Toy places the Malay kris in her hand, was also excised, so that Mae's dispatching of her Chinese employer/lover happens completely off screen and can only be inferred by the plot.

Mae's escape from Chan Lo cuts directly to her coming aboard the tramp steamer *Java Maid* together with her faithful Chinese servant, Fah Wong, played by Soo Yong, the only credited Chinese person in the cast. This returns us to the main setting of 1930's *Frisco Kate* and the originally bestial captain, Bull Brackett, described in the play as 'a bully of the seas'. He is played in the movie by Victor McLaglen, already an action-man in silent movies, including a number of early John Fords (*Mother Machree* and *The Black Watch* among them), though he was yet to become Ford's archetypal cavalry sergeant with a heart of gold. (McLaglen, though he almost always played an archetypal Irishman, was, in fact, born in Tunbridge Wells, England, in 1883, the son of a clergyman.) McLaglen's first American film had been *The Beloved Brute* (1924), and he excelled in the character of a soft-hearted hulk. The casting alone rendered Bull Brackett tenable as a love interest for Mae, despite the roughness of the captain on the page. Posters for the film played up the 'beauty and the beast' aspect: 'Most girls want their men to look good to them, but not too good,' blared one, and another: 'You're no erl paintin' . . . but you're a fascinatin' monster!'

The overwhelming seediness and sexual threat of the play's *Java Maid* has been dropped, and the brutish seamen rendered into one comic figure, the cockney ship's cook, played by Chester Gan. The ship's company are a group of stock sailors who gather around the bilges complaining – but not to his face – that the captain has gone barmy with the dame he has living in his cabin.

There is no hint of Mae's savage call to arms, her anarchic speeches or her chronicle of sins in every port, which would have made *Frisco Kate* unfilmable. Instead, Mae, aware of the obstacles in her own original material, sought out another strand to her story that would transform the original on-board sleaziness into a more acceptable story. The irony was that it was precisely this addition that caused the major clash with the Hays Code and the resulting furore.

Mae had obtained, from her co-writers on *Goin' to Town*, Marion Morgan and George B. Dowell, a story which they had titled 'Hallelujah! I'm a Saint!' or 'How About It, Brother?' as well as an Alaskan story called 'Lulu Was a Lady', by one Frank Mitchell Dazey. Morgan and Dowell's full-length narrative treatment was set in Shanghai in 1888 and was introduced thus:

This is the story of Lily Larsen, a modern Jezebel, who rose from the drab

Chinese Mission to be the most talked of woman in Shanghai. Beautiful, ruthless – the admiration of men and the envy of women – she became known as the 'White Lily' – sought after by diplomats and titled officials of high rank.

Her one passion was gold, and for this obsession, she became a fugitive from justice, hunted and hounded by the law which traced her from relentless China to the underworld of the Barbary Coast and from there to the gold rush shores of Alaska.

Through a cruel trick of circumstance, she became the victim of fate which later proved her redemption, and by a glorious transmutation of character, she slowly changed from the adventuress known as the 'White Lily' to become the 'Angel of the Yukon.'

Like the path of man's evolution, she goes from glory to glory, ever rising higher, until at the summit, she fulfills her destiny and is lost in the recorded names of those we call 'saints' – and when the Good Book is one day opened, we shall find a name inscrolled in large letters – a name devoted to good deeds and tender mercies – and the 'White Lily' will be forgiven and the name will read 'Soul Savin' Annie' – she who once was the Jezebel of Shanghai and became the Magdalen of the Klondike . . .

'Soul Savin' Annie' may have had many origins. The true-life Klondike Kate was the origin, as we have seen, of the twice-made *Flame of the Yukon*, the script which made its way into Mae's files. A northern 'Diamond Lil', she was probably flickering in the back of Mae's mind for a long time. Biographer Emily Wortis Leider has unearthed a vaudeville playlet, *Salvation Sue*, of 1915, 'set in the Alaskan gold fields' and concerning 'a female Salvation Army leader who works at soul-saving in the town's dance halls and saloons'. The previously noted 1928 play *The Shanghai Gesture* also played its obvious part, as well as Marlene Dietrich's *Shanghai Express*, produced in 1932, and perhaps even James Cagney's dance with Ruby Keeler as 'Shanghai Lil' in 1933's *Footlight Parade* – a classic Busby Berkeley number.

Morgan and Dowell's tale, however, is a firmly straight-laced affair with, they later claimed emphatically, a pious and most serious intent. The image of the real-life soul-saver, Aimee Semple McPherson, was never far from the surface. Dispatching the first treatment of the Mae West script, still titled 'Frisco Doll' (another title, 'Klondike Lou', had been dropped), to the censor, John Hammell wrote to Will Hays about the character:

She takes passage on a passenger steamer and has for a cabin companion a mission worker from the slums of San Francisco, who is on her way to the Klondike to engage in mission work there. In their close contact on board ship, we have the contrast and clash of the two characters – the earnest devout mission worker, and the flippant product of a hard, cruel upbringing – West.

During the voyage, we see the gradual impression the mission worker makes on West . . . She tells the story of her life of service and sacrifice. West becomes, little by little, deeply impressed with it all.

The Hays Office, however, was not. Hays wrote back, a few days later, on 2 July, to Hammell:

Dear Mr Hammell,

I have received and read carefully the outline dated June 29, 1935, of your proposed next Mae West picture.

After careful consideration and discussion, we believe that this outline contains one element which is very questionable from the standpoint of general industry policy and audience reaction. We judge from your letter that during part of this picture, Miss West will be masquerading as an exponent of religion or a religious worker . . . It is our belief that it is imperative that you make clear throughout the script that Miss West is *not* in any sense masquerading as a preacher, revivalist or any other character known and accepted as a minister of religion, ordained or otherwise. Rather, her assumed character should be that of a social service worker, rescuing unfortunate girls etc., along the lines of numerous rescue missions which are basically philanthropic and not especially identified with, or promoted by, organised religious bodies.

Hays had picked up on the plot point in which Mae, having nursed the frail missionary Annie Alden aboard the ship till she dies, takes on her identity when a Mountie, Jack Forrest (played by Philip Reed), comes on board in search of the fugitive San Francisco Doll. When she steps off the ship in Nome, Alaska, the Doll takes on Annie Alden's mission to assist the local evangelical settlement in its bid to save the Yukon roughnecks' souls. This was the nub of Mae's idea for the plot: that she would be seen, on screen, to be atoning for the 'bad' life she had been leading to that point.

'Sister' Mae's recipe for promoting religion became the centrepiece of the film. The studio had assigned her one of the best craft directors in the business, one-eyed Raoul Walsh, who had been directing since his collaboration with Christy Cabanne in 1914's *The Life of General Villa*. Walsh would later, in 1941, direct perhaps the best of Hollywood's 'Gay Nineties' pictures, *The Strawberry Blonde*, with James Cagney, Rita

Hayworth and Maureen O'Hara, and he was at his best when dealing with rip-roarin', robust communities of 'ordinary' folk. French critics idolized him for the qualities of 'whirlwind and passion . . . His characters are projected on the world by their own energy and committed to a space that only exists for their actions, fury, spirit, craft, ambition and unbridled dreams.' These characters were, of course, supplied by the screenwriters – and performers – but Walsh was able to imbue them with that extra oomph, which is evident in the settlement scenes of *Klondike Annie*. The missionaries of the settlement are a cast of well-meaning bumblers, derided by the tough townspeople and unable to raise a cent for their efforts until Mae commands attention with a rousing address to 'all of you barflies, that revel and wallow in sin' and her own version of a spiritual pep talk: 'I ain't here to blame you for what you've done . . . I'm leavin' it up to your conscience to be on the level with yourself and the world in everything you do. It's human nature to have a certain amount of weakness. It's an uphill fight tryin' to be good. It takes plenty of courage and spirit to play it that way. What you win in the end is worth it.'

A hearty chorus of 'It's Better to Give Than to Receive' precedes the passing of the collection box, which is filled with the prospectors' pokes, donated watches and cash. In the background, Bull Brackett seethes and waits for the Doll to get back to her senses, while an old veteran of the San Francisco joints, Big Tess, congratulates the Doll on her new act, only to be told that, this time, it's on the level – 'There's somethin' about liftin' people upward that gets yer – I ain't hypocritin' either.'

Given the cuts, which lost about eight minutes of the original eighty-five-minute running time of the film, it is difficult to gauge the full intention of the character Mae was creating in the story. Scenes between the Doll and Bull Brackett suggesting the sexual attraction between them are absent, and the full impact of the dichotomy between the 'sinful' life of the town and the struggling missionaries has been blunted. As the censor ordered: 'It is imperative that you do not designate Fanny Radler and her dance hall girls as prostitutes.' Joseph Breen's response to the full script, dated 4 September 1935, runs to seven packed pages of objections: 'Doll's speech, " . . . you can't save a man's soul if you don't get close to him. It's the personal touch that counts. That's my experience," has a double meaning and most certainly will be deleted by censor boards everywhere . . . The miner's remark to Forrest "That thar's the queerest salvation song I ever did hear," should be rewritten and the word "evangelist" should be deleted from Forrest's speech . . . Doll's expression "Judge not, lest you be judged," should be rewritten . . .'

The entire thrust of Breen's objections was to fillet out of the script the idea of Mae taking over as a missionary and to omit religion from the tale completely. 'Convertin'', 'sermon', 'salvation', 'soul', 'Bless you', 'preacher' or even Biblical lines had to go: 'Definite quotations from the Bible "The Lord is my Shepherd, I shall not want . . ." will be deleted by censor boards in this country and – definitely – by the censor boards in London.' Instead, Breen embarked on the somewhat forlorn task of trying to suggest alternative activities for Mae as a 'social worker' in the settlement, 'working into this script . . . shots of Doll playing games, possibly with the rough miners, teaching them Mother Goose rhymes, etc. Settlement workers make it a practice to gather children around the settlement house to cut out paper dolls or to play charades. Why not have Doll giving the rough miners a bit of the same instruction? Why not inject into this picture a few Eskimo or Chinook Indians? How about Doll as a sort of Carrie Nation, cleaning out the saloon and building up the settlement house as a rendezvous for the workers?' and so forth.

Sometimes the rigours of the Code are, even in its known puritanical zeal, quite outlandish. Why is it that 'the word "bedbug" is always deleted by censor boards'? Or why would civilization collapse at the inclusion of the line 'He's just one of those guys that get you in a corner and breathe in your face'? But Breen saw himself as drawing the line at the outermost perimeters of the public's perceived moral squeamishness. It is difficult perhaps to believe, but Breen always presented himself as the protector of the movie producers against external forces who were much more zealous than he. And he was right, for even after the Board approved *Klondike Annie*, after much disputation and argument, the roof fell in on the Hays Office's 'laxity'.

The Code's dictums on religion were that *(1) No film or episode may throw ridicule on any religious faith. (2) Ministers of religion in their character as ministers of religion should not be used as comic characters or as villains. (3) Ceremonies of any definite religion should be carefully and respectfully handled.* But the combination of both sex and religion became the ultimate offence, the reddest rag to the bulls. There were even, the censors felt, hints in the script that more than just the suggestion of sex was contemplated:

We wish again to repeat our general caution, as set forth to you in our letter of October 19, regarding the photographing of Miss West's breasts. We again remind you that there is a definite code provision which ordains that the breasts must never be exposed, either in whole or in part – nor should these be emphasized in the costume.

All this leaves the question, which censors and critics alike preferred to ignore, of what Mae's genuine intentions were for the movie? The official Paramount press book sidestepped all the clerical pitfalls and presented the film as 'a gay and gusty story of the "nineties" like "She Done Him Wrong" and "Belle of the Nineties." Mae goes north, to Alaska and the Gold Rush – and what a rush there is for Golden Mae!' The publicists suggested frozen north-style merchandise tie-ups, like 'Klondike Store Windows', 'Soda-Fountain Tie-Ups', vending Baked Alaska under the slogan 'Mae's the gal who makes Alaska bake!', and even 'Refrigerator Tie-Ups' – 'the refrigerator season will be just getting under way when "Klondike Annie" is released . . .' Taglines like 'Boys, You Sleigh Me!' and 'Mae Answers the Call of the Wild' were set beside the usual Mae West Wisecracks contests, though not many of her characteristic lines had survived into the picture: 'Sheets are cold when only one sleeps under them,' 'I could tell everything that King Solomon knew and didn't tell' and even 'Give a man a free hand and he'll try to put it all over you' were chopped out, and we are left with only one sure-fire gem that survived the censor: 'Between two evils, I always pick the one I never tried before.'

Several songs had also been dropped or rejected by the censor, including 'My Medicine Man' ('When life's no bed of roses / there's no one who diagnoses / like my medicine man . . .') and 'I Hear You Knocking but You Can't Come In': 'You never missed my lovin' / Till I said goodbye / Now I'm a busy woman / So you'd better run along / It's too late to holler / 'Cause the train's done gone.' Only one great song scene remains in the film: the astonishing opening number, in which Mae sings 'I'm an occidental woman / in an oriental mood for love' in Chinese headdress in front of a grand circle flanked by dragons and gigantic vases.

It is, I think, reasonably clear, however, that Mae intended *Klondike Annie* to be a sincere story of a woman who, after a lifetime of straying, commits one authentically pious act as a tribute to the example of the missionary woman whose own life was beyond reproach. This sincere act sits in the midst of a whirlpool of moral confusion, social chaos, rampant greed and unavoidable lust. Mae's world is a strange concoction, part real life, part fantasy, part opium dream, part moral tract. Out of an 'oriental' world of lust and pain – mostly excised – that was to segue into the foggy mist of the tramp steamer gliding over the ocean, the San Francisco Doll floats towards the frontier, where desperate men and women dream of gold in a haze of liquor. While the moral reformers stamp their feet as they belt out 'There'll Be a Hot Time in the Old Town Tonight', the sinner woman calls her fellow sinners to a communion of salvation and healing. The theatrical stage and the movies combine in a strange marriage of the mundane and the bizarre. A yearning for structure underlies, undercuts and is undermined by this jumble of clashing images and sensations.

The San Francisco Doll, at the end of the movie, has a choice between two men – the upright cop, Forrest, who discovers her true identity but has fallen in love with her, and the bullish Captain Brackett. In the original play, Brackett's lust for 'Frisco Kate' was the aggressive desire of a degraded would-be rapist. But Victor McLaglen's Bull is a gentle giant, whose male belligerence is brought to heel by the love of a beautiful dame.

The Doll's choice is to allow Forrest his unsullied reputation as a lawman and choose the captain, who must transport her back to San Francisco, where she can confess her killing of Chan Lo in self-defence. (Bull's killing of the Tong avenger who follows her to Nome has been cut from the movie.) For the first time in her movie narratives, Mae sacrificed a man she wanted for his own good rather than hers. But she had done it before – on stage, in *Sex*, when her then heroine, Margy Lamont, decided to mend her ways and gave up the love of a rich young man to sail into the sunset with her Navy boyfriend.

Everything that goes around comes around. Throughout the movie, after her encounter with Sister Annie, Mae keeps emphasizing her decisions as 'paying a debt', squaring the pain in her conscience. Are we catching a glimpse here of the other, private Mae West, who, unrecognized by the public, attended the Church of Christ the King in Hollywood, according to her own account, every Sunday? Was this a rare, in fact unique movie sighting of the contemplative, even doubting Mae, that old-fashioned girl she always claimed was hidden behind the libertine's mask?

In Mae's unpublished manuscript of the novelized *Sex, Margy Lamont*, she included a significant chapter, not based on the play, describing a Spanish church mass in Cuba, which Margy visits before the tale's familiar Trinidad scenes. At the church, 'amid the murmur of praying voices', Margy becomes 'absorbed in the mystery of worship . . . She had never known what the word "holy" meant, and she didn't now. If she had, she might have told herself that what she sensed in the candle-lit chapel was "holiness." At any rate, she had never experienced anything like it before . . .'

If *Klondike Annie* was that elusive, spiritually hungry Mae West, authentically questing for a religious meaning, she certainly got no appreciation for it. In an ironic twist, it was Mae's very act of repentance that brought the wrath of the godly down upon her.

As usual, the censor's shafts kept falling right up to the final days of editing, with the last lines, on cold sheets and Solomon, dropping out in early February 1936. When the censors viewed the film, however, they discovered, 'because of certain private information' and preview notices in *Daily Variety* and the *Hollywood Reporter* indicating the inclusion of excised lines and scenes, that 'the picture, as we saw it on Friday last, was quite definitely *not* the picture which had been approved'. Breen therefore informed John Hammell of Paramount that 'our certificate of approval would have to be withdrawn and the print re-submitted'.

Whether this was a genuine mix-up or a last-ditch attempt by Emanuel Cohen to thwart the censor and blow a razzberry at Breen for his suggestion that Mae should be portrayed as Mother Goose in Alaska, Paramount was very swiftly put in its place. The movie was released in its recut version on 21 February, but by this time William Randolph Hearst had already issued his fatwa and an open season was declared on *Klondike Annie* and Mae West in all of his twenty-eight newspapers.

In the week commencing 20 February, the same article, emanating from Catholic journals known as 'the Paul Block newspapers', was reprinted in the Hearst press:

IS POLITICS INFLUENCING CENSORSHIP?
Last week an official board in Ohio saw fit to ban an animated cartoon because it poked fun at the New Deal . . . This in line with the influence brought to bear upon radio stations to restrict programs that might be displeasing to political powers . . . It would seem that the Hays organization, or

whoever is responsible for judging pictures on the basis of possible political complications, would serve the American public better if they were to outlaw indecent and immoral pictures such as the film, 'Klondike Annie.' Here is a picture which lauds disreputable living and glorifies vice. Censors may cut a few of the worst scenes in some states, but they cannot clean it up, for the whole story is on the lowest possible level.

On February 22, the *Pittsburgh Sun-Telegraph* weighed in with its own broadside:

The latest of the West exploits is questionable in taste to say the least, it is choked with double-entendre gags, and it becomes, when Mae turns evangelist à la the Aimee Semple McPherson mold, practically sacrilegious, the unforgiveable sin in the anything-but-prudish eyes of this observer . . . The entire mess is not only a throwback to the very things that got Miss West in bad on the stage, but it is generally a dull affair . . .

If Paramount were smart, it would recall such prints of 'Klondike Annie' as are out immediately and forget as quickly as possible about the sorry business. The company should also give Miss West less to say, if it can, about just what she will and will not appear in on the screen in the future.

On 29 February, the Hearst papers pitched in again with 'STOP LEWD FILMS! . . . The film industry itself should be the FIRST to combat and stop any return to the salacious productions that brought upon it just rebuke . . . ONE INDECENT FILM MAY TEAR DOWN MUCH OF THE GOOD WILL THAT HAS BEEN BUILT . . . It is to be hoped that the churches of this country are awake to the necessity of BOYCOTTING such a picture as "Klondike Annie" and denouncing its producers . . .'

On 2 March, the Atlanta Better Films Committee registered 'a strong vote of condemnation of the Mae West picture "Klondike Annie." It is a violation of all codes of decency and a burlesque on religion.' Similar attacks came in from all over the country. Breen, stung by the onslaught, went so far as to defend the movie, writing to Will Hays that 'in the past few days I have asked a number of our local folks, many of whom saw the picture at the Cathay Circle last Friday night, if they got out of it the suggestion that it was an attempt to burlesque or travesty religion. Not a single one I talked with about the matter suggested that they did get any such flavor . . . You will have in mind that this picture was passed as the result of the approval, not once, but twice, of our *entire* staff.'

But the entire staff were just New Deal wimps to Hearst, and

Klondike Annie was an ideal peg on which to tie together Hearst's dislike of President Roosevelt's encroachments on capitalism's unbridled freedom and his diatribe on the moral health of the nation. The theatre-owners' weekly, *Motion Picture Herald*, however, speculated on a more personal reason for Hearst's outburst: 'The grapevine from Hollywood reports that the production community . . . saw as a possibility Production Code Administration attention to "Ceiling Zero," produced by Mr. Hearst's Cosmopolitan Pictures.' (This presumably refers to the Howard Hawks flying picture with James Cagney and Pat O'Brien, another innocuous movie that for some reason fell foul of the Code.) An even pettier reason reported by the *Herald* was that 'Miss West had not so long before declined an invitation to appear as a guest star on a "Hollywood Hotel" program, the radio hour sponsored by Campbell Soups and conducted by the influential Louella Parsons, motion picture editor of Mr. Hearst's Universal News Service.'

Hearst had, of course, been raging on about tightening motion-picture censorship for years, and he knew how to galvanize the zealots. On 5 March, the Legion of Decency had listed *Klondike Annie* in its 'B' classification, denoting 'objectionable in part', which still meant a ban on Catholics viewing the movie. Sunday sermons from Catholic pulpits castigated the movie, and the director of the Legion of Decency in Washington, Father Joseph B. Buckley, welcomed the Protestant Federation of Churches' decision to make common cause with the Legion's campaign to 'clean up the motion picture industry'.

These were heavy guns. Mae West had become a political football on several fields, as the *Motion Picture Herald* commented:

Mae West was the real issue last week in the arguments in Washington before a Senate sub-committee hearing on the Neely-Pettengil bill to abolish block booking. Minority exhibitor interests . . . contended that compulsory block booking forces exhibitors to play 'Mae West pictures' – symbolizing a type – or else, pay and not play, which, they added, they could not afford to do.

The complaint was symptomatic of the limits of the Hearst policy, as box-office figures showed that his newspaper editorials merely added to Mae's publicity. Refusing to advertise the film was easier than preventing the mention of her name if the editors wished to continue their attacks. Even without ads, the *Herald* revealed that *Klondike Annie*'s gross was several thousand dollars more than average at almost every movie theatre it played. Audiences rushed to see

THE DEVIL'S DAUGHTER REVISITED

the sinful 'Mae West' pictures, whereas movies designated 'high standard' by the Legion of Decency – such as *Alice in Wonderland*, *Peter
Ibbetson*, *Abraham Lincoln* and the like – had been dropped after
short runs.

Bad reviews did not seem to deter audiences either. The *New York
Times*'s Frank S. Nugent wrote that '"Klondike Annie" does not
merit the agitation it has caused. Neither as healthily rowdy nor as
vulgarly suggestive as many of her earlier pictures, it emerges . . . as
a tiresome and rather stupid combination of lavender and old japes.
Although we are prepared to debate the blue noses on Mae West's
right to wave, we cannot accept undulation without wit or negligee
without reason.' *Variety* found it 'badly told, insincerely acted and
largely lacking in the salty quips anticipated'.

Mae may well have winced at the unfairness of being slated for omis-
sions wholly forced by the censors. Pressures at Paramount were in any
case mounting, and not only over the moral turmoil. Before the film
had been shot, changes were made at the top and director–producer
Ernst Lubitsch was brought in to replace Emanuel Cohen as the executive in charge of production. Mae did not get on with Lubitsch, who
had no intention of giving her the sort of special treatment she had
come to expect from Cohen. There were tales that she had chased him
off the set with a hand-mirror. The brash Mae West approach – which
we would today call 'in your face' – was anathema to the director who
excelled in suggesting vice by means of the most elegant subterfuges. By
the time *Klondike Annie* was made, Emanuel Cohen had been fired by
Paramount and was known to have been wooing Mae over to his own
new company, Major Pictures.

In 1935, Mae had been judged to be the top salaried female in the
US, earning a gross of $480,833, the only person surpassing her
being, ironically, Hearst himself, with a cool half million. She even
topped General Motors President Alfred P. Sloane, who took
$374,505 (himself just clipping Dietrich at $368,000, with Bing
Crosby the richest male star at $318,000). *Klondike Annie*, however,
had cost more than a million dollars to make, well over its original
$750,000 budget, and the constant bludgeoning by the Hearst press
and the churches was taking its toll, even with 'B.O. bonanza.'
Paramount was, after all, a corporation with many favourite sons
and daughters, producing dramas, westerns, thrillers, musicals, featuring Bing Crosby, Maurice Chevalier, Jeanette MacDonald, Carole

Lombard, George Raft, Claudette Colbert, to name but a few. Cecil B. DeMille had made his epics *The Sign of the Cross* in 1932 and *Cleopatra* in 1934 at Paramount, among a slew of other box-office winners.

Comedy, in any case, was itself moving on, with Frank Capra's *It Happened One Night*, made for Columbia in 1934 with Clark Gable and Claudette Colbert, winning five major Oscars and establishing a new romantic but socially more realist format. The Marx Brothers had decamped to MGM, and W. C. Fields would lumber on for a while at Paramount before looking for a new home.

Time was taking its toll on Mae, despite all her endeavours to ignore the incoming tide. Her fans might choose to embrace her defiance, but her detractors remarked the signs. As a note in Breen's files emphasized, quoting a 'liberal minded and intelligent social worker about thirty years of age . . . not connected with the motion picture industry':

Whatever this picture cost, it is too much. Frankly I think Mae is definitely through. In this picture she looked old and hard and fat and so definitely 'typed' that she cannot express any genuine emotion . . . As to the audience reaction, they laughed at her, and, from her point of view, at the wrong places. They laughed when she was trying to be serious and they roared at the love scenes . . . She's not half as seductive as she thinks she is . . . Mae is like a cartoon. She's all veneer and trappings. She could be so much more effective in playing her type of lusty, big, buxom, sexy women and make them real and sympathetic characters if she had the ability to inject a bit of humaness and kindness in her portrayals . . . Mae seems to be losing ground. This picture may make money but she cannot hope to remain popular much longer. I have talked to a few people who saw the present picture and they said it bored them. This boredom will increase and many people will not know why. It seems to be the reason is that she is too UNREAL.

It appeared that Paramount agreed, despite the continued support of William LeBaron, and was ready to terminate her contract and cede her services to Emanuel Cohen's Major Pictures. Cohen was reported to have made a distribution deal with Columbia but, within a few weeks, turned around and concluded a better deal with Paramount to release and finance his productions, albeit by a flat fee for every picture. Nevertheless, it was a technical divorce. If Hearst and the churches wished to continue whipping Mae West, they would have to note a new address for their scourge.

The Fifty Monkeys, and Other Primates

The parade, nevertheless, marched on. From the *New York Herald Tribune*, 21 July 1936:

MAE WEST TYPE OF POSTURE IS HIT BY DOCTOR

. . . The Mae West posture and the 'society slouch' for women, and the military carriage for men, were condemned as menaces to health by Dr. Olive B. Williams, of Worcester, Mass., closing the first day's program of the fortieth annual convention of the American Osteopathic Association at the Waldorf Astoria yesterday.

The Mae West figure, with its wasp waist and held-in abdomen, its squared-back shoulders and upper body bent forward, is as bad for feminine health, said Dr. Williams, as the drooping posture of more recent decades, which she described as 'knees anteriorly bent, chest dropped, abdomen dropped, chin uplifted and a general loss of tone' . . . The high chest is responsible for disarrangements of the anterior lumbar area, and the held-in abdomen is responsible for narrowness of the sacro-iliac interspace and the narrowing of floating ribs and diaphragm, and sinus troubles that come from too slender a waist. Turned out toes lead to practically all foot troubles.

For perfect posture, she advised, one should look to a baby who is learning to walk.

Alas, Mae was way past babydom. Long a subject for adulation and curiosity, she now had to endure the downturn of her celebrity status and the accompanying back-biting and resentment. She was said to be depressed and taking refuge in her new family ranch. Reports that she intended to return to the New York stage in a current Broadway hit, *Jubilee*, were quickly denied. Travelling east to promote *Klondike Annie* she was still accompanied by her tenacious guards. James Timony kept briefing reporters that Mae was fine and could afford her break with Paramount, and in any case 'money doesn't mean everything to her'. But Frank Wallace continued to dog her heels. In the midst of the Hearst denunciation campaign, he won a round in his legal battle to be declared her husband, obtaining an order enjoining her from denying that she had ever been his wife. Mae managed to wriggle out of that one and continued her dismissive denials.

She continued to hold forth to all and sundry on her favourite topic – men – declaring to Dorothy Calhoun of *Motion Picture* that 'Blondes Prefer Gentlemen':

'It isn't only manners and tricks that go with being a gentleman,' Mae murmured, while a dozen mirrors gave back her secret smile. 'Sometimes I think too much schooling and polishing educate the sex out of people. The great lovers of history weren't professors, were they? They were the he-man type . . . Scratch a prize-fighter and you'll often find a real gentleman under an East Side accent – if you don't scratch him too hard! And he's got a title, too, even if it isn't "Count" or "Duke" . . .'

'A man is no less a gentleman because he gives a woman a ten carrot stew instead of a twenty-five carat ring,' Mae continued. It was perfectly true that Mae preferred to splash out on her own gems. And her penchant for fighters was becoming well known. As she related of one of her conquests: 'I met Vincent Lopez, the handsome young World's Heavyweight Wrestling Champion . . . There was something about a handsome brute crushing other brutes in a ring I couldn't resist . . .' The morality of Hollywood, Mae said, puzzled her. 'Good and bad, right and wrong, are as clear to me as sweet and sour, or black and white. But the trouble is that no moral question is either sweet or sour or just black and white. It's often bland and tepid, or gray and tan.' Emotions in Hollywood, Mae observed, 'always follow salary brackets'. The rich and famous could get away with multiple marriages and affairs, while still searching for 'romantic perfection'. Mae clearly preferred to leave the marriages aside and do honestly what others did under masks. By showing up such subterfuges and mocking them she knew she was making enemies and overstepping social boundaries. Hearst's war against her, Mae was convinced, was born of pique and annoyance, given that her salary almost matched his own: 'He hated to see a woman in his class.'

Her own life, however, continued to reflect the contradictions of her starry status. Besides being denounced by churchmen and osteopaths, she ploughed the Hollywood furrow of conspicuous spending and shopping: 'Once she was actually asked to leave a swanky store,' runs one unsourced clipping in her scrapbook. 'It appeared that Miss West, still buying clothes and looking at others, was still going strong a full hour after closing time. They really hated to ask her to leave . . . but they did have to lock up for the night.'

Behind the scenes, Mae was trying to maintain her hapless sister Beverly and her more hapless husband Vladimir Baikoff, at one point bankrolling Beverly to run a 'Chinese chow-mein factory in Los Angeles . . . Mae has purchased ten pure white delivery cars, and sends fine Chinese dinners on order to private homes.' But this brief glimpse of Mae the Chinese Takeaway Queen is all that remains of this intriguing enterprise. In May 1936, Mae was reported to have packed Beverly and Vladimir off on a 'bring-'em-back-alive expedition' to Ecuador 'in search of fifty matched monkeys. The couple sailed from Los Angeles Harbor aboard the *Talamanca* for Ecuador, where they will organize a band of hunters to snare the animals. "These are special monkeys that a fellow from Ecuador told me about," explained the film actress. "I need them for the picture I'm writing and I can't find enough that look exactly alike in this country." Miss West, writing the screenplay for the picture which Emanuel Cohen will produce for Paramount release, was at the dock to give her relatives last-minute instructions and bid them bon voyage. She expects it will be two months before the cargo of monkeys can be returned to Hollywood.'

While this was a fantastic wheeze to get rid of Bev and Vlad for a few weeks, no more was heard about the fifty monkeys. They certainly did not figure in Mae's first film of her new partnership with Emanuel Cohen, with Randolph Scott as her new romantic lead.

While Mae had been ruminating on several projects that she might favour for future productions, Cohen found a vehicle which he hoped would avoid the *Klondike Annie–Diamond Lil* obstacles. It was a play called *Personal Appearance* by Lawrence Riley, which had starred Gladys George on the stage. The story was of a prima-donna movie star, Mavis Arden, who has an affair with a rising politician but then falls in love with a local young man, Bud Norton, whom she meets when her car breaks down at a rural Pennsylvanian guest house. Cohen cast Scott, then a minor western star and upcoming heart-throb, in the role – 'What large and sinewy muscles!' Mae exclaims, as she spies him through the guest-house window.

The Hays Office, however, was not ready to give any Mae West film an easy passage and gave an early warning that the play was not fit for the screen. After reading the original script, Breen wrote to Cohen: 'The whole flavor is that of a nymphomaniac, treated for comedy, and has to do with her attempts to seduce a fine clean boy . . .'

The usual detailed exchange of fire proceeded from February 1936 through to August, when the film began shooting under a new title: *Go West, Young Man*. Cohen assured Breen the story would be altered, but Breen rejected the first script, writing, on 3 June, that it was 'definitely *not* acceptable under the provisions of the Production Code'. The usual objections about suggestions of immorality, men coming out of women's rooms, desire, vulgarity and so forth were tendered: 'Scene D-39 is very dangerous, with all the business of Bud panting; and the dialogue between them; the putting out of the light; the fixing up of the cushions . . .' etc., etc. On 17 June, the script was still unacceptable, but by this time Cohen had been beaten and did whatever was required for approval. At least Mae was spared the anguish of the battle being fought over her own original lines, as, although she was credited with the screenplay, there was little scope in the story for the standard Westian quips, gags or jokes. The nearest we get is the star, Mavis's answer to her publicist's line that 'You're a great star and you can't risk a scandal, your life has to be an open book': 'It is. I'm just lookin' for someone to read it.'

In the film, Mavis is watched over zealously by her press agent, Morgan, played by a somewhat stiff if battered Warren William. He has to hold her, by force or guile, to her unbreakable contract with her off-screen producer, A. K. Greenfield (of Superfine Pictures Incorporated), which forbids her marrying for five years. The 'sinewy' Bud Norton no longer has a barn with hay to roll in but is a garage mechanic who has invented a new method of recording sound for motion pictures and is seduced, not so much by Mae's charms, but by her promise to take him and his invention to Hollywood. Most of the story takes place in a rural guest house, The Haven, run by two Depression-hit women, the snobby Mrs Struthers (Alice Brady) and her down-to-earth Aunt Kate (Elizabeth Patterson). A star-struck waitress and rather clumsy farmhand add to the hicksville atmosphere, which is debased by a dumb negro boy, 'Nicodemus', whom Mae herself – one hopes – would never have written into the plot. The politician-lover's part in the play has been so truncated that he only appears at the front and end of the tale. In two signs of the straitened times, Mae was to work with the Xavier Cugat band, rather than Duke Ellington, and the black maid was replaced in the story by a white French maid, who is merely decorative and contributes no repartee.

Randolph Scott's somewhat glazed performance is amiable, if no precursor of his late-life blooming as the West's most grizzled loner. The best part of the film is probably the opening sequence, a film within the film of Mavis starring in a torrid South American romance – featuring her *Diamond Lil* stalwart Jack La Rue as a rejected latin lover – which is followed by Mavis's curtain speech, thanking her fans with unctuous insincerity:

MAVIS: That, my dear friends, was 'Drifting Lady,' but it was not, please believe me, the real Mavis Arden. I often say to my producer, Mr A. K. Greenfield, President of Superfine Pictures Incorporated, A. K., I say, I always call him A. K. – please oh please let me play a part that expresses the real me, a simple, unaffected country girl who finds her happiness in a garden and a swimming pool, but Mr Greenfield always says: No, no, Mavis, you are a great artiste, and it wouldn't be fair to deprive the world of your genius. So that is why I play these fascinating sirens which you seem to like to see, but oh I'm such a different person really – beneath all the glitter Mavis Arden is a very human person, like yourselves. If you, my dear pub-

Randy and Mae

lic, could only come up and see me in my little Eye-talian villa in Hollywood, I'm sure you'd be disappointed in the dullness and simplicity of my life there. I know it's cruel to disillusion you this way, but I have to be honest, and you must take it in the right spirit . . .

The irony of Mavis Arden's plight is that in the end it turns out that her press agent, Morgan, has been in love with her all along, and it is he who gets the fade-out clinch. One feels that this, too, has been written in by Mr A. K. Greenfield of Superfine Pictures Incorporated, even if Mae gets the name muddled with 'Stupefyin' Pictures'. There is little doubt that she would have preferred to flounce off the screen with muscly, 'panting' Randolph, even if recent gossip on the co-star's housing arrangements with Cary Grant suggests a somewhat flexible sexuality on his part. One senses, throughout the movie, that Mae's heart is not really in it, and she extends the minimum necessary to act the part of Mavis Arden rather than of Mae West. In her auto-biography, Mae spends two short dry paragraphs on the film, merely stating that 'it went into general release in 1937'.

Go West, Young Man is generally considered the weakest of Mae's 1930s movies, although it is directed competently by another Hollywood stalwart, Henry Hathaway, who had already directed Scott in several westerns and had just had a box-office hit with the Technicolor *Trail of the Lonesome Pine*, starring Henry Fonda and Sylvia Sidney. Cohen had recruited Hathaway to beef up the picture, but according to the director's account in Eels and Musgrove's 1984 biography of Mae: 'By the end of the first day [of shooting] I was completely disillusioned . . . She came on the set in a skintight satin dress. I took one look and asked our cameraman, Karl Struss, if her belly would show. He assured me it indeed would. So I took Mae aside and suggested maybe she should put on a girdle. She was out-raged. "You're a very sexy woman," I said, trying to soothe her, "but in the camera it looks as if you have a potbelly. We don't know how to drape it." With the patience of a great teacher she took my hand and placed it on the bulge. She proceeded to wiggle it sideways, up and down, crosswise. "Don't worry about me," she said. "It took me a long time to develop that. You just worry about yourself."'

Like her fellow vaudevillian, W. C. Fields, Mae scorned direction when it suited her and arranged her own moves. Hathaway claimed that in her scenes with Scott, he was so tall that he towered over her and had to stand in a hole. Hathaway told Musgrove that, in his opinion, all that interested Mae was 'Power . . . the power she got from making a picture was more important even than money. Her requirements demanded that she have authority, not material things.'

Hathaway was speaking of Mae's professional life, but the pursuit of power appeared to reflect Mae's approach to her private life as well. Gossip about her affairs with prizefighters was clearly so common now that Paramount had to allude in a press release to her 'generosity' in finding a job for a Filipino boxer, Speedy Dado. Dado (reportedly born Diosdado Posados) had a wife and five-year-old son and had been a noted flyweight and bantamweight fighter before his waistline took him out of both categories. Paramount explained that 'Dado is now chauffeur for the star after a series of disastrous attempts to pick which horse would finish first in a given race.' Mr Posados was soon in trouble with the police, as his penchant for violence in the ring spilled over into threatening and gun-waving behaviour at a traffic snarl-up on Beverly Boulevard. No doubt Mae helped to smooth this over, but her interest in pugilists continued with an alleged appeal to her old flame Owney Madden to assist in getting contender Joe Louis the fight that, in June 1937, won him the world heavyweight title.

Go West, Young Man was released in November 1936 to mixed notices. *Daily Variety* was pleased, noting that 'no Mae West picture has been more Westful or more zestful. It is earthy, erotic, pungent – broad comedy pitched at its most entertaining level . . . a production of lavish and sparkling quality.' The *Hollywood Reporter* was less impressed, calling it 'strictly for the Mae West fans . . . Director Henry Hathaway is the victim of the script but adroitly saves individual episodes. The production as a whole lacks distinction and is hardly an auspicious start for Emanuel Cohen under his new Paramount releasing contract.' The Legion of Decency was still not mollified by the new morals-friendly Mae and gave the film its 'B' rating for 'morally objectionable in part for all'.

The question of what next loomed quite heavily. Paramount was at a loss how to promote Mae now that her all-American sex appeal was formally off-limits. Any flimflam was worth a try. On 13 November, the studio even put out a press release stating that 'Mae West will go to Egypt to make a harem picture if she accepts the offer of a fez-wearing movie director from Cairo, who has been interviewing her for the past week.'

Aficionados of world cinema might have a frisson of regret that Mae was not, in the event, brought into proximity with the Egyptian cinema's star singer-actress, Umm Kulçum, who was flourishing in Cairo at this time. The fez-wearing Egyptian director turned out to be one of the winners of a 'Most Eligible Bachelor' contest sparked by the *Go West, Young Man* press book, the eight finalists of which were to 'meet in Hollywood and be Miss West's guests . . . Come on, you Romantic Romeos, you lagging Lotharios!' When the day came, Mae was recovering from flu, but six winners were nevertheless ushered into her presence and each handed 'a handkerchief with her name embroidered on the corner . . . "You know," Mae said, "there's nothing I like like my daily half dozen," and she stretched her white arms toward the mirrored ceiling . . . Jack Bassilli, of Cairo, Egypt [said] "Miss West is the most gorgeous and intelligent woman I have ever met in my life. I shall tell all – Egypt – and we've had Cleopatra to think about in the past."'

Mr Bassilli's invitation to Mae to come down and see Egypt some time was skilfully fended off: '"Well buddy . . . I can't say that I can make it now, but if you are a sample of the kind of men they grow there, I can't understand why Cleo let that sap get to first base with her. Mark Antony surely didn't have it on the Egyptians." And with that she pinned a rose on Mr. Bassilli's lapel.'

Mae had already recruited Cleopatra once for a Paramount press puff about powerful women, counting the Egyptian Queen among predecessors of a possible woman President of the United States, though Mae assured the public that she wasn't a candidate for the job herself. However, 'Why not? . . . Women have been running men for years. One could handle a country just as well . . . Queen Elizabeth – Cleopatra – Catherine of Russia – and a dozen others got along all right in the past . . .'

Catherine of Russia was becoming a particular bugbear of Mae's, as she was already lobbying Emanuel Cohen to take on development of a film project on the subject of the Russian Queen, who had ruled the steppes from 1762 to 1796, cantering through a multitude of lovers. Cohen, however, did not want to make 'Catherine the Great', particularly as Marlene Dietrich had already made a film on the same subject, *The Scarlet Empress* in 1934 with director Josef von Sternberg.

A long hiatus ensued while Cohen pursued other projects and Mae had to fight yet more rounds in her legal battle with Frank Wallace. She was edging towards an inevitable admission of her 1911 marriage by filing a brief in the New York Supreme Court 'charging that Wallace was a bigamist on the basis of the arguments he himself had presented to the court', since he had married Rae Blakesley in 1916 without evidence of a previous divorce. Citing similar reasoning, the New York judge hearing the case did indeed refuse Wallace's application for Mae to be declared his wife.

The case came to a head in May 1937, as Wallace petitioned a Californian court to rule on his status and 'define the rights of each party to the alleged nuptials'. Mae would not answer questions in a deposition to the plaintiff's counsel in Los Angeles and was ordered into court to answer the case under oath. In June, Wallace extended his suit to claiming joint ownership of Mae West's assets, 'community property worth $100,000'. Faced with so direct a threat, Mae had to bow to reality, and on 7 July she filed a formal answer, admitting that she had married Frank Wallace on 11 April 1911 in Milwaukee but denying that 'they ever had lived together as man and wife'.

Once again, the press could indulge in a Mae West feeding frenzy, as the 'bombshell' struck home, establishing, once and for all – and to Mae's obvious chagrin – her true age as forty-four, not thirty-seven. Copies of the original Milwaukee marriage licence were published, as well as old photographs of the couple in their youthful honeymoon glow. 'At Last "Mr. Mae" Gets Recognition,' cried out the *Los Angeles Examiner*, though Mae's attorney, Charles Milliken, tried to argue that in legal fact her denials of the marriage, 'although frequent and pointed, never have been official'. Nevertheless, Mae was in a tight spot. Wallace was reported to be planning to ask the Californian courts to force an accounting of Mae's personal fortune and sue for his half. At the same time, a letter he had allegedly written her stated that 'I still love you as my wife, in spite of the things you have said about me, and I do not see why we cannot openly assume the relations of husband and wife again and live together as married people should.' To twist the knife a little further, Wallace threatened to sue James Timony for 'alienation of affections'.

The heart of Wallace's case was his insistence that rather than Mae being a 'kissless bride', they had lived together as man and wife for three years until she left him in 1914. Our researches into Mae's vaudeville life from 1912 indicate that this was most unlikely. The press continued to follow the story avidly. A woman from New York, Mrs Eugene Perkins, the *Los Angeles Examiner* reported on 12 July, advised Mae of her own success in fending off a similar case by an estranged husband by obtaining a finding under New York laws that a wife could own separate property. Mrs Perkins prided herself on being 'the first woman to beat that community property law' and had kept half a million smackeroos from real-estate deals. Mae, on the other hand, simply claimed that, for the reasons she had given, there were no issues between her and Wallace. The Californian judge did not rule on the money but did rule that the 1911 marriage was still valid.

The *Citizen-News* reported on 29 July that Mae's studio had 'announced 98 per cent of her fan mail had been "favorable" since the song and dance man filed his declaratory suit here. Letters doubled in volume during July. Male admirers, the studio said, volunteered to lick her persistent mate. Few blamed her for trying to keep the marriage secret. Few were disillusioned that her admission of wedlock fixed her age as in the middle 40's.'

Once again, Mae benefited from her success in keeping both her male and female fans loyal. The women saw her not as a rich actress living in pampered luxury but as a woman wronged like so many others. Men saw her chivalrously as the victim of a money-grubbing heel. It was enough, for the moment, to carry her through to her next project, which was to be her last solo major Hollywood studio film and her swansong with Emanuel Cohen and Paramount.

The title was *Every Day's a Holiday*.

Flutter By, Little Butterfly

It's *déjà vu* all over again – 3 August 1937, Emanuel Cohen to Joseph Breen:

Dear Joe,
   I am attaching herewith a copy of the first draft of the Mae West musical. Naturally there will be some changes made, particularly in the latter part. Miss West, in trying to overcome the censorship problems of the past, has bent over backwards to take a clean political viewpoint – in fact, so much so that it marred the entertainment value.
   However, I am sending you this script now so that you can get an idea of the type of story and its treatment. It is our belief that there is not a single line or situation which can be considered objectionable from a censorship standpoint or from a public standpoint . . .

Breen to Cohen, 6 August:

Dear Mr Cohen,
   We have received the yellow script, dated July 29, 1937 . . . for your production titled *Mae West Musical*, and I regret to be compelled to advise you that, in its present form, the material is not acceptable under the provisions of the Production Code. It is likewise enormously dangerous from the standpoint of political censorship . . .

Breen objects to:

The large number of offensively suggestive, or double-meaning lines . . . the excessive and unnecessary drinking and drunkenness . . .
(*Detailed examples, from six-page letter*)
SCENE 6: The bartender should not spit on the floor.
SCENE 8: The piano player should not pat his forehead with his handkerchief, dipped in whiskey.
SCENE 9: We recommend that you change the word, 'sloppy', in Feet's line, to some other less offensive word.
SCENE 13: All the business of the girl blocking Nifty's way by the 'rear part

of her anatomy' should be deleted . . .

SCENE 35 et sequence: We recommend that you delete, entirely, the Italian character. If you do not do so, your picture will be rejected, in toto, in Italy.

SCENE 37: The same thing goes with reference to the word 'sphagetti . . .'

SCENE 72: We recommend that you change the word 'rotten' in Van's speech.

SCENE 81: Please eliminate the word, 'profession,' from Peaches' speech, and also the words 'on and off . . .'

SCENES 92, 93 . . . delete entirely the scene of the Chinese joint. If you do not do this, your picture may be rejected in China . . .

SCENE 105: It will be necessary that you do not indicate at any time that Peaches is a thief. If she is to be so characterized, you will have to indicate her punishment, later on . . .

SCENES 260-A, et seq.: We urge and recommend that you consult your legal department regarding the acceptability of the scenes which seem to indicate that the District Attorney of New York, the commissioner of police, and the mayor, at the turn of the present century were dishonest. It may be that some of these people, or their next of kin, are still alive, and may take serious objection to these characterizations . . .

Cohen's capitulation, this time, was swift. By 10 August, the internal files of the Motion Picture Producers and Distributors Association noted with satisfaction that the studio had made all the necessary deletions in the script for the new Mae West picture. The following day, an advance guard of the Board, Messrs Auster and Shurlock, had even gone to the studio 'to look at a Salome costume to be worn by Miss West in this picture. The costume was incomplete, but the description of the finished costume sounded satisfactory. We cautioned them, and finally left with the understanding that we would see a test of the costume made with two different materials before final approval is given.'

The lyrics and music for two songs, 'Fifi' and 'Flutter By, Little Butterfly', both by Sam Coslow, were also approved, and by 31 August Cohen sent Breen the second draft of the movie, now titled *Every Day's a Holiday*, with a grovelling note: 'I think you will find that we have complied with all of the changes suggested in your previous letter. If there are any other changes that you desire made, please let me know and I assure you we will be only too happy to comply . . .'

On 1 September, Breen approved the script, subject to further cavils, such as that, in the film, the producers 'must not overexpose the bodies of the dancing girls' and 'have in mind that the censor boards in London will not allow scenes depicting negro spirituals . . . I understand that the Salome, John the Baptist speciality is not to be included in the picture.'

It certainly wasn't. We can be mystified, and intrigued, as to the exact nature of the 'Italian character', the 'sphagetti', the 'Chinese joint' or the omitted 'Salome speciality', all of which would have certainly given us a very different picture from the sanitized, if vibrant, entertainment the movie turned out to be. The characterization of the New York police chief 'Honest' John Quade as corrupt has been retained by suggestion, and he is portrayed as more of a buffoon than a villain. What remains is, however, a return to form for Mae as comedienne rather than social reformer, although the robust character of Peaches O'Day, con artist and heartbreaker *par excellence*, still manages to mock the Code.

To quote from the movie's official press-book synopsis:

On New Years's Eve, 1899, the New York Police Department, outraged at Peaches O'Day for selling the Brooklyn Bridge over and over again, sends Captain McCarey out to bring her in. Also seeking Peaches is 'Nifty' Bailey, shoestring producer, who wants her to star in his new show. On the way to sell the bridge again, Peaches meets Graves, Butler to Van Reighle Van Pelter Van Doon, eccentric millionaire, woman-hater and leader of a reform movement. Graves makes a date with Peaches for a New Year's celebration.

After selling the bridge, Peaches meets McCarey. He advises her to get out of town. Peaches keeps the date with Graves and meets Van Doon. The three go to Rector's to celebrate the New Year. They meet 'Nifty' and it isn't long before Van Doon agrees to angel the show. In order to kill two birds with one stone, Peaches leaves town and returns as Mlle. Fifi, the rage of Paris . . .

Cohen surrounded Mae with an especially strong cast of 'eccentric' players, and her interaction with them contradicts the legend that Mae was ever jealous of her fellow actors and moved to reduce their impact and scenes. Veteran Ziegfeld Follies comic Walter Catlett, as distinctive a figure on the screen as he had been on the stage (he was to appear in Howard Hawks's *Bringing Up Baby* later the same year), played the ebullient 'Nifty', whose continual backslapping leaves stickers for his show on the backs of passers-by, prominent citizens and cops. Charles Winninger, who had portrayed 'Cap'n Henry' in the stage and screen versions of the hit *Show Boat*, was the reforming millionaire Van Doon, whose lifelong dream of pulling the

tablecloths from dining tables is fulfilled in spades on New Year's Eve. Edmund Lowe is the staunch, authentically honest cop McCarey, and Lloyd Nolan a suitably sneering Quade. Charles Butterworth, a character actor known mostly for his supporting roles, portrays a stolid motor-car driver who helps Peaches remove some choice gowns and hats from a clothes store, as he muses: 'Say, hasn't this a slight touch of larceny?'

Veteran Keystoner Chester Conklin appears in three short scenes as Peaches' carriage-driver, Herman Bing is the r-r-r-r-ridiculous sucker Frrritz Krrrausmeyer, who buys the Brooklyn Bridge, and Louis Armstrong turns up for a rip-roaring closing parade. Of Herman Bing, the encyclopaedist Ephraim Katz relates a sad trajectory: 'A former circus clown, vaudevillian and stage actor, he entered German films as an assistant to F. W. Murnau and in the late 20s accompanied the master director to Hollywood. Here he assisted Murnau on *Sunrise* (1927), then became a character comedian, turning on his heavy accent and excitable manner in numerous films of the 30s and 40s. With his career declining, he shot himself (in 1947).' Not every day was a holiday in the real-life movie business.

To direct the melange, Cohen brought in Eddie Sutherland (credited this time as A. Edward Sutherland), another vaudevillian, stuntman and jobbing actor who had grazed at Sennett's Keystone and with Chaplin before directing two of W. C. Fields's silent features – *It's the Old Army Game* (1926) and the lost remake of *Tillie's Punctured Romance* (1928). He had returned to The Great Man several times in talkies, directing *International House, Mississippi* and *Poppy*. So close a knowledge of the foibles of Fields must have stood him in good stead for handling Mae West, and there is every sign that the shooting of the movie was harmonious. Ructions rose mainly over the script, which had originally been written by Jo Swerling and then adapted by writer Alan Rivkin, who was eventually paid $5,000 to relinquish his screen credit to Mae. Mae herself claimed she had written the whole story in a rush of inspiration sparked by Sam Coslow's song 'Mademoiselle Fifi from Gay Paree'. Her extrasensory perception, she later said, must have been at work, as the whole story, characters and dialogue came to her in a flash, as if seen in her 'psychic eye'. Yet another tale has the entire piece deriving from the fact that Emanuel Cohen had a ready-made sumptuous set of the famous New York restaurant Rector's, which had to be used, complete with maestro George Rector playing himself. In the event, the screenplay credits Mae West alone.

Sutherland whipped the film along at a cracking pace, and the film editor, Ray Curtiss – editors being yet more unsung heroes of these Breen-swept projects – made the film flow regardless of the ongoing cuts and changes. Again, there are few vintage Westian quips, apart from the well-known 'My mom always told me to keep a diary and some day it'll keep you.' But there is good give and take between the characters – Mae to McCarey: 'You got me wrong, I might crack a law now and again but I ain't never broke any.' McCarey: 'The only law you ain't never broke is the law of gravity.' Mae: 'I'll go to work on that right away,' as she hands him the badge which she has just lifted from his coat.

Peaches' return as Mademoiselle Fifi, the blonde metamorphosed to brunette, clad in the most *outré* fashions by oh-so-chic Schiaparelli, is another unique late-Mae moment. Ooh-la-la-ing like crazy, she flounces on, looking for once genuinely like the male impersonators she has latterly been seen by some as portraying. Did she relish the echoes of her act as 'La Belle, the Paris damzel' who 'speak a little one English' in 1921's *Whirl of the Town*? The stage settings certainly did her proud, with flashing lights of the Folies Bergère, Moulin Rouge and Palais Royal, and squads of flower women, palette-bearing painters, flash doormen and Parisian cops marching around to 'If you like to meet Fifi / why don't you come up and see me . . .' as the gown and hat billow and sway . . .

The good cop McCarey sees through Peaches' disguise but keeps it a secret, while 'Honest John' Quade is smitten and woos her with flowers. 'Fifi', who is 'so temperamental she even annoys herself', rejects him and, in revenge, he orders McCarey to shut the theatre as a fire trap. McCarey refuses and is fired by Quade. 'Fifi' launches a charm-blitz on Quade, reducing him to jelly in his own office and chasing him out, so she can rummage through his filing cabinet and lift her own police record from its drawer.

The plot now moves to wrap up the story: Quade has been planning to run for city mayor, so Peaches suggests to her 'angel' Van Doon and his reform committee that they run McCarey for mayor against him. Parades and shows using all the city's actors, jugglers and tumblers will sell McCarey to the public: 'LAUGH, SING AND VOTE, SAYS PEACHES O'DAY.' Quade orders his men to take McCarey out of the running, and after a farcical attempt by the reformers to kidnap McCarey for his own good, he is snatched by what appears to be a band of Quade's men. 'What shall we do?' the reformers wail to Mae, having guaranteed their candidate's appearance at a mass rally in Madison Square.

'If he don't come back I'll be the Mayor!' she exclaims.

'You can't do that,' she is told, 'it's unconstitutional.'

'Not for my constitution,' says Peaches, 'I'm a suffragette.'

Every Day's a Holiday was Mae's most expensive picture, budgeted at a million dollars, with a large slice of that going into the final torchlight parade scene, including a spectacular reconstruction of the famous square at the turn of the twentieth century. Louis Armstrong led a phalanx of black musicians down the great studio set, playing Hoagy Carmichael's tune of 'Jubilee', followed by Mae in a throne set aboard a great carriage, lashing away somewhat unconvincingly

Mae the brunette: Mademoiselle Fifi of gay Paree

319

at a set of jazz drums. Once again, Mae had convinced Cohen to insert a popular jazz performer of the day into one of her pictures, although it should be noted that the pristine white uniforms and helmets the band cavorts in were those of the 'white wings' – the city street-cleaners.

McCarey escapes from his captivity – which is revealed to have been engineered by Peaches to keep him safe from Quade (she had bribed Quade's own goons with their stolen criminal records) – to make his date on the podium and slug Quade in the puss. The crowd roars, 'Vote for McCarey!' Once again, Mae West has won the day.

Getting the fictional 'good cop' elected mayor on celluloid, however, proved far easier for Mae than regaining her status as a 'member in good standing' in show biz. As if fate were recreating the jinxes of her early stage-revue years, a new scandal erupted within days of the end of the film shoot from an unexpected source.

The medium of this threat was neither stage nor screen but radio. Radio had been the salvation of more than one stage or screen star who was experiencing that sinking middle-age feeling of being left behind by shifting fashions and tastes. Fanny Brice, who failed to make the leap from stage to screen, had nevertheless remained famous on radio. Radio stars of the early 1930s found it a stepping stone to the movies. The latest beneficiary of the wireless had been W. C. Fields, who, languishing in hospital after 1936's *Poppy*, lunged at the microphone 'and seized it by the throat'. Fields was teamed with the young ventriloquist Edgar Bergen and his obnoxious dummy, Charlie McCarthy, in a series of enormously popular routines broadcast throughout 1937, as well as recycling his old sketches, such as 'The Pharmacist' and 'The Golf Game'. The Bergen–Charlie McCarthy show was hosted on the *Chase and Sanborn Hour*, sponsored by the coffee manufacturers of that name and broadcast by NBC.

There was no reason why Mae West, too, should not be able to exchange ribald repartee with the little wooden boy on air, and she was booked for a Sunday show broadcasting from Los Angeles on 12 December. The portion of the show featuring banter with Charlie was fairly tame, with Mae recounting her invitation to Charlie to 'come up and see me some time' and then saying: 'You weren't so nervous and backward at my apartment . . . You didn't need any encouragement to kiss me.' 'Did I do that?' asks Charlie. 'You certainly did, I got the marks to prove it, an' the splinters too.' This did not appear to cause the public too many conniptions. But the central sketch, specially written by Arch Oboler (later to direct the first 3D feature, *Bwana Devil* in 1952), sparked a firecracker that lit up the bluenoses from coast to coast.

The scene of the sketch was the Garden of Eden. Mae, of course, was Eve, with dashing Don Ameche as Adam and Edgar Bergen's Charlie moonlighting as the Snake. The sketch was introduced thus:

Under a spreading fig tree rests one Mr. Adam – sprawled out lazily in the hot sun. Eve, obviously, is bored beyond endurance as they play a game of cards with a deck of fig leaves.

EVE: Listen, tall, tanned and tired. I think it's about time to tell you a thing or three. Ever since creation what have I done? Do I go any place? Do I do anything? No – just sit here playin' double solitaire! I tell you it's disgustin'!

ADAM: Oh, we've got a nice place here!

EVE: That's the trouble – it's too nice! . . . I want somethin' to happen! A little excitement – a little adventure! A girl's got to have a little fun once in a while . . .

Adam and Eve banter a little more, Eve finally saying:

EVE: Adam, you don't know a thing about women!

ADAM: Ahh! You apparently forget you were originally one of my ribs.

EVE: A rib once, but I'm beefin' now! . . . A couple of months of peace and security and a woman's bored all the way down to the bottom of her marriage certificate.

Eve is tempted to the fenced-off apple tree while Adam goes off fishing, only to encounter the Snake ('Hello, long, dark and slinky . . .'), the angle being that it's Eve who tempts the Snake to get her the forbidden fruit, rather than the other way around:

SNAKE: But, forbidden fruit!

EVE: Get in there and get those apples! Are you a snake or are you a mouse?

SNAKE: I'll – I'll do it!

EVE: Now you're hissin'! Here, right between these pickets!

SNAKE: I'm – I'm stuck!

EVE: Shake your hips! . . . There, you're through . . . Get me two big ones . . . I feel like doin' a big apple! . . .

SNAKE: Say, wait a minute . . . Adam'll never eat that forbidden apple . . .

EVE: He will if I feed him what women'll feed men for the rest of time!

SNAKE: What's that?

EVE: Apple sauce!

Adam quaffs the apple sauce, gets groggy, noise of pandemonium.
Adam and Eve have been dispossessed for 'forbidden apple sauce'.

ADAM: Eve, what have you done?
EVE: I've just made a little more history, that's all. I'm the first woman to
have her own way – and a snake'll take the rap for it!

The whole thing might be regarded today as child's play and
should have read that way on the page. Given Mae's usual sultry
delivery, however, it seemed more suggestive, with a final smacking
kiss between Eve and Adam representing the original 'sin'. In the
heated moral ambience of the day, all hell broke loose. The wrath of
the righteous was conveyed in no uncertain terms by the *Baltimore
Catholic Review* of 17 December:

> CHASE, SANBORN SPONSORS HOUR OF INDECENCY.
> MAE WEST EXPOUNDS HER SEXUAL PHILOSOPHY IN
> CARICATURE OF BIBLICAL STORY.
> DR. MAURICE S. SHEEHY URGES SPEEDY PROTEST.

The following letter has been received by The Review from the Rev. Maurice
S. Sheehy, head of the Department of Religion, the Catholic University of
America:

May I solicit your editorial support on a matter I consider of grave importance at this time when religious ideals and moral standards are being openly flaunted [*sic*] in the press, on the screen, and over the radio? On Sunday
evening, over a national hook-up, the Chase and Sanborn Coffee Company
presented the most indecent, scurrilous and religiously irreverent program
that it has been my misfortune to hear . . . In her peculiarly indecent style,
Miss (or is it Mrs.?) West introduced her own sexual philosophy into the
biblical incident of the Fall of Man.

In the name of all 'decent people', the *Review* and other religious
protestors demanded that the hapless coffee-makers and NBC be
brought to account. The attacks piled up from all over the country,
forcing the Federal Communications Commission to order a 'complete investigation' of the sketch. NBC Chairman Frank R. McNinch
admitted that 'there is marked uniformity of thought in the letters of
protest, which variously categorize the skit as "profane," "obscene,"
"indecent," "vulgar," "filthy," "dirty," "sexy" and "insulting to the
American public."' The FCC pointed out that although it had no
'power of censorship over radio broadcasts', it had a 'moral duty and
obligation to protect the public from offensive broadcasts'.

Emanuel Cohen was sent reeling by these unexpected broadsides. He had hoped for a trouble-free release of *Every Day's a Holiday* in January and now had to consider a postponement. The studio, trying to limit the damage, issued a statement in Mae's name that she had herself objected to the script – 'she wanted to play a part from her recent picture, but the producers of the show ruled otherwise. They insisted on the "Adam and Eve" skit. Miss West objected to it on the ground that anything connected with Adam and Eve is too closely associated with religion to be made into a comedy.'

Nobody believed this disclaimer, although Mae West fans rallied to her cause and wrote NBC counter-letters pointing out that 'the script was typical "West" comedy and was highly enjoyable'. The advertising company, J. Walter Thompson, representing the sponsors, nevertheless issued a grovelling apology for the incident and stated: 'we can assure the public at large that the same error will not be made again'.

Unschooled in the politics of radio, Mae had misjudged the speed with which an enterprise broadcasting into people's homes, sponsored by companies made easily vulnerable by pressure on advertisers, could be reduced to quivering jelly. The revenge of the reformers, this time round, was ferocious, as the *Los Angeles Examiner* related in its 'Views and Reviews' column on 4 January 1938:

The name of Mae West – much more of a miss than a hit – has been banned from use on its radio programs by the National Broadcasting Company.

Such action is the only proper protection for the homes of decent American citizens.

Banned from the air by a great broadcasting chain and jailed for her performances on the stage, Mae West finds refuge only in motion pictures.

Is it not time, indeed, that film producers learned that impropriety is not acceptable to the American people and that there is not even a satisfying supply of tainted money in questionable films and performances to warrant risking the condemnation of the better elements of the public?

Moving picture people have always found that money, prestige and popularity are the rewards of films that are clean and wholesome.

Box office receipts, if nothing else, should show the moving picture people that salaciousness is not only bad morals, but bad business, and should teach them to be clean, wholesome and American.

Every Day's a Holiday was nevertheless released on 14 January, having been previewed just before Christmas 1937 to mixed reviews.

Mae by Al Hirschfeld in *Every Day's a Holiday*

The *Hollywood Reporter* unusually praised it as 'sumptuous in atmosphere and setting . . . Mae is Mae as always, sartorially magnificent in the stunning wardrobe designed for her by Schiaparelli . . .' *Variety* noted that though the film was 'less flagrantly sexy than previous Mae West screen exhibits . . . indeed, quite conservative – a model of discretion', it was 'a robust piece of entertainment, lush and colorful, displaying Miss West's unmatched burlesque gifts luxuriantly'. Non-trade newspapers were less enthusiastic, the *New York Times* bewailing 'a witless period comedy', and Howard Barnes in the *New York Herald Tribune* blowing it the ultimate razzberry by calling it 'clean and dull'. Audiences were likewise divided, and the usual Mae West lift appeared to be absent. Emanuel Cohen and Paramount saw swiftly that the film was not going to recover its cost. A double decoupling, of Paramount from Cohen's Major Pictures and of Cohen's Major Pictures from Mae West, followed in the weeks and months ahead. The movie press book's promotional stunts were to be a rather fading echo of the great ballyhoos of the past:

WELCOME A CUTOUT OF MAE TO TOWN
The Mae West 'welcome' stunt has always been popular with showmen – and it has demonstrated its value at the box office! Use the life-size cutout of Mae West from the exchange three-sheet, mount it on compoboard, and bring it into town for a city-wide welcome, just as if you were entertaining Mae West herself . . . Have your reception committee at the station or edge of town escort a bannered open car, in which 'Mae' is riding, to the spot where she will be greeted officially by the civic officials in charge of the welcome . . . Follow this visit to the Mayor with a pre-arranged welcome as guest of honor at a civic or service club luncheon, where the club's comedians can make speeches of welcome. After the lunch, have 'Mae' make a tour of the city and pose her with local business men, well-known cops or other local personalities for pictures to be planted in the newspapers . . .

Alas, no amount of parading paper cut-outs of Mae through the towns and cities of America could bring her back to life in the movies – yet.

In Mae West's long life, and a career nearly as long in show business, the six years between 1932 and 1937 were the apex, the top of the curve. Hollywood had taken the raw material of Mae's stage passion and transformed her, by its celluloid magic, into a unique figure, a stranger even to herself, a flesh-and-blood cut-out to whose image she would have to live up, while at the same time bowing to the censor's yoke. This was no easy task. In the years to come there would be four comeback movies, only the first, *My Little Chickadee*, acknowledged as a *bona fide* classic in its double-headed romp with W. C. Fields; the second, 1943's *The Heat's On*, registering as an odd blip on an erratic trajectory; the third and fourth, *Myra Breckinridge* and *Sextette*, to appear much later – bizarre elements of a Salvador Dalí-like landscape of a 'persistence of vision'.

But, in 1938, Mae West was still brimful of plans and projects, unwilling to accept defeat and fully determined to remain the focus of the spotlight that she had vowed, as 'Baby Mae' of amateur night in Brooklyn, never to allow to shift from herself.

PART FIVE

Herself Alone

32

Off Screen as On . . .

On the front page of the *Mansfield (Ohio) News Journal*, 7 March 1938, a selection of important world events of the last week:

WOMAN BARES FANTASTIC DEATH PLOT IN RUSSIA.
REVEALS PLAN TO KILL BOTH LENIN, STALIN –
First Feminine Soviet Official Blames Conspiracy on One of 21 Treason Suspects . . .

GOVERNOR SAYS STATE ENGINEER AIDING 'SMEAR CAMPAIGN'
FOR PERSONAL GAINS . . .
MARRIAGE TOUTS FACE JAIL . . .
ON SCREEN AND OFF, THIS WEST GAL IS ALWAYS SAME –
WORDS, GESTURES, CLOTHES

Mae West is Mae West off and on screen, 24 hours a day. And if there are scattered moments when she isn't – only the gal of the undulating hips knows. And maybe Timony . . . Before you meet her you are prepared for everything and anything – except what you find. And that is the identical personality and makeup that you see on the screen. She never steps out of character. She wears the same kind of clothes off the screen as on. She slurs her words and has the same gestures in her off-screen conversation . . .

Once the mask is created and set in the imagination by that sixty-foot screen that makes nostrils look like subway tunnels, it proves difficult to slip on and off at will. Even stars who played different dramatic roles, like Garbo or Dietrich or Cagney or Edward G. Robinson, found the fantasy fixed in public reality. So much more so the comedians, who, like Groucho Marx, slap on a dash of greasepaint and are then remembered for that face alone, or W. C. Fields, who laboured many years to create his own character and was then trapped in his own invention. Mae West found, despite her years on the stage trying on her masks, from The Hussy to Margy Lamont, Babe Carson-cum-Gordon to Diamond Lil, that

329

she had become to the world a character called Mae West and surrendered herself to the image.

Mae's great boast, in many interviews, was that she never allowed a negative thought to take root in her mind: in work, play, sex and health matters she always accentuated the positive – that most American of religions. Positive thinking enabled her to sail through the bad times and make the most of the good. 'I never wanted to be

330

anybody else,' she would say. 'If I wanted to be somebody in history – Florence Nightingale or Madame de Pompadour or Catherine the Great, who was a preincarnation of myself – I'd just write a play for myself about 'em . . .' When the interviewer for *Playboy* magazine who extracted this from her thanked her for her generosity and her time, she told him: 'It was fun for me, dear. I always enjoy talkin' about myself . . . Come up any time.'

But this air of eternal optimism did not entirely conceal the obvious fact that there were troughs as well as peaks in Mae's mood. She had weathered the assaults of the New York stage reformers largely due to the immediate support of audiences who were palpable on the other side of the footlights, a living, breathing, applauding throng. This could not be repeated on the screen. Mae's screen-life supporters may have been a vast multitude but they were a faceless crowd out there, somewhere in the gloaming of Depression America, manifest by fan letters and statistics. In her immediate surroundings Mae had the paraphernalia of the movie studios, the flesh-and-blood casts and crews, and also the phalanx of producers, supervisors and executives, who were subject directly to the pummelling and jostling of the legions of scourgers and scourers. The massed editorials, denunciations, rebukes, insults and threats could not fail to make an impact on even the most positive soul.

The fact that these denunciations came thick and fast from the most powerful organized churches in the country was – as well as threatening to Mae's future as a performer – much more hurtful than she ever let on. As we have seen in examining *Klondike Annie*, there was a strong strand of Mae's private morality that derived from a personal faith that perhaps only James Timony could fully appreciate, he who accompanied her to Sunday services and remained her most faithful retainer. Timony continued to suffer the obloquy of being added to Frank Wallace's ongoing suit against Mae, as the man who had 'alienated' her affections and defamed her ever-loving ex-husband. This case was set to run for four more years.

The drip, drip, drip of endless legal processes continued, too, with the old jewel-theft case of 1932, when the chief suspect, Harry Voiler, returned to California to enter a plea of Not Guilty. Put on trial in March 1938, he was swiftly exonerated when the court was told that Edward Friedman, already serving his sentence for the robbery, repudiated his earlier naming of Voiler as the instigator of the crime and would not testify in the case. Voiler was free to go.

Another lawsuit featured an old aquaintance, playwright Mark Linder, suing Mae for a million dollars' profit from *She Done Him Wrong*, on the basis that he had written the original script from which the original *Diamond Lil* emerged. The *Los Angeles Citizen-News* gave a snapshot of the scene on 15 June, as Mae dropped in on the offices of attorney Joseph Rosen, where she had been ordered by the court to give her deposition:

The clock said two and Hollywood boulevard was at its busiest when the slightly incredible proceedings began. A limousine the size of a freight car, but shinier, rolled to the curb. A Filipino chauffeur in a mauve uniform opened the door and saluted. Out stepped Mae. What a Mae!

Covering her curves, but not concealing them, was a brown dress with diamond shaped white spots on it. Covering her shoulders was a white cape of close-clipped fur, as if an Albino calf had made the supreme sacrifice. On her left lapel were two orchids of palest lavender, entwined with some maiden's breath. On her head was a hat so wide and so big it almost engulfed her golden curls – but not quite. On her feet were tan slippers with heels so tall, she almost slipped off the running board . . .

Miss West posed on the curb for the photographers, while her red faced business manager, James Timony, bulking large in a double-breasted checked coat, glowered. They walked into the elevator and more flashlights popped. Upstairs another contingent of photographers did their work on the run, because Miss West was walking in a hurry. She walked into Rosen's office. So did the photographers. So did Timony.

'This is a publicity frameup,' he shouted. 'It is unethical. You are trying this case in the newspapers. If you hadn't let the newspapers know, there never would have been these photographers. They make Miss West nervous. It isn't right . . .'

As ever, Hollywood is as Hollywood does. Timony, having been accused in the past of orchestrating Mae's contacts with New York's organized crime, appeared to be a shadow, albeit a bulky one, of his former self. Denied a significant role in Mae's relations with the studios, he had continued to dabble with his Hollytown Theater, mounting the plays Mae wrote for him anonymously.

In July, columnist Sidney Skolsky noted that there were five actresses 'declared poison at the box office', naming 'Mae West, Marlene Dietrich, Katharine Hepburn, Joan Crawford, Kay Francis and Greta

Garbo'. Apart from totalling six, this list merely showed how little gossip columnists – or theatre owners, who had compiled the list – understood the concept of any creative staying power. By that summer, in fact, Mae had completed the first of her personal-appearance tours, which had kicked off in February when she headed east to Chicago. Mae's agent Murray Feil had booked the tour, which would include one-week stands at Columbus, Washington, Baltimore and other east-coast venues. This tour was to set the template for future Mae West road circuses, with several supporting vaudeville acts and an entourage of male singers attached. When Mae reached New York in April, the act included Jack Powell, blackface comedy-drummer, Moore and Revel, 'satirical ballroom dancers', Frakson the magician and 'Juanita and her Champion, skating marvels', along with Milton Watson and 'six leading men'.

This was the tour that caused near riots and ructions as, in Boston, 'a clutching, squealing crowd of 3000 eager admirers . . . turned the South Station into a mob scene'. In Hartford, 30,000 turned out for a 'Mae West Safe Driving Week' parade, which 'created one of the wildest and maddest crowd scenes in several years. Not since Lindbergh came to town has there been such a tumult . . .' In Columbus, Ohio, Mae played the Palace Theater, whose other attraction that week was the movie *Love, Honor and Behave*, not quite the full motto for Mae West. Orchestra leader Lionel Newman recalled the show and his recruitment by Mae, speaking to Stanley Musgrove and George Eels forty years later:

I was a tall, skinny young guy, and when I went to her apartment for the interview, I was scared to death. I was still a virgin, and I thought she was going to rape me. She received me in her bedroom. She didn't look young, or old either. She showed no sexual interest in me whatever. I was such a kid she never called me Lionel or Mr. Newman. It was always, 'Hey, Newman!' On those tours we didn't carry an orchestra. We'd go into a town and hire musicians. But whatever they wore, she demanded I wear tails.

Another clipping describes the set: 'Attractive velvet backdrops, with a chaise longue the only piece of furniture, her six leading men in toppers, tails and canes, advance to center mike from the wings and sing the praises of the Sultana of Sex . . . Her voluptuous figure, clothed in glittering black jet costume with black ostrich feather headdress, the whole designed to give her conception of Catherine the Great . . . Sure and certain of herself, she does a typical West strut to the mike and sings "You Must Come Up and See Me Sometime" . . .'

Newman remembered the show attracting what he called the Overcoat Brigade – 'she told me to watch the first couple of rows . . . and you'd see these guys scattered around masturbating under their coats. And that, to her, was the greatest compliment you could give her.' Well, perhaps, at forty-five years of age. Newman also recalled to Musgrove and Eels that on one of the train journeys the train was rocking so hard the star was having orgasms. 'They had to get her some pills to prevent that,' he recalled. Which only demonstrates, once again, the pitfalls of oral history.

Mae's tour certainly proved to her that, whatever the moral guardians and the movie moguls thought, there was still an audience in America that wanted more, not less, Mae West. And not only in America, since Mae was a favourite abroad, too, most evidently in Great Britain, which had no domestic substitute in the drab, depressive 1930s apart from the robust Gracie Fields. But a putative deal for a trip to the Palladium, London, in mid-1938 fell through, and her arrival in the British Isles had to wait until 1947.

Nevertheless, Mae's exile from movies was irksome, and her troubles deepened her interest in the familiar range of mental and spiritual disciplines that might provide balm in the rat race. ESP and seances continued to be one form of escape. One session described in *Mae West on Sex, Health and ESP* involved communicating with the aviatrix Amelia Earhart, who had disappeared in 1937 during a flight over the Pacific Ocean. At the 'posh resort at La Cinta . . . a place for private people', where many movie mavins relaxed and made their real deals, Mae joined what she claimed in her book – falsely – to be her first seance to contact the lost pilot. As the table tipped in her direction, Mae recalled, it seemed that Amelia Earhart had a message from Mae's dead father. Another participant in these seances, Mae wrote, was a Jewish executive from a devout family, who had never married his Catholic girlfriend. A message in Yiddish, however, from his dead mother enjoined him to 'do what your heart tells you . . . and never mind your father'. This, for some reason, convinced Mae that 'there might be something to the psychic world', rather than suggesting that frauds come in many forms and languages.

Mae's attraction, or gullibility, to spiritual mentors led her down a very dangerous path in the summer of 1939, when she received the leader of the Moral Rearmament movement, Dr Frank Buchman, in her apartment. It was her birthday, 17 August, and Mr Buchman 'went up to see her . . . to discuss the principles of the world spiritual crusade he heads'. At the end of their meeting, Mae proclaimed herself a disciple. Eels and Musgrove, the only previous Mae biographers to give this mention, play Buchman down as a 'famous but naïve religious' leader whom Mae had persuaded to give her credibility, but the benefit was all the other way. Buchman, a Pennsylvania-born evangelist and ordained Lutheran minister, had visited England in 1921, where he formed among his students in Oxford ('The Oxford Group') a movement dedicated to 'world-changing through life-changing'. They stressed the four qualities of Honesty, Purity, Love and Unselfishness but rejected any form of secular collective ideas, becoming fiercely anti-communist and evangelizing in churches, colleges and people's homes. In 1938, the movement was formalized as 'Moral Rearmament'. But, in 1936, Buchman had already been led by his anti-communism to praise Adolph Hitler, stating, in the *New York World-Telegram*: 'I thank heaven for a man like Adolph Hitler, who built a front line of defense against the anti-Christ of Communism . . . Of course, I don't condone everything the Nazis do. Anti-Semitism? Bad, naturally. I suppose Hitler sees a Karl Marx in every Jew. But think what it would mean if Hitler surrendered to the control of God?' This became Buchman's mantra, that only 'God-controlled' people were sane in an insane world. 'The true patriot,' he would state in 1961, 'gives his life to bring his nation under God's control.' Buchman's 1936 view that 'a God-controlled Fascist dictatorship' could be valid frightened off many at the time, though he ended up counting such good Americans as Henry Ford, Harry Guggenheim, Mayor Fiorello La Guardia, Joe DiMaggio, Senator Harry Truman, General Pershing and Mae West among his acolytes.

One offshoot of Buchman's Oxford Group was Alcoholics Anonymous, who broke away from his religious and political dictums but adopted his practical self-help methods as the basis for their '12-Step Recovery' plan. It is possible that Mae, ever a zealous non-drinker, wished to encourage this positive element. Her comments on Buchman's visit were tied in, for the press pack, with her latest promotion, the forthcoming double-headed comedy in pre-production with W. C. Fields. 'Moral Rearmament is just the thing he needs,' she said. Fields, of course, was not present or he would have poured a bucketful of sick on this particular idea.

The Fields–West project, which became *My Little Chickadee*, has been subject to a familiar inundation of mythology and charades. The question of what to do next after her tour was vexing Mae through the early months of 1939. By now, she had completed her first screenplay of 'Catherine the Great' but still had no takers. Questioned by journalists, she said, hopefully: 'That was some gal, that Catherine. Ruled a country and kept her men going at the same time. Really a swell story. And I'm going to do it. Maybe in one year, two, three or five. But the picture will have to be one of those million dollar affairs in technicolor. That's why we've postponed production. Later on the setup will be better.'

In the meantime, there were reports that Mae would play another lady of the past, heading back to Broadway for a stage production of Aristophanes' *Lysistrata*, which would be 'tricked out with tunes and dancing as a musical comedy. The artist, Russell Patterson, and the Shubert producing organization are reported to be backing the venture.' But this did not happen either. In the interim, Universal Studios, with whom Mae had flirted with no result since 1915, came up with a proposal for the movie with Bill Fields.

As Paramount stars, Mae and Bill were no strangers to each other, particularly as during the height of her fame their dressing rooms were adjacent to each other on the lot. A clipping from Mae's archive, undated but referring to Fields's 1935 work, reveals an intriguing early offer:

'Some day I shall contribute to literature my treatise on the subject of beds – if I can get out of bed long enough,' said W. C. Fields between the scenes of a Pullman berth sequence in Paramount's 'The Old Fashioned Way' . . . 'I have been approached by Mae West to consider collaborating. But I want my work to stand out individually. Besides Mae has the wrong slant on this thing. She says she does her best writing in bed. Well, I do my best loafing there, and consider that that is the primary purpose of a bed.'

The legend of *My Little Chickadee* remains in many minds a tale of two rivals slugging it out for credits and power. Bill wrote his own lines, Mae wrote hers, and seldom the twain did meet. In fact, as vaudeville babies, both Fields and West had a long stage past in common. In private they were poles apart: he liked his liquor abundant and his female companions young and pliable; she liked the liquor locked in the cupboard and her men young, sober and hunky. Nevertheless, they also shared another powerful common interest, that of performers fighting to get their own way in the face of studio procedures.

Universal, founded by Carl Laemmle, had been run until 1935 by his son, Carl Junior, who eventually sold his studio interests to a group of businessmen who struggled to keep the company viable. In 1938, a new team headed by Nate Blumberg took over, with Cliff Work as the production executive. Within a year Universal emerged from the deficits that had dogged it throughout the Depression. Compared with the giant Paramount, this was a second-rank enterprise, notable chiefly for its low-budget horror hits of the early 1930s, *Dracula* and *Frankenstein,* and some first-rank musicals, such as 1936's *Show Boat.* By 1939, though, it had inherited some of Paramount's stars, with Marlene Dietrich heading the cast of the western *Destry Rides Again* with James Stewart and Charles Winninger (of Mae's *Every Day's a Holiday*). In the spirit of repeating a successful formula, the studio adopted the project of a western with Mae and Bill.

The kernel of the idea allegedly came from an early story named 'December and Mae' concocted by Fields while on one of his many drying-out cures. This combined his old reprobate circus trickster with Mae's 'Gay Nineties' character. Some of Fields's drafts, under titles such as 'Honky Tonk', 'The Little Lady', 'The Sheriff and the Little Lady' or 'Husband in Name Only', incorporated a character often cut from his own films, a trapeze-artiste 'wife' named Gorgeous. Fields suggested his good friend Gene Fowler should develop the screenplay, but the studio passed the parcel to a more pliable writer, Grover Jones. When Jones's script arrived in July, Fields waxed furious and denounced it as 'a cross between The Drunkard and Nick Carter'. In quick response he dashed out a lampoon, entitled 'Corn With the Wind, a Cinema "Epic-Ac" of Long Ago. Based on the novel idea that movie audiences have the minds of 12 year olds.'

Mae later claimed that she had written the whole script herself, leaving Fields room to construct his own dialogue in the scenes they had together. Original credit is further muddled by the claim of producer Lester Cowan, who said he had developed the basic plot himself from a play by Ferenc Molnár called *The Guardsman*: 'I swiped

the idea and helped Grover Jones with the screenplay.' This was calculated to enrage both his stars.

There can be no doubt that Mae wrote her own lines, since Fields
knew quite well that, to a comedian, one's jokes are the nub of one's
soul. But adrift on her own, with no powerful mentor like the ever-
shrewd Cohen to back her, it appears that Mae, in this case, was less
eager than Fields to fight tooth and nail with the studio. Fields was
fiercely, obsessively hostile to Lester Cowan, a brusque individual
who, ten years later, achieved the incredible feat of arousing so calm
a soul as Harpo Marx to venomous fury.

Fields's feud with Universal (related previously both in my own
work and that by James Curtis) can now be seen in a more poignant
light thanks to a series of letters, hitherto unknown and found in
Mae's archive, written by Bill to Mae between September and
October of 1939, just before shooting commenced. There do not
appear to be any answers by Mae. Fields wrote to her on 11
September:

Dear Mae,

I have a story or the epitome of one which I think we could work to our
satisfaction. I do not know whether Cowan has shown it to you or not. But
we will have to get together and talk it over at your convenience and
wherever you say.

I purposely left out writing your scenes. The following excerpt from my
letter to Cliff Work of August 30 will explain why I did not write more
scenes in my script for you:

'No matter what you hear to the contrary you know that I am not a hog
or a thief and that I can be trusted. Miss West will take care of herself and
she has only to wave her little finger to have me pitch in and write scenes
for her or collaborate with her or leave her entirely alone, as she desires
. . .' [handwritten: 'She knows and can write for herself better than anyone
else.']

Mr Jones in the two scripts I have seen has failed by a country mile to
get either of our characters. He is not confident and fancies himself no end.

All this is only one man's opinion. Further, Mr. Cowan who has just
recently graduated from the Screen Actor's Guild as an executive, seems to
want to grab the wheel. He has aligned himself with Mr. Jones and Mr.
Cline, our director. They all seem very smug and assured they are going to
tell me just when to sit on my hind legs and when to roll over. I am now
giving them absent treatment . . .

I feel we must understand each other thoroughly and that we must get together for a chat if we are to make this opus. I am so thoroughly disgusted I have asked them several times to let me out of my contract. When I am to be placed in the tender mercies and to be guided by the trio of Jones, Cowan and Cline, it's time to take a laminster.

Best wishes as always to Timmony and yourself,
Bill Fields

Mae did not seem to respond to Fields's request for a meeting, but he continued writing to her, sending on copies of his blistering correspondence with Cowan:

My idea of starring with Miss West, even taking practically second billing, was done in the interests of Universal. I was and still am, willing you shall be given credit for anything your whimsical mind dictates. I felt I had in you a young friend and to think you should align yourself with the director and writer and make false or evasive statements to me is inconceivable. Maybe Leo Tolstoy summed it up when he said: 'All the Gods were there

Al Hirschfeld's Mae and Bill

and they all knew each other, except two, who were never introduced –
Benevolence and Gratitude' . . .

On 6 October, Fields once again wrote to Mae appealing for her
support, stating, 'between you and me, Mae, I will be a pushover for
giving up this point if we can get supervision and a director that is
compatible to you . . . I have great enthusiasm for this picture and my
only hope is that we can do it without interference from outside interests who have not really got the success of the picture at heart, but
their own aggrandizement.' On 12 October, Fields sent her a copy of
his letter to Universal executive Matty Fox, asking to be let off the
assignment if Lester Cowan continued to be in charge – 'but I insist
on Miss West going along with me'. There was an added P.S.: 'The
fact that Lester has just lost his wisdom teeth, vide local Zeitungs, has
nothing to do with this letter.'

In the end Cowan, perhaps pleading his aching molars, did not
oversee the shoot, though he still maintained the producer's credit.

Mae kept out of this feud for the simple reason that she had her
own recurring problems with Joe Breen at the Hays Office, which
had moved to Red Alert at the sight of a new Mae West script with
added Fieldsian impedimenta. A six-page letter from Breen to
Universal executive Maurice Pivar enumerated all the familiar details
which rendered the script 'not acceptable': 'Scene 12: The "revealing
white lawn blouse" worn by Miss West in this scene, must not expose
her breasts. Scene 12, page 5: We suggest that you re-write the qua-
train, "He who sins, and runs away, Must die in sin, Another day."
In this same scene, please delete in toto the entire speech regarding
the traveling salesman.'

Strange censor fetishes abound: 'Scene 51: The acceptability of this
scene with the dancing figures on rubber, will depend entirely on how
it is shot . . . Scene 85, with Baxter "broken out in sweat." Any such
scene will, of course, not be approved . . . Please eliminate the "daring costume" of Lita . . . The word "punk" is always deleted by the
British Board of Film Censors, and the word "lousy" is included in
the list of words which must be omitted . . . Page 93: Please eliminate
the seemingly endless kiss . . . Scene 313, page 117: Please eliminate
Munbane's line, "Go ahead and shoot, I've seen everything . . ."'

None of these intriguing titillations have survived into the movie,
which was finally shot between November and December 1939 and

released in February 1940. The Fields and West ideas have been incorporated into the tale of Flower Belle Lee, kidnapped in the first scene by the Masked Bandit in a stagecoach hold-up, who returns to town on her own steam, saying only: 'I was in a tight spot but I managed to wriggle out of it.' Caught out meeting the bandit at night by town busybody Miss Gideon (Margaret Hamilton, fresh from portraying the Wicked Witch of Oz), Flower Belle is ordered to leave town and 'not to return until you're respectable, and married'. The train to Greasewood City, however, makes an unscheduled stop to pick up Fields – borne across the track by his Indian bearer – alias Cuthbert J. Twillie, 'Novelties and Notions'. 'What kind of notions you got?' coos Flower Belle. 'Some are old, some are new,' grates the old soak, his nose fully grown to its mythologically bulbous proportions. Flower Belle spots what appears to be a pile of cash in Twillie's bag and eggs on travelling companion Amos Budge (Donald Meek), a card sharp dressed as a preacher, to fix a marriage of convenience. Meanwhile, the putative Sheriff of Greasewood City has been killed aboard the train in a shoot-out with Indians (all dispatched by Flower Belle as in a shooting gallery) and Twillie becomes the town's new sheriff.

Sheriffs do not last long in Greasewood City, which is run by big shot Jeff Badger (played by Joseph Calleia), who is, in fact, the Masked Bandit. There goes the plot. Twillie and Flower Belle fence with each other, especially after she discovers his money is fake and keeps him at more than arm's length. Fields gets into bed with a goat by mistake, a scene which generated his own contretemps with the Hays Office, which objected fiercely to him 'fondling it, remarking about its smell, etc.'.

On the set, the vaunted rivalry with Fields was not in evidence. *Picture Play* reported on 13 November upon the first day of shooting:

FIRST 'TAKE' WITHOUT SPARKS

'That's Eddie Cline, the director,' said a guide, 'he is the man who, when asked if he was the director of the West–Fields picture, replied: "No, I'm the referee."'

This is how it looks: Mae, curvesome as ever, is wearing a long, form-fitting blue dress with a bustle.

Fields is resplendent in top-hat, dark striped coat and trousers, spats and yellow gloves . . .

The first scene is in the lobby of a typical frontier hotel. The stars cross the lobby and Mae says to the clerk: 'Two rooms please.'

'The bridal suite,' Fields adds. 'We're married, you know.'
'I'll take the suite,' puts in Mae. 'Give him the rooms.'

'We realize that our comedy styles are just different,' Mae explained to her interviewer, 'and we understand that the more we build each other up the better our picture will be.' Harry Evans, for the magazine *The Family Circle*, was smit with both Bill and Mae: 'I was charmed, fascinated, and hooked. Every move she made was the Mae West I had hoped she would be. Not only the gestures, the voice, and the strut, but what she said and how she said it. The upward tilt of the eyes, the palm of the hand on the hip . . . "I have to dominate the action in my scenes, or they won't go over . . . I usually play the character of a woman who is, well, not exactly a church worker. At the same time, I must carry out some sort of love interest. In order to play this shady character and keep the sympathy of the audience there's one thing I must have – dignity . . . If I allow other characters to dominate me, where's my dignity?"'

In the event, Mae had her own scenes, with the townspeople, the local newspaper editor, Carter, played by Dick Foran, and the boss-cum-bandit, and Fields had his, with the barflies, the card players ('Is this a game of chance?' 'Not the way I play it') and his great hanging scene which occasioned – as he is mistaken for the bandit and about to be strung up – one of his immortal comments: when asked, 'Have you any last wish?' he replies: 'Yes, I'd like to see Paris before I die!' and, as the rope tugs: 'Philadelphia will do!' At which point the real bandit rides in and Flower Belle shoots the rope off Twillie's neck. Bandit escapes, fake marriage exposed, and Flower Belle can sashay back to her room, wiggling her rump at Twillie as they switch lines:

TWILLIE: If you get up around the Grampian hills, you must come up and see me some time!
FLOWER BELLE: Oh yah . . . I'll do that, my little chickadee . . .

Right to the end of the shoot Mae and Bill continued to relate to each other amicably, with Fields continuing to ply her with notes and suggestions, such as the following, marked 'Dressing room, December 11, 1939':

Dear Mae,
    Eddie told me that you asked him if I had any suggestion for the finish. This is it. This finish leaves just the two of us at the end of the picture with

no attempts at comedy or wise cracks from either of us. I think it will leave a nice, human, homey feeling in the audience's mind.

An old-fashioned hug, Bill

(*At railroad station – train is about to pull out.*)

MAE: I'm sorry there's been a misunderstanding. It's been good knowing you. Do you mind if I keep the little heart pin you gave me on the train?

FIELDS: Not at all – not at all. If I hadn't been so busy, I would have had it gold-plated for you.

MAE (*smiling*): Never mind – it's all right as it is.

(*Fields kisses her hand – walks away – disappears along the platform.*)

MAE (*shakes head*): What a man, what a man.

(*Train whistle blows, indicating departure of train. Mae walks back and sits down on a trunk, a small grip by her side. She leans her head on her tall parasol. There is nobody at the station. A stranger enters and looks at her, tips his hat – very politely.*)

STRANGER: Did you miss your train, ma'am?

MAE (*very quietly*): No – I'm going the other way.

FADE OUT

As we can see, this was not used. But although, even in their scenes together, close-ups were shot separately, a process Mae preferred even when playing with Cary Grant – preserving her main love affair as that with the camera – the scenes in which Bill and Mae spark off each other are, for many, the best in the film. Bill Fields could play with a lamp post, an umbrella, a swinging door or a lightbulb as a protagonist, but Mae was at her best when sparring with a worthy partner, whether it was Grant or Fields. Fields's comedy was of the most basic root of the clown – the perplexed human faced with the chaotic absurdity of the world: society, other people, made objects, existence itself; even one's own body refuses to behave as we wish, one's head being in the wrong place for one's hat. Mae's comedy was of the human root of manners and expectations, the social follies of convention versus desire. Fields's clown could not care less how people behaved; their peculiarities would always confound his own personal logic. Social reality was dangerous and perverse. For Mae, social reality was a challenge to overturn the received wisdoms of what was, from Adam, a man's world that Eve was dedicated to confound. As her response to the schoolhouse blackboard provides: 'I am a good boy, I am a good girl – what is this, propaganda?'

343

My Little Chickadee became, ironically, the best known of Mae West's films, its double-headed status giving it a unique place in the annals of screen comedy, though Mae was always piqued at the perception that she had made more than one film with Fields. Revivals and television resurrections made it a perennial hit. Reviews of the time were a familiar mixed bag, the *Hollywood Reporter* praising a 'Sure Fire B.O. Hit – Story Limps but Laughs are Plenty,' while *Variety* griped that the 'gags are rather slim', bemoaning 'some monotonous stretches and footage hung onto too long'. The *Los Angeles Examiner* found that 'some moments are funny – others are embarrassing', noting that the scene where the Masked Bandit makes love to Mae 'brought forth laughter where it wasn't intended'. The combined fan clubs of Bill and Mae, however, ensured the film a warm welcome.

The movie incorporated the last of Mae's risqué on-screen songs of her golden age, her saloon ditty 'Willie of the Valley', altered as per tradition by Joe Breen. Instead of 'Willie was a good man / Too bad he had to go / I said he was a good man / And boys I ought to know,' the verse became 'Willie was a good man / Too bad he didn't last / He hasn't got a future / But boy, he had a past . . .' Which at least expressed, in hindsight, the poignant truth of the movie. On screen, the lines were sanitized further: 'Willie was a good man / The best man that I've found / I said he was a good man / He should have hung around.' Another attempt by Mae to insert a 'Samson and Delilah' scene was stamped on by the censors' board, which also added, with an almost audible sigh:

. . . Delete the line 'Snow White was all right but she drifted' . . . It is an old gag, and has always been cut out . . .

'Mae West Haunted by Dead Romance . . .'

Fitting historical periods neatly into archetypal decades can often be misleading, but both the 1920s and 1930s, the vital years of Mae West's prominence, ended with cataclysmic events: the 1920s with the Depression; the 1930s with the outbreak of World War II in Europe. The shock of the Depression had an unexpectedly invigorating effect on Hollywood movies, coinciding with the coming of sound, in the few years before Will Hays and Joe Breen shut the air vents of social comment and satire. The war, in turn, cast its gloom west from the 'Old World', signalling that all that had seemed certain till now was in flux and values that had been taken for granted would have to be fought for, at great cost.

Of all places upon the planet, Hollywood seemed the least equipped to realize this. For twenty years it had built its dream factories, gathered together fey and talented people, many of whom, as the Fatty Arbuckle scandal of 1921 and later affairs demonstrated, drifted uneasily in a soap bubble of the audiences' fabricated fantasies. They could rise on the hot breath of adoration but collapse if the bubble was pricked.

For a brief period, from 1931 to 1933, Hollywood had found a voice that was unexpected for those who assumed the movie colony was, or should be, nothing more than a frothy confection of consumer-led entertainment. Films of robust social criticism, like Mervyn LeRoy's *I Am a Fugitive from a Chain Gang*, the gangster cycle, from William Wellman's *The Public Enemy* to Howard Hawks's *Scarface*, or Frank Capra's early satires *The Miracle Woman* and *American Madness*, appealed to audiences that knew very well that something had gone badly awry with the American dream. The Empire State Building was about to rise to the heavens, but bread lines snaked around the block down on the ground. How could the mighty fall so low, and was recovery just round the corner, as so often promised? What kind of society contained such a paradox?

Suddenly the American screen was full of movies that asked that very question. Even the quickly made 'short' features, running barely seventy minutes and including Jimmy Cagney in *Taxi* or Edward G. Robinson in *Two Seconds* (the first directed by Roy Del Ruth, the second by Mervyn LeRoy), crackled with social comment and anger at the injustice of the times. The sleaziness of dance halls, women reduced to prostitution or the invasion of crime into ordinary working lives were highlighted again and again in movies that cut through the paper prohibitions of Hays' 1930 Code.

Mae West found herself, all too briefly, at the crest of this wave, which enabled *She Done Him Wrong* and *I'm No Angel*, before the tide began to turn and the censors reconstructed their tools to make sure the moment of freedom – or licence – was short.

In 1935, when Paramount sought to re-release *She Done Him Wrong* and *I'm No Angel*, Joseph Breen wrote to Will Hays, on 1 October, that 'both pictures are now so thoroughly and so completely in violation of the Code that it is utterly impossible for us to issue a certificate of approval for them . . . It is our judgement that no successful effort can be made to cause them to be entirely unobjectionable under the Production Code.' Just a month before, the US Customs service had banned Mae's 1932 novel of *Diamond Lil* as obscene. The two movies were classified by the Production Board as Class One: 'Pictures which should be withdrawn immediately, and not again released.'

It was in this atmosphere that Mae laboured to produce the rest of her 1930s movies, from *Klondike Annie* through to *My Little Chickadee*. World War II itself and the great shaking that it gave to American life did not move Joe Breen one inch. In 1949, he was again writing to Paramount, this time to executive Luigi Luraschi: 'With further reference to the question of the reissue of the Mae West 1933 production, *I'm No Angel* . . . no good will accrue to the industry among right thinking people with a release of a Mae West picture. On the contrary, it would appear to me that we would expose ourselves to the charge that we were "letting down the bars"; that we were again making "filthy pictures," as was the charge levelled against the industry, from a thousand sources, back in 1933–34.'

The gates were shut, and all but padlocked, on Mae West and on an entire strand of Hollywood film-making for more than three decades. The Code's provision that foreign nations should not be offended constrained the making of movies that would be overtly critical of Nazi Germany, or fascism in general, until the US entered the war. Of course, there were exceptions and courageous breakthroughs, and many fine movies, great directors, exciting actors – and Rita Hayworth and Marilyn Monroe – and new tricks at the lower end of the budget to find ways to express the shadow-and-light of post-war life. But the kind of audacity that showed Walter Huston, in Capra's *American Madness*, as a banker loaning money to poor people with no collateral, thus endangering the whole principle of profit, was rarely seen upon the American screen for a very long time – the fate of *Citizen Kane*'s director demonstrating the hazards of stepping out of line. And for those who still dreamed of movies that nevertheless challenged the status quo and hit hard, whether above or below the belt, the era of Senator Joseph McCarthy and the Hollywood Ten would soon provide further deterrence. Without Joe Breen's zealous witch-hunting in the 1930s, McCarthyism might not have had so potent a precedent to root out transgression in American cultural life.

Mae was to make one wartime comeback movie, *The Heat's On* in 1943. But at the beginning of the 1940s her creative energies were focused on her return to the stage. The chosen vessel was to be Mae's oft-rejected film project on Catherine the Great. As a play, this, too, would take some years to reach production.

Meanwhile, Mae's personal archive now reveals that she continued, on a regular basis, come war or peace, to shore up her collection of jokes. The old vaudeville joke annuals had ceased publication, but Mae filed away a book of *1,000 Jokes*, published 1940, and a typewritten 'Digest of Humour', copyrighted in 1941 by Mildred Meiers, the latter containing 3,718 jokes categorized from Absentmindedness, Actor, Adam and Eve, etc., through to Sucker, Suffrage, Suicide, X-Ray and Zoo. Joke 2,214: 'Was your marriage one of those trial and error things? – Just the opposite, first came the error, then the trial.' More jokes are contained in notebooks, each of around 200 pages, classified in different categories in which Mae has, as was her habit, ticked off certain lines for possible use.

GOSSIP:
'I've heard lots about you.'
'Well, you can't prove anything.'

THEATRE:
'What did the censors have to say about my last film?'
'Several cutting remarks.'

As well as jokes that featured Mae herself, now well established in the canon:

'Your girl is Mae West's double.'
'Yeah? How do you figure?'
'She's twice as big.'

Few of these would have been much use, but Mae diligently logged them all, including endless aphorisms:

'I try to turn my best thoughts into actions.'
'You can't really kill time, you can only kick it around a little.'
'Men who are backward make a woman look forward.'
'Love is the only fire against which there is no insurance.'
'Vanity has no sex. Anybody can be vain about something.'
'He has a voice that sounds like progressive jazz.'
'War is such a waste. I hate to waste anything, especially men.'

These notebooks stretch well into the 1950s and beyond, with some collected thoughts veering towards the fashionable right, such as 'I notice a lot of people are in favour of Government ownership of something as long as it belongs to someone else.' Or a quote by 'Ebeneezer Elliott': 'What is a Communist? One who hath yearnings / For equal division of unequal earnings / Idler or bungler, or both, he is willing / To fork out his copper and pocket your shilling . . .'

It is clear that Mae continued to consider herself a working writer, though her pace had slowed somewhat. The legal battle with Frank Wallace lingered into the war years, with Wallace's suit against Timony for interfering with his career and 'threatening his life' dismissed in December 1940, and his claim for alimony thrown out of court in September 1941. Superior Judge Charles M. Allison, sitting in San Bernardino, found that 'there is no question that the plaintiff, in filing this action, did not act in good faith. Nothing in this case has convinced me that he was not motivated by profit.'

The judge accepted Mae's point that Wallace, in marrying Miss Rae Blakesley in 1916, had shown no interest in finding out whether Mae had filed for divorce from him or not and had lived with his second wife for nineteen years. The judge also seemed swayed by Mae's

plea that she was 'as things go in Hollywood, just about broke . . .
"All I have," she said, "is a bank account that's a few thousand dollars overdrawn, a pile of receipts for the jewels I've had to sell in the
past few months, this piece of costume jewelry I'm wearing on my
finger, and a purse with less than $50 in it."' She slapped aside any
queries about her purchased stocks and bonds: '"Look, I haven't got
a bookkeeper's mind. I can't remember what I paid for those things
five or six years ago." . . . Although she once earned $400,000 a year
on the screen, she said her income in 1940 was "zero."'

Mae's plea of poverty and ignorance to the court was more than a little ingenuous. She was not above playing the dizzy innumerate dame
when circumstances required. Insurance documents in her personal
archive relating to this period reveal the extent of the property owned
by 'Mae West and Hollywood Enterprises'. Personal assets insured
included $10,000 'miscellaneous', $13,315 for Furs, $24,065, $8,500
and $32,565 separately for Jewelry, all these at 570 North Rossmore
(the Ravenswood apartment). There are five cars, including a 1934
Cadillac Town Cabriolet and 1937 Terraplane Coupe, real estate at
'Various locations', including 1745 North New Hampshire – site of
Timony's Hollytown Theatre – and farm property at 16022 Rayen St.,
San Fernando, the latter occupied by sister Beverly and her husband
Baikoff. The Terraplane Coupe was also Baikoff property. There was
insurance for two workpersons, one chauffeur and one in-servant. Mrs
Baikoff's residence had one in-servant.

In April 1940, some more properties were added to the insurance,
including two more apartments at 1743 North New Hampshire and
a Gasoline Service Station at the south-east corner of Chandler and
Van Nuys Boulevard.

These chronicles reveal that, although not fabulously wealthy,
Mae's poverty in the early 1940s was relative to Hollywood's best-
heeled. Other receipts, undated, show 'income from 13 apartments at
$19,860', with other interests in a location on Olympic Boulevard,
'in finest rental section of Beverly Hills'. Documents from 1945 show
Mae disposing of several items of jewellery, to wit: 'Star Sapphire and
diamond fancy ring, $750; Star Sapphire and diamond brooch,
$10500; One platinum ladies ring set with 1 large aquamarine stone
approx. 125 cts. 26 small baguette diamonds and 280 small round
diamonds – $7000 . . .' ('Sounds like a six-course dinner,' W. C. Fields
might have growled.) In short, the loose $50 cash in Mae's handbag

was most likely for valet parking. The yen for real estate clearly saved Mae from the hazards of the stock markets long after the shockwave of the Great Crash had faded.

In 1942, after Pearl Harbor and with America in the war in deadly earnest, Mae moved to wrap up her own long struggle with the legacy of that rash day in Milwaukee, thirty-one years before. 'MAE WEST HAUNTED BY DEAD ROMANCE,' headlined the press in July, when Mae's suit for a formal divorce from Frank Wallace came to court and, for the first time, she faced her ex-husband in the same courtroom. Mae's appearance in the court 'was somewhat belated . . . the fans who crowded the courtroom were quick to observe that the word "curvesome" was not inappropriate in describing the actress . . . emphasized by a tailored black crêpe street dress. The ensemble was composed of a huge green, off the face straw hat, a large green bag, plain black shoes. Costume jewelry there was in abundance, most conspicuous being a wide bracelet with an inch square topaz setting, and a ring with topaz to match.

'To Judge Paonessa, Wallace declared that for more than 30 years he zipped his lip about his marriage. In a slightly tear laden voice he said: "I complied with every wish of Miss West. She wanted a career. For over 30 years I have held our secret in my heart."'

This was a little rich of Wallace, as he had been shouting his secret from the rooftops for seven years. Intriguingly, Wallace named five men who, as the press put it, 'had been privileged to come up and see his wife'. These were Timony, the boxers Speedy Dado and Chalky Wright, another 'fistic', Alex Haver, and one Boris Petroff Lerman, whose wife had subsequently divorced him. Wallace also alleged Mae had been 'associated with "criminals"', naming Bugsy Siegel, Carl Weiss, Frank Carbo, Leslie Tannenbaum, Kid Twist Reles and Harry Voiler but, curiously, not Owney Madden – who was still alive at the time.

Wallace got his case postponed for a day because his lawyer had toothache, but on 21 July 1942, he withdrew his suit for separate maintenance, and the judge swiftly granted Mae her divorce, 'on her cross-complaint of cruelty'. On the witness stand, Mae claimed that she and Frank had only lived together for 'several weeks' and then 'he left me'. She had not seen him again until he showed up in San Bernardino, where he brought his first action for maintenance. The judge wrapped the show in just half an hour. In September,

Mae spoke her mind to Robert J. Rhodes of *The American Weekly*:

'I think,' said Mae West, thinking, 'a woman may owe a man a lovin'. But not a livin' . . . Things would certainly come to a pretty pass if any husband could go into court and get alimony simply because his wife happens to have more money . . .

'A man once used to be proud to be recognized as a gentleman. I hear now that some men are flattered if you call them "heels."

'I also hear that nowadays if a man opens a door for a lady to go through first, he's only the doorman. Some women are thrilled to pieces when a man gets up on a streetcar or a bus and gives them the seat. But they shouldn't be. Generally the guy gets up to keep the crease in his trousers.'

'I don't hold a grudge against Frankie,' said Mae, 'but I would just as leave he wouldn't come up to see me sometime. In fact, I do not want to see him any time.'

This was almost, but not quite, the last word, as the formalized Final Decree of Divorce from Frank Wallace was granted on 7 May 1943. This was indeed the final act of that saga, granted by the amazingly well-named Judge Goodwin J. Knight.

By this time, Mae West was a brand not only in the realm of entertainment. British Royal Air Force officers had renamed their inflatable lifejackets 'Mae Wests' and her image was adopted among soldiers everywhere as a prime pin-up. The first soldiers to have taken up Mae's name were, oddly, Italian troops in Ethiopia in 1935, who had occupied a place called 'Mai Uecc', which, according to her archive clipping, 'officers insisted on calling Mae West', but this was not a military engagement Mae would have been proud to be associated with. She had aired her views on Signor Mussolini and Herr Hitler in a bizarre sketch found in her archive entitled 'Mae West Meets Hitler and Vice Versa', which may have been intended for radio. Admitted to Hitler's 'spacious office . . . with Nazi pomp and flourish', Mae receives the Führer's salutation of 'Well, Fraulein West, you have come up to see me' with 'Wait a minute, 'Dolph, you're stealin' my stuff.' Some tit for tat over German and American patrotism ensues, as Hitler tries to woo her round:

HITLER: America has everything.

MAE WEST: Yeah, and she's going to keep it.

HITLER: Have you not read 'Mein Kampf'?

MAE WEST: No, have you read my diary?

HITLER: Read 'Mein Kampf' and you will see how I am going to set the world on fire.

MAE WEST: Well, read my diary and consider it burnt.

HITLER: Ah, Fraulein, I have to tell you that I find you extremely fascinating.

MAE WEST: And I have to tell you that I find you rather repulsive.

Goebbels and Mussolini enter to matching insults about their characters. 'You're fighting to glorify your ego and to realize your own selfish ambitions . . .' Mae scolds the Führer.

Politics were clearly not Mae's forte. But in 1943, with the war raging on all fronts, her hopes for a comeback were about to be fulfilled, courtesy of producer–director Gregory Ratoff. Ratoff had played the lawyer Benny Pinkowitz in *I'm No Angel* and had since 1936 directed over a dozen pictures, mostly romances, including *Rose of Washington Square* and *Intermezzo – A Love Story* in 1939. He was also a cousin of sister Beverly's husband, Baikoff. Mae described him as the kind of man who 'has an accent that has an accent' – a man with a 'borscht and sour cream personality'.

The movie Ratoff proposed was to be called 'Tropicana', based on a known Broadway show. It soon turned out Ratoff could not obtain the rights to this but had some other ideas about a show-based film instead. Perhaps because he was family, or perhaps because she was still consumed by her Catherine project, Mae did not get involved in the writing of the script, which turned up in June 1943. This went through the usual Hays Office mangle, with Breen rejecting various lyrics in song numbers, including the line, 'And then came the blackbirds and bombed with precision,' which he observed had a 'vulgar connotation'. The rest was the usual stuff:

It is very important that you exercise the greatest possible care in the staging of the various dance numbers . . . there should be no offensive suggestiveness in gesture or movement . . . please have in mind the provisions of the Production Code, which make it mandatory that the 'intimate parts of the body must be fully covered at all times' . . . The business of the cop 'eyeing Fay's leg,' should be eliminated; also Fay's line 'It looks like you're watching it for me, big boy' . . . Please eliminate the word 'jerk' . . . Fay's appearance, 'dressed in a filmy, low-cut negligee which accentuates and even flatters the lines of her figure,' appears to us to be highly questionable . . . certain it is that the negligee should not be a 'daring' negligee . . . Fay's line, 'I like a man who takes his time,' should be entirely eliminated . . .

Mae was downcast when she set eyes on the script, as it seemed 'nothing but a hodgepodge of banal situations'. She claimed she asked to be released from the project. 'Ratoff pleaded in three languages,' she wrote, but she gave in, much against her better judgement.

The film was indeed a 'cold turkey', as announced by the *Los Angeles Examiner* when it opened, renamed *The Heat Is On*, in the New Year of 1944. A proper feast it was and remains only for Xavier Cugat fans, who are blessed with interminable sessions of the mellow Latin's numbers. Most of these do not feature Mae West at all but a succession of 1940s crooners. Pianist Hazel Scott and a full ensemble of soldiers boogie on stage in an all-black swing piece called the 'Caisson Number'. The plot is the convoluted concoction of writers who have lost their way: Mae is Fay Lawrence, a stage star whose producer, Tony Ferris, loses her to a rival, Forrest Stanton, producer of the show *Tropicana*. Ferris tries to cover his losses by getting a reformers' group, the Bainbridge Foundation, to raid his own show, having been approached by the batty deputy head of the Foundation, Uncle Hubert, who wants his niece to sing on stage. The rival producers score off each other by exploiting Hubert, who is played in cloying fashion by Victor Moore. Ferris gets Hubert to embezzle Foundation money – while his sister Hannah, the chief reformer, is out of town – to back his own show, replacing Fay with the niece, Janey. Ferris also uses Hubert to threaten Stanton with blacklisting Fay, thus tricking him into selling *Tropicana* to him, and so forth. Mae has some languid scenes, chiefly with the bumbling Hubert, whom she outs as a wannabe 'stage-johnny'. None of her lines pass the test of time, unsurprisingly, since, as far as we know, she wrote none of them. Best in show: Aunt Hannah: 'My ancestors came over on the *Mayflower*!' Mae: 'You're lucky, now they have immigration laws.'

In the end Mae charms reforming Hannah into backing the *Tropicana* show, while Ferris's last trick to escape his debtors – pretending to have gone mad to make Fay feel sorry for him – backfires and leaves him in the nut house. Mae sashays on stage for her finale, 'Hello Mi Amigo', closing her movie career – until 1969 – with the very un-immortal 'If you want things put in order / You can come and see me south of the border.'

Mae might well have fled to Mexico for all the good *The Heat Is On*

generated. Box office was poor and the notices poorer. The *Hollywood Citizen-News* wrote: 'There's nothing specially wrong with Miss West's performance. She hasn't lost her knack for doing what she's noted for doing so well; all she needs is a story with a tailored role.' But *Daily*

Variety pronounced, scathingly, that 'producer–Director Gregory Ratoff lacks any semblance of smoothness in the unreeling'. Indeed, he seems to have directed the film in some kind of stupor. It was a sad epitaph for Mae to read in the *Hollywood Reporter*: 'Her insinuatin' comedy ain't what it could be.'

But Mae West was not finished yet.

Mae generating no heat with Victor Moore

34

Catherine Was Great – But She Drifted . . .

Mae still had one resource that was not measured in immediate box-office receipts: her great base of loyal fans. Though Mae's personal archive contains little correspondence, one letter to a fan from this period has been kept (although the letters that prompted the reply have not):

February 12, 1943

My dear Mr. Jackson-Craig,

No one could help being moved by your always beautiful letters and the fineness of the sentiment they express. The most recent of your letters presents a problem, however, that cannot, I am afraid, be solved in the way that you wish. Not that I do not value the loveliness of your intentions, nor regard your depth of feeling with anything but the utmost appreciation and sincerest respect.

A life such as mine is anything but simple. It is hedged around with so many complexities and ramifications that if I were to discuss them in detail they would surely give you a headache as they occasionally give me. And times being what they are, I am convinced that a person is wise to be as realistic as possible, and avoid all sorts of complications. It is my belief anyway, that Destiny takes care of most things: that whatever is to be will be and vice versa.

Actually, we know very little about each other, although you apparently know lots more about me than I do about you. I suppose that is true, because in the position I happen to be in, there is very little privacy to my life. But I have never met you, personally, and your very enjoyable letters talk more about me than they do about you. Won't you write me more about yourself and about your life so that I may have have [sic] a full length character portrait of you in my mind?

As I intimated above, I believe in placing things in the hands of Fate. So far it has been very good to me.

With all good wishes, sincerely, Mae West

Clearly Mae was not ready for everyone to come up and see her. But she was careful to keep her fans sweet. One intriguing entry, two years earlier, in 1941, sheds light on Mae's ongoing interest in an issue which had concerned her since 1916: the rights of prison inmates. On 4 February 1941, the *San Quentin News*, a unique prison journal that had sprung from the policies of a reforming warden, Clinton T. Duffy, printed a letter Mae had sent to California Governor Culbert Olson. Mae wrote that she had received a great deal of fan mail from prisoners at San Quentin, all praising Duffy's reforms. 'It is my feeling that Warden Duffy is the right man in the right job,' Mae told the Governor, 'doing great work making prisoners less bitter toward society and placing them in a frame of mind to become worth while people when they are released. I hope your excellency will feel as I do and let Warden Duffy continue making bad men good, while I continue making good men bad – I mean in my pictures.'

In response, Governor Olson invited Mae to 'come up and see me some time', and Warden Duffy invited her to visit San Quentin. Mae returned a polite compliment, and added a P.S. to 'the Men at San Quentin':

I want to thank you for your beautiful Valentine. It was a lovely thought . . . Maybe I can return the compliment by 'comin' up to see you' in person. Of course, I don't think I can improve your minds. I'm afraid that's a little out my line. But I would try and cheer you up a little. In fact, my gentlemen friends have told me I cheer them up a whole lot. And I guess if I get up there to see you I can at least be a kind influence, although I can't exactly say what kind. Somehow, I always seem to make a good impression in the worst way!

But kidding aside, boys, I would like to see you. It would certainly be a fascinatin' experience to call on so many men – usually they call on me. There must be a lot to learn about San Quentin – but that takes time.

Thanks again for being so nice to me, boys.

Sin-sationally yours, Mae West

History does not record a visit by Mae West to San Quentin in 1941, but we can certainly conjure the scene, if not in the lurid images of the prison visit in *She Done Him Wrong* . . .

Another surviving letter, of 16 August 1944, was written on Mae's behalf by a secretary to a Miss Liboria Romano, who had defended her from her detractors over the stage production of 'Catherine the Great':

Miss West wishes to thank you for your letter and copy of your article which appeared in Arthur Pollock's column in the *Brooklyn Eagle*, and also to express her sincere appreciation for the manner in which you recognized and paid tribute to the qualities which have brought fame to Miss West throughout the world as a unique personality, and, in fact, even more than that, as an 'institution' in the entertainment world . . .

No one has been able to write a play or a picture for Miss West, but herself. The studios found that out, although they were willing to pay enormous amounts of money to find new material for her. But any play or picture in order to give the public what they expect from Mae West – and it is the full benefit of her unique personality that the public demands – has to be especially patterned in such a way that her personality dominates all else in play or picture if its value isn't to be lost . . .

Surely such unique personalities (and unique means only one of a kind) are above and beyond being judged by ordinary standards of comparison and criticism. Can for instance such a recognized unique personality as Charles Chaplin be criticized, because in some picture he might decide not to wear his big shoes? It is just as ridiculous to criticize Miss West for not having the great Empress of Russia slouch through three acts with the hip movements of Diamond Lil.

To paraphrase an old saying, 'Those who can, do; those who can't, criticize . . .'

In a P.S. the letter adds: 'There will never be another Duse. There will never be another Shakespeare. And there will never be another Mae West.'

This imperial approach by Miss West followed her long-awaited anointment as Empress Catherine of all the Russias, which took place at the Shubert Theatre on Broadway (after an early run in Philadelphia), on 2 August 1944. After years of futile attempts and rejections, Mae had finally found a producer with ideas as grandiose as her own, showman Michael Todd. Todd announced that he would produce Mae's play, as well as Gypsy Rose Lee and a Cole Porter show, all in the 1944 season. Apart from cheering up audiences in a gruesome phase of the war, with American and Allied troops dying in Europe in the aftermath of the D-Day invasion, Todd also devised a scheme of 'selling tickets only to the purchasers of war bonds', gathering $4 million worth of bonds for the opening night alone.

The play was billed as a 'romantic comedy with historical overtones', though Mae saw it as her opportunity, finally, to prove herself a great dramatic actress. According to biographers Eels and

Musgrove, Mae claimed to have received a direct message, courtesy of her spiritual advisers, from Catherine the Great herself, urging her to take the role seriously.

Mae's spiritualist tendencies had grown apace since the early days of attempted contact with Valentino over Ouija boards in New York City. In the autumn of 1941, she later wrote, she had met a Reverend Thomas Jack Kelly, who impressed her, and many others, with his prowess at extra-sensory perception. Mae thought he was a 'serious man, neither vivid nor a fanatic'. According to Mae, he predicted the attack on Pearl Harbor, or at any rate on Hawaii. Mae was at this time, as she said, 'satiated with success' and (despite her protestations of poverty in court) not lacking in any material things. 'I had reached a point where I began to feel that I would either live a very wicked life, or develop spiritually.' Neither Catholic nor Protestant churchmen appeared to have answers for her. She wanted, she wrote, 'tangible proof' of the hereafter, and, in the Reverend Kelly, it seemed, she found its demonstrator. Another spiritual mentor, 'a woman of recognized psychic ability' whom Mae did not name, taught her to meditate. Though she did not know it, Mae was mapping out a path that would be followed, twenty years later, by vast swathes of questing performers and 'civilians'. The *sri* whom she had met in Chicago in the 1920s continued also to be a guide.

All this was at least less harmful a practice than Buchmanism, which Mae seemed to have left behind, probably wary of Moral Rearmament's political ambitions. Perhaps her imaginary encounter with Herr Hitler was designed to clarify her own thoughts on the gap between Americanism and fascism. Whatever the sources of her beliefs, the spiritualist mindset helped Mae to feel her way much more closely, as she saw it, into the character of the Russian Empress Catherine, while arguably preventing her from applying the usual professional scepticism and self-enquiry an actor needs to see his or her mask from both within and without. The result, as critics saw it, was both impressive and puzzling. Apart from messages from the beyond, Mae had prepared for the job by reading a dozen books on Catherine and embedding historical research into her stage version. Mae's archive contains numerous versions of *Catherine Was Great* (as the play was eventually named), all close variations on the text that she sent for copyright submission at the Library of Congress in April 1944.

Despite publicity puffs that Catherine was the 'Diamond Lil' of her day, the Empress of Russia had been a very different kettle of caviar, having succeeded to a throne steeped in blood and intrigue in 1762 by the time-honoured method of having the real heir to the throne, Peter III, her husband, bumped off by her lover Orlov. She was considered historically to be a great reformer, grafting onto a sprawling, anarchic and backward country the seeds of European organization. She introduced new agricultural methods, developed mines, crafts and textile factories, modernized the army and civil service and revolutionized Russian education. Of course, as all fans of Rudolph Valentino know, she also dropped her pants for all and sundry but always remained in control. She was thus tailor-made, Mae thought, for her own unique persona.

By all accounts, the production was lavish, with little spared on sets and costumes. Veteran drama critic Howard Barnes reported on the première that 'Mae West returned to Broadway last night, decked out like a battleship in a swimming pool.' Photographs show Mae with extraordinary coiffures, hairdos in which the entire Russian army might have been able to hide. The performance was regarded as much more uneven, probably reflecting rehearsal battles between Mae and her producer. Mike Todd wanted a Mae West comedy, but Mae had become obsessed with Catherine both as an alter ego and a female role model. *The New Yorker*'s critic commented that the actors 'behaved sometimes as if they thought they were mixed up in a solemn historical document and at others as if they would hardly be surprised by a visit from the police'. Mae's behaviour on and off stage was eccentric, her penchant for 'sex at least once a day' was noted, as she fondled and ogled the male extras, the imperial guard whom, Eels and Musgrove reported, were 'recruited off the beaches and out of prizefight rings for their appearance rather than their acting ability'. In Art Cohn's *The Nine Lives of Michael Todd* (published in 1958), the author describes one of many typical Mike–Mae tangles:

'Mike, I'm not happy about my leading man,' she said, a plaintive note in her voice. 'I told you to find me the biggest, handsomest brutes in town.'

'I did my best,' he said, 'but I warned you, the biggest, handsomest brutes are in the Army.'

'I know one brute who isn't, and who would make a great leading man.'

'Who?'

'Wee Willie Davis . . .'

'Can he act?'

'Can he act? He's one of the best wrestlers on the Pacific Coast!'
Mike brought him to New York and tested him for the lead.

'He's a big, handsome brute all right, Miss West,' Mike said, 'but he seems incapable of reading difficult lines like "Yes" and "No." Or is he going to grunt the part?'

Actor Don de Leo, who played the Turkish Ambassador, confirmed to Musgrove that Mae lacked all inhibition: 'When she met somebody she liked, she went. If it was a cabdriver, a wrestler, a Park Avenue playboy or an actor. Black or white, it didn't make any difference.' De Leo also recalled Mae's yoga exercises with her *sri*, which, Eels and Musgrove relate, 'ended with the *sri*, fully clothed, lying on top of Mae while she experienced an orgasm'.

A vintage Hirschfeld of Mae as Catherine

Clearly nothing as exciting as this was occurring on stage, with Mae further confounding critics and audience by delivering her lines in her standard wide Brooklyn tones. Howard Barnes denounced the script as 'incredibly boring and monotonous' and panned Mae's performance as 'more limited than ever'. The problem was that Mae had spent so much time and effort on her text that she would accept few changes. The Library of Congress script contains acres of explanation, exposition and monologues:

CATHERINE: You see, Panin, I have plans. There are so many things I want to do for Russia. Russia has been robbed of her virtue, but not of her passion. She will rise again! . . . In foreign and domestic affairs, in education, science, medicine, the arts – new, fresh ideas and methods must be tried and encouraged. We need hospitals, schools, an intelligent banking system – we need so much . . .

We need a few laughs, everybody agreed, but they were few and far between: 'The Turkish situation interests me, Prince Potemkin. You may return later for a private audience. Come to the Royal Suite, and we shall talk Turkey . . .' That wasn't going to go far. Nor was Mae's tame discussion with her maid about meeting Voltaire: 'They say Monsieur Voltaire is a very naughty writer – that he says very wicked things – in French.' Catherine: 'Nonsense, why the man's a genius. He's the "divinity of gaiety," – and gaiety suits my temperament. He makes one laugh, and that is a blessing in any language.'

Quite so. One of the few comic scenes in the script revolves around the peasant leader, Pugacheff, who is brought before the Empress, who marvels at the natural cross of hair on his chest, which the peasants take as a heavenly sign of his 'divine right to rule'. Mae, going incognito to an inn, *à la* Garbo's Queen Christina (though not in male attire), flirts with him:

CATHERINE: How strange and wonderful! Is it real? (*She feels the hair on his chest and gives it a little yank. He jumps.*) Yes it is. When did it appear there?

PUGACHEFF: (*proudly*) After I had boils – there it came.

CATHERINE: Heaven sent you boils? How marvellous!

PUGACHEFF: At once I knew I could be Tsar by divine right.

CATHERINE: Of course, after that how could you be anything else?

Later, when Pugacheff is brought to her in chains, he mourns: 'I was a leader. I had an army even with banners. I was something. Now

I am nothing.' Catherine replies: 'Well, you are the biggest chunk of nothing I have ever seen . . . Muscle! Strength and muscle – and you wasted it on a filthy rebellion . . .' Pugacheff is poisoned by her courtiers, another lover, Mirovich, is caught out in treachery, but Catherine continues with Prince Potemkin on her upward trail of triumphs for Russia – 'I shall go on and on, and with my great men I shall do *more* and *more* and *more!*' (THE MUSIC SWELLS UP POWERFULLY AND MAJESTICALLY AS CATHERINE MAKES HER GRAND EXIT. CURTAIN.)

Throughout the script, Mae was determined that her views on the equal right of women to power, her thoughts on history and the underlying causes of World War II as she saw it should be highlighted. In the prompt script, the version definitely used upon the stage, she had added her thoughts on fascism as male power somewhat more forcefully than in her Hitler sketch:

CATHERINE: The world will never be safe or at peace, as long as we have dangerously ambitious military-minded men. Their career is war – their aim is power. They can only feed their ambitions by destruction and slaughter, because they have no talents that can be recognized in time of peace . . . They care not if they destroy a state, a country, a nation, with all that it has taken ages of toil and sacrifice to accomplish. They care not what, nor whom they strike down as long as they may rise. The world is full of these dangerously ambitious military-minded men. Every country has them. And as long as they do have them and do not control them, there will only be short periods of peace between horrible periods of war . . .

Despite all its manifest flaws, *Catherine Was Great* ran for thirty-four weeks, closing in the spring of 1945. The *Washington Daily News* reported in February that a local benefit matinee for wounded soldiers was packed out: 'They came by jeep, Army trucks and on foot and . . . reacted delightfully to her seductiveness on the Steppes . . . Miss West didn't play to an empty seat thruout the engagement.'

Mae had demonstrated that she was still a box-office draw, but also that there was no point in producers trying to impose on her any style or story that she did not fully endorse or that did not flow from her own pen. Some said that ghostwriters, like Larry Lee, had a hand in her manuscripts, but this cannot be fully verified. Projects and treatments were still flowing from Mae's mind, as her personal archive shows, but there was a distinct sense of narrowing options.

The problem, amply revealed, was the shift in her own self-percep-
tion. Gone for ever was the Mae West who had started life with the
hoochie-coochie and shimmy, 'the finest woman who ever walked the
streets'. Gone was Margy Lamont, friend of the disenfranchised and
marginals, The Hussy, Babe Carson/Gordon of rags to riches and
anything goes, or the real Mae who might have gone on a cab ride
around the docks and found inspiration for her stories and plots in
the sight of boozy sailors and women with their bodies to sell. What
had emerged from this rough cocoon was a bejewelled beast, Mae as
star and celebrity, the latest in a determined line of Famous Women
of History, a kind of sacred monster whose fabulous nature and qualities could not be challenged or misconstrued. In Diamond Lil, Mae
had found, for a decade, a character poised between both worlds, a
glittering icon who was still only one step up from the streets. But
now Diamond Lil, too, had been surpassed – though she was to
return in a series of revivals commencing late in 1947.

Catherine Was Great ended its run at the same time as the spectacular close of World War II in Europe, though the Pacific war thundered on. Mae's portrayal of a sympathetic Russian ruler most
probably benefited from the alliance with Stalin, who was neither
sexy nor progressive but was the American ally of convenience *par
excellence*. The post-war reality had no place for such sympathies, as
the 'cold war' would soon begin to bite. Exhaustion with war, and
delirious relief following Hiroshima and Japan's surrender in August,
were palpable throughout America. Mae West was marooned, however, on her own planet. Her own skirmishes continued apace. Two
obscure writers, George S. George and Vadim Uraneff, sued her for
$450,000 in July 1945, claiming plagiarism of their own text on
Catherine. No sooner had this claim fallen away than another
loomed, from writers Edwin K. O'Brien of New York and Michael
Kane of Hollywood, who claimed they had supplied Mae with material for her Catherine script in California in 1938. This annoyance
would linger in her lawyers' inbox until 1948.

Meanwhile, Mae moved to capitalize on her stage revival by
appearing in another new play, presented over the years under a
number of titles: *Ring Twice Tonight, Come On Up* and *Come On
Up, Ring Twice*. This was credited as a play by Miles Mander, Fred
Schiller and Thomas Dunphy, but Mae inserted her own lines on
stage, as the audience would expect. The *Washington Evening Star*

described it thus on 24 September 1946:

While Miss West's current vehicle scorns to change the subject of last season's 'Catherine Was Great,' it does put it into a new and more congenial setting. This time the star sets up in an elegant Washington apartment, of all places, and she presides over it much more comfortably. As a buxom blonde . . . she always seemed somewhat out of place in the semioriental splendor of Catherine's palace boudoir. She and her current place have a classic unity, if 'classic' does not mind being borrowed for such an occasion.

Another factor which eliminates the ersatz effect of Miss West's last season's adventure is the architecture of the males. That the manpower shortage, particularly harrowing in the casting of wartime West plays, is over is occasion for a downright celebration in 'Come On Up.' The cast amounts to virtually a review of the whole male sex to which, naturally, Miss West acts as a common denominator. From Washington cab drivers to Senators, Nazi agents to heirs of steel tycoons, Miss West is ready for them with no more than a dextrous, undulating twist from one negligee to the other.

The plot line – which the *Evening Star* described as 'half a jigger of a story' – was pretty threadbare, establishing Mae as an internationally famous nightclub singer who turns out to be a 'Mata Hari for the FBI and clearly much more active and successful than the original glamorous spy of the same name. There are references – once every dozen smouldering, two-toned speeches – to the money Nazi bigwigs are supposed to have stashed in Argentine . . .' This was a plot which Mae had tinkered with before, among her 1930s treatments, a story set originally during the Spanish–American war in Cuba in 1898. To spice up the current stew, Mae was given a saucy French maid who suggests to her the trick of an old former mistress 'who filled the air of Paris with toy balloons carrying the message "come on up to Suite B-3, Bellflower apartments, and ask for Carliss."' Naturally, various male suitors 'come up'. To entertain every one of them, Mae as Carliss Dale dashed on and off stage in a variety of sightly gowns.

At a Washington press conference to mark her show's début in the capital, Mae demonstrated what she now called 'The Personality', the mask she donned on stage, denigrating her impersonators, who tended 'to make it too broad'. Asked whether she might play a burlesque queen, Mae said: 'No . . . I gotta watch the kind of people I have around me. You get too many tough burlesque characters hangin' around makin' wisecracks and you don't stand out . . . I don't go for any of this real low stuff.'

Changed tunes indeed. To the assembled hacks, Mae added, some-what wistfully: 'You know, I think this play'd make a good movie.' But there were no takers.

Nineteen forty-six was the first year in which Mae got to help pick Mister America in what she called 'a male beauty contest', a publicity gimmick that was to become a stock-in-trade in years to come. Holding forth to Marjory Adams of the *Boston Globe* when her play opened in the city, she openly ogled the traffic policeman who waved her on: 'What a man! . . . Isn't he handsome? I'm going to steal him for my show . . . There are too many shows for men,' she explained, 'producers pick out beautiful girls of all types to please the male patrons. But I like to think of the women – so I pick out good look-ing men of all types so the ladies will have fun when they come to a Mae West play . . . The more men there are the better, I say . . . Me, I like all types. The men I don't like don't exist.'

Mae was certainly not pleading her poverty on this tour, as Miss Adams noted a diamond bracelet on her arm 'that must have con-tained more diamonds than there are stars on the Milky Way. On one finger blazed a modest little ring with a 22-carat diamond which would knock out the eye of the average beholder.'

But Mae was providing for women not only a model of a commer-cially successful feminist but hope on a more creative level, as one plaintive letter from a fan in 1947 – a rare instance of preserved fan mail in Mae's archive – recounts:

March 2 1947

Dear Miss West,

When you were at our English Theater last year, you had a write up in the paper, wanting some plays, but the right kind.

I have written a short play and by the time it was performed could be made into a long play – which I am sending to you.

Not bragging but I think you are the most wonderful and most beautiful actress and to my estimation the best liked. If anyone says they don't like you, it would be because they couldn't take it and are, shall we say jealous. I'm not saying this because of my play, I wouldn't miss a picture or play of yours for anything . . .

I have been writing for sometime but have never done anything with my stories of which I have many, and am about to complete a book entitled *Light Keeps Flickering*.

I'm hoping very much to sell some of them to surprise my son and be able to help him. He was in the Marines three years, tall dark and handsome and I'd like to do something in my own little way to kinda pay for what he has helped do for all of us.

Now Miss West, don't think me begging, I'm only telling what I would like and if we don't tell the things on our minds, no one will know, isn't that correct. I've played mother and father both to my son and would like to be worth while.

So with all the luck in the world to you and coming straight from my heart, I shall close. Hoping to hear from you.

Thelma Salter

35

Mae West, with Diamonds, Arrived . . .

The new Mae West, Queen of all she surveyed, was, in 1947, fifty-four years of age. When he was just that age, W. C. Fields, her male vaudeville shadow, had been giving of his best via Paramount Pictures, though he was forced by the image in the mirror to construct his own mask as a robust plum pudding that had seen many Christmases come and go. A male actor of fifty-four can flaunt his scars and his calluses, construct comedy from his liquory tones and staggering gait or the sunset climes of an undimmed debauchery in the grand manner of Groucho Marx. A woman is expected to begin playing grandmothers, if she can get employment at all. Yet at this stage Mae began the boldest of all her grand career plans – a project to remain young for ever.

From now on, Mae would be ageless, rejecting all offers to play mature ladies, matronly types, mothers of any age or, as was reputedly offered her by Billy Wilder, the decaying silent star of *Sunset Boulevard*. Her mantra would be, as repeated almost to her last breath, that she would never play any woman over twenty-six. The Sex Goddess was to reign supreme, giving forth her nostrums and ideas on sex, health, beauty, skin care, exercise, sex, psychic forces, sex, even marriage, and male and female energies. These thoughts would flow both in public and private – little notes found in files and folders in Mae's archive contain jottings about issues like skin treatment, such as this barely decipherable two-inch strip of paper with the scribble:

1. Clip hair very close.
2. Wash skin with rubbing alcohol.
3. Vaseline the edges of skin.
[4.?] Scrub [???] on real well, up & down across [hair?]
5. Not too much [????] on brush.

6. Repeat treatment for 3 days small amounts each day . . . End of [?] day remove [?] scales [?] With rubbing alcohol apply vaseline for 3 days. Do not use water or wash of any kind at any time.

Jokes and gags continued to be stockpiled, as if by force of habit. The full-scale playscripts and screenplays are all versions of previously performed material, including more versions of *Come On Up*, which morphed into 'Embassy Row', also proposed as a screenplay. In 1952, a new play, *Sextette*, makes its appearance and would play an ongoing role. The rest consists of a slew of sketches and fragments, including treatments for a proposed weekly TV show portraying Mae as famous (or infamous) ladies of legend. The most complete of these, at forty-two pages, is the fable of Bluebeard's eighth wife, Fatima, the Sultan's daughter, in an Arabian Nights-style tale. Fatima appears after an Announcer calls upon 'the mystic maze of Mae West's Museum of Historical Humbug . . .' to opine: 'That's the trouble with history. It only tells you the man's angle – how tough this Bluebeard was . . . it's all *his* story – but not one word what Fatima did – that's why I want you to see *her* story – because herstory is the real lowdown . . .' The real lowdown turning out, of course, to be more skimpily costumed harem stuff, with Fatima's 'traditional veil' described as 'tiny and sheer and transparent and does not hide her features, but is chic and provocative . . .' At the end the barker calls: 'Come to visit us at the museum, again next week, when Mae West will once more set the record straight for you with another classic from history.' Alas, this delight never materialized, despite Mae producing her veteran backer, William LeBaron, from her battered Aladdin's lamp.

Another sample, a nineteen-page 'farce-comedy in one act', is titled 'Lady Godiva's Modesty', and features Mae as Lady G., in bed after her ride and refusing to come out for her husband Leofric, as she declares:

GODIVA: I've caught a cold, you know. Perspiring in this clammy weather . . . After ages I reached the other side of town. I had ridden through Coventry naked, just as you said. But I forgot to bring any clothes with me, so I had to do it all over again on the way back . . .

'Peeping Tom' Thomas, the Tailor, begs an audience, tells her of his dream and is bidden undress behind a screen. 'How fare you there?'

she asks. Tom, behind the screen: 'I am becoming like a newborn child.' Godiva: 'Ah – but not as tiny, I trust.' And, seeing his physique: 'Gadzooks! . . . are you quite sure you are a tailor and not a smith?'

Yet another of these sketches, 'Madame Pompadour', is written for Beverly to give an impression of her sister Mae West as another of the 'great ladies of history'. Madame Pompadour tries to get the King to get her the crown jewels, but the King protests: 'Nay, not the crown jewels . . . for they are in the Queen's boudoir and I haven't been there in forty years.' Pompadour: 'Very well, I shall bandy words with you no longer, but I will sell the story of our love to the Police Gazette.'

At the cusp of the 1940s, however, after the pomp and circumstance of *Catherine Was Great*, Mae was hungry for more substantive fare. Her solution, to keep her legend and her livelihood going, was to find a new lease of life in tried and true material: the revival of her greatest hit, *Diamond Lil*.

The impetus for this was Mae's long-desired and long-postponed trip to Britain, which finally took place in September 1947. Mae sailed from New York on the *Queen Mary* on 11 September and arrived at Southampton to be greeted by a small party of press people, who reported to her transatlantic fans:

MAE WEST, WITH DIAMONDS ARRIVED AT 2 A.M.
Mae West reached Southampton at 2 o'clock this morning. She was too excited to see Britain to go to bed. I recognized her by her diamonds. With a pink scarf over her platinum blonde hair, Miss West came down from the top deck between her bodyguards, Hal Gould and Dick Bailey. She was a frail, almost ethereal figure in black chiffon and had almost no make-up except for gigantic eyelashes shadowing demure blue eyes.

She stretched out her arms to the little British Press party and said: 'Oh! how lovely of you to come and see me.' She denied that she had been slimming, and said that the change was due to 'period costumes.'

Miss West has brought with her two trunks of costumes for her show, 'Diamond Lil,' which she is putting on in London.

The hack from the *Star* was equally struck by the eyelashes, remarked on the 'most schoolgirlish complexion, gentlest voice and demurest manner in London' and detailed the evening gown of 'black georgette, high to the throat, with a pale pink yoke embroidered with bugle beads . . . A 22 carat diamond glittered on her right hand and she had a two-inch diamond bracelet.' Mae revealed to the press that she was six pounds overweight, but would 'exercise – dumb-bells, horseback riding and walking' to get in shape for the show. The *Star* noted: 'Her measurements are, bust 38, hips 38, waist 28$^{1}/_{2}$, height 5 ft. 5 in.' Miss West had come to England 'because of your men. I love the way they talk.' She hoped to meet 'John Bull, the King and Queen, and some of her ancestors in the north of England. Mae West is her real name. "A name for lights," she said.'

Coincidentally, two other famous Hollywood stars were in town – Laurel and Hardy, playing at the Empire Finsbury Park and Chiswick the week of 22 September. But there is no record of these three meeting, one of the many might-have-beens of show business. Mae's diamonds were a perennial wonder, occasioning headlines about the headache provided Scotland Yard to safeguard the $250,000 worth of sparklers. The two 'bodyguards', Gould and Bailey, were, in fact, the actors she had brought over (with Timony, as ever, in trail) to base her London cast upon, the other sixty-seven actors to be auditioned locally.

The British run of *Diamond Lil* was produced by Val Parnell and Tom Arnold, and played in Manchester, Blackpool, Birmingham and Glasgow before opening at the Prince of Wales Theatre in London on 24 January 1948. Casting was by all accounts chaotic, and, practically by definition, there could be little natural rapport between Mae and her unfamiliar colleagues. Bruno Barnabe was cast as the latin lover Juarez and Noele Gordon became 'Russian Rita', but neither seemed to get close to the 'real Mae'. Noele Gordon recalled her as 'that horrible woman', and Barnabe recalled getting the role after being asked by Mae to clasp her breasts in his hands. He also remembered getting paid £40 per week as against Mae's £2,000.

The cast were so estranged from the star that rumours abounded off stage about the real character of the person behind all the make-up. Was Mae West bald underneath her blonde wigs? Was Mae West a man? One make-up girl who had seen Mae's breasts said they were scarred 'as though she had had an operation'. Other performers noted Mae's short-sightedness, which, with her refusal to wear glasses, did not help make relationships easy. James Timony was yet another obstacle, his brusque way of shielding Mae and representing her often bordering on rudeness.

British audiences, however, lapped up the visit of Hollywood's legendary diva. Mae played the star on and off the stage, compiling a

'Personal Social Register' of the friends she made across the ocean: these ran from Alexander, Prince of Yugo-Slavia, through Lady Aberconway and Frederick Ashton to the Duchess of Buccleuch, Ladies Cunard and Colfax, Henry Channon MP, Lady Diana Duff-Cooper, Peter Glenville, the director, who introduced her to many of these 'British swells', Lord Hesketh, Mr and Mrs Hulton, HRH the Duchess of Kent, Alf Robens MP, Sir Louis and Lady Sterling, and Mrs Georgia Sitwell. Like so many successful Americans, Mae was like melted butter in the presence of titles, although there are a number of standard folk in the 'Register', such as one Bill Mollison (phone Regent 2872), Hannen Swaffer, journalist and fellow spiritualist, and Clem Butson, of the Savoy Hotel. Other ordinary people Mae only saw from the stage, blurred shadows across the footlights.

The British *Diamond Lil* ran for a full three months and convinced Mae that she had found the right vehicle to make another American comeback. This opened in Montclair in New Jersey in November 1948, courtesy of a stock company run by Albert H. Rosen and Charles K. Freeman, and moved to Philadelphia at the end of December. The play opened in New York at the beginning of February, after a health scare that saw Mae's abdominal pains 'cured' again by her favourite *sri*. She had also endured the six-week trial of the plagiarism suit over *Catherine Was Great* brought against her by writers Kane and O'Brien – which ended in jury deadlock and a mistrial. Mae wrote letters to the seven jurors who had rooted for her, saying that, 'I'm sure if the Empress Catherine the Great was looking down or "up" on us during the recent trial, she feels all the friendliness towards you that I do . . . as Catherine the Great, herself, has said: "I have learned to complain quietly, and to praise loudly."'

Mae had little cause to complain over the New York reception of the new *Diamond Lil*, as the *Hollywood Citizen-News* summed it up: '"DIAMOND LIL" FAILS TO PLEASE CRITICS – BUT MISS W. SLAYS 'EM!' The reviews were, in fact, not that bad: the *New York Times* called her act 'performing in the grand manner'. The *Mirror* wrote: '"Diamond Lil" is no great shakes of a play, but it is an excellent vehicle for the display of Miss West's amazing talents.' The *Post*: 'Mae West is one of the comic legends of our time, and in "Diamond Lil" you can see why.' The *Journal-American*: 'Mae still slinks. As a slinker, she is wonderful.' The *Sun*, however, thought it 'sheer rubbish', though 'consider it merely as a museum piece and you find that it offers a measure of entertainment'. John Chapman in the *News* had an angle that would become more and more common in critiques of Mae West from now on: 'Mae West, the most gifted female impersonator since Julian Eltinge, returned Saturday evening in her 20-year-old shocker "Diamond Lil" and had me and the rest of the Coronet Theater audience laughing fit to kill. If you'll pardon the expression – it is the same old Mae in the same old play – and now it is funnier and so is she.'

This was the point at which Earl Wilson, of the *World Omaha Herald*, came up to see Mae in her New York hotel and was greeted with a full view of her perfectly preserved molars. 'Yuh ask me muh age – Uh'm over 21,' she said, musing to her journalistic fan about her ongoing love life: 'Uh'm still lookin' for the right man . . . Muh trouble is, uh find so many right ones, it's hard to decide.'

Mae's right man, for the moment, was one David Lapin, one of her actors, who appeared to have breached Timony's defences. Another name mentioned was Patsy Perroni, yet another ex-boxer who could get through multiple condoms. It was clear that Mae was becoming increasingly isolated from what anyone might call a normal life, dependent on devotees who would lavish her with non-stop praise and addicted to her own self-made image. Friends noticed that she was becoming paranoid, convinced that rivals and colleagues, particularly her fellow actresses, were plotting to do her down. 'Who's Marilyn Monroe?' she would ask in 1953, when preparing to play Cleopatra in a new show planned by her old mentor William LeBaron called 'Herstory' – probably a version of the 'Fatima' script. 'Marilyn Monroes may come and Marilyn Monroes will go but Mae West will always be the standard by which they judge sex.'

Like many cursed by fame, Mae had reasons for her anxieties, as she was often at the receiving end of ludicrous lawsuits. The most absurd surfaced in October 1949 when two Los Angeles promoters, Arthur Van Wyke and A. E. Harrison, sued her for over $10 million for preventing them calling their new resort 'Diamond Lil'. This was the least of their lawsuits, as they were suing one defendant for $72 billion over 'a metallic lubricant' and another set of unfortunates, ex-business associates, for a mere $12 billion, according to the *Los Angeles Herald Express*. In 1950, an actress called Sara Allen sued for $1 million, charging Mae, 'in verse', for preventing her getting stage jobs as a 'Diamond Lil' impersonator. For good measure, Mae had sued the Chatham Hotel

Hirschfeld 'Diamond Lil', 1949
© AL HIRSCHFELD/MARGO FEIDEN GALLERIES LTD., NEW YORK.
WWW.ALHIRSCHFELD.COM

in New York for $250,000 over a 'defective bath' that caused her a fractured leg in February 1949, claiming losses for her play's cancellation – but at least that involved a real injury.

Despite all the hazards, the revival of *Diamond Lil* played on for over two years, climaxing at the Biltmore in Los Angeles in March 1951, where the *Los Angeles Times* described her parading 'across the boards in a succession of gowns of lavender, cerise and every other sinful shade, the feathers nodding and bouncing with each step and she herself suggesting the constrictor that goes with the boas'.

In January 1950, with the old Adam and Eve skit long forgotten, Mae had another go at radio, appearing on NBC as a guest of Perry Como on the *Chesterfield Supper Club*. 'Garbed in a bandage-white beaded evening gown cut to reveal a discreet midriff, with reflections from an enormous diamond lavaliere and ring lighting her way,' quoth *Newsweek*, omitting to point out the futility of such plumage on an aural medium, 'Mae last week sidled onto the stage of NBC's studio 8H in Radio City . . . this time, in a script with all possible blue bleached out. Miss West appeared as Juliet opposite Como's "Comeo." But even had she overstepped, there was the saving grace

374

of tape recording. The Thursday night show was recorded on Tuesday. A snip of the scissors would have deleted any rough stuff.'

Nevertheless, there were still some echoes of Mae's old troubles when the Atlanta Library Board banned *Diamond Lil* from the local Roxy Theater at the end of January 1951. The city censors had requested the script after hearing that the play and the movie *She Done Him Wrong* were 'one and the same story,' said movie having been 'kicked . . . out of the city limits' two decades before. Atlanta therefore remained pure and unsullied. In March, Mae gave the *Los Angeles Herald Express* another vintage look at her home life and concerns in:

MAE WEST TELLS HER VIEWS ON LIFE AND LOVE AND TAX FORMS
Writes in Bed, Keeps in Shape
By Jack Smith

Two imperishable institutions came together today – the income tax and Mae West. In her elegant Hollywood apartment, a satiny world of cream rugs, gigantic mirrors, nude statues, egg shell walls and bear skins, Mae fought the last minute battle against the only form she hasn't been able to tame.

'And I thought I knew all about figures,' she said.

Mae was in bed, sheathed in a nude colored lace and satin negligee, reclining under a canopy of rich silk and a breath-taking arrangement of wall and ceiling mirrors.

'I do all my writin' in bed,' she explained. 'That's how I wrote "Diamond Lil." I got the inspiration one day so I went in bed and wrote it.'

Mae threw back a satin cover and unwound from bed, walking across the thick blonde rug with more sex in every step than a platoon of starlets in a belly dance.

At the wall, she bent over and pulled at a pair of exercisers.

'I believe in keepin' in shape,' she said. 'On the road I knock everybody out . . .

'You take "Diamond Lil,"' she said, 'I haven't changed a line in years, but the young people kick and scream. They come backstage and tell me they think I'm marvelous.

'Twenty years ago only the sophisticates liked it. Other people were shocked. Now the young people are educated. They've heard about life on the radio and seen it in the movies. They know what's going on.

'I've been years ahead of my time, that's all.'

But it was arguable whether Mae had been ahead of her time for so long that she was now falling far behind it. Since Mae was committed to denying the ageing process she was sinking into a time warp of her own, a place where, indeed, people 'heard about life on the radio and seen it in the movies' rather than experienced change and flux in the real world. Mae's world now almost exclusively consisted of her dreamland apartment, her limousines, her dressing room and the stage, with an occasional foray into attorneys' offices. Gone were the days when the newspapers could pick out so affirming a nugget as this from her mid-1930s heyday:

About a year ago Mae and Jim Timony, enroute to Frisco by car, eyed the chicken dinner spots dotting Ventura blvd., finally selected one called 'Mrs Pattee's' which looked like a good bet. The proprietress was a sweet old woman who served them well, and the food was excellent. Mae and Jim made the spot a 'regular,' and grew fond of the old woman. A few weeks ago they stopped and found it closed and dark. Mae climbed out of her limousine. She found the old woman and her one waitress seriously ill. She shipped them to Hollywood Hospital, paid all the bills and visited them daily. The waitress recovered but Mrs Pattee, alone and without funds, died. Mae had her buried at Hollywood cemetery and has paid for permanent care. The chicken dinner house is reopened now and operating as the Colonial Grill – with Mae footing the bills!

Now it was all news of disputes over money and lucrative entertainment deals that kept the Queen of Sex in the spotlight in the manner to which she had grown accustomed and entitled to by dint of her uniqueness and stardom. In September 1950, *Variety* announced that Mae had signed 'one of the most fabulous contracts in recent showbiz history to cover her participation in an upcoming Las Vegas nitery to be known as the "Diamond Lil."' The deal would assure Mae $2,000 per week for a minimum sixty days of performance annually and $1,000 when she was not performing, for 'mere use of the "Diamond Lil" billing. Miss West has also been given 45,000 shares of "Diamond Lil" corporation stock which . . . has been floated on the market at $6 a share.' Mae would also receive free living quarters at the casino and free costumes, and would 'not be held personally responsible for any debts or liabilities' in connection with the operation of the new joint. The casino 'edifice', along the Las Vegas strip, would cost $300,000 to construct. Another report valued the resort at $1 million, saying that Mae would 'settle here and run it herself'.

This turned out to be a fantasy contract. 'Mae West's Diamond Lil

Casino and Restaurant' was never built. But Mae had her eye on this glittering hub of amusements, which was continuing to expand in the heat of the Nevada desert. The gambling barons who constructed this new American frontier of money were willing to pay top dollar for entertainers who were getting too old for Hollywood's eternal wheel of youth in order to entice the suckers to unload their dollars and cents into the maws of the casino Molochs.

In 1954, Mae arrived in 'Sin City' itself to begin the latest phase of her rejuvenation.

36

Crossing the Sahara . . .

On 5 April 1954, James Timony died of a heart attack at his home in Los Angeles. He had been ill for some years and unable to advise Mae as both would have liked. His death severed the last connection Mae had to the beginnings of her show-business life. Timony had, after all, been around since the vaudeville tours of the 'Original Brinkley Girl' and her shimmy-shawobble in the small time. He had seen her through agents, managers and lovers, through fallow and break-through years, her success in revues, her fallback years and the hazards of her self-authored plays. Where others had been fickle or temporary, he had been unflinchingly loyal, submerging his own personality and subordinating his entire life to the greater glory of Mae. The *Los Angeles Times* reported that she 'was prostrated by news of his death, and her secretary said she was unable to receive callers'. High Mass was celebrated for him at Our Mother of Good Counsel at Vermont Avenue, and his body was flown back east to Brooklyn for interment in his family plot at the Holy Cross cemetery.

In July, Mae opened in Las Vegas, alone apart from her retinue of supporting male singers, musclemen, stage crew and the host of Vegas punters and gamblers. In 1954, Las Vegas was in the midst of its greatest period of expansion. Founded in 1903 by Charles 'Pop' Squires along the route of the San Pedro and Los Angeles Railroad, Las Vegas had seen its first resort hotel, the El Rancho, opened in 1941. Nineteen forty-six saw the opening of the legendary Flamingo, 1950 the Desert Inn, and 1952 the Sands and the Sahara along what was known as The Strip. This was the supreme heyday of the mobsters who controlled the country's most glittering and overflowing money box. Bugsy Siegel had built the Flamingo but didn't live to see its fabulous profits, as he was gunned down in 1947. Meyer Lansky, Frank Costello, Moe Dalitz and Gus Greenbaum were only a few of The Strip's multiple godfathers. Coincidentally, nuclear tests in the southern Nevada desert in the early 1950s were transformed into another attraction, as tourists were welcomed to watch the explosions from the top floors of the hotels and a chorus girl was elected 'Miss Atomic Blast'. Onlookers reported that 'gamblers rushed out of the casinos to watch the desert sky glow in the light of an artificial sun'.

In the summer of 1954, however, the main blast was Mae West, booked by 'Mr. Entertainment Agent extraordinaire' William Miller, hoofer turned entrepreneur who was said to have invented the 'lounge show', which brought Mae and later Elvis Presley, as well as the 'Rat Pack' – Sinatra, Dean Martin, *et al.* – to Vegas. Once again, Mae was blazing a trail.

'Comeback? She's Never Been Away,' said *Variety*, reporting on Mae's new act, with its number entitled 'I'd Like to Do All Day What I Do All Night' and her new *bons mots*, such as 'Why marry a ballplayer when you can get the whole team?' For once, there was no censor to tell Mae what not to say. 'The 45-minute melange of songs and sketches that comprises the West act is concerned with only one thing. And anyone who doesn't know ahead of time what that one thing is, is wasting good table space.' Accompanying Mae West were a troupe of singers in tuxedoes, veteran actress Louise Beavers, reprising her old role as Pearl in *She Done Him Wrong* and playing the maid Beulah, and Mae's nine 'athaleets', as she called them, culled from Muscle Beach, Venice, and from the 1954 Mr America contest. The winner, Richard Du Bois, had wanted to see Mae, and a whole gang trouped into her apartment. Mae described this encounter rather oddly in her soon-to-be-penned autobiography, noting 'this magnificent herd of males' and the declaration of love from the winner, who told Mae: '"You are the end of my search for an ideal . . ." "I find you very lovable indeed," I said.' This love, Mae wrote, 'a perfect union of the mental, physical and spiritual', scared her off, as she never wanted to lose her sense of self-possession. But it would do for a while.

Special sketches and songs were written for the Las Vegas show, including a straight steal from Eva Tanguay's turn-of-the-century hit 'It's Not What I Say, It's the Way that I Say It', boasting stanzas such as: 'Now maybe they picture me as a little Snow White / With seven dwarves to entertain I might do all right / But should I concentrate on one dwarf a night? / That's all, brother, that's all!'

A finale with Liberace was carefully scripted, the other Queen of Las Vegas gushing: 'Miss West, you're wonderful!' West: 'Call me Madame DuBarry, she's my favorite queen of tarts – or hearts. You may kiss my hand.' Liberace: 'Only your hand? . . . Wow – that started a fire!' West: 'I'd rather have you hot than all wet. Besides, Lee baby, if you're in a mood for romance, you're a match for my mood!' Liberace: 'Ladies and gentlemen – this is The End!' And curtain.

Mae's act, the tuxedoed singers, the disrobing musclemen and her tit-for-tat routine with Louise Beavers was a wow – 'Sensational Hit,' headlined the *Los Angeles Times*, 'a show to stop all shows . . . The men in loin clothes furnished all the Ball-type décor. Mae was amply clothed except for moderate seminude effects under net. She looked askance at duplicating diaphanous Dietrich results or anything like that in the aftershow interview. She also said, "I'm getting the highest salary yet paid"' – rumoured to be $10,000 a week.

Success without Timony galvanized Mae, who was already eyeing another new departure – television. Mae had told Hal Humphrey of the *Los Angeles Mirror*, on 30 April, that she was 'going to begin filming a half-hour TV series with Producer Bill Le Baron right after [my] engagement at the Sahara Hotel . . . Doncha think TV is a perfect medium for me? After all, I've always entertained the masses – all ages and mentality.' This was doubtless the 'Mae West Museum of Historical Humbug' project, which was never produced. Television, like radio, was coralled by restrictions that would not allow Fatima's 'chic and provocative' veil.

In February 1955, Mae was struggling with yet another domestic crisis when her chauffeur, Ray Wallace, was found dead of carbon-monoxide poisoning in her car on a farm near Patoka, Indiana. The *Chicago American* sensed a scandal of some kind, but could not pin it down: 'In the car was a sealed metal box inscribed with Miss West's name. Miss West, who is now appearing at a Chicago nightclub act, said she didn't know what the box contained. She said Wallace left Los Angeles on a drive to Chicago seven days ago and telephoned her Monday that he had taken the wrong road and would be late arriving.' Wallace had only been Mae's chauffeur for seven months and his death was noted as an unexplained suicide. Meanwhile, the *Chicago Sun-Times* related, on 20 February, that Mae was 'wreathing middle-aged males at the Chez Paree in their happiest leers since they leafed through Captain Willy's Whizz Bang or the Police Gazette . . .

Slinking through an entourage of five Adonises in white tie and tails
and nine Lionel Strongforts in breech-clouts, she simpers: "Spread
out boys, I feel like a million tonight, but one at a time." The nine
musclemen beat Tarzanlike tattoos on their breasts . . .'

Pictures of Mae from this period show her struggling both with her
age and her much younger rivals, sporting a hairdo that more than a
little resembles that of her bête noir, Marilyn Monroe. Continuing
the nightclub tour, the march of testosterone led in Washington D.C.
to an unseemly internal brawl. According to Eels and Musgrove: 'The
body builders lived strictly regimented lives, economizing by piling
three or four in a room, eating tinned high protein foods, drinking
milk out of cartons and sleeping long hours. When not resting or performing, they pumped iron to inflate their muscles.' Meanwhile,
Mae's bodyguard-cum-lover, ex-boxer Vincent Lopez, was inflating
another anatomical part in her suite. But she was not averse to sam-
pling the wares of the iron pumpers too. Two in particular took her
fancy on the 1955 tour. One was an ex-Navy and merchant Marine
who had served in Korea, thirty-two year-old Chester Ribonsky,
a.k.a. Chuck Krauser. (Featured as 'Grouser' on the cover of May
1955's *Strength and Health* magazine.) The other was Mr Universe,
Hungarian-born Miklos 'Mickey' Hargitay. The press announced the
contest thus:

Washington June 7 (AP) – 'Mr Universe,' sporting a shiner and limping,
today filed assault charges against a fellow muscle man who knocked him
out last night in Mae West's dressing room.

Mickey Hargitay, Budapest-born weight lifter who came to the United
States eight years ago, filed the charges against Chuck Krauser. Both are
members of the Mae West troupe . . . Krauser pleaded self-defense. His
lawyers said they will seek a trial by jury when the case comes up June 28.

Miss West, garbed in a pink duster over full black slacks, sat in demure
silence throughout a hearing before the charges were filed. She kept silent
even when another muscle man in the act, George Eiferman, suggested
Krauser 'planted a tremendous haymaker on Mickey's head' because he is in
love with Miss West and was defending him against abusive language by
Hargitay.

Hargitay, 26, is a weight-lifter with a build that won him the 'Mr.
Universe' label in a competition at London last year. He recently has been
seen often with Jayne Mansfield, New York stage actress with quite a
physique of her own.

Both Hargitay and Miss Mansfield were married, though not for long, to other people, and their tempestuous liaison has become part of Hollywood lore. It should not be surprising that, surveying Jayne Mansfield on one side and sixty-two-year-old Mae West on the other, Hargitay made the expected choice. Jayne was appearing in George Axelrod's Broadway show *Will Success Spoil Rock Hunter* – filmed by Frank Tashlin in 1957 – at the time. Mae had to find an exit from this humiliation, and the intimation that two musclemen were fighting over her favours suited her fine. At the trial, Mae testified that she had dropped Hargitay from the show for missing a rehearsal, and Hargitay's reaction sparked Chuck Krauser's act of self-defence. The judge became fed up after three days of frivolity and dismissed the case. Mae left on Krauser's strong arm, en route to Atlantic City to continue the show, which the publicity had boosted nicely.

Krauser himself described the incident in a blow-by-blow essay found in Mae's archive, 'Why I Beat Up the Amateur Mr Universe of 1955 and Put Him in the Hospital', which recounts the tricks and wheezes tried by suitors to get round 'that big gorilla', Vince Lopez. Krauser kept making himself useful, delivering packages to her room, playing the 'strong silent type' that appealed to her, so that she began giving him the task of answering fan mail, then promoted him to 'secretary and all-round assistant'.

Much to everyone's surprise, the musclemen's dogfight turned out to be another turning point in Mae's life. Instead of being just another passing beef steak for her swift consumption, Chuck Krauser was to remain at Mae's side until the end of her life. Changing his name, at her suggestion, once again, to Paul Novak, he became 'her lover, bodyguard, driver, cook and anything else to prove his love for her'. The incident at Washington was to be his only moment in the limelight as Mae's consort, after which he moved into the background. Like Timony, he subsumed his own personality in the glow of her persistent lustre. Unlike Timony, he performed the most intimate services without any open gossip or complaint – although close acquaintances were aware of mighty spats between them that were, nevertheless, always smoothed over.

Krauser/Novak supplied a still centre that Mae required absolutely in the continuing turmoil of her public life. In November 1955, *Hollywood Confidential*, the ferociously malicious scandal magazine, zeroed in on her under the heading 'Mae West's Open Door

Policy'. *Confidential* had previously savaged Liberace, prompting a lawsuit over allegations of his homosexuality, and Mae was taken to task for her affairs with boxers, the 'tan warriors'; black fighters like 'California's rugged Negro battler, Watson Jones, in 1954,' and 'bronze' Albert 'Chalky' Wright: 'Chalky would take his mistress to the fights every Tuesday and Friday, for example, at which times Mae would give him $100 to $200 for betting money . . . She even came to the rescue when Chalky's brother Lee was arrested for shooting another pug.' Also in the roll-call was 'Speedy' Dado, 'the berry-brown Mexican bantam-weight'. The magazine concluded its sneer with 'Wright's no different from all of the boxing boys along California's muscle row. They all have a stock answer when they hear that silken voice purring, "Why don'tcha come up and see me some time?" The reply is, "How about now?"'

Mae, and everybody else, issued writs, but *Confidential*'s downfall did not come till August 1957, when a California State Senate sub-committee (the Kraft Commission) charged the journal with criminal libel, wielding as star prosecution witness a former editor, Howard Rushmore, who testified that police informants had been used to dig dirt on Robert Mitchum, John Garfield, Dick Powell, Ava Gardner, Maureen O'Hara, Mae West, *et al.* *Confidential* agreed to stop publishing exposés of celebrities and folded the following year, but the Pandora's box of scandal sheets had been opened, with *Hush-Hush*, *The Lowdown*, *Tipoff*, *Uncensored* and others taking up the slack, the forerunners of our modern tabloids.

Confidential's assault clearly galvanized Mae into concentrating on the latest of her writing projects, the autobiography which would be published in 1959 as *Goodness Had Nothing to Do with It*. Now she could tell her own story. One senses, in the book, a defence mounted against a lifetime of unwarranted charges: accusations of selfishness, crudity, wantonness, self-indulgence, vulgarity, lewdness. By choosing her title, perhaps Mae was pleading that, in her multiple attacks on hypocrisy and dumb conformity, she was stating that, in fact, Goodness had everything to do with it, but it was a Goodness that was not recognized. Others had claimed that Mae had led a wicked life, and her own play titles often rebelliously evoked the problems and issues she made into her subject: *Sex*, *The Wicked Age*, *The Constant Sinner*. In the movies, others kept imposing safer titles on her, like *She Done Him Wrong* for 'Ruby Red', or *Belle of the Nineties* for 'It Ain't No Sin'.

The *New York Times* review by A. H. Weiler stated that the book could be termed 'Mae West's own refutation of her quotation of another famed thespian's remark to the effect that "actors are people but not human" . . . The lady is nothing but vivid flesh and torrid blood enhanced by candor, narcissism, experience, brains, independence and a healthy bank account,' though the reviewer noted that the book was 'basically clean'. The more zestful tales of long-lasting lovers and multiple condoms would have to wait for *Mae West on Sex, Health and ESP*. After *Confidential*'s attack, Mae had omitted any hint of cross-racial coupling, even to the degree of downgrading her knowledge of black stage life in her account of *The Constant Sinner*, as we have seen.

Mae credited her writing partner, Larry Lee, as well as agents Murray Feil and James J. Geller, 'editorial assistant' Stephen Longstreet and her close fan and later confidante, Dolly Lyons (later Dempsey), for helping in her project. There was also an acknowledgement to astrologist Jerome Criswell for his research in newspaper archives and libraries. Criswell was a noted character in Hollywood circles, not so much for his research abilities but his long career of 'Predictions'. He appeared in two of 'golden turkey' director Ed Wood's movies, *Plan 9 from Outer Space* (released in 1959) and *Night of the Ghouls* (shot in 1959). In 1955, he had apparently predicted that Mae West would be elected President in 1960 on a pro-space-travel platform and then visit the moon with Criswell and Liberace in 1965. Some might say that metaphorically these events indeed happened, but Criswell continued to be one of America's most colourful shamans well into the 1960s and 1970s. He set the End of the World for August 1999, but left it well ahead of time in 1982.

It might be argued that Mae, in the 'Sunset Boulevard' mode of Hollywood stardom – with the echoes of greatness long past metamorphosed into grotesque and caricature – was quietly, and often not so quietly, going mad in her own perfectly sane way, were it not for the question that might be asked of the movie colony in general or of much of celebrity America: who could tell, and who could judge? A few months before the publication of Mae's autobiography, the *Las Vegas Sun* spoof-headlined: MAE WEST ENTERS PRESIDENTIAL RACE: 'Mae's Move Busts Up Political Status Quo With Third Party Bid', the other candidates, of course, being Richard Nixon and John F. Kennedy. Mae launched her campaign, the *Sun* announced, from the

Sahara Hotel, where she once again cavorted with the musclemen as she coined her slogans: 'A chick in every pot' and 'A man in every bed.' '"I am well aware that ill-advised taxes can take the incentive out of any activity," she said. "I plan no new tax affecting love . . . As far as the rumors are concerned, I'm certain someone is quoting me into syn-tax," the presidential aspirant declared.'

To mark her book launch, Mae planned in October 1959 to make her long-awaited 'official' television début on CBS's *Person to Person* talk show. This was not her very first appearance on TV, as she had been sighted, unannounced, on 1958's Academy Awards ceremony. The show's producer, Jerry Wald, asked her to sing a duet, 'Baby It's Cold Outside', with Rock Hudson. What this might refer to for those in the know about Mae's troubles with *Hollywood Confidential* and Hudson's close shave when he was spared the revelation of his secret gay life by the same magazine after studio pressure, who can tell at this distance from the events. The slot lasted two minutes but stopped the show until the next item of razzmatazz.

Mae's chat with presenter Jack Collingwood on *Person to Person* was recorded in her Ravenswood home on 4 October 1959, but, after a viewing by CBS executives, its transmission was cancelled because 'some parts of the program "might be misconstrued."' Once again, Mae was put on to the defensive, arguing that 'I was asked questions from my autobiography, which is honest and frank and deals with sex all the way through the book. In my apartment I have a nude statue of myself and maybe they objected to that. The program showed my bedroom and bed and I was standing by it. But I did wear a very sedate, dignified gown.'

Portions of the banned exchange were published in the *Los Angeles Herald-Express*, proving that Mae had not lost her bite:

COLLINGWOOD: 'Is the book about your private transgressions?'

WEST: 'Transgressions is a long word for sin. Nowadays you don't hide the past. You print it . . .'

COLLINGWOOD: 'Have you ever given advice to the lovelorn?'

WEST: 'Lots of times – especially my telephone number.'

COLLINGWOOD: 'What do you enjoy reading?'

WEST: 'Biographies, metaphysics and psychology.'

COLLINGWOOD : 'Straight fiction?'

WEST: 'Never. I can dream up my own.'

COLLINGWOOD: 'Man in space?'

WEST: 'That's a waste – of man, I mean.'

COLLINGWOOD: 'Any advice for teenagers?'

WEST: 'Grow up.'

COLLINGWOOD: 'Do you have some reflections on life?'

WEST: 'Yes, I'd rather have life in my men than men in my life. Hmmm. And a man in the house is better than two on the street . . . There are no withholding taxes on the wages of sin . . .'

COLLINGWOOD: 'How does it feel like to be an American institution?'

WEST: 'Great, and I have the constitution to prove it.'

That even a sixty-six-year-old woman joking about sexual desire could not be countenanced by the guardians of television showed how short a distance America had travelled, in its moral discourse, since the days of Will Hays.

Mae finally made it onto the small screen as a talk-show guest in the *Dean Martin Show* in 1959 and the *Red Skelton Show* of March 1960. On both shows she was carefully scripted, though in the latter she reportedly got away with the comment that 'a smart girl never beats off any man'. In her on-stage appearances, however, Mae could still poke fun at the whole thing. The nightclub tours were constructed for an audience that cared not about stories, dialogue or ideas but only the garish Spectacle of Celebrity, the repetitive coronation of the Sex Empress by her gyrating male slaves.

Mae was still shrewd enough to know, however, that this, too, had a limited life and would have to be topped with something new. Several times, when the Las Vegas show palled, Mae had revived her stalwart *Come On Up*, touring it again in stock theatres. But, in 1961, she had a new playscript, or rather an adaptation of the one she had flirted with in 1952, *Sextette*. This was Mae's last self-authored play, though the copyrighted 1961 version reads 'based on a story idea by Charlotte Francis'.

Still observing the golden rule of her agelessness, Mae cast herself as a movie star on the eve of her sixth marriage who is plagued by the return of her 'exes'. Once again, as in *Come On Up*, the character is Queen Mae, alias Marlo Manners, visiting London to wed her latest conquest, a rich and titled English nob, Sir Michael Faraday. Sir 'Mike' is appalled to discover, from the newspapers, that he is sixth in line:

MIKE: You can't feel exactly pretty after being headlined in catastrophe for being also-ran number six. I shall be the laughing stock of the Stock Exchange.

MARLO: Don't forget you've married a famous woman. Many men will envy you.

MIKE: Envy me taking on a job that five others have been thrown out of?

MARLO: They gave up – resigned. They released me for a better life with a better man. And I thought *you* were the man.

Mae blended her fantasy England with shards of the plot line of *Go West, Young Man* – namely, the character of the star's breathless manager, who is in love with her himself and jealous of all others. Two previous husbands turn up inconveniently, one a still ardent Hungarian film director and the second an Owney Madden-like American gangster. Everything, however, is sorted out in the end, and Mae bonds with her titled spouse without giving up her waiting room full of other panting available males.

As was now standard, the obsession with the star's glamour, sexiness, unstoppable allure and staying power was paramount. Mae's now famous quips on men were once more repeated but with none of the social or character-based observation that so marked her early plays. The *Chicago Daily News* noted that two of Mae's finer lines – 'Tact is knowing how far to go too far' and 'He is every other inch a gentleman' – were borrowed uncredited from Jean Cocteau and Rebecca West. Which only suggested that Mae was at least picking her material from better sources than *McNally's Bulletin* or Mildred Meiers' *Digest of Humor*.

The show opened at Chicago's Edgewater Beach Playhouse, on 7 July 1961, amid much chaos after Mae's absence from many rehearsals with a cold affected her first-night performance. Nonetheless she still had her press fans: 'She is a trouper of the old order,' wrote William Fulwider, 'unflustered by a couple of tangled bits of dialogue and the almost complete flubbing of half a dozen or so lines by a character in the third and best act . . . Mae West is still queen, an American institution, and they loudly applauded her.' The *Chicago Daily News* called her 'a Wagnerian heroine . . . emerging out of a mountain of marshmallow'.

The play toured Detroit and venues in Ohio, arriving in Miami in August, where it wowed the punters at the Coconut Grove Playhouse. 'The entrance alone called forth sustained applause for at least two minutes,' quoth *The Miami News*. 'It would be safe to call the reception an ovation. The audience came prepared to laugh and laugh they did . . . She changes negligees three times, wears two other gowns, makes good use of her diamonds and ermine wrap. Her men – and a fine lot they are too – wear white tie and tails.'

Trailing Mae was old trouper Jack La Rue, who had partnered Mae in the original *Diamond Lil*, playing the Yank gangster husband. 'MAE WEST OOMPH CREATES NEW INTEREST IN THEATER', wrote the *Miami Beach Sun*. 'When the final curtain rang down, not a single customer made a rush to the exit. Everybody sat glued to his seat and Miss West took repeated curtain calls, from about the most enthusiastic audience I have ever seen in this theater . . . Everybody present expressed amazement at the fabulous appearance of Mae West, at her enthusiasm, at her dominating personality.'

Anyone else might have rested on these laurels, bowed gracefully and retired to the shadows of ceremonial dinners, tributes of her peers, movie revivals, tending the garden, chuckling wistfully over the old scrapbooks. But not Mae West. Like Billy Wilder's fictional

Norma Desmond, she could retort that she was still big; it was only the pictures that had got smaller. The small screen, and the large stage, were still beckoning. Baby Mae was still not ready to leave the spotlights, even if her sight might blur, her make-up thicken, her wigs slip off, her gait begin to falter. Immortality imposed its own obligations, and the performer's duty still called.

Is This the End – Or Are We Just Beginning?

In 1964, Mae reappeared on the TV screen – in partnership with a horse. This was Mister Ed, the loquacious equine, who was in his third season for CBS after winning a Golden Globe award in 1963. Mister Ed not only talked but gave birthday parties, drove a truck, flew a plane, surfed and, of course, met celebrities, making trouble all along for his long suffering owner, Wilbur. 'Mae West Meets Ed' aired on 15 March, episode 102 in the series, directed by Arthur Lubin. The plot line: when Ed hears Mae commissioning Wilbur to design deluxe stables for her own horses, he turns up on her doorstep for adoption and gets a perfumed bubble-bath in her apartment. 'For her boudoir scenes,' *TV Guide* related, 'she insisted on transporting her own canopied bed – all gilt and crêped and white satin – from her home to the set.' Mr Ed, however, was one stud who did not progress beyond the ablutions.

It would have been a cautionary moment for Mae to realize she could eke out a twilight career as a sidekick to talking horses and other TV 'personalities'. However, despite her realization that show business had turned the corner to be dominated by the new medium, no one offered her this podium in her own right. There was still the stage, upon which she was planning once again to revive her old perennial, the immortally shameless Diamond Lil. Mae had invested a great deal in preserving the title to her creation, waging war against plagiarists and imitators, however obscure. For years she had pursued a stubborn court case against one Marie Lind, who had performed as 'Diamond Lil' at a nightclub, Gorman's Gay 90's, in San Francisco. In 1960, Mae had lost the first battle in her war against Lind when the California District Court of Appeals held that she had no exclusive right to use the name, because Miss Lind had registered her act with the AGVA and Miss West had not. Mae blamed incompetent lawyers and retained private detectives, who provided some entertaining, if frustrating, gossip about Miss Lind's disarranged life: Marie Lind, true name Alice Marie O'Loughlin, reported Detective J. Lockwood Albright (on 11 November 1961), 'was engaged for 6 weeks at Gorman's Gay 90's, and was so well received that she remained 32 weeks . . . She is short and fat, about 200 pounds; she did a comic burlesque dance on her toes . . . she has a big, powerful voice and resembled Sophie Tucker . . .' Her ex-husband, found in a 'very run-down . . . cheap tract area', said, 'Frankly she is kinda nuts, and I do not want her to know where I am. She might get a gun and shoot me.' She sounded like a dame after Mae's old heart, but the new Mae was not amused at all.

Marie Lind/O'Loughlin claimed she had got the name 'Diamond Lil' from researching the old gold rush Calico Saloon, fifteen miles from Barstow, California, and had been using the name since she was 'singing and selling boysenberry juice in a "medicine show" at Knott's Berry farm'. Mae's lawyers went so far as to locate a Mrs Lucy Lane, who had lived in Calico between 1885 and 1889 and had never heard 'Diamond Lil' mentioned. Meanwhile, Mae was updating the original script and copyrighted a new version in September 1964. This opened with a lengthy recital of the plot to come:

> *In the days of wicked whiskey*
> *When New York was wild and frisky,*
> *Lived a lady by the name of Diamond Lil.*
> *At a place along the Bowery*
> *Lived this dame with name so flowery*
> *In a dive alive with women song and gin . . .*

On her first entrance, Lil looks 'the height of fashion and fabulously expensive, all a-glitter with diamonds on fingers, wrists, throat and ears . . .' When one of the awed men says to her, 'You're a great lady, Miss Lil. You're a fine woman,' Lil revives the movie line of 'Yeah, one of the finest women who ever walked the streets.'

The new script is more outspoken than the old, portraying Suicide Hall as 'a lowdown dive, where murder and rape and white slavery thrived', commenting on the Salvation Army man Cummings that 'He said over at the Mission he'd make a saint of Diamond Lil / Did he say when I looked at him, I gave his tambourine a thrill?' and referring to 'a Chinese hop joint run by Hung Low Lee':

But where Lil was really dexterous
Was in matters ambisexterous,
When it came to that she never could be beat.
And at plain or fancy lovin'
She was such a human oven
Folks for miles around would suffer from the heat.

This revival meeting, however, never came to be. Mae might convince herself that age had not dimmed her, she might regale interviewers with her belief that Diamond Lil was eternal and that audiences were clamouring for her return to the stage or to the movie of Lil that she continually urged her agent Stanley Musgrove to foist upon the reluctant studios, but the world of entertainment had inevitably moved on. Although Mae won her case for title of 'Diamond Lil' in November 1964, she had to be content, in the same month, with another kind of revival, a carefully censored version of the old 1937 Edgar Bergen–Charlie McCarthy show, rebroadcast from recut tapes. In any case, Mae had fallen ill in September, diagnosed as diabetic, and retired to her apartment and the reclusive beach house, with Paul Novak at her side. In October, her brother Jack, John West II, died of a heart attack and his body was transported back to Brooklyn to the family vault at Cypress Hills. Of her immediate family, now only sister Beverly was left. If Mae pondered that she might be joining her loved ones in the Brooklyn vault soon, she did not confess, publicly, to any ideas of mortality, and Paul Novak, as ever, remained discreet.

Nevertheless, at the end of the year, writer Lewis H. Lapham was granted, for the *Saturday Evening Post*, another of Mae's home interviews. Lapham related how a friend, Joe Bardo, photographer, editor, one-time circus strongman, chauffeur and bootlegger, had arranged the engagement at Mae's beach abode:

Her house, protected by a high wall, is on the Pacific Coast highway, about a mile north of the Santa Monica Pier. Bardo announced our arrival over a telephone embedded in the wall. The heavy gate, controlled by an electronic device within the house, opened with a polite, swooshing sound. As we walked through a narrow courtyard overgrown with vines and leaves, Bardo seized me nervously by the arm.

'Don't louse it up,' he said.

We were met at the front door by Grayson, the butler, who, smiling through his gold teeth, showed us into a large room presumably fronting on the ocean. I say, presumably, because, although early in a bright, sunny after-noon, all the curtains had been drawn. The room was illuminated by electric candles set in gilded sconces. There were a lot of mirrors in gilded frames; also a number of Louis XIV chairs covered in white satin, assorted cream-colored sofas and couches and a white fur rug on the floor. On the white piano sat a sculptured nude (Miss West in the 1930's); photographs and paintings of herself decorated the walls and tables.

Lapham was taken into an adjoining room to see the monkeys, Baby and Pretty Boy, old Boogie's replacements, swinging from gym-nastic bars. According to Bardo, Mae had sent one of her monkeys once 'to Bullock's to be fitted for a camel's-hair coat and a beret'. Small heaps of porcelain broken by the monkeys lay on a sideboard. 'Very valuable stuff, but she never gets mad at them,' said Bardo. His tone suggested would that humans were so lucky . . .

After about 20 minutes Grayson came to conduct us into Miss West's pres-ence. We followed meekly up the circular stairs, like captives being brought before a barbarian queen . . . She received us in her bedroom, seated on a gold chair in front of her round bed. Over a pink satin nightgown of the type preferred by movie stars of the 1930's she wore a negligee of fine lace. Her corsets held her figure rigidly in place. She wore a long, blonde wig and exaggerated false eyelashes. The only sure marks of her age were the deep wrinkles in her throat and the lines around her eyes and wrists. Sitting motionless in her chair, she conveyed an impression of immense strength and solidity, almost as if she had been carved from stone.

'How are ya?' she said, grandly extending her hand.

Her voice was slurred and rough, the same suggestive drawl with which she always delivered her most successful ripostes and asides.

'There was no interview in the usual sense of the word,' wrote Lapham. 'Miss West spoke only as the spirit moved her, revealing whatever she thought within reach of our masculine – and therefore limited – intelligences.' Sex was natural to her, she said, her basic style was one she never changed – 'half the women in the world have copied me. I stimulated 'em. Those other actresses, those imitators, who are they? What have they done? Who ever heard of 'em?' Only Mae reigned supreme. 'I was the first person to bring sex out into the open. Before I came along nobody could even print the word on bill-boards.' She told her breathless two-man audience the tale of her encounter with the sailors and the girl with the bird-of-paradise hat that sparked off her first stage sensation. 'Sex is like a small business;

you gotta protect it, watch over it. It's a matter of timing.' She had never suffered guilt or regret over her many gentlemen callers: 'The score never interested me . . . only the game.'

The further Mae retreated into her shell, at Ravenswood or the beach house, the more she invited the journalists to imprint upon the receding audience her status as an icon and pioneer. Extended in-depth interviews were granted to Helen Lawrenson of *Esquire* magazine in 1967, to Richard Meryman for *Life* in 1969, to *Playboy* magazine in 1971, with many shorter pieces in between. Later claims that Mae was reclusive and seldom opened up were absurd, since she would give an interview to a hat stand. Playing hard to get was part of the routine of the lady who wished to advertise that she was still around to be got. Offers of the craved spotlight were becoming rarer. An appearance on NBC's *Truth or Consequences* turned out to be a hoax by an imitator. Old scenes were reshown in a documentary, *The Love Goddesses*, in 1965. Mae made two records in 1966, *Way Out West*, which featured Beatles songs and Bob Dylan, and *Wild Christmas*, which had to feature the ditty 'Santa, Come Up and See Me'. In 1968, she recorded another album, *Great Balls of Fire*, for record producer Ian Whitcomb, but it was not released until 1972.

Nineteen sixty-eight, of course, was recalled as the swingingest year of the so-called 'swinging sixties', and Mae once again rediscovered herself as an icon of rebellious youth. In February that year, the Delta Kappa Alpha 'cinema fraternity' of the University of Southern California held a special caper in her honour. *Variety* reported the 'turnaway event, with about 800 crammed into school's Town and Gown building'. Hollywood old hands Robert Wise, Jimmy Stewart, George Cukor and Mervyn Le Roy were in tow, but Mae 'held court for 55 minutes, seated in a chaise-lounge in a simulated bedroom setting. The standing ovation which she received – with humble thanks for, in her words, the "generous applause" and also the "heavy breathing" – underlined her professional ability to remain a star, despite inactivity, even in the sometimes jaded, cynical, what-have-you-done-lately atmosphere here.' James Bacon of the *Hollywood Reporter* waxed more lyrical about the event:

As vignettes from three of her pictures were shown on the screen, stagehands hurriedly set up a silky double bed, a full length mirror and all the other accoutrements that surround the Queen of Sex . . . At precisely one minute

Still Swinging – the eternal West

before the house lights went up, a chauffeured limousine pulled up to a side door and out stepped Mae wearing a dress that revealed more curves than Sandy Koufax ever threw . . . On her fingers were roughly $250,000 worth of diamonds. Some of the ringsiders were so blinded they never did see the show . . . Up come the house lights and there's three USC All-Americans around the bed in a huddle . . . O. J. Simpson among them . . . The huddle broke and there was Mae on the bed. Where else?

Giving her Diamond Lil spiel, Mae climaxed, as ever, with 'Frankie and Johnny', which she had first sung in vaudeville before the First World War. It was as if she had indeed vanquished Time, Space and Entropy. At home, in private, these elements slithered gloomily in the house she shared with sister Beverly, who continued a long alcoholic decline. Increasingly more paranoid than Mae, she held onto life just as stubbornly behind the drawn curtains. Perhaps Mae shunned the sunlight because artificial light was all she required. There was another *Red Skelton Show* and, on 14 May 1968, a *Night with Mae West*, at Universal City Studios, in which she performed her skit 'Lady Godiva's Modesty'. Plans for a grand show along the lines of her nightclub tours were put on paper, with an M.C. introducing: 'In our center ring . . . that alluring, electrifying Queen of the Beasts . . . Lady Mae and her tigers!', Mae reprising her prime time of lion-taming glory as enacted by her toy boys in tiger skins. Plans to shoot *Sextette* and *Diamond Lil* in colour, plans to produce 'Catherine the Great' as a rock opera . . . none of these came to fruition. But something else did happen. Out of the blue an offer came from Twentieth Century Fox for Mae's return to the big screen. The production was to be supervised by Darryl F. Zanuck, adapted from a sensational best-selling novel by Gore Vidal and directed by a young Englishman with flared pants named Michael Sarne. This was an offer that could not possibly be refused, though as Mae told the tale, she consulted her psychic advisors before responding. In true Hollywood style, they gave their assent.

And thus was begat *Myra Breckinridge*.

Something Left Over, or Who Do You Sleep With to Get Off This Film?

From the script by Michael Sarne (revised first draft, 3 July 1969):

'Myra Breckinridge' begins with a strip cartoon version of the conquest of the Trobriand Islanders. Myra is clad in underpants and wields a stone axe. The Islanders, exquisitely formed young men, are wearing the tattered remnants of The Flag. The series of cuts bears our credits as well as the story of the heroic conquest. Finally, with the dead and bleeding all around her, a bubble is seen at Myra's mouth containing the words: 'Myra Breckinridge is a dish, and never forget it, you mothers.'

Once upon a time, actor-writer-film critic Michael Sarne had directed a film called *Joanna* about a young girl looking for happiness in 'swinging' London. The film was shot in the tricksy mode that motion-picture executives had been told appealed to the younger generation – superimpositions, disorienting colour shifts, overlapping dialogue, the works – and was bought by Twentieth Century Fox for distribution in the US.

Once upon the same time, Gore Vidal, *enfant terrible* of American letters, published a book called *Myra Breckinridge* about a homosexual young man, Myron, who has an operation to change his sex and rampages through the entertainment world, satirizing decaying American values by the verbal, and sometimes not so verbal, whip of his/her transexual rebellion. Fox bought the film rights, but the studio executives could not figure out how to turn so transgressive a book into a movie, even in the promiscuous 1960s. Then, in 1969, the iconic film of the new generation, *Easy Rider*, was released, transforming the base metal of Dennis Hopper *et al.* into box-office gold. The solution for Fox, clearly, was to hire a director as young and dishevelled as possible, as long as he could, in a good light, distinguish between the front and back of a camera. Sarne's film had not made any money, but he was full of vim and strange ideas. As he told

Vanity Fair in March 2003:

I was penniless in New York, basking in the critical success of my first feature, *Joanna*, but without enough change to buy a cup of coffee, when I spotted an article in *The Hollywood Reporter* stating that Gore Vidal, the celebrated misanthropist, was unable to come up with an acceptable screenplay of his novel.

I had a brainwave. Walked across Manhattan to 20th Century Fox, saw David Brown, the head of acquisitions and, after the usual pleasantries, said, 'You know that dirty book you're having so much trouble with? It's actually about a film critic who gets hit by a car and, while he's unconscious, imagines he's a woman, then wakes up and says, "Where are my tits . . .?"'

He stopped me there, his face betraying a Damascene revelation. 'You mean the whole thing's a dream?'

This notion, one of the first 'don'ts' of film-school narrative tuition, seemed to inject the Fox management team with unrestrained enthusiasm. It had worked for Lewis Carroll in *Alice in Wonderland*, after all, and it could get them out of a hole. Casting Raquel Welch – who had looked pneumatically beautiful in a wolf pelt in *One Million Years B.C.* (1966) and had just acted in the Britishly incomprehensible *The Magic Christian* – as transexual Myra was another apparently brilliant idea. The next idea, casting Mae West as the sexually rapacious casting agent, Leticia Van Allen, allegedly came from Sarne himself, though the offer was formally made by Robert Fryer, the film's producer.

Mae disliked the dream idea, telling her agent Stanley Musgrove, 'someone tells you a story and you get all interested. They they say, "then I woke up and it was all a dream." – You want to smack 'em in the face.'

Sarne's first script, with its comic-strip Myra among the Trobriand islanders, rang alarm bells at Fox, despite the fact that the opening faithfully mirrored the first chapter of Vidal's book. Producer Fryer swiftly assigned another writer, David Giler, who shifted the focus of the credit scene to mythological Hollywood:

Fade in images of stars –
JOHN WAYNE – ONE MIGHTY OAK TREE,
CLARK GABLE, GARY COOPER & JOAN CRAWFORD *(crosscut with sawing of tree)* JAMES CAGNEY & JEAN HARLOW, ROBERT TAYLOR & VIVIEN LEIGH . . .

Meanwhile, Sarne set out to woo Mae, writing to her, on 13 September:

Dear Mae,

As you know, our script has been going through a lot of changes, and I shall need to have your criticism within the next day or two. Bobby Fryer and I agreed on two very exciting ways to include a production number in the film and also how to involve the Leticia Van Allen part more strongly in the plot. As you know, it has been my conviction from the very earliest days that you come out of this picture with a triumphant, classic success . . .

Mae was, however, as was her wont, engaged in rewriting her own part, pulling her age-old collection of quips, one-liners and vintage dialogue out of mothballs. To wit:

'The wages of sin are sables and a film contract.'
'Hollywood brides keep the bouquets and throw away the grooms.'
'I don't expect too much from a man – just what he's got.'
'I not only know all the answers, I make up the questions.'
'I didn't read "Fanny Hill." I'm not interested in amateurs.'
'I warn you boy, Hollywood is fickle. One day you put your foot in Grauman's cement and the next day you're mixing it.'

(*at party*) 'I saw you arriving with two boyfriends.'
'Yeah – I always carry a spare.'

'Don't your past sins keep you awake at night?'
'No, only my present ones do.'

'You certainly have a lot of mirrors around.'
'Yes, I hate to be alone.'

For good measure, Mae included some more up-to-date, 'with it' lines in her notes:

'At my place I don't have the grass cut any more. I just have a bunch of hippies come round to smoke it.'
'Who needs marijuana when sex is a more groovy habit?'

As well as old stalwarts:

'How's business?'
'Well, you know how it is. This business is like sex. When it's good it's wonderful. When it's bad – it's still pretty good.'

None of these is in the movie, which was pulled this way and that by its competing creators. Sarne's conception of Leticia as a force to forward the plot line and Mae's desire to slow her down and make the movie a showcase for her gags might have merged if cast and director had enjoyed a better understanding. Both Mae and Raquel Welch, however, were in agreement that the studio should dump Sarne and hand the direction of the picture to someone more experienced, namely the veteran George Cukor – himself seventy years old at the time. Stanley Musgrove's diary notes of August 1969 reveal this muttering behind the scenes, with Mae becoming more and more fretful of Sarne's attempts to mould her to the image in his mind. Mae was also obviously anxious about being upstaged by the young Raquel Welch, despite Welch's earnest overtures to Mae to 'become friends before rumors and expectations of feud could cause real trouble'. Musgrove's notes portray a West very different from the deluded, decaying and half-blind character drawn by her detractors in this period:

AUGUST 13: I went to Mae's at 2. For the first time I saw her own hair. Always before she'd been in wigs . . . in fact, somebody a few months back said she was bald. She's not. She has lovely blonde hair, fairly short, and the look of her in it is charming – so much fresher than that long straight style of her wigs . . .

Mae insisted I stay for dinner – another first . . . While Paul cooked, we talked script some more . . . Paul is a good cook, if stingy with salt. We had sautéed fillet of sole – light, not overdone and encrusted with, Mae said, crushed cornflakes. There also was mushroom and barley soup, salad, broccoli in cheese sauce, stewed tomatoes, boiled potatoes, fresh peaches and apple tarts, topped off with Sanka. I wasn't very hungry, so ate little, but Mae and Paul put away plenty . . .

AUGUST 16: The Ruth Waterbury–Robert Brown–Mae West interview – in Mae's bedroom – the most candid I've ever known. Mae said Timmoney [sic] used to keep her isolated from men so her sex drive would be chaneled into writing. This would cause her to have sex dreams, so she'd have to take a sedative to make her sleep deeply enough that she wouldn't dream.

I asked her why she objected to sex dreams. She said because you couldn't control who'd crawl into bed with you. Her first such dream, age 12, was with a bear. It was her first climax. She described the penis – about 4" diameter of her thumb and reddish brown. She couldn't understand why it was a bear – she'd never been interested in them. Lions had fascinated her though, always . . .

Mae continued to take advice from her spiritual mentors, at this stage mainly Dr Richard Ireland, a psychic who had taken the place of the Reverend Jack Kelly, deceased in 1964. But whatever box-office clouds they might have seen in the future, she was deeply committed to the picture. Production began at the end of September, with a budget rising to $5 million – the most expensive movie Mae had ever appeared in. But the atmosphere on the studio set was as fraught as the uneasy preparation. Writer Calvin Trillin, for *Life* magazine, described the scene, in March 1970:

On the set of *Myra Breckinridge*, amateur bitchiness is so common that Rex Reed, the only professional present, seems somewhat removed from it . . . It is true that Reed was quoted by Hollywood columnist Jean Haber as saying that Sarne looks like 'a wolf with rabies,' but by the standards of discourse on the *Myra Breckinridge* set that was not a particularly unfriendly thing to say. Fryer's most representative comment about Sarne in the same piece was 'God, I hate him.'

Mae and Raquel vied with each other over their costumes – who could or couldn't wear the black and white that, it was said, stood out in Technicolor – Mae's favourite costumier, Edith Head, once again designing her gowns. Everyone apart from Sarne wanted to shoot a straight comedy; Sarne called his style 'fantasy'. Trillin wrote:

What Sarne calls fantasy Fryer calls '1964 Antonioni,' Giler calls 'Women's Magazine Pirandello' and Miss Welch sums up as 'a festival of freaks.' Gore Vidal, upon whose novel the film is based, wrote a script that was rejected. The present script, according to most of the combatants, is basically Giler's script being systematically destroyed by Sarne, but parts of it were identified to me as 'something left over from Gore's script.'

The only neutral was John Huston, brought in to play the film teacher-cum-old western star Buck Loner, who 'somehow managed to put in a day's work every day without becoming involved in his surroundings – like a piano player in a whorehouse'. Mae had submitted eight non-negotiable script demands, including 'the instruction that Leticia cannot, as the plot requires her to, know that Rusty Godowsky, her final partner, was the boyfriend of an innocent girl named Mary Ann, since "Mae West never takes a man away from another woman."' Of the original novel she was reported to have said, 'To tell you the truth, I never got through it.' When writer Giler suggested to Mae that Leticia might have known Buck Loner 'in the old days', he got the inevitable frozen riposte: 'I never play a character who is over 26.'

In the event, it was astonishing that Sarne survived the movie without being assassinated, or that anything resembling a movie was actually assembled in the end. To be fair to Sarne, it must be said that the problem derived largely from the original material: Gore Vidal's mock-trashy vision of a morally and physically polluted America, drawn through the transexual's eyes – and, in particular, the subculture of Los Angeles, inhabited by a rogue's gallery of phoneys and grotesques. George Cukor would have foundered as deeply, albeit in quite another manner.

Sarne preserved the novel's first-person narrative by presenting it as Myra/Myron's account to her psychiatrist Dr Randolph Spencer Montag (who appears late in the movie in the guise of actor Roger C. Carmel), opening with Myra's words: 'I must write it down. Exactly as it happened . . . Not only for its own sake but also for you, Randolph, who never dreamed that anyone could ever act out totally his fantasies and survive.' A pre-title sequence then shows Rex Reed, as Myron, in the surgical chair, waiting for the cut of John Carradine's scalpel – 'You realize once we cut it off it won't grow back . . . How about circumcision? It'll be cheaper.' But Myron waves him on. Titles begin, over black-and-white clips of Shirley Temple singing 'You've got to S-M-I-L-E, to be H-A-double-P-Y,' as she skips over Hollywood Boulevard's brass sidewalk stars. And following the credits – the Atomic Bomb.

These visual tics, interspersed throughout the film – more bomb shots, someone being stabbed when a particularly weak verbal barb gets through, clips from Laurel and Hardy's *Great Guns* intercutting a scene between Mae and her stud clients, and so forth – remain perhaps the most infuriating element in the disjointed cutting style of the movie, and its most misguided departure from the novel. The storyline sticks to Vidal: Myron-become-Myra goes to his/her uncle Buck Loner's dramatic academy to claim her part in his enterprise, staying on to become a tutor for 'deportment and empathy' – 'I'm the widow of your later nephew Myron, and I've come to collect half a million dollars.' Buck hires a legal team to find out that Myron was never married, only to be flabbergasted at the end when Myra climbs onto his desk and reveals – to him but not to the audience – the proof that

Raquel and Mae – black and white in Technicolor

Myra and Myron are one. This principle is undercut by Sarne elsewhere, however, with shots in which Rex Reed as Myron moons
about, like a solid ghost, in scenes where Myra is also present.

Mae first enters this melange as LETICIA VAN ALLEN, PRESIDENT –
ARTIST MANAGEMENT – LEADING MEN ONLY, swanning in her office
and sashaying down the ranks of waiting studs with the murmur, 'I'll
be right with you, boys, get your résumés out.' A very young Tom
Selleck gets selected (intercut with a particularly inappropriate leering Richard Widmark clip), with Leticia's comment: 'I don't care
about your credits, as long as you're oversexed . . . mmm, I'll keep
you in mind as a summer replacement. Next!'

Gore Vidal's Letitia is an aggressive lush who arrives halfway

403

through the book, almost as an afterthought. Myron/Myra bonds with her as a fellow transgressive: 'Two masterful women had met and there is no man alive capable of surviving our united onslaught.' As written, she is in the prime of womanhood. Mae approved of the sentiments but would have no hint of Letitia's 'drinking problem' on the screen. (She also allegedly changed the second 't' of 'Letitia' to 'c' to avoid the 'tit' reference.)

Aged seventy-six, Mae looks like nothing so much as a living wax-work, wound into life by the mere thought of any sexual endeavour. It was as if Mae's Sex Queen status required that she should make a sexual comment every time she appeared in a scene. In her *Playboy* interview of 1971, Mae admitted that she revelled in the thought of 'doin' and sayin' things that woulda given Adolph Zukor apoplexy when I was at Paramount'. By virtue of make-up, she finally does appear ageless, an indeterminate figure oozing a kind of raw power.

As she so often repeated, Mae claimed the most important clue to her life was that she never allowed a negative thought to pass through her mind. Exaggerated as this no doubt was, it nevertheless expressed a truth about her prodigious self-confidence – in public, on stage and screen, as her self-invented persona. It is the supreme validation of The Act that took so long to perfect. Like all great performers, and particularly clowns – Fields, the Marx Brothers, Laurel and Hardy – who found their own unique masks to define them for ever, Mae utters the age-old cry of 'I Am That I Am.' Thus the inner strength that enabled Mae to claim that she could triumph over the march of time itself, preserving her smooth skin, silky hair, her vital vigour, which all the world, particularly its male subjects, should pay court to and worship:

'Hi, Cowboy! How tall are you without your horse?'
'I'm six feet, seven inches.'

'Well, never mind the six feet – let's talk about the seven inches!'

And as she swans back to the lobby –

'I can't wait to get back to bed. If that doesn't work, I'll try sleepin'.'

Whatever massacre of script and story took place on the set con-tinued in the cutting room, where a great deal of Mae's scenes were left in out-bins. What remains is frustratingly curtailed: another scene in her office with an Italian stud sent with a recommendation by

Fellini – 'Hmm, he's my fan . . .' Then, to her assistants: 'Get a test on this guy.' 'Screen test?' 'No – blood test.' A party scene, for which Mae assembled pages of scribbled notes, shows her only as a fleeting presence. Then Leticia visits Buck Loner's academy for a brief exchange with Myra, who offers her the hunky but exceedingly dumb Rusty Godowski – 'the last stronghold of masculinity in this Disneyland of perversion'. Leticia is in a contemplative mood: 'I think all the gay boys are going to run the business,' she murmurs. 'There's no more studs any more. Everybody's poppin' pills and smokin' grass.'

Mae takes over Rusty, who has already been emasculated by the most potentially outrageous scene in the film, his 'medical examination' by Myra which climaxed, literally, with Raquel Welch penetrating the stud from behind, although the instrument of this humiliation is left to the imagination.

'My purpose in coming to Hollywood,' says Myra Breckinridge in book and film, 'is the destruction of the American male in all its particulars.' So might Michael Sarne have said that his purpose in coming to Hollywood was to destroy the American motion-picture industry, but it was a robust, ruthless and well-armoured beast, and even Twentieth Century Fox survived the inevitable debacle of *Myra* the movie.

For Mae, of course, the destruction of the male was never her purpose or intention. She sought, as a pioneering feminist in her own right, to make her mark in her chosen profession, to have as much fun with the opposite sex as powerful men saw as their right from time immemorial, and to control her own destiny. Right at the end of the shoot, she was granted her own much-vaunted production numbers: the first as, to a crescendo of clip-shots of massed bananas from a Carmen Miranda saga, she enters in a palanquin supported by male bearers, dressed in a flimsy but suitably concealing number, crooning, 'Do something just for the thrill of it / You've gotta taste the fruit,' while in the second, attired in Edith Head's bravura black-and-white cossack-like gown, she sways on stage as an ensemble of African-American studs in tuxedoes floats around her, oozing, 'I'm gonna have you baby / Gonna love you every day . . .'

'Sex is an emotion in motion,' Mae stated to Kevin Thomas of the *Los Angeles Times*, when interviewed in August about *Myra Breckinridge*. And once again, Mae was in the spotlight. 'Too Much of a Good Thing Can be Wonderful' ran the heading of a long article in the *Times' West* magazine of 21 December, recounting, once again, her thoughts on life and men, her tips on health and beauty: 'I wash my face with bottled water and good Castille soap. And I pat a little lanolin oil, cocoa butter and rosewater on my face in the morning and at night, leave it on for about an hour each time. I don't need lots of face powder like other actresses do. I clean up the makeup with vegetable oils – a little coconut oil, avocado oil; and I steam my face . . .'

Mae didn't recount, in public, the secret that her friends were privy to in private: her assertion that a colonic irrigation, once per day, cleansed her inside to match the out. But interviewers were encouraged to examine the surface: 'Face lifts? . . . If you need a face job, why not? . . . No, I haven't had a lift. Look at my hairline, there isn't a scar. But feel my skin, feel my arm. The quality of young skin is there, isn't it? Here, look at my cleavage, see how tight the skin is? . . . I've taken good care of myself all my life . . .' It was not only Myron/Myra Breckinridge who acted out fantasies totally – and survived.

The première of *Myra Breckinridge*, in June 1970, proved that Mae's legend had become established. Outside New York's Criterion Theater a ten-thousand-strong crowd waited for her. Many surged forward and broke through police lines as she drove up with her musclemen escorts to make, in the words of the *Los Angeles Herald-Examiner*'s admiring Earl Wilson, 'the greatest comeback in history . . . "It was the last of the red hot premières,' gushed Wilson, 'a terrible push and rush to the car . . . somebody saying, "Mae! They're running up the street after you!" Like a champ, Mae stood up at the theater entrance and waved and took it, never running like some of the kids do now . . .'

Deac Rossel, in *Boston After Dark*, wrote: 'There is no doubt that Mae West has the sex personality, parcels of valuable land, a unique career and the adulation of filmgoers both young and old. She also seems to have the stamina and desire now to begin a second movie career. Mae West is still, as Will Rogers once defined her, "The most interesting woman in Hollywood."'

'The Last of Living Legends'

But it was, nevertheless, almost the end. The critics tore into *Myra Breckinridge*, Vincent Canby of the *New York Times* declaring that it only showed 'the lengths to which today's moviemakers will go to try to be different and dirty'. The audience did not warm either to the disjunctions of 'swinging London' turning up in their familiar Hollywood. Twentieth Century Fox pulled the movie out of the theatres within a few weeks of its release. Michael Sarne was given the equivalent of a one-way ticket to Devil's Island, returning to acting and film writing, with a co-directing credit on a Brazilian movie (*Intimidade*, with Perry Salles) in 1975 and then small parts in movies and TV series (the low point: SS Captain Schwartz in the mini-series *War and Remembrance*, 1988). He returned to directing in 1993 with a British film, *The Punk*. Nevertheless, he would enjoy something of a last cackle, as *Myra Breckinridge* became – and remains – one of Hollywood's rarest cult movies, a subject of wonder, awe, adulation and numerous websites paying homage to its bizarre anti-narrative and its freakish, hallucinogenic appeal.

Myra inaugurated the final phase of Mae's career: an icon of the elusive quality that goes under the heading of 'camp', that curious place where impersonation and subterfuge meet to celebrate transgressions that may or may not be real – the crossing of borders, of gender, of the 'authentic' and its imitation, though Mae West was never an imitator of anything other than Mae West. This, in the end, was the most peculiar of her attributes as seen by the public in these last years: where once had been, indubitably, a living, breathing Mae West, who danced and sang and cavorted on stage and screen, there was now a slightly less than believable, almost ersatz copy, elegantly or clumsily, as differing views had it, going through those celluloid motions. When Joyce Haber, in the *Los Angeles Times Calendar* of 30 August 1970, celebrated 'the Last of Living Legends', a hostile reader, one J. Gorrell, riposted in a letter to the editor:

Joyce Haber's interview with Mae West . . . somehow missed, but only
because Mae has become a tiresome old bore, forever talking about how
wonderful she was, and thinks she still is . . . At almost 80, I can put up
with her ego to some extent, for she is a gabby old girl, but at her present
age, she is not the Mae West of 40 years ago and I was a fan of hers then.
She belongs in the past, and only in the past. An old lady who thinks of
herself as a sex symbol is sad and somewhat revolting.

But to Mae, of course, she was still the same person inhabiting the
skin she had been born in. Her personal search for meaning in spiritual gimmickry continued undimmed, with the loyal Joyce Haber
invited to a demonstration of ESP at her home. Ninety persons paid
five dollars apiece to attend a demonstration of the occult skills of her
advisor, Dr Richard Ireland. With two-inch adhesive tapes and a
blindfold Dr Ireland 'read' the questions in the guests' letters and
answered them to their amazement. 'There are forces in the room
that speak to him,' Mae told Ms Haber, as her musclemen-athletes
hovered around her, watched carefully by Paul Novak.

Mae told interviewers she was engaged in writing a biography of
her deceased former mentor, Thomas Jack Kelly, but this probably
referred to the tome published in 1973 as *Mae West on Sex, Health
and ESP*, which contained some of her raunchiest revelations, as we
have seen. Another prose project, co-written with Larry Lee, was her
long-promised third novel, *The Pleasure Man*, a version of her 1928
play with the gay subplots cut out. It was a strange throwback to the
age of fading vaudeville and rapacious male cads, her most stilted
and quipless book. At least she could at last refer openly to the villain
Rodney Terrill's emasculation – 'And Rodney Terrill was as cocky as
ever, although now he had nothing to back it up with . . .' Not something one could suggest of Mae, as in the last page of her *Sex, Health
and ESP* manual she was still at it: 'As a final word, let me remind
you that you should always save a lover for a rainy day . . . and
another one in case it doesn't!'

In 1973, the war in Vietnam was on temporary hold, President
Richard Nixon's Watergate cover-up was unravelling with sensational testimony from his own staff, another war was brewing in the
Middle East, icons of liberal America like President Kennedy, his
brother Robert and Martin Luther King had been gunned down years

before, the country was still torn between different forms of patriotism and the Cold War maintained its nuclear threat. Eighty years before, Mae had been born into a very different nation, one that had yet to experience its first major overseas war, against the Spanish in Cuba and the Philippines; a world still dominated by the horse-and-buggy, where the first crackle of telephones was still fresh in the ear, the movies were just about to move, flying machines were only a gleam in the inventors' eyes, trolley cars were a new infernal engine, John Philip Sousa conducted his band in the parks and Miss Lillian Russell was appearing in local halls with her Opera Comique.

Mae had lived through two world wars and revolutions in technology, culture and style, the growth of mass media – cinema, radio and TV – the political emancipation of women, the lifting of taboos on sexual practices and discourse, and the rise of women's and gay 'lib'. This final phase of Mae's fame, as a cult gay icon, was something she could only explain by her own stereotyped view of gay men as essentially effeminate – the old 'third sex': 'They're crazy about me 'cause I give 'em a chance to play,' she told *Playboy*, 'it's easy for 'em to imitate me, 'cause the gestures are exaggerated, flamboyant, sexy, and that's what they wanna look like, be like, feel like. And I've stood up for 'em. They're good kids. I don't like the police abusin' 'em, and in New York I told 'em, "When you're hittin' one of those guys, you're hittin' a woman . . .," 'cause a born homosexual is a female in a male body . . .'

Gay men might have been less enamoured of Mae had they seen some of her late notes for raunchy lyrics in her nightclub tours – undated verse like 'Rub-a-dub-dub, Three Fags in a Tub', which may or may not have ever been performed. Mae could not help being of her own generation, and her revolt against inhibition still bore the marks of the prejudices and mores of her time. As she grew older, in fact, she often became more coarse, as one can see from the dialogue of *Myra Breckinridge* and verses like the following from the same tour material:

> *Yankee Doodle, came too soon*
> *Unless he had some brandy*
> *Sometimes he would have too much*
> *Like a kid has too much candy.*
> *Oh, yank yer doodle, doodle boy,*
> *Yank yer doodle, it's a dandy,*

If you've got to be alone,
You might as well be handy!

Asked by Robert Jennings of *Playboy* in January 1971 how she would like to be seen and how she saw herself, Mae replied: 'I see myself as a classic. I never loved another person the way I loved myself. I've had an easy life and no guilts about it. I'm in a class by myself. I have no regrets . . . A reporter asked me recently what I wanted to be remembered for and I told him, "Everything." That about sums it up.'

In May 1971, Mae was named 'Woman of the Century' by students of the UCLA council and handed a gold winged statue: 'Sheathed in white faille and sparkling with diamonds, the star was accorded several standing ovations by the approximately 1,700 students who crowded the ballroom. In a question and answer session with the young people Miss West declared that she would not consider running against Gov. Ronald Reagan in the next election. "I don't know much about politics," confessed Miss West, hand on hips ("I'm just restin' 'em"), "but I know a good party man when I see one."'

Seances continued, with the mother of murdered actress Sharon Tate 'hoping to reach her dead daughter through the spirit world'. But though Mae might be thought as close to the spirit world now as might be, she continued rolling along. In August 1972, she travelled to Venice to receive a special 'Lion of San Marco' award at the Venice Film Festival, alongside Billy Wilder. If his invitation to her to play Norma Desmond still rankled, she showed no sign of it. A month later, she received an honorary King David Award on behalf of Israel Bonds, though no one could quite figure out why. In 1973, the Masquers Club celebrated 'Mae Day', at which she reminisced about W. C. Fields and gave her 'recitative' from *Diamond Lil*. George Raft, Lloyd Nolan and Jack La Rue were among the survivors attending. A small item in *Variety* noted, on 21 May, that Mae was 'writing a new book, largely autobiographical, "Sex Drive." Will include real names in her personal experience . . . Meanwhile, Warner Toub and Harry Weiss have a film option on Mae's "Sextet" until June 10 for a proposed $2–3,000,000 production . . . Following her one-niter for friends at the Masquers, La West has again received Las Vegas offers . . .'

Nothing came of this option . . . yet. In 1974 and 1975, Mae was more reclusive though seeing some interviewers, such as the young

Anjelica Huston and Peter Lester. She had her famous apartment redecorated, so that 'it now boasts several dishy male nudes alongside the bare-breasted maidens', revealed George Haddad of *Coronet*, to whom she mused: 'We are in the liberated 70's, so what's wrong with enjoying a little male anatomy, hmmm? As far as I'm concerned a woman is never too old . . . to do whatever she has in mind. You're not only as old as you feel, you're as old as you want to be. None of us feels great all the time, but if you make up your mind to live a young life, you've got it made!'

In March 1976, Mae returned to Paramount to take part in a CBS special, *Dick Cavett's Backlot USA*, a 'nostalgic retrospective on Hollywood's golden days'. Mae sang 'After You've Gone' and 'Frankie and Johnny':

Wearing a black crêpe gown and black velvet feathered hat designed for her by Edith Head, Miss West emerged from her dressing trailer on the arm of her muscular bodyguard, Paul Novak. Spontaneous applause broke out as she made her way to a bordello-red Victorian saloon set that looked as if it had been saved from one of her movies. With only one long break between numbers, she worked almost constantly for the next six hours under the guidance of director Dwight Hemion and choreographer Mark Breaux.

Starting out at the bottom of a sweeping staircase, Miss West surveyed some 50 male extras (including her frequent escort, Playgirl's Man of the Year Lou Zivkovich) and observed 'This is the kind of room I always liked: wall-to-wall men . . .'

Under the blazing lights and the chronic hurry-up-and-wait of filming, the essential Mae West emerged. Beneath the diamonds and feathers and outrageous quips was a tireless trouper, a born entertainer who loves to perform and who is a consummate pro. Relaxed, confident, quick to laugh at a fluffed line or a muffed piece of business, Miss West was eager to get everything just right.

The spotlight – ever the spotlight. At home, the faithful Paul Novak had set up a programme of exercises to enable Mae to stay fit. As Stanley Musgrove described: 'To preserve her muscle tone, he placed a pair of small dumbbells beneath her bed. Each morning after studying an attractive photo of herself and setting that image in her consciousness, she would reach for the dumbbells and work out . . . At some point during the day she would ride her stationary bicycle to keep her legs firm and shapely.' Novak performed the tasks of secretary, cook, butler and husband in all but name. To most of their friends, they 'conducted themselves like a conventionally married couple'. In her private moments, though, Musgrove related, she was becoming more and more paranoid, manifesting an unreasonable fear of fire to the extent that she 'applied full makeup before retiring so that she would look attractive should she have to flee the burning apartment house in the middle of the night'.

In 1976, Mae was eighty-three years old, time to fade out for any performer. The obituary writers might have fairly felt that they had updated their Mae West file for the last time. But on the first day of December 1976, Mae was, against all expectations, once again in the movie spotlights, commencing the shoot of her long-awaited *Sextette*.

Of Short Weddings and Long Honeymoons

The story opens in the heart of London, England, recreated – with a few stock shots of the major sites, Big Ben, Trafalgar Square, etc. – at Paramount Studios, Los Angeles. Real-life TV host Regis Philbin introduces us to the social event of the year: the wedding of screen glamour queen Marlo Manners and her sixth husband, Sir Michael Barrington – 'the year's most romantic newlyweds'. Crowds besiege Saint Martin's Church as the Rolls-Royce arrives, with the Sex Goddess stepping out to frenzied applause. Meanwhile, Mr Philbin informs us, the world's leaders are meeting in a secret conference – coincidentally in the same hotel Miss Manners is staying at – to solve the many crises and tensions which are threatening world peace. They have 'no time', the announcer solemnly tells us, 'for a world of fantasy and romance'.

The 'World Leaders' were part of a new plot line inserted by scenarist Herbert Baker to beef up the original play/screenplay that Mae had been offering for years. Two very young men, Daniel Briggs and Robert Sullivan, both in their early twenties, were the producers found by Mae's attorney, Harry Weiss. The director, after a detour around George Cukor and Irving Rapper, was the British veteran Ken Hughes, who had made the successful *Chitty Chitty Bang Bang* in 1968 (as well as co-helming 1967's bizarre *Casino Royale*).

The movie commentator reveals Marlo Manners' gold swan bed, set up in her hotel room ready for the first night with Sir Michael, played by the young and zesty Timothy Dalton. Marlo's affairs, however, are being run by her manic agent Dan Turner, played by Dom DeLuise (Danny Kaye allegedly having been turned down for being too old). Turner informs the press brusquely that Marlo Manners 'loves short weddings and long honeymoons; by the time she gets out of bed there may be a new administration'. He is also impatient to arrange a screen test for a new actor for Marlo's next movie, as well as an assignation with the Russian delegate to the peace conference,

'Sexy Alexei', coincidentally her second husband, who is holding up world peace with his *'niet'* – a role filled by a most hammy Tony Curtis. Marlo, it appears – shades of *Come On Up/Embassy Row* – was once a top US special agent, as shown by a montage of her hob-nobbing with world leaders, including Israel's Moshe Dayan, the spoof headline in the Yiddish newspaper *Forwaerts* proclaiming, for those able to read the Hebrew lettering: 'Marlo Banget Moishe.'

In the hotel lobby, the crowd, bellhops and receptionists wheel about in a 'Hooray for Hollywood' chant as Marlo rolls on in dazzling white. Marlo's answer to the question 'How do you like it in London?' – 'I like it anywhere' – inadvertently anticipates a spontaneous quip by the century-old George Burns at an Oscar-night query: 'Are you happy to be here?' – 'I'm happy to be anywhere.' Which was not quite Mae's intention, though it could well have been. Critics and viewers noticed that most of her progress in the film appeared to be by a kind of gliding motion, with the floor-hugging garments totally concealing her feet. The result is most odd, till one notices she is either holding onto a door or moving on the arm of a man or, better, one on each side propelling her along.

Having triumphed over time – and reality, as must have been stark in her mirror, with Paul Novak the sole witness to the pitiless advance of mortality – Mae was making her last stand, like the last sunset of the last gunfighter, against her greatest ally so far – the camera lens. The task – conjuring the conviction that a host of perfectly sane, handsome, virile men are all madly in love with an eighty-three-year-old woman and are leaping over each other to bed her – was something the combined efforts of lighting cameraman, make-up artist and publicist strained to achieve as if they too had succumbed to the mirage. But gossip emanating from the production could not be stilled: Mae was crotchety, snappy with her designers, uncomfortable with the gowns and immense wigs, unable to remember her lines, unable to carry out simple movements like hitting an elevator button. Lines had to be fed her via a concealed radio headphone, so that she once, legend has it, repeated a police hold-up announcement that broke through onto the studio's wavelength.

The film's plot revolves ironically around Marlo's memories, record-ed on a cassette tape upon which she has dictated her entire life, recalling every peccadillo of ex-husbands and lovers. The tape must be found because it can prove whether she had, in fact, formally divorced husband number five, gangster Vance Norton – hammed by George Hamilton – who turns up alive rather than dead as another honeymoon spoiler. But the tape has been thrown out of a window, seized by a dog, speared on the javelin of a member of the US Olympic team – also staying at the hotel – and then trampolined up into a stone lion's mouth, before being placed in a cake for the World Leaders.

In the meantime, there is husband number four, eccentric film director Laslo Karolny, played by none other than Ringo Starr. Adding to the roster of 'with it' pop icons, Keith Moon appears as a gay dress designer given to talking like Robert Newton in *Treasure Island*, and Alice Cooper looms briefly as a piano-playing waiter. Old partner George Raft greets Mae in the lift with the murmur, apropos the new husband: 'Let me know if this dude gives you a hard time.' 'Oh, that's what I'm hoping he'll do,' Mae coos. To complete the roster, we have the aforementioned Olympic athletes, gyrating for her in the hotel gym in what must count as one of Mae's strangest scenes. The players in this team included one Mr Universe, one Mr America, one Mr USA, two Mr Californias and one Mr Pennsylvania. Paul Novak remained behind the scenes, making do with a credit for 'Production Liaison'.

To stir the concoction, the producers added some musical numbers – Timothy Dalton crooning 'Love Will Keep Us Together' to Marlo, and Mae herself delivering 'After I'm Gone, and Left You Cryin'' to a besotted Tony Curtis, 'Happy Birthday, Twenty-one' to the US Olympic team and 'Baby Face' to the rest of us.

Sextette, oddly enough, contains the most Mae West in a Mae West movie since *My Little Chickadee* of fully thirty-eight years before. Holding their breath, producers and crew waited for Mae to keel over, crumble under the pressure or her fabled natural never-ending battery to finally fail and fizzle out. On screen, Mae is clearly slowed down, her delivery often stilted and slurred, the power of the old voice curtailed. As if to make up for lost time, she grinds out a solid set of her tried and true quips: 'It's not the men in your life, it's the life in your men'; 'When I'm good I'm very good, but when I'm bad I'm better.' She also finally delivers the world-famous line that does not, in fact, feature in any movie except this one: 'Is that a gun in your pocket or are you just glad to see me?' As well as some new ones: 'You gotta get up early in the morning to catch a fox, but you have to stay up late at night to get a mink.' Or replying to 'I'm British, stiff upper lip' – 'Well, you gotta start somewhere.' Another first, and last, in a Mae West movie is an opportunity for her to utter the 'F'-word, stating, apropos of no particular plot line: 'I'm the girl that works at Paramount all day – and fucks all night.'

In the end, Marlo's taped memoirs of the nocturnal indiscretions of the world's VIPs, headed by a suave Walter Pidgeon, force them into a peace pact, and Marlo Manners has saved the world. Against all obstacles, she has also found true love with Dalton, who is finally revealed to be a top British agent ('He's bigger than double-o-seven!' 'I never got a chance to take his measurements,' says Marlo). Reunited with him on his yacht, she delivers her very last quip in the movies, as Dalton tells her she's done more for her country than Paul Revere: 'Well, as he said – the British are coming.'

Marlo's boat sails off down the Thames, as onlookers and sailors of the old moored warships hold up placards proclaiming the 'Marlo Manners Fan Club', and the last credits roll.

Although billboards went up all over Los Angeles with the legend MAE WEST IS COMING, the movie languished unseen throughout 1977. The major distributors, Warner Brothers, Universal, Fox, *et al.*, viewed the finished cut and turned it down. The producers, Briggs and Sullivan, finally opened it themselves at the Cinerama Dome on 2 March 1978. The film was next shown in San Francisco in November, then went on a limited release in June 1979 in New York and other east-coast theatres. Criticism was vitriolic. Vincent Canby called the movie a 'disorienting freak show', and Rex Reed, still smarting over his entry in the Golden Turkey stakes with *Myra Breckinridge*, wrote that 'it will probably be shown decades hence as a monument of ghoulish camp'. Mae West, he ranted, 'looks like something they found in the basement of a pyramid'.

Time magazine dubbed *Sextette* 'one of those movies rarely seen these days, a work so bad, so ferally innocent, that it is good, an instant classic treasured by connoisseurs of the genre everywhere'. Randy Shilts, in the *Village Voice*, bemoaned the live appearance that Mae had made at the San Francisco opening:

A procession of musclemen in satin bikinis slowly walks from the wings, like a train of young virgins clearing the way for a grand potentate. Then, the tip of a white feathered boa, the sparkle of diamond rings, bracelets, and the rhinestoned sleeve of a white satin floor-length gown – and Mae West, one of our last dwindling supply of silver screen starlets-cum-living legends, saunters slowly across the stage . . .

Yes, Mae West is a legend still living – but only barely. Once robust and lovely, the 86 [*sic*]-year-old West now seems petite and fragile, like a grandmother who needs to be escorted from chair to chair . . . Yes, her face looks ageless – ageless because it is impossible to make out any feature, even age, under the pounds of pancake make-up which only partially conceal the inevitable erosion of years.

The crowd hushes as she begins to speak. The voice is pushing with all its might to achieve the level of what was once a sultry, subdued murmur. 'I hope you enjoy . . .' Mae West starts, the sentence tapering into words that none can hear.

'Louder,' shouts someone in the audience.

But by then, after this one sentence, Mae already is being gingerly escorted off the stage. The crowd roars in gratitude anyway. Even the shells of legends are hard to come by these days . . .

The last hurrah – Mae and the U.S. Olympic team

Every last movie has its fade out. Back in Hollywood, Paul Novak nursed Mae through her last months of occasional parties and excursions. She became less and less lucid, forgetting names and faces, disoriented and frail. There were few further appearances during 1979 and 1980, just brief sightings, as of a lingering mirage.

A week before Mae's eighty-seventh birthday, on 10 August 1980, a fall out of bed led to a diagnosis of a minor stroke. According to Stanley Musgrove, Mae was signed into a room at the Good Samaritan Hospital, with Novak taking an adjacent room, the couple registered as 'Gloria and Paul Drake'. Her last reported quip was recounted by Novak, who said that Mae had attributed her fall from the bed to a dream – 'When asked whether it was a bad one, she responded, "No, a good one. How bad can a dream about Burt Reynolds be?"'

On 25 August, Mae was reported to be 'doing fine' after her stroke and was expected to leave the hospital, but she remained in place. Novak walked her slowly along the corridors. On 10 September, the press reported that the stroke had caused Mae 'a speech impairment'. On 18 September, she suffered another stroke and was placed in intensive care. The next day, Musgrove reports, Novak approached Mae's hospital room to hear 'unearthly sounds emanating from it. When he entered, the only light came from two candles, and the sounds were being made by five Filipino faith healers, who were talking in tongues.'

In early November, Novak arranged for Mae to be transferred back home to her Ravenswood apartment, with the great canopy bed replaced by a hospital one and a team of three nurses. Her friends, Paul Novak, Tim Malachovsky and Dolly Dempsey, saw her through her last days. A copy of She Done Him Wrong was projected in the apartment; Mae seemed to recognize her image on the screen.

On the morning of Saturday 22 November, her condition was such that Novak hurried to arrange the last religious rites, from a Catholic priest who was the closest on hand.

At 10.30 a.m., she was gone.

After hinting at a lavish Hollywood funeral, the shell of Mae was instead transported, as was her evident wish, to the family vault she had paid for and kept up since the 1930s at the Cypress Hills Cemetery, where she was interred beside her mother, father and brother. A hundred friends gathered at the Old North Church at Forest Lawns in Los Angeles, including a group of her musclemen attendants, directors

Robert Wise and Arthur Lubin, designer Edith Head, comedienne Joan Rivers, and less famous loyalists, like casting director Marvin Paige, Judy Canova, Terry Robinson and Warner Toub, executive producer of *Sextette*. Ross Hunter delivered a eulogy which paid tribute to the bond between Mae West and Paul Novak: 'In both her professional and private life [she] liked us to believe that she belonged to no man, yet she was actually caught up in a singularly tender love story.' No one, it seems, mentioned James Timony.

Beverly West lasted till March 1982, after many months of hospital care following a stroke. When, in the previous September, she was forced to abandon the West ranch in the San Fernando Valley, an orgy of looting erupted: people pulled up in cars and broke into the house, some staying for half a day, according to neighbours, driving pick-up trucks onto the property and taking out 'old letters, dresses, family photographs and other memorabilia'. It is possible that Mae's correspondence, or part of it, was lost in this rampage. Mae's own beach house in Santa Monica had been sold, in July 1981, to one Francis de Menil, 'a bachelor whose fortune derives from the Schlumberger oil drilling equipment empire'.

The usual squabble over the inheritance ensued, with Paul Novak suing for a million dollars rather than the paltry $10,000 he was left by Mae in her will. Her fortune, he said, 'had been left to relatives, charities and such groups as the defunct Mae West Fan Club of Canada'. Novak claimed that in her last years Mae had continually asked him to get an attorney to change her will in his favour, but he had always said, '"Not now, dear, there's plenty of time to do that." I guess I thought she would live forever.' He added poignantly: 'How did she ever pick me – just a wrestler and roustabout?' Novak died in 1998. Characteristically, his obituaries were almost wholly about Mae West, Chester Ribonsky having remained in discreet shadow even in his own demise.

To sum up – is there a need to sum up? Mae's life speaks for itself, a fantastic, almost phantasmagoric saga, spanning entire generations of show business and a world that alternated, as ever, between shadow and light, dreams and nightmares, hope and anxiety, ecstasies and dread. She was multifaceted, presenting herself as entertainer, showgirl, singer, star, writer, performer, sex educationist, feminist icon, role model, comedienne, metaphor, glamour object, spokeswoman for the marginalized of society, national symbol and 'American

Institution'. When Timothy Dalton serenaded her in her last movie, crooning 'You'll be young for ever' to her eighty-three-year-old figure, he was expressing her own impossible dream. And is it not in the search for the impossible that America is so often lauded and worshipped or, equally, derided and feared?

'Make love, not war' might well have been a slogan invented by Mae West, as she pioneered so many staples of our wobbling civilization: women's liberation, self-reliance, spiritual fads, the search for individual perfection, but always, unlike the politician or the evangelist, with a sense of fun, a balancing self-deprecation, a satirical take-off of pomposity, self-aggrandizement, the worship of mammon, the pursuit of earthly desires.

In 1935, when the Spanish surrealist Salvador Dalí – without ever meeting her – painted his *Mae West's Face Which Can Be Used as a Surrealist Apartment,* he portrayed her as a universal receptacle: her eyes gaze out of framed city landscapes, her lips form a blood-red sofa, which was also constructed as a full-sized surrealist artifact. Her nose is a fireplace topped by an ornamented clock, her blonde hair as drapes or curtains drawn back from the lower part of her face, which is represented as bare stage boards. The stage is ready for the play, the divan for romance.

You can have it all, Mae suggests, but perhaps only in illusion.

In 1998, *Los Angeles Magazine* reported the strange experiences of the man who had taken over Mae West's unit 611 of the Ravenswood Apartments at 570 North Rossmore Avenue. Mr N. had moved in two years before and 'filled the place with bird's-eye maple deco furnishings. Soon he discovered that his TV wouldn't work in West's former bedroom and that the phone would ring again and again without a caller on the line.' One night, returning with his friends from a comedy-club outing, a snapshot was taken of N. and his friends in the flat. 'When the film was developed, a bosomy apparition appeared in a mirror . . . "I've never doubted anything metaphysical, but I've never had it so blatantly in my face," N. says.'

Strange things continued to happen: 'The chandelier in the foyer flashed when someone West didn't like was present. N. had to remove many doors because they were always slamming shut.' Then, at dusk on a July evening in 1996, 'a form N. describes as a "computer-generated, slow-motion miniature tornado" rose from an electrical outlet. "I sat down and watched it for 45 minutes," he says.'

Mr N. persuaded the telephone company to allow him to use Mae's old phone number and 'reinstalled some of her Louis XIV-style white and gold bedroom suite, including a dressing table and bench'. He took to leaving a glass of water out for her and began using 'her favorite perfume as an air freshener'. Later, he gave a party on her 105th birthday, and a visiting psychic 'spotted West standing with her hand on N.'s shoulder'. The article was published just before Halloween.

In a cemetery in Brooklyn, in a family vault, lies the husk of an old actress who died at the age of eighty-seven in Hollywood. But Mae West, liberated from her *prima materia*, flies around the world, on her never-rusting celluloid broomstick, forever cracking her old corny joke-book quips:

'Being good is an awful lonesome job . . .'
'Vulgarity's just doin' in front of people what you do when nobody's around . . .'
'Don't ask me to follow the straight and narrow, it's too slippery . . .'
'She has plenty of class but it's all low . . .'
'How did you ever come to fall for him?' 'I guess his line was just low enough to trip . . .'
'Haven't we met somewhere before?' 'I don't know, but you certainly taste familiar . . .'
'Would you marry a fellow for his money?' 'Not if there was any other way to get it . . .'
'What are your views on love?' 'I haven't any views, I just love . . .'
'Marriage is really intended to join you together until you fall apart . . .'
'He's a self-made man, and he worships his creator . . .'
'All he does for a living is breathe . . .'
'He has a lot of dough, but he's only half-baked . . .'
'Something tells me you know the quickest way to a man's heart.' 'Sure, but I always like to detour a bit . . .'

And the finale:

I'm free and easy, my life's my own,
I come and go as I choose.
Just look me over, I'm plenty known,
I take what I want or refuse!

I sing a passionate strain,
Then I'm low down again,

EPILOGUE

I'm fire and I'm flame,
So be careful of this dame,
'Cause they call me Sister Honky Tonk!

Boys, you know you're only human,
Give yourself a break and let's be gay –
I'm not looking for a true man,
All I want to do is have my way.

I walk and talk like a queen,
Man, that's just what I mean,
If you ask me how I'll tell,
Here's a lovin' tip, it's swell –
And they call me Sister Honky Tonk!

CURTAIN

APPENDICES

Notes on Sources

Abbreviations

AMPAS: General files, Margaret Herrick Library, Academy of Motion
Picture Arts and Sciences, Los Angeles.

AMPAS-MW: Mae West Collection, Margaret Herrick Library, Academy
of Motion Picture Arts and Sciences, Los Angeles.

BDE: *Brooklyn Daily Eagle*.

BFI: British Film Institute Library, London.

GHNTDWI: *Goodness Had Nothing to Do with It*, Mae West, Prentice-
Hall, Englewood Cliffs, NJ, 1959.

LOCPC: Washington Library of Congress Periodical Collection.

MPPDA: Motion Picture Producers and Distributors Association.

NYPL: New York Library of the Performing Arts, New York.

NYDM: *New York Dramatic Mirror*.

NYT: *New York Times*.

PWT: *People Will Talk*, John Kobal, Aurum, 1986.

Prologue

xi   'Things I'll Never Do . . .' typewritten note, undated, AMPAS-MW.

xii   'Clutching, Squealing Crowd . . .' *Boston Herald*, 29 April 1938,
      AMPAS-MW.

xii   'created one of the wildest . . .' 20 April 1938, clipping, AMPAS-MW.

xiii 'Being invited to "Come up and see me . . ."' *Los Angeles Times-
      Herald*, September 1946, AMPAS-MW.

xiii 'encrusted with what is said . . .' *New York Herald Tribune*, 15
      September 1951, AMPAS-MW.

xiii 'If all the men in the world . . .' 'Connecticut Sunday Herald, 20
      July 1952, AMPAS-MW.

xiii 'MAE STILL HAS ALL HER TEETH . . .' *World Omaha Herald*, 12
      February 1949, AMPAS-MW.

xiv   'I have often been accused . . .' etc., *The Parade*, September 1929,
      AMPAS.

xvi   'Mae West's formula for writing a play . . .' *American*, 8 July 1928,
      AMPAS-MW.

xvii 'THE TROUBLE WITH MEN . . .' *Movie Mirror*, February 1933,
      AMPAS-MW.

Chapter 1

3   'The Brooklyn I was born in . . .' GHNTDWI, p. 1.

3   '"BREAD AND WORK" THEIR CRY . . .' etc., BDE, 17 August 1893.

4   'I tell you . . . the horse car is less likely . . .' etc., BDE, 18 August 1893.

4   'It is a radical question of independence . . .' BDE, 17 August 1893.

5   'An epic figure in Brooklyn . . .' GHNTDWI, p. 2.

6   'I was crazy about my mother . . .' PWT, p. 161.

7   'postilion basques . . .' etc., *Harper's Bazaar*, magazines in Mae West collection, AMPAS-MW.

7   'a child that has to be humored . . .' GHNTDWI, p. 4.

8   'We went to a store . . .' Charlotte Chandler, *The Ultimate Seduction*, Doubleday and Company, New York, 1984, Quartet, London, 1985, p. 47.

8   'a pink and green satin dress . . .' GHNTDWI, p. 9.

8   'I heard the applause . . .' Chandler, op. cit., p. 51.

Chapter 2

9   'I had a natural singing voice . . .' PWT, p. 161.

9   'some 200 different characters . . .' BDE, 15 April 1907, NYPL.

10 'the school for our future . . .' NYDM, 29 June 1907, NYPL.

10 'Her Christian name was Mary . . .' quoted in Emily Wortis Leider, *Becoming Mae West*, Farrar Straus and Giroux, NY, 1997, p. 19.

11 'the popularity of Mr. Clarendon's . . .' NYDM, 6 July 1907, NYPL.

11 'lost heirs, lost virtues . . .' GHNTDWI, p. 15.

11 'the Eastern Detective . . .' NYDM, 23 July 1907, NYPL.

13 'a beautiful girl . . .' etc., NYDM, 20 July 1907, NYPL.

13 'more than two hundred Indians . . .' *The Billboard*, 4 May 1907, NYPL.

13 'the Place Where Chorus Girls . . .' *The World*, 8 July 1906, NYPL.

14 'It is system, system, system with me . . .' undated clipping, NYPL.

14 'The text of a musical show is woman . . .' *Theatre Magazine*, May 1920, NYPL.

14 'In the past the man has been first . . .' Frederick W. Taylor, quoted in Donald Crafton, *Before Mickey*, the Animated Film 1898–1928, MIT, 1982, p. 163.

Chapter 3

17 'Murderesses (found not guilty) . . .' etc., GHNTDWI, p. 19.

18 'due to the exploitation of her personality . . .' Douglas Gilbert, *American Vaudeville, Its Life and Times*, Whittlesey House, McGraw-Hill, 1940, p. 329.

18   'even doing Salome's dance . . .' GHNTDWI, p. 19.

19   'While no documents . . .' Jill Watts, *Mae West, an Icon in Black and White*, Oxford University Press, 2001, p. 4.

19   'I rushed in, looked at this man . . .' Charlotte Chandler, op. cit., p. 52.

20   'Belobed black brodren . . .' William J. Mahar, *Behind the Burnt Cork Mask, Early Blackface Minstrelsy and Antebellum American Popular Culture*, University of Illionois Press, p. 59.

21   'Den hoe it down . . .' Hans Nathan, *Dan Emmett and the Rise of Early Negro Minstrelsy*, University of Oklahoma Press, 1962, p. 254.

21   'the most racially integrated . . .' *Mahar*, op. cit., p. 318.

22   'Ned C. Weyburn sings . . .' *Milwaukee Daily News*, clipping, NYPL, Ned Wayburn Scrapbooks.

22   'that past master . . .' clipping, August 1897, NYPL, Ned Wayburn Scrapbooks.

23   'we adopt as ours the melodic idiom . . .' NYT, 1 December 1901.

23   'leader of the Handel Musical Society . . .' NYT, 13 November 1904.

24   'sings rag melodies . . .' etc., *Variety*, 25 May 1912.

Chapter 4

25   'He was never in any way unkind . . .' etc., GHNTDWI, p. 17.

25   'at eight she joined . . .' *Brooklyn Home Builder*, September 1928, AMPAS-MW.

26   'I was neither one thing nor the other . . .' *Movie Classic*, February 1934.

26   'He was about seventeen . . .' PWT, p. 162.

27   'divide my attention . . .' etc., GHNTDWI, p. 22.

27   'organised in January . . .' etc., *Variety*, 3 June 1911.

30   'To the majority of burlesque managers . . .' *Variety*, 10 December 1910.

30   'Huck Finn . . . painted freckles . . .' George Eels and Stanley Musgrove, *Mae West, the Lies, the Legend, the Truth*, Robson Books, London, 1984, p. 27.

31   'Back in 1909 . . .' Scrapbook No. 10, AMPAS-MW.

32   'Mae never was in Milwaukee . . .' etc., ibid.

33   'I couldn't sleep the night before . . .' *New York Daily Mirror*, 12 May 1935, NYPL.

Chapter 5

35   'He wanted to marry me . . .' *Movie Classic*, February 1934, op. cit.

35 'We never used any swearing . . .' etc., PWT, p. 161.
36 'As soon as the doors of the theatre . . .' Bernard Sobel, *A Pictorial History of Burlesque*, Bonanza Books, New York, 1956, p. 50.
37 'The audience listened reverently . . .' ibid., p. 53.
38 'had a fine show in the New York roof . . .' GHNTDWI, p. 31.
39 'bitten by the writing microbe . . .' etc., *New York Sun*, undated clipping, NYPL.
39 'the burlesque satirizes . . .' NYDM, 27 September 1911, NYPL.
39 'who played the part . . .' *Variety*, 23 September 1911.
39 'A girl named Mae West . . .' Eels and Musgrove, op. cit., p. 44.
40 'FOLIES BERGERE EXPERIMENT . . .' *Variety*, 30 September 1911.
40 'At the Wintergarten in Berlin . . .' Jesse Lasky, *I Blow My Own Horn*, with Don Weldon, Victor Gollancz Ltd, London, 1951, p. 82.

Chapter 6

41 'Frank kept on pressing me . . .' etc., PWT, p. 163.
42 'there was no room in New York . . .' Brooks Atkinson, *Broadway, Limelight Edition*, 1985, p. 63.
42 'into a never-never-land . . . 'ibid., p. 104.
42 'VERA: I am a woman of fire . . .' playscript, Shubert Archive, New York.
43 'Gaby Deslys in "Vera Violetta" . . .' *Variety*, 25 November 1911.
43 'The new Winter Garden show . . .' *Variety*, 16 September 1911.
44 'With her famous rope of pearls . . .' *New Haven Evening Register*, 18 November 1911, LOCPC.
44 'a wet hen was never madder . . .' ibid., 20 November 1911.
44 'After seeing "Vera Violetta" . . .' etc., *Variety*, 25 November 1911.
46 'Mae West and Girard Bros . . . .' *Variety*, 20 January 1912.
47 'like a broken greyhound . . .' GHNTDWI, p. 38.
47 'The real surprise of the bill . . .' *New Jersey World*, 19 January 1911, NYPL.
47 'Mae West, late of the Folies . . .' *The Player*, 29 May 1912, NYPL.
48 'May West Monday evening . . .' *Variety*, 9 March 1912.
48 'The girl, I remember . . .' etc., *Screen Play*, September 1933, AMPAS-MW.
49 'HER WRIGGLES COST MAE WEST . . .' GHNTDWI, p. 41.
49 'I immediately removed her from the act . . .' *Screen Play*, op. cit.
49 'SHOW GIRL . . . HEARD SMACKS . . .' *New Jersey Morning Telegraph*, 24 February 1912, NYPL.
50 'unnecessary grist . . .' NYDM, 17 April 1912, NYPL.
50 'a tip-top show . . .' quoted in John Tuska, *The Films of Mae West*, Citadel Press, Secaucus, NJ, 1973, p. 23.

50   'a poor performance . . .' *Variety*, 20 April 1912.
51   'Mae West is a single now . . .' *Variety*, 25 May 1912.

Chapter 7

55   'I believe I'll go to Paris . . .' unsourced clipping, 1912, NYPL Locke Collection.
56   'The man single . . .' *Variety*, 23 December 1911.
57   'The elements that went to make up . . .' Fred Allen, *Much Ado about Me*, Little Brown and Company, Boston, Toronto, 1956, p. 240.
57   'foaled on trains . . .' ibid., p. 241.
57   'Mae West, the comedienne at the Grand . . .' etc., *Atlantic Journal*, 25 February 1913, NYPL.
58   'lithesome and willowy . . .' unsourced, NYPL Locke Collection.
58   'the original Brinkley girl model . . .' *Baltimore News*, 3 June 1913, NYPL.
58   'by singing a repertory . . .' unsourced, 5 August 1913, NYPL.
58   'Now Sam McKee . . .' etc., songsheet, AMPAS-MW.
59   'Mae West . . . is plainly vulgar . . .' *Detroit News*, 26 August 1913, NYPL.
59   'nut comedienne . . .' *Philadelphia North American*, 29 September 1914, NYPL.
59   'with a terrific personality . . .' GHNTDWI, p. 52.
59   'DEIRO. ACCORDIONIST. 13 MINS . . .' *Variety*, 10 December 1910.
60   'used to sit by my side . . .' GHNTDWI, p. 56.
60   'This guy had quite an act . . .' etc., *Mae West, on Sex, Health and ESP*, W. H. Allen, London, 1975, p. 19.
61   'tubercular condition of the spine . . .' *Variety*, 17 March 1916.

Chapter 8

62   'a spoiled, rich . . .' GHNTDWI, p. 61.
62   'connected with some firm . . .' *Movie Classic*, February 1934, op. cit.
63   'MAY WEST IN PICTURES . . .' *Variety*, 20 August 1915.
64   'NEW ACTS THIS WEEK . . .' *Variety*, 7 July 1916.
66   'VAUDEVILLE MUST "CLEAN UP" . . .' *Variety*, 27 October 1916.
66   '[Mother] was French . . .' *New Movie Magazine*, May 1933, AMPAS-MW.
67   'a child singer on the Loew circuit . . .' *Screen Play*, December 1933, BFI.
67   'blacklegs and scamps . . .' *Variety*, 15 September 1916.
67   'MAE WEST'S NEW NAME . . .' *Variety*, 17 November 1916.

68   THEATRE – PROCTOR'S TWENTY-THIRD . . .' *The New York Clipper*, 25 April 1917.

69   'OUR BOYS NEED SOX . . .' etc., Time-Life Books, *This Fabulous Century*, Volume II, 1910–1920, pp. 228, 236.

69   'some flag – waving into my act . . .' etc., GHNTDWI, p. 61, 63.

Chapter 9

70   'Personally speaking, lots of different men . . .' *Mae West on Sex, Health and ESP*, op. cit., p. 18.

70   'who was to help guide . . .' GHNTDWI, p. 63.

71   'ACTORS, LISTEN TO THIS! . . .' *Variety*, 11 May 1917.

72   'There was no radio . . .' George Burns, *All My Best Friends*, G. P. Putnam's Sons, New York, 1989, pp. 22, 60.

72   'big black men with razor-slashed faces . . .' GHNTDWI, p. 64.

73   'women of the streets . . .' *Variety*, 25 December 1914.

73   'Brother Bill, Sister Kate . . .' advertisement, AMPAS-MW.

74   'loud, slapstick, comedic nature . . .' Alyn Shipton, A New History of Jazz, Continuum, London/New York.

75   'Jazz suited me . . .' GHNTDWI, p. 63.

75   'Thrive On Life in the Trenches . . .' *Chicago Sunday Tribune*, 2 September 1917.

Chapter 10

77   'I'm getting awful fed up . . .' Sometime script, Shubert Archive, New York.

79   'I was born a scamp . . .' etc., ibid.

80   'And if . . . the public don't want that . . .' *Variety*, 11 October 1918.

80   'Women much prefer to be feminine . . . 'NewYork World-Telegram, 31 October 1933.

81   'MAE WEST. SONGS. 16 MINS . . .' *Variety*, 19 September 1919.

81   'given a solar plexus . . .' *Variety*, 13 December 1918.

82   'more than 114 specific spots . . .' *Variety*, 11 July 1919.

82   'Demi Tasse revue . . .' etc., *Variety*, 31 October 1919.

82   'booze joints . . .' etc., *Variety*, 8 April 1925.

83   'indecent material . . .' etc., *Variety*, 18 February 1921.

84   'Chief – the kid's a wonder . . .' etc., *The Whirl of the Town*, Shubert Archive, New York.

84   'In Paris all the decent people . . .' etc., *The Mimic World of 1921*, Shubert Archive, New York.

84   'as if it were an attempt . . .' etc., clippings, Shubert Archive.

85   'French prima donna of temperament . . .' etc., *Variety*, 23 June 1922.

Chapter 11

87 'The smallest cast . . .' and subsequent gag lines, joke folders, AMPAS-MW.

89 'SCENE 1 . . .' etc., *The Ruby Ring*, Mae West scripts, LOCPC Washington.

89 'how different types of vamps . . .' *Variety*, 23 June 1922.

90 'Gloria: Do I look so wicked . . .' etc., *The Ruby Ring*, op. cit.

92 'an episodic picture . . .' Kevin Brownlow, Behind the Mask of Innocence, Jonathan Cape, London, 1990, p. 31.

92 'avoid scenes of murder . . .' William Lewis Gordon, *How to Write Moving Picture Plays*, Atlas Publishing Co., Cincinnati, Ohio, 1915.

93 'the stage is given over to . . .' BDE, 27 August 1893.

94 'MRS SOMERVILLE . . .' and other citations, *The Hussy*, Mae West scripts, LOCPC.

Chapter 12

97 'It is hard to believe . . .' unnamed movie magazine, October 1934, AMPAS-MW.

98 'One day in 1922 . . .' Harry Richman, *A Hell of a Life*, Duell, Sloan and Pierce, New York, 1966, p. 38.

99 'In one of them she played . . .' ibid., p. 39.

99 'Mae West, once known to vaudeville fans . . .' *Variety*, 23 June 1922.

99 'If you don't like my peaches . . .' Harry Richman, op. cit., p. 41.

100 'lying on the bed . . .' ibid., p. 44.

100 'For years, my manager was wild . . .' *Playboy*, January 1971.

101 'It was through this knowledge . . .' ibid.

101 'He knew Mae wanted to make it . . .' Eels and Musgrove, op. cit., p. 42.

101 'MAE WEST, AUTHOR, LOSES HER PIANIST . . .' *Variety*, 8 September 1922.

102 'Mae West, who was with . . .' *The New York Clipper*, 23 August 1922.

102 'Mae West and Harry Richman also . . .' *The New York Clipper*, 25 April 1923.

103 'The Dynamic Force of Vaudeville . . .' *Variety*, 17 January 1924.

105 'Her next to shut impression . . .' *Variety*, 2 July 1924.

105 'clean up on films . . .' etc., *Variety*, 30 July 1924.

106 'popular hangout for boxers . . .' Jill Watts, op. cit., p. 66.

106 'West and Owney had a "hot romance" . . .' *Los Angeles Times*, 23 December 1984.

108 'What brings you here so early . . .' Perry Bradford, *Born with the*

Blues, New York, Oak Publications, 1965, pp. 131–2.

109 'Broadway has little to hold . . .' *Variety*, 26 August 1925.

Chapter 13

113 'I got started in plays . . .' etc., *Life* magazine, 28 April 1969.

114 'the San Pedro harbour district . . .' and subsequent quotes, *The Albatross*, script, AMPAS-MW.

116 'as they stand talking . . .' untitled fragment, miscellaneous papers, AMPAS-MW.

117 'I write my plays in rehearsal . . .' *San Francisco Examiner*, 17 November 1929, AMPAS-MW.

117 'MARGY: Mrs Stanton . . .' *Sex*, script, AMPAS-MW.

118 'something out of an EdgarAllan Poe . . .' GHNTDWI, p. 81.

118 'the slow, hard work . . .' ibid., p. 83.

119 'asking for an investigation . . .' etc., *Variety*, 25 February 1925.

119 'superfluity of hits . . .' etc., *Variety*, 7 October 1925.

119 'the most sensational drama . . .' *Variety*, 23 December 1925.

120 'immoral magazines . . .' *Variety*, 24 February 1926.

120 'Never has disgrace fallen so heavily . . .' *Variety*, 28 April 1926.

Chapter 14

123 'Margy: Why ever since . . .' Sex, script, AMPAS-MW.

124 'MAE WEST, 3-STAR SPECIAL . . .' *Variety*, May 5, 1926

124 'talked with them concerning . . .' *Variety*, undated, 1926.

124 'a married woman . . .' *Variety*, 9 June 1926.

124 'persons connected with the management . . .' *Variety*, 2 June 1926.

126 'a millionaire's home in Westchester . . .' etc., *Variety*, 16 June 1926.

127 'DAVID: Always, from the earliest . . .' *The Drag*, script, AMPAS-MW.

127 'I admit that in my play . . .' *The Parade*, September 1929, AMPAS.

128 'forced this vice into a corner . . .' *The Drag*, script, op. cit.

128 'the two-faced . . .' etc., GHNTDWI, p. 94.

128 'glorified homosexuals . . .' *Playboy*, January 1971.

129 'WENT TO BE SHOCKED . . .' unsourced clipping, 1 February 1927, AMPAS-MW.

130 'the dramatization of a wild party . . .' *Variety*, 2 February 1927.

Chapter 15

132 'I enjoyed the courtroom . . .' GHNTDWI, p. 97.

132 'After considerable of a squabble . . .' quoted in John Tuska, *The Films of Mae West*, op. cit., p. 35.

132 'This is not an attempt to provide . . .' *New York Daily News*, 10 February 1927.

132 'Censorship Epidemic . . .' etc., *Variety*, 23 February 1927.
133 'He . . . searched his mind for chaste circomlocutions . . .' NYT, 16 February 1927.
133 'This is a woman I admire . . .' NYT, 19 February 1927.
133 'outsiders . . . visitors . . .' etc., NYT, 22 February 1927.
134 'frequently, under the instructions . . .' NYT, 31 March 1927.
134 'volunteered that he had seen . . .' NYT, 2 April 1927.
135 'addressing the jury . . .' *Daily News*, 2 April 1927.
135 'These people were given sufficient notice . . .' clipping, 20 April 1927, NYPL.
135 'I never expected to be sent to jail . . .' ibid.
136 'Asked if she might write a play . . .' ibid.
136 'Because they wouldn't help the police . . .' *Daily News*, 20 April 1927.
136 'Give my regards to Broadway . . .' *Daily News*, 21 April 1927.
136 'I was ushered into a waiting room . . .' etc., *Liberty*, August 1927, NYPL.
137 'Upon entering the reception-room . . .' etc., ibid.
138 'A night club wants her to mop . . .' *Daily News*, 23 April 1927.

Chapter 16
140 'Midas Saloon and Dance Hall . . .' etc., script, AMPAS-MW.
142 'FERGUSON: The basis . . .' etc., *The Wicked Age*, scripts, AMPAS-MW.
145 'theatrical tripe . . .' etc., *Variety*, 9 November 1927.
146 'dat woman ain't got no spah time . . .' *Hollywood Magazine*, January 1934, AMPAS-MW.
146 'Miss West is well fortified . . .' etc., *Variety*, 9 November 1927.
147 'failure to pay salaries . . .' *Variety*, 16 November 1927.
147 'Mae West paid off her shoes . . .' ibid.

Chapter 17
149 'ME: Miss West, as the most persistent . . .' *San Francisco Examiner*, 17 November 1929, AMPAS.
150 'It's still wild and crazy . . .' GHNTDWI, p. 107.
151 'The Linders got a break . . .' clipping, 1929, AMPAS-MW.
151 'There were Chinamen dancing . . .' *NYT*, 19 December 1903.
151 'Paddy the Fake . . .' *NYT*, 17 December 1898.
151 'found a beautiful bar . . .' *Yonkers Herald*, undated clipping, AMPAS-MW.
152 'Big Jack Howard . . .' clipping, 14 September 1928, AMPAS-MW.
152 'actually was a singing waiter . . .' ibid.

153 'Jo-Jo, the Dog Faced Boy . . .' etc., *New York World-Telegram*, 17 December 1935, NYPL.

153 'AT AN OLD CONCERT HALL . . .' clipping, AMPAS-MW.

153 'In the early stages of "Diamond Lil" . . .' *New York Herald Tribune*, 8 July 1928, AMPAS-MW.

154 'pure trash, or even impure trash . . .' *The New Yorker*, April 1928.

154 'It is one of the "hits" . . .' *New York Herald Tribune*, 29 April 1928.

154 'so blonde, so beautiful . . .' *New York Evening Telegram*, 5 April 1928.

155 'GLAMOR MISS WEST UNDOUBTEDLY HAS . . .' *The New Republic*, 27 June 1928, AMPAS-MW.

156 DIAMOND LIL, scripts, AMPAS-MW and Library of Congress

Chapter 18

162 'The first thing I remember . . .' 1935 interview with Maude Cheatham (quoted in S. Louvish, *Man on the Flying Trapeze: The Life and Times of W. C. Fields*, Faber and Faber, 1997, p. 53.

163 'The wicked women of old . . .' *Chicago Evening American*, 10 February 1929, NYPL.

163 'the most unusual, most curious . . .' etc., BDE, 24 June 1928.

164 'bedroom eyes . . .' etc., GHNTDWI, p. 121.

165 'I carried twelve protectors . . .' *Mae West on Sex, Health and ESP*, op. cit., p. 21.

165 'We all sat round a big table . . .' *Variety*, 11 July 1928.

166 'lean, dark man . . .' GHNTDWI, p. 134.

166 'OH, MY DEAR . . .' *Variety*, 19 September 1928.

168 'EDGAR: You know . . .' etc., *Pleasure Man*, scripts, AMPAS-MW.

168 'Stan Stanley and Brother . . .' *Variety*, 11 June 1910.

168 'The Drawing room . . .' *Pleasure Man* scripts, op. cit.

169 'MAE WEST SHOW RAIDED . . .' *Daily News*, 2 October 1928.

169 'Before the performance . . .' *New York Herald Tribune*, 2 October 1928, AMPAS.

169 'MAE WEST RAID OPENS CRUSADE . . .' *New York Evening Post*, 2 October 1928.

170 'full of a curious native wit . . .' quoted in introduction by Lillian Schlissel to *Three Plays by Mae West*, Routledge, New York, 1997, p. 22.

170 '"PLEASURE MAN" – SOMETHING OF A DESCRIPTION . . .' *New York Sun*, 2 October 1928.

434

Chapter 19

172 'an obscene, indecent and immoral . . .' quoted in Schlissel, op. cit., p. 222.

173 'Negroes had become the rage of society . . .' GHNTDWI, p. 141.

174 'Babe Gordon leaned against . . .' *Babe Gordon*, a.k.a. *The Constant Sinner*, version of Virago Press, London, 1995, p. 1.

175 'Think what passed through . . .' ibid, pp. 207–8.

176 'Yes, hell had broken loose . . .' ibid, p. 108.

176 'Babe was the type that thrived on men . . .' etc., ibid, p. 5.

177 'he wanted the whitest . . .' ibid, p. 110.

177 'hell ship Java Maid . . .' etc., *Frisco Kate*, script, Library of Congress.

178 'is done in the height of Oriental splendor . . .' fragments, *Frisco Kate* file, AMPAS-MW.

178 'CHAN LO: Pearl of pearls . . .' ibid.

179 'There ain't been nothing so awful . . .' etc., ibid.

Chapter 20

181 'her death was the greatest shock . . .' GHNTDWI, p. 143.

181 'collapsed in her dressing room . . .' *Daily Mirror*, 3 February 1930, NYPL.

181 'Do you have any prejudice . . .' *New York Sun*, 17 March 1930, NYPL.

182 'baldish, yet domestic-looking jurors . . .' clipping, NYPL.

182 'small hat and long coat . . .' *New York Herald Tribune*, 18 March 1930, NYPL.

182 'in a circus for a while . . .' etc., *New York Sun*, 21 March 1930, NYPL.

182 'lines that the police found quite blue . . .' etc., *New York Sun*, 1 April 1930, NYPL.

183 '"Oops!" said Lenzen . . .' clipping, 1 April 1930, NYPL.

183 'that the police who testified here . . .' *New York Sun*, 2 April 1930, NYPL.

184 'MAE WEST BEAT IT . . .' *Variety*, 9 April 1930.

185 'Shows closed, backers blew out their brains . . .' GHNTDWI, p. 136.

186 'I went to Miss West's dressing room . . .' Testimonial, Mae West, Friends of the USC Libraries, University of Southern California, 1983, p. 15, USC archive.

187 'Mae West Employs . . .' *Pittsburgh Courier*, 17 October 1931, LOCPC.

187 'the aroma of Mae West's . . .' *Washington Herald*, 24 November

1931, LOCPC.

187 'to arrest the entire company . . .' *New York Herald Tribune*, 26 November 1931.

187 'The play settles into a slough of boredom . . .' NYT, September 1931, Shubert archive.

188 'mastered the rick of complete restraint . . . 'New York Herald Tribune, clipping, Shubert archive.

189 'HARRY: We're fixin' to go . . .' *The Constant Sinner*, script, Shubert archive.

189 'There has been a change in the attitude . . .' *New York Herald Tribune*, 4 October 1931.

190 'The woman has got something . . .' clipping, BDE, Shubert archive.

190 'strange fan letters . . .' etc., *Evening Graphic*, 23 October 1931, Shubert archive.

Chapter 21

195 'THE ROSSMORE APARTMENT . . .' etc., Interview, December 1974.

197 'DIAMOND LIL IN TOWN . . .' *Illustrated News*, 20 June 1932, AMPAS.

198 'Mae West, according to dispatches . . .' *Los Angeles Herald*, June 13, 1932.

199 'it was my intention to appear in my play . . .' notes, AMPAS-MW.

199 'NOTE: Of course, for Miss Dietrich . . .' notes, AMPAS-MW.

200 'Universal is considering . . .' MPPDA files, 11 January 1930, AMPAS.

200 'To exercise every possible care . . .' ibid., 22 April 1930.

201 'dark, well-appointed cafés . . .' etc., Lewis Yablonsky, *George Raft*, Mercury House, San Francisco, 1989, p. 17.

203 'YOUNG MEN: We're going in with you . . .' etc., off-screen script, *Night After Night*.

204 'I've never loved but once . . .' etc., gag/joke folders, AMPAS-MW.

204 'REPORTER: Your second husband . . .' Night After Night gag folder, AMPAS-MW.

205 'Joey, Joey . . .' etc., off screen, op. cit.

207 'Suggested ad lines for your lobby . . .' etc., *Night After Night*, Paramount Press Books, Library of Congress, Washington.

Chapter 22

208 'ball-bearing shaped . . .' GHNTDWI, p. 153.

208 'It was a new medium . . .' etc., ibid., p. 152.

209 'In re "Diamond Lady" . . .' MPPDA files, 18 October 1932, AMPAS.

209 'Please wire immediately . . .' etc., ibid., 19 October 1932.
211 'Zukor and Hertz promised . . .' ibid., 5 November 1932.
211 'It is taken for granted . . .' note in Paramount scripts, *Ruby Red*, a.k.a. *She Done Him Wrong*, AMPAS.
212 'The basic story of Ruby Red . . .' MPPDA files, 11 November 1932, AMPAS.
212 'Inter-Office Communication . . .' etc., ibid., 9 November 1932.
213 'We have three basic suggestions . . .' ibid., 29 November 1932.
213 'major contribution . . .' ibid., 2 December 1932.

Chapter 23

215 'MAE WEST SEES HOLLYWOOD . . .' clipping, 7 July 1932, AMPAS.
215 'GEM MISSING – MONKEY HAS IT . . .' *Los Angeles Times*, 10 October 1932.
216 '$16,000 in jewels . . .' etc., clipping, 13 October 1932, AMPAS.
216 'The majority of Mae West's evenings . . .' *Los Angeles Times*, 12 December 1932.
217 '[suggest] you rewrite Cummings . . .' MPPDA files, 13 January 1933, AMPAS.
217 'I went last night to see . . .' ibid., undated.
217 '*The Gay Nineties* . . .' and subsequent quotes, off screen, She Done Him Wrong.
219 '"Who's that?" I asked . . .' GHNTDWI, p. 160.
220 'CUMMINGS: You remind me . . .' etc., off screen, *She Done Him Wrong*.
222 'Glitter and Squalor . . .' etc., She Done Him Wrong, Paramount Press Books, op. cit.
222 'Mae West in pictures . . .' *Variety*, 14 February 1933.
222 'for a picture of its type . . .' Harrison's Reports, 4 February 1933, USC archive.
222 'hearty, hilarious . . .' *New York Herald Tribune*, 19 February 1933, USC archive.
222 'Let's . . . make some reference . . .' MPPDA files, 2 August 1933, AMPAS.

Chapter 24

224 'HERMIT PETE SCOFFED AT MAE . . .' *New York World-Telegram*, 15 February 1933, NYPL.
225 'you never hear about . . .' *Variety*, 31 January 1933.
225 'Hollywood has thinned Mae . . .' *Daily News*, 11 February 1933, AMPAS.
225 'I'll never try to go sweet . . .' *Citizen-News*, 14 March 1933,

AMPAS.

226 'I'm well educated . . .' clipping, 13 April 1933, AMPAS.
226 'she takes long drives . . .' etc., *Motion Picture*, July 1935, NYPL.
227 'Her next picture will be . . .' *Los Angeles Times*, 19 April 1933.
228 'Why brother –' MPPDA files, AMPAS.
228 'I'm free and easy . . .' etc., ibid.
229 'The underlined words . . .' ibid., 11 July 1933.
230 'ALICIA (cattily): I don't suppose . . .' etc., gag folder, *I'm No Angel*, AMPAS-MW.
231 'Joe the turtle boy . . .' etc., off screen, *I'm No Angel*.
236 'Clayton agrees to settle in full . . .' *I'm No Angel*, Paramount Press Books, LOC.
237 'I must confess . . .' etc., ibid.
238 'Mae West – the lady who was known as Lou . . .' *Variety* (undated).

Chapter 25
240 'the basic secret of sex . . .' *Mae West on Sex, Health and ESP*, op. cit., p. 31.
240 'CAPRICORN . . .' ibid., p. 33.
241 'I've always been a bit put off . . .' ibid., p. 42.
244 'the naughtiest show . . .' *Ontario California Outlook*, clipping, 1935, AMPAS-MW.
244 'two husbands who fear their wives . . .' *Loose Women*, playscript, AMPAS-MW.
244 'MARSTON: My trusted wife . . .' ibid.
245 'conducting an illegal theatrical . . .' clipping, 31 December 1935, AMPAS-MW.
245 'IRENE: You're awfully old-fashioned . . .' *Havana Cruise*, playscript, AMPAS-MW.
247 'Velvet Royal is the wife of . . .' synopsis, untitled files, AMPAS-MW.

Chapter 26
249 'JUST SAW ANGEL PICTURE . . .' MPPDA files, 16 September 1933, AMPAS.
249 'the general flavor of the story . . .' ibid., 23 February 1934.
250 'the picturization of crime, sex . . .' *Motion Picture Herald*, 17 June 1933, NYPL.
251 'financial institutions like the Chase . . .' quoted in Leonard J. Leff and Jerold L. Simmons, *The Dame in the Kimono, Hollywood, Censorship and the Production Code from the 1920's to the 1960's*, Anchor Books, 1991, p. 43.

251 'there may be an element of the public . . .' *Motion Picture Herald* (undated).

252 'IT AIN'T NO SIN. In police headquarters . . .' etc., MPPDA files, February–March 1934, AMPAS.

253 'This is where you become . . .' ibid.

253 'we are quite aware that . . .' ibid., 17 February 1934.

254 'Dear Mr Botsford, We have read . . .' ibid., March 7, 1934.

254 'The company officials . . .' ibid., 7 March 1934.

255 'Dear Mr Botsford, It is difficult for us . . .' ibid., 13 March 1934.

255 'In the scene in which Scratch . . .' etc., ibid., 7 March 1934.

256 'to reject in toto . . .' ibid., 28 March 1934.

256 'slowly raises her dress . . .' ibid., 26 April 1934.

256 'INTERNAL MEMO: I think you will readily see . . .' etc., ibid., 2 June 1934.

257 'OUR JUDGEMENT IN REJECTION . . .' ibid., 4 June 1934.

257 'Mr John Hammel, Paramount Studios . . .' ibid., 6 June 1934.

260 'Don't ask me to follow . . .' *Belle of the Nineties* notes, AMPAS-MW.

260 'I'm gonna drown . . .' *Belle of the Nineties*, off screen and MPPDA files, ibid.

261 'It's a tingle that goes . . .' *Motion Picture*, September 1934, NYPL.

262 'Mae West's kisses . . .' *Belle of the Nineties*, Paramount Press Books, LOC

Chapter 27

267 'Dynamite Lady – Mae West . . .' *Screen Play*, November 1932, NYPL.

267 'Call her sexy, call her siren . . .' *Picture Play*, April 1933, NYPL.

268 'Mae West designed every bit of furniture . . .' Hollywood Magazine, January 1934.

269 'Three Men – and ALL Kissed . . .' etc., *Motion Picture*, November 1933, NYPL.

270 'latest rumor that I am jealous . . .' ibid., January 1934, NYPL.

270 'Mae West take a back seat . . .' ibid., June 1934, NYPL.

271 'WILL I LAST? ASKS MAE . . .' ibid., June 1934, NYPL.

271 'He had his meals . . .' clipping, 28 September 1933, AMPAS.

271 'I have known Voiler . . .' *Los Angeles Times*, 5 December 1933, AMPAS.

272 'a wealthy Parisian . . .' *Los Angeles Examiner*, 22 November 1933, AMPAS.22

272 'She swayed into court . . .' *Los Angeles Times*, 17 January 1934, AMPAS.

273 'will spend her vacation in Hawaii . . .' *Movie Mirror*, July 1934.
274 'In a dance hall . . .' *Goin' to Town*, Paramount Press Books, LOC.
277 'masseur and physical culturist . . .' etc., Paramount press release, 1933, AMPAS.
278 'seems to us to be a definite violation . . .' MPPDA files, 16 January 1935, AMPAS.
278 'I used to dig for gold . . .' etc., ibid.
279 'GOIN' TO TOWN: This latest Mae West picture . . .' ibid., 1 May 1935.
279 'compares favorably . . .' *Variety*, clippings, 1935, Doheny Library, USC.
279 'Mae West's poorest . . .' *Variety*, 1 May 1935.
279 'Writing Is shoddy . . .' *Hollywood Reporter*, clippings, USC.
279 'I'M AN ANGEL, REALLY . . .' etc., *Sunday Dispatch*, 6 January 1935, BFI.

Chapter 28

282 'there were three Mae Wests . . .' *Los Angeles Times*, 21 April 1935, AMPAS.
282 'I've gotten a lot of bunnies on Easter . . .' *Los Angeles Examiner*, 22 April 1935.
283 'I hate to spoil a good story . . .' *Los Angeles Times*, 23 April 1935.
283 'He wouldn't spill it because . . .' *Los Angeles Herald*, 24 April 1935.
284 'By the P.A.'s contrivings . . .' *Los Angeles Times*, 4 May 1935.
284 'motion-picture editors . . .' ibid., 19 May 1935.
285 'With women trying to look like . . .' *Los Angeles Herald*, 3 July 1935.
285 'MISS WEST WE TOLD YOU . . .' etc., *Los Angeles Herald*, 8 October 1935.
285 'come up and see her . . .' etc., *Los Angeles Sunday Times*, 22 December 1935.
285 'all the coffee tables and consoles . . .' NYT, 9 June 1935, NYPL.

Chapter 29

287 'COPY TO ALL MANAGING EDITORS . . .' MPPDA file, *Klondike Annie*, AMPAS.
287 'I hear he is madly jealous . . .' etc., *Klondike Annie*, off screen.
288 'sex relationships between . . .' Article II (Sex), section 6 of the Motion Picture Code, quoted in Leff and Simmons, *The Dame in the Kimono*, op. cit., p. 285.
288 'There is to be no implication . . .' MPPDA files, 29 June 1935,

AMPAS.

290 'There should be no suggestion of excessive . . .' ibid, October 22, 1935.

291 'This is the story of LILY LARSEN . . .' Paramount scripts, *Klondike Annie*, AMPAS.

292 'a female Salvation Army leader . . .' Emily Wortis Leider, *Becoming Mae West*, Da Capo Press, 2000, p. 319.

292 'She takes passage on a passenger steamer . . .' MPPDA files, 29 June 1935, AMPAS.

293 'Dear Mr Hammell . . . 'ibid., 2 July 1935.

294 'whirlwind and passion . . .' David Thomson, *A Biographical Dictionary of Film*, Andre Deutsch, 1994, entry on Raoul Walsh, p. 789.

294 'I ain't here to blame you . . .' *Klondike Annie*, off screen.

294 'It is imperative that you do not designate . . .' etc., MPPDA files, 4 September 1935, AMPAS.

296 'We wish again to repeat our general caution . . .' ibid., 22 October 1935.

296 'a gay and gusty story . . .' *Klondike Annie*, Paramount Press Books, LOC.

298 'amid the murmur of praying voices . . .' *Margy Lamont*, book ms, AMPAS-MW.

298 'because of certain private information . . .' etc., MPPDA files, 10 February 1936, AMPAS.

299 'IS POLITICS INFLUENCING CENSORSHIP? . . .' ibid., 21–25 February 1936.

299 'The latest of the West exploits . . .' *Pittsburgh Sun-Telegraph*, February 22, 1936.

299 'STOP LEWD FILMS! . . .' *Los Angeles Examiner*, 29 February 1936.

299 'a strong vote of condemnation . . .' MPPDA files, March 2, 1936.

300 'in the past few days . . .' ibid., Breen to Hays, 2 March 1936.

300 'The grapevine from Hollywood . . .' etc., *Motion Picture Herald*, 7 March 1936.

300 'Mae West was the real issue last week . . .' ibid.

301 '"Klondike Annie" does not merit . . .' NYT, 12 March 1936, Doheny Library, USC.

301 'badly told, insincerely acted . . .' *Variety*, 18 March 1936.

302 'Whatever this picture cost . . .' MPPDA, typed note by Breen, undated, AMPAS.

Chapter 30

303 'Mae West Type of Posture . . .' *New York Herald Tribune*, 21 July

1936, NYPL.

304 'It isn't only manners and tricks . . .' etc., *Motion Picture*, September 1936, NYPL.

304 'Once she was actually asked . . .' unsourced, undated, scrapbooks, AMPAS-MW.

305 'Chinese chow-mein factory . . .' ibid.

305 'a bring 'em-back-alive . . .' *Los Angeles Times*, 17 May 1936, AMPAS.

306 'The whole flavor is that of a nymphomaniac . . .' MPPDA files, 17 February 1936.

306 'definitely not acceptable . . .' ibid., 3 June 1936.

307 'MAVIS: That, my dear friends . . .' Go West Young Man, off screen.

308 'By the end of the first day . . .' Eels and Musgrove, op. cit., p. 160.

309 'Power . . . the power she got . . .' ibid., p. 163.

309 'Dado is now chauffeur for the star . . .' Paramount Press Release, 29 December 1936, AMPAS.

309 'no Mae West picture has been more Westful . . .' *Variety*, clipping, USC archive.

309 'strictly for the Mae West fans . . .' *Hollywood Reporter*, clipping, USC archive.

309 'Mae West will go to Egypt . . .' Paramount Press Release, 13 November 1936, AMPAS.

310 'meet in Hollywood . . .' *Go West, Young Man*, Paramount Press Books, LOC.

310 'a handkerchief with her name . . .' *Daily News*, 31 October 1936, AMPAS.

310 'Why not? . . . Women have been running men . . .' Paramount Press Release, 1936.

311 'charging that Wallace . . .' *Evening News*, 9 December 1936, AMPAS.

311 'define the rights of each party . . .' *Los Angeles Citizen-News*, 3 May 1937.

311 'At Last "Mr. Mae" gets recognition . . .' *Los Angeles Examiner*, 8 July 1937.

312 'announced 98 per cent of her fan mail . . .' *Los Angeles Citizen-News*, 29 July 1937.

Chapter 31

313 'Dear Joe, I am attaching . . .' MPPDA files, 3 August 1937, AMPAS.

313 'Dear Mr Cohen, We have received . . .' ibid., 6 August 1937.

314 'to look at a Salome costume . . .' ibid., 11 August 1937.

314 'I think you will find that . . .' ibid., 31 August 1937.

314 'must not overexpose . . .' ibid., 1 September 1937.

315 'On New Year's Eve, 1899 . . .' *Every Day's a Holiday*, Paramount Press Book, Library of Congress, Washington.

317 'A former circus clown . . .' Ephraim Katz, *The Macmillan International Film Encyclopedia*, London 1994, p. 127.

320 'come up and see me some time . . .' etc., *Chase and Sanborn Hour*, 12 December 1937, Radio Script, USC archive.

321 'Under a spreading fig tree . . .' etc., ibid.

322 'CHASE, SANBORN SPONSORS . . .' *Catholic Review*, 17 December 1937.

322 'there is a marked uniformity . . .' *Sunday Morning Herald* (Washington DC), 19 December 1937, AMPAS.

323 'she wanted to play a part . . .' undated clipping, MPPDA files, AMPAS.

323 'the script was typical "West" . . .' undated clipping, ibid.

323 'The name of Mae West . . .' *Los Angeles Examiner*, 4 January 1938, AMPAS.

325 'sumptuous in atmosphere . . .' *Hollywood Reporter*, 20 December 1937.

325 'less flagrantly sexy . . .' *Variety*, 20 December 1937.

325 'WELCOME A CUTOUT OF MAE . . .' *Every Day's a Holiday*, Paramount Press Books, Library of Congress, ibid.

Chapter 32

329 'WOMAN BARES FANTASTIC . . .' *Mansfield News Journal*, 7 March 1938, USC archive.

330 'I never wanted to be anybody else . . .' *Playboy*, January, 1971.

332 'The clock said two . . .' *Los Angeles Citizen-News*, 15 June 1938.

332 'declared poison at the box office . . .' clipping, 22 July 1938, AMPAS-MW.

333 'a clutching, squealing crowd . . .' *Boston Herald*, 29 April 1938, AMPAS-MW.

333 'I was a tall, skinny young guy . . .' Eels and Musgrove, op. cit., p. 187.

333 'Attractive velvet backdrops . . .' clipping, scrapbooks, AMPAS-MW.

334 'she told me to watch the first couple of rows . . .' Eels and Musgrove, op. cit., p. 189.

334 'do what your heart tells you . . .' *Mae West on Sex, Health and ESP*, op. cit., p. 121.

335 'went up to see her . . .' *Los Angeles Citizen-News*, 18 August 1939,

AMPAS.

335 'I thank heaven for a man like Adolph Hitler . . .' *New York World-Telegram*, 26 August 1936 (cited from Thornston Deusbury, *The Open Secret of MRA*, from www.morerevealed.com/quotes/buchman_qte.htm).

335 'The true patriot . . .' ibid., from Buchman, Frank, *Remaking the World*, Blandford Press, London 1961.

336 'Moral rearmament is just the thing he needs . . .' *Los Angeles Citizen-News*, op. cit.

336 'That was some gal, that Catherine . . .' Paramount press release, AMPAS.

336 'tricked out with tunes . . .' *Daily News*, 28 July 1939, AMPAS.

336 'Some day I shall contribute . . .' clipping, scrapbook (#10), AMPAS-MW.

337 'a cross between The Drunkard . . .' Ronald Fields, *W. C. Fields by Himself*, Prentice Hall, Englefield, NJ, 1973, p. 342.

337 'I swiped the idea . . .' Eels and Musgrove, op. cit., p. 195.

338 'Dear Mae, I have a story . . .' W. C. Fields correspondence file, AMPAS-MW.

339 'My idea of starring with Miss West . . .' ibid.

340 'between you and me, Mae . . .' etc., ibid.

340 'Scene 12: The "revealing white lawn blouse" . . .' etc., MPPDA files, 26 September 1939, AMPAS.

341 'fondling it, remarking about its smell . . .' ibid., 31 October 1939.

341 'FIRST TAKE WITHOUT SPARKS . . .' *Picture Play*, 13 November 1939, AMPAS-MW.

342 'I was charmed, fascinated and hooked . . .' *The Family Circle*, 22 March 1940, AMPAS-MW.

342 'TWILLIE: if you get around . . .' *My Little Chickadee*, off screen.

342 'Dear Mae, Eddie told me . . .' W. C. Fields correspondence file, op. cit.

344 'Sure Fire B.O. Hit . . .' *Hollywood Reporter*, 7 February 1940.

344 'gags are rather slim . . .' *Variety*, 7 February 1940.

344 'some moments are funny . . .' *Los Angeles Examiner*, 9 March 1940.

344 'Delete the line "Snow White" . . .' MPPDA files, ibid.

Chapter 33

346 'both pictures are now . . .' MPPDA files, 1 October 1935, AMPAS.

346 'With further reference to the question . . .' MPPDA files, 2 September 1949, AMPAS.

347 'GOSSIP: I've heard lots about you . . .' etc., gag books, AMPAS-

MW.

348 'there is no question that the plaintiff . . .' *Los Angeles Examiner*, 24 September 1941, AMPAS.

349 'Mae West and Hollywood Enterprises . . .' etc., financial files, AMPAS-MW.

350 'MAE WEST HAUNTED BY DEAD ROMANCE . . .' etc., clipping, 7 July 1942, AMPAS.

351 '"I think," said Mae West . . .' *The American Weekly*, 6 September 1942, AMPAS.

351 'Mai Uecc . . .' clipping, 31 October 1935?, scrapbooks, AMPAS-MW.

351 'Mae West Meets Hitler . . .' etc., miscellaneous files, AMPAS-MW.

352 'It is very important . . .' MPPDA files, 29 June 1943, AMPAS.

354 'There's nothing specially wrong . . .' *Hollywood Citizen-News*, 17 January 1944.

355 'producer–director Gregory Ratoff . . .' *Variety*, 17 January 1944, USC archive.

Chapter 34

356 'My dear Mr. Jackson-Craig . . .' correspondence files, 12 February 1943, AMPAS-MW.

357 'It is my feeling . . .' *San Quentin News*, 4 February 1941, AMPAS-MW.

357 'I want to thank you for . . .' 18 February 1941, miscellaneous files, AMPAS-MW.

358 'Miss West wishes to thank you . . .' correspondence, 16 August 1944, AMPAS-MW.

358 'selling tickets only to the purchasers . . .' *New York Herald Tribune*, 2 August 1944, AMPAS.

359 'serious man, neither vivid . . .' etc., GHNTDWI, p. 212.

360 'Mae West returned to Broadway . . .' *New York Herald Tribune*, August 1944 (undated).

360 'behaved sometimes as if . . .' *The New Yorker*, 12 August 1944, NYPL.

360 'Recruited off the beaches . . .' Eels and Musgrove, op. cit., p. 217.

360 'Mike, I'm not happy . . .' Art Cohn, *The Nine Lives of Michael Todd*, Random House, New York, 1958.

361 'When she met somebody she liked . . .' ibid., p. 218.

362 'Catherine: You see, Panin . . .' etc., scripts, *Catherine the Great*, LOC, AMPAS-MW.

365 'While Miss West's current vehicle . . .' etc., *Washington Evening Star*, 24 September 1946.

www.fortunecity.com.
379 'Comeback? She's Never been Away . . .' *Variety*, 28 July 1954.
379 'this magnificent herd of males . . .' etc., GHNTDWI, p. 245.
380 'Miss West, you're wonderful . . .' Liberace and Mae West sketch, AMPAS-MW
380 'a show to stop all shows . . .' *Los Angeles Times*, 28 July (?) 1954, AMPAS.
380 'going to begin filming . . .' *Los Angeles Mirror*, 30 April 1954.
380 'In the car was a sealed metal box . . .' clipping, Chicago American, 1955, AMPAS.
381 'The body builders lived . . .' Eels and Musgrove, op. cit., p. 246.
381 '"Mr Universe", sporting a shiner and limping . . .' clipping, June 1955, AMPAS.
383 'Chalky would take his mistress to the fights . . .' etc., Hollywood Confidential, November 1955, LOCPC.
384 'Mae West's own refutation . . .' NYT, 11 October 1959.
384 'Mae's Move Busts Up . . .' *Las Vegas Sun*, 22 March 1959, USC archive.
385 'some parts of the program . . .' *Los Angeles Times*, 15 October 1959.
385 'COLLINGWOOD: Is the book about . . .' *Los Angeles Herald-Express*, 16 October 1959.
387 'MIKE: You can't exactly feel . . .' *Sextette*, script, AMPAS-MW.
388 'She is a trouper of the old order . . .' clipping, AMPAS.
388 'a Wagnerian heroine . . .' *Chicago Daily News*, 12 August 1961.
388 'The entrance alone called forth . . .' *Miami News*, 12 August 1961, AMPAS.
388 'When the final curtain rang down . . .' *Miami Beach Sun*, 13 August 1961, AMPAS.

Chapter 37
390 'For her boudoir scenes . . .' *TV Guide*, 29 February to 6 March 1964, AMPAS.
391 'was engaged for 6 weeks . . .' report, 11 April 1961, AMPAS-MW.
391 'In the days of wicked whiskey . . .' etc., *Diamond Lil*, 1964 script, AMPAS-MW.
392 'Her house, protected by a high wall . . .' etc., *Saturday Evening Post*, 14 November 1964, AMPAS.
394 'turnaway event . . .' *Variety*, 13 February 1968.
394 'As vignettes from three of her pictures . . .' *Hollywood Reporter*, 13 February 1968.
396 'In our center ring . . .' notes, miscellaneous files, AMPAS-MW.

Chapter 38

397 'Myra Breckinridge begins . . .' script notes, 3 July 1969, USC archive.

398 'I was penniless in New York . . .' *Vanity Fair*, March 2003.

398 'someone tells you a story . . .' Eels and Musgrove, op. cit., p. 272.

398 'Fade in images of stars . . .' script notes, Myra Breckinridge, USC archive.

399 'Dear Mae, As you know . . .' ibid.

399 'The wages of sin are sables . . .' etc., Myra Breckinridge notes, AMPAS-MW.

400 'become friends before rumors . . .' Musgrove diary notes, 2 September 1969, USC archive.

400 'AUGUST 13: I went to Mae's . . .' etc., ibid.

401 'On the set of Myra Breckinridge . . .' *Life magazine*, 6 March 1970.

401 'What Sarne calls fantasy . . .' etc., ibid.

405 'Sex is an emotion in motion . . .' *Los Angeles Times*, 31 August 1969, AMPAS.

405 'Too Much of a Good Thing . . .' *Los Angeles Times*, 21 December 1969.

406 'the greatest comeback in history . . .' *Herald-Examiner*, 1 July 1970, AMPAS.

406 'There is no doubt that Mae West . . .' clipping, 3 June 1970, AMPAS.

Chapter 39

407 'the lengths to which today's moviemakers . . .' NYT, 5 July 1970.

408 'Joyce Haber's interview . . .' *Los Angeles Times*, 30 August 1970. AMPAS.

408 'And Rodney Terrill was as cocky as ever . . .' Mae West, *Pleasure Man*, Dell Publishing Co., New York, 1975, p. 247.

408 'As a final word . . .' *Mae West on Health, Sex and ESP*, op. cit., p. 160.

409 'They're crazy about me . . .' *Playboy*, January 1971.

409 'Yankee Doodle came too soon . . .' miscellaneous notes, AMPAS-MW.

410 'I see myself as a classic . . .' *Playboy* interview, op. cit.

410 'Sheathed in white faille . . .' *Los Angeles Times*, 15 May 1971, AMPAS.

410 'hoping to reach her dead daughter . . .' *Herald-Examiner*, 13 June 1971, AMPAS.

410 'writing a new book . . .' *Variety*, 21 May 1973.

411 'We are in the liberated 70's . . .' *Coronet*, September 1975, AMPAS.

411 'Wearing a black crêpe gown . . .' *Los Angeles Times*, 2 March 1976, AMPAS.

411 'To preserve her muscle tone . . .' Eels and Musgrove, op. cit., p. 294.

Epilogue

416 'disorienting freak show . . .' NYT, 8 June 1979.

416 'it will probably be shown . . .' quoted in Eels and Musgrove, op. cit., p. 307.

416 'one of those movies rarely seen . . .' *Time magazine* (undated).

416 'A procession of musclemen . . .' *Village Voice*, 27 November 1978, AMPAS.

418 'When asked whether it was a bad one . . .' etc., Eels and Musgrove, op. cit., p. 309.

419 'In both her professional and private . . .' *Los Angeles Times*, 26 November 1980.

419 'old letters, dresses . . .' NYT, 30 September 1981, NYPL.

419 'a bachelor whose fortune . . .' *Daily News*, 28 July 1981, NYPL.

419 '"Not now dear . . ."' obituary of Paul Novak, *Independent* (London), 20 July 1999, BFI.

420 'filled the place with bird's eye maple deco . . .' etc., *Los Angeles Magazine*, October 1998.

Chronology, Stage Plays and Filmography

19 January 1889: marriage of Matilda (Tillie) Delker and John West, Brooklyn.
August 1891: birth of first child, Kate, died after four months.
17 August 1893: birth of Mary Jane West.
1898: birth of Mildred, later called Beverly West. First amateur appearance of 'Baby Mae'?
1900: birth of brother John Edwin.
To 1908: Mae attends school.
Summer 1908: Mae appears in Hal Clarendon's Stock Company.
1909?: Mae's first ventures into touring shows. Hogan and West act?
1910–11: Mae's tour with Frank Szatkus (Wallace) in burlesque.
11 April 1911: marriage of Mae West and Frank Wallace.
June 1911: first press mention of Mae, in *Variety*, with the Big Gaiety Company.

Stage Appearances

A La Broadway

Folies Bergère, New York, opened 22 September 1911. 8 performances.
Music by Harold Orlob. Book by William Le Baron. Lyrics by William Le Baron and M. H. Hollins.
Cast: Agostino Baci, James Bradbury, Octavia Broske, Ernest Collins, James Cook, Glenn Eastman, Virginia Gunther, Ida Harris, Kitty Kyle, Harriet Leidy, John Lorenz, Emily Monte, Wallace Nedringhaus, Mae West, Will Phillips, Margaret Taylor, Ted Westus.

Vera Violetta

Winter Garden, New York, 20 November 1911. 112 performances (Mae West only in previews).
Music by Edmund Eysler. Writers Leonard Liebling and Harold Atteridge, from the German play by Leo Stein.
Cast: Gaby Deslys, Barney Bernard, Al Jolson, Harry Pilcer, Billee Taylor, Doris Cameron, James B. Carson, Edward Cutler, Florence Douglas, Harry Fisher, Mae West, Clarence Harvey, Van Rensselaer Wheeler, Stella Mayhew, The Gordon Brothers.

End of 1911: Mae and Frank Wallace separate?

January 1912: Mae begins appearing with the Girard (Gerard) Brothers.
February 1912: Mae, off stage, assists detective father John?

A Winsome Widow
Based on *A Trip to Chinatown* by Charles H. Hoyt. Music by Raymond
Hubbell. Opened April 1912. 172 performances. Mae West only at open-
ing.
Cast: Fawn Conway, Katherine Smythe, Lottie Vernon, Marie Baxter, Ethel
Kelley, Harry Kelley, Charles King, Charles J. Ross, Leon Errol, Frank
Tinney, Elizabeth Brice, Ida Adams, Natalie Dugwell, Emmy Wehlen,
Sidney Jarvis, the Dolly Twins, Mae West as La Petite Daffy.

May 1912: 'Mae West is a single now . . .' first solo vaudeville appearances.
1912: Mae's vaudeville career begins, through the next decade.
December 1914: Mae West and Deiro the accordionist.
July 1916: 'Mae West and Sister,' with Beverly.
April 1917: Mae back as single act; US declares war on Germany.
1917: Mae's relationship with James Timony begins.
1917–18: Mae touring, in Chicago?

Sometime
Shubert Theatre. 4 October 1918. 283 performances.
Produced by Arthur Hammerstein. Writers Rida Johnson and Rudolf
Friml. Music by Rudolf Friml.
Cast: Mae West as Mayme Dean. Ed Wynn as Loney Bright. With Harrison
Brockbank, Beatrice Summers, Francine Larrimore, Frances Cameron,
Charles DeHaven, Fred Nice, John Merkyl, Mildred LeGue, William
Dorrian, George Gatson, Francis Murphy, Albert Sackett, Betty Stivers,
Harold Williams.

1919: Mae resumes vaudeville tours, through to 1921.
March 1921: Mae registers playlet, *The Ruby Ring*, with Library of
Congress copyright.

The Mimic World of 1921 (a.k.a. *The Whirl of the Town*)
Century Promenade, 17 August 1921. 26 performances.
Book by Harold Atteridge, James Hussey and Owen Murphy. Lyrics by
Harold Atteridge. Music by Jean Schwartz, Lew Pollack and Owen
Murphy.
Cast: El Brendel, Peggy Brown, Flo Burt, Cliff Edwards, Lou Edwards,
Clarence Harvey, Gladys James, Frank Masters, William Moran, Beth
Stanley, Albert Wiser, Mae West as Cleopatra, Shimmie Dancer and La
Belle (later renamed Madelon).

1921: Mae's resumes vaudeville tours again.

1922: Mae registers play, *The Hussy*.

June 1922: Mae's act includes pianist Harry Richman, to September.

1922–4: Mae tours vaudeville act.

22 March 1924: unused Mae West–Bud Burmester marriage licence.

1925: Mae's 'missing year'. Affair with Owney Madden? Writing of *Sex*.

Early 1926: rehearsals of *Sex*.

Plays by Mae West (before the movies)

Sex
A Comedy Drama in Three Acts. Written by 'Jane Mast' (Mae West).
Staged by Edward Elsner. Produced by C. W. Morganstern. Opened Daly's
63rd Theatre, 26 April 1926. 375 performances.
Cast: Mae West as Margy Lamont. Barry O'Neill as Gregg. Warren Sterling
as Rocky Waldron. Edda Von Beulow as Clara Smith. Ann Reader as
Agnes. Lyons Wickland as Jimmy Stanton. Pacie Ripple as Robert Stanton.
With Al Rigali, Conde Brewer, Gordon Burby, Gordon Earle, D. J.
Hamilton, Frank Howard, Michael Markham, Constance Morganstern,
Mary Morrisey, George Rogers.

The Drag
A Homosexual Comedy in Three Acts. Written by 'Jane Mast' (Mae West).
Staged by Edward Elsner. Produced by C. W. Morganstern. Opened 31
January 1927, Poll's Park Theatre, Bridgeport, Connecticut. 2 preview per-
formances.
Cast: Elmer Grandin, Emily T. Francis, Allan Campbell, Leo Howe, A.
Francis Lenz, Margaret Hawkins, Jay Sheridan, Charles Townsend, Charles
Ordway, Harry Shlegle, Marshall Bradford, Marion Davis, Arthur Rowse,
Jane Young, Sam Mass, George Du Vall. Drag ball guests: Herbert Sullivan,
Bobby D'Andrea, Allan Gray, Dick Gray, Gus Shiling, Eugene Casali,
Stuart Callaghan, Ed Hearne, Harry Carroll, Frank Carroll, Edi Ellis, John
Mangum, Sylvan Repetti, John Rosimer, James King, Howard Ditley, Fred
Dickens, Jimmy Barry, Charles Langston.

The Wicked Age
A Comedy in Three Acts. Written by Mae West. Staged by Edward Elsner.
Produced by Anton F. Scibilia. Opened Daly's 63rd Street Theatre, 4
November 1927. 19 performances.
Cast: Mae West as Babe (Evelyn) Carson, Doris Haslett as Ruth Carson,
Ruth Hunter as Gloria Carson, Hal Clarendon as Robert Carson, Peggy
Doran as Peggy, Hassell Brooks as Willie, Robert Bentley as The Count,
Augusta Perry as Mrs Carson, Mike Jackson as Jazzbo Williams, with

Carroll Daly, Emily Francis, Raymond Jarno, Louise Kirtland, William Langdon, David Newell, Hub White, Harry W. Williams.

Diamond Lil

A Drama of the Underworld. Written by Mae West. Period and locale suggested by Mark Linder. Produced by Jack Linder. Staged by Mae West and Ira Hands. Opened Royale Theater, New York, 9 April 1928. 176 performances.

Cast: Mae West as Diamond Lil, Curtis Cooksey as Captain Cummings, Ernest Anderson as Dan Flynn, Rafaella Ottiano as Rita Christiana, Jack LaRue as Juarez, J. Merrill Holmes as Gus Jordan, Herbert Duffy as Chick Clarke, Jack Cheatham as Spider Kane, Lois Jesson as Sally, Jo-Jo Lee as Steak McGary, Pat Whalen as Ragtime Kelly, Helen Vincent as Flo, Ronald Savery as Pete the Duke, Jack Howard as Bill the Waiter, James F. Kelly as Officer Doheny, Harold Glarry as The Bowery Terror, Chuck Connors II as Lefty Eddie, with Joseph A. Barrett, Clara Cubitt, Marion Day, David Hughes, Richard Keith, Patsy Klein, Thelma Lawrence, Mark Linder, Mary Martin, Agnes Neilson, Louis Nusbaum, Frank Wallace (?) as Jimmy Biff.

The Pleasure Man

A Comedy Drama in Two Acts. Written by Mae West. Staged by Charles Edward Davenport. Produced by Carl Reed. Biltmore Theatre, 1 October 1928. 2 1/2 performances.

Cast: Alan Brooks as Rodney Terrill, Stan Stanley as Stanley Smith, Jay Holly as Tom Randall, William Augustin as Steve, Camelia Campbell as Dolores, Leo Howe as The Bird of Paradise, Ed Hearn as Toto, William Selig and Herman Lenzen as the Otto Brothers, with Chuck Connors II, Harry Armand, Edgar Barrier, Elaine Evans, Lester Sheehan, Wally James, Martha Vaughn, Julie Childrey, Margaret Bragaw, Anna Keller, Jane Rich, Frank Leslie, William Cavanaugh, Charles Ordway, Fred Dickens, Sylvan Repetti, Gene Drew, Albert Dorando, Lew Lorraine, Jo Huddlestone, Walter MacDonald, James F. Ayres, Augusta E. Boylston, Marguerite Leo, Kate Julianne, May Davis, Mae Russell, Edward Roseman, Paul South, Herman Linsterino as Pork Chops and Robert Cooksey as Sugarfoot.

26 January 1930: death of Tillie West.
November 1930: publication of Mae's first novel, *Babe Gordon*.

The Constant Sinner

A Comedy in Three Acts. Written by Mae West. Produced by Constant Productions Inc. Staged by Lawrence Marsden. Opened Royale Theater, 14 September 1931. 64 performances.

Cast: Mae West as Babe Gordon, Russell Hardie as Bearcat Delaney, Adele Gilbert as Cokey Jenny, George Givot as Money Johnson, Arthur R.

Vinton as Charlie Yates, Walter Petrie as Wayne Baldwin, with Hubert Brown, Ollie Burgoyne, George Bush, Allen Cohen, William Daly, James Dunmore, Walter Glass, Joseph Holicky, Harry Howard, Paul Huber, Donald Kirke, Billy Kohut, Florence Lee, Leona Love, Henry Matthews, Jack McKee, Paul Meers, Cora Olsen, Harry Owens, Grey Patrick, Billy Rapp, Marie Remsen, Ralph Sanford, Trixie Smith, Bernard Thornton, Rudolph Toombs, Christine Wagner, George Williams, Lorenzo Tucker as Headwaiter and Robert Rains as Liverlips.

Unproduced play: Frisco Kate, 1930–1.

1932: Mae's second novel, *Diamond Lil*, published.

The Movies – 1932 to 1943

Night After Night

Paramount Publix, 1932. Produced by William LeBaron. Directed by Archie Mayo. Based on *Single Night* by Louis Broomfield. Screenplay by Vincent Lawrence (with Kathryn Scuola). Additional Dialogue by Mae West. Cinematography by Ernest Haller. Camera Operator Guy Bennett. Original Music by Ralph Rainger and Bernhard Kaun. Sound by Don Johnson. Costume Design by Travis Banton.

Cast: George Raft as Joe Anton, Mae West as Maudie Triplett, Alison Skipworth as Mabel Jellyman, Constance Cummings as Jerry Healy, Roscoe Karns as Leo, Louis Calhern as Dick Bolton, Wynne Gibson as Iris Dawn, with Bradely Page, Harry Wallace, Al Hill, George Templeton, Marty Martin, Tom Kennedy, Mary Boland, Bill Elliott, Dennis O'Keefe, Patricia Farley as Hat-check Girl.

Released 29 October 1932. 70 minutes.

She Done Him Wrong

Paramount Publix, 1933. Produced by William LeBaron. Directed by Lowell Sherman. Written by Harvey F. Thew and John Bright from *Diamond Lil* by Mae West. Cinematography by Charles Lang. Camera Operator: Robert Pittack. Art Direction by Robert Usher. Costume Design by Edith Head. Edited by Alexander Hall. Original Music by Ralph Rainger, Shelton Brooks, John Leipold and Stephan Pasternacki. Assistant Director: James Dugan. Sound by Harry M. Lindgren. Stills by Elwood Bredell and Eugene Richee.

Cast: Mae West as Lady Lou, Cary Grant as Captain Cummings, David Landau as Dan Flynn, Louise Beavers as Pearl, Rafaela Ottiano as Russian Rita, Gilbert Roland as Serge Stanieff, Noah Beery as Gus Jordan, Owen Moore as Chick Clarke, Dewey Robinson as Spider Kane, Rochelle Hudson as Sally, Tammany Young as Chuck Connors, Fuzzy Night as

Ragtime Kelly, Grace LaRue as Frances, Robert Homans as Doheny, with
Ernie Adams, Wade Boteler, Jack Carr, Mike Donlin, James Eagles, Harold
Entwistle, Mary Gordon, Aggie Herring, Al Hill, Tom Kennedy, Lee
Kohlmar, Michael Mark, Tom McGuire, Frank Mills, Frank Moran, Leo
White, Harry Wallace as Steak McGarry, Frank Sentley as Tenor, Arthur
Housman as Hungry barfly, and Heinie Conklin as Street Cleaner.
Released 27 January 1933. 66 minutes.

I'm No Angel
Paramount Publix, 1933. Produced by William LeBaron. Directed by
Wesley Ruggles. Written by Mae West and Lowell Brentano.
(Contributions to early screenplay by Claude Binyon and Frank Butler.)
Cinematography by Leo Tover. Art Direction by Hans Dreier and Bernard
Herzbrun. Edited by Otho Lovering. Sound by F. E. Dine and Philip
Wisdom. Original Music by Harvey Brooks, with Karl Hajos, Herman
Hand, Howard Jackson, Rudolph G. Kopp, John Leipold and Heinz
Roemhold. Lyrics of 'They Call Me Sister Hony-Tonk', 'Nobody Loves Me
Like That Dallas Man', 'I Found a New Way to Go to Town', 'I'm No
Angel' by Gladys DuBois and Ben Ellison. Continuity by Harlan
Thompson. Sound by Phil Wisdom, F. E. Dine.
Cast: Mae West as Tira, Cary Grant as Jack Clayton, Edward Arnold as
Bill Barton, Ralf Harolde as Slick Wiley, Gregory Ratoff as Benny
Pinkowitz, Gertrude Howard as Beulah, Libby Taylor and Hattie
McDaniel as Maids, Kent Taylor as Kirk Lawrence, Gertrude Michael as
Alicia Hatton, William B. Davidson as Brown, Dorothy Peterson as
Thelma, Russell Hopton as the Barker Flea Madigan, Nigel De Brulier as
Rajah, with George Brugeman, Morrie Cohan, Monte Collins, Ray Cooke,
Nell Craig, Edward Hearn, Lew Kelly, Tom London, Edmund Mortimer,
Dennis O'Keefe, Lee Phelps, Larry Steers, Laura Treadwell, Walter Walker,
Duke York, Irving Pichel as Bob's attorney, and Nat Pendleton as Harry the
acrobat.
Released November 1933. 88 minutes.

Belle of the Nineties Paramount Publix, 1934. Produced by William
LeBaron. Directed by Leo McCarey. Written by Mae West. ('Contribution
to dialogue' by Grant Garrett. 'Contribution to treatment' by J. P.
McEvoy.) Cinematography by Karl Struss. Camera Operators: George
Clemens and Hatto Tappenbeck. Edited by LeRoy Stone. Art Direction by
Bernard Herzbrun and Hans Dreier. Costume Design by Travis Banton.
Sound by Harry Mills. Original Music by Arthur Johnston and Sam
Coslow, with Howard Jackson, John Leipold and Tom Satterfield. Sound
by Harry Mills.
Cast: Mae West as Ruby Carter, Roger Pryor as Tiger Kid, Johnny Mack

Brown as Brooks Claybourne, Katherine DeMille as Molly Brant, John
Miljan as Ace Lamont, Libby Taylor as Jasmine, with James Dolan, Stuart
Holmes, Harry Woods, Frederick Burton, Augusta Anderson, Benny Baker,
Morrie Cohan, Warren Hymer, Tyler Brooke, Wade Boteler, Sam Flint, Ed
Hearn, Tom Herbert, Mike Mazurski, James Pierce, Frank Rice, Walter
Walker, George Walsh, Sam McDanile as Brother Eben, Duke Ellington as
Piano player, Gene Austin as Crooner, Eddie Borden and Fuzzy Night as
Comedians.
Released 21 September 1934. 73 minutes.

5 January 1935: death of father, John West.
April 1935: Mae's marriage to Frank Wallace, and her true age, exposed.

Goin' to Town Paramount Pictures, Major Pictures, 1935. Produced by
William LeBaron. Directed by Alexander Hall. Written by Mae West from
a story by Marion Morgan and George B. Dowell. Cinematography by
Karl Struss. Edited by LeRoy Stone. Art Direction by Hans Dreier and
Robert Usher. Costume Design by Travis Banton. Sound by M. M. Paggi.
Original Music by Sammy Fain, Irving Kahal, with John Leipold, Stephan
Pasternacki, Ralph Rainger and Tom Satterfield. Make Up by Dorothy
Ponedel. Special photographic effects by Dewey Wrigley.
Cast: Mae West as Cleo Borden, Paul Cavanagh as Edward Carrington,
Gilbert Emery as Winslow, Marjorie Gateson as Mrs Crane Brittony, Tito
Coral as Taho, Ivan Lebedeff as Ivan Valadov, Fred Kohler as Buck
Gonzales, Monroe Owsley as Fletcher Colton, Adrienne D'Ambricourt as
Annette. Morgan Wallace as J. Henry Brash, Lucio Villegas as Ricardo
Lopez, Mona Rico as Dolores Lopez, Luis Alberni as Signor Vitola, Grant
Withers as Young Fellow, Wade Boteler as ranch foreman, Paul Harvey as
Donovan, Joe Frye as Laughing Eagle, Francis Ford as Sheriff, Dewey
Robinson as Bartender.
Released 17 May 1935. 74 minutes.

Klondike Annie
Paramount Pictures, Major Pictures, 1936. Produced by William LeBaron.
Directed by Raoul Walsh. Written by Mae West based on her play *Frisco
Kate*, story by Marion Morgan and George B. Dowell, and 'material sug-
gested by' Frank Mitchell Dazey. Cinematography by George T. Clemens.
Edited by Stuart Heisler. Art Direction by Hans Dreier and Bernard
Herzbrun. Set Decoration by A. E. Fredeman. Sound by Harold Lewis and
Louis Mesenkop. Original Music by Victor Young, Gene Austin, Sam
Coslow, with John Leipold, Heinz Roemheld and Tom Satterfield.
Cast: Mae West as Frisco Doll, Victor McLaglen as Bull Brackett, Philip
Reed as Inspector Jack Forrest, Helen Jerome Eddy as Sister Annie Alden,

Harold Huber as Chan Lo, Soo Yong as Fah Wong, Esther Howard as
Fanny, John Rogers as Buddy, Lucille Gleason as Big Tess, Conway Tearle
as Vance Palmer, Harry Beresford as Brother Bowser, Ted Oliver as
Grigsby, Vladimir Baykoff as Marinoff, George Walsh as Quartermaster,
Chester Gan as Ship's Cook, Jack Daley as Second Mate, Jack Wallace as
Third Mate, with Lawrence Grant, Gene Austin, Philip Ahn, Richard
Allen, Edna Bennett, Edward Brady, James Burke, D'Arcy Corrigna, Nell
Craig, Guy D'Ennery, Pearl Eaton, Arthur Turner Foster, Huntley Gordon,
Russ Hall, Otto Heimel, Philo McCullough, Jack Mulhall, Marie Wells,
Mrs Chan Lee as Blind Woman and Mrs Wong Wing as Ah Toy.
Released 21 February 1936. 77 minutes.

Go West, Young Man
Paramount Pictures, Major Pictures, 1936. Produced by Emmanuel Cohen.
Directed by Henry Hathaway. Written by Mae West. Cinematography by
Karl Struss. Edited by Ray Curtiss. Art Direction by Wiard Ihnen and Hans
Dreier. Costume Design by Irene Jones. Sound by Hugo Grenzbach.
Original Music by Arthur Johnston, with Leo Shuken, George E. Stoll and
Herbert Taylor. Lyrics by John Burke. Musical Director: George Stoll.
Cast: Mae West as Mavis Arden, Randolph Scott as Bud Norton, Warren
William as Morgan, Alice Brady as Mrs Struthers, Elizabeth Patterson as
Aunt Kate Barnaby, Lyle Talbot as Francis X. Harrigan, Isabell Jewell as
Gladys, Margaret Perry as Joyce Struthers, Etienne Girardot as Professor
Rigby, Alice Ardell as Jeanette, Maynard Holmes as Clyde, Nick Stewart as
Nicodemus, John Indrisano as Chauffeur, Charles Irwin as Master of
Ceremonies. In film within film: Jack LaRue as Rico, G. P. Huntley as
Philip, Robert Baikoff as Officer, Xavier Cugat as Orchestra Leader, with
Eddie Dunn, Dick Elliott, Si Jenks, Jack Perrin, Lee Shumway.
Released 13 November 1936. 82 minutes.

Every Day's a Holiday
Major Pictures, released by Paramount Pictures, 1938. Produced by
Emanuel Cohen. Directed by A. Edward Sutherland. Screenplay by Mae
West. Original story by Jo Swerling and Mae West. Cinematography by
Karl Struss. Edited by Ray Curtiss. Art Direction by Wiard Ihnen. Gowns
by Schiaparelli. Wardrobe by Bassia Bassett. Sound by Hugo Grenzbach.
Production Manager: Joe Nadel. Assistant Director: Earl Rettig. Special
Effects by Gordon Jennings. Choreography by Leo Prinz. Music (songs) by
Hoagy Carmichael and Sam Coslow, incidental music by Leo Shuken.
Musical Director: George E. Stoll.
Cast: Mae West as Peaches O'Day, Edmund Lowe as Captain McCarey,
Charles Winninger as Van Reighle Van Pelter Van Doon, Walter Catlett as
Nifty Bailey, Charles Butterworth as Larmadou Graves, Lloyd Nolan as

John Quade, Herman Bing as Fritz Kraysemeyer, Roger Imhof as Trigger Mike, Chester Conklin as Cabby, George Rector as Himself, Louis Armstrong as Himself, with Lucien Prival, Adrian Morris, Francis McDonald, John Indrisano, Johnny Arthur, William Austin, Edgar Dearing, Maude Eburne, Dick Elliott, Weldon Heyburn, James C. Morton, Ferdinand Munier, Herbert Rawlinson, and Irving bacon, Allen Rogers, John 'Skins' Miller and Otto Fries as the Quartet. Released 14 January 1938. 80 minutes.

My Little Chickadee
Universal Pictures, 1940. Produced by Lester Cowan and Jack J. Gross. Directed by Edward F. Cline. Written by Mae West and W. C. Fields (or W. C. Fields and Mae West) with material by Grover Jones. Cinematography by Joseph Valentine. Edited by Edward Curtiss. Art Direction by Martin Obzina and Jack Otterson. Set Decoration by Russell A. Gausman. Costume Design by Vera West. Sound by Bernard B. Brown and Joe Lapis. Special Effects by John P. Fulton and James V. King. Original Music by Ben Oakland and Frank Skinner. Lyrics by Milton Drake. Musical Director: Charles Previn. Sound by Bernard B. Brown and Joseph Lapis.
Cast: Mae West as Flower Belle Lee and W. C. Fields as Cuthbert J. Twillie, Joseph Calleia as Jeff Badger/Masked Bandit, Dick Foran as Wayne Carter, Margaret Hamilton as Mrs Gideon, Ruth Donnelly as Aunt Lou, Donald Meek as Amos Budge, George Moran as Indian, Sy Jenks as deputy, James Conlin as Squawk Mulligan (Bartender), Bob Burns and Bob Reeves as Barflies, Fay Adler as Mrs 'Pygmy' Allen, Morgan Wallace as gambler, Fuzzy Night as Cousin Zeb, Willard Robinson as Uncle John, Jackie Searl as Schoolboy, Gene Austin as Saloon Musician, Otto Heimel as Coco, Russell Hall as Candy, William B. Davidson as Sheriff, Al Ferguson as Train Passenger, with Addison Richards, Mark Anthony, Jan Duggan, Dorothy Vernon, Wade Boteler, Harlan Briggs, Chester Gan, George Melford, Ed Hearn. Released 9 February 1940. 83 minutes.

The Heat is On
Columbia Pictures, 1944. Produced and Directed by Gregory Ratoff. Associate Producer: Milton Carter. Written by Lou Breslow, Fitzroy Davis, George S. George, Boris Ingster and Fred Schiller. Cinematography by Franz Planer. Edited by Otto Meyer. Production Design by Nicolai Remisoff. Art Direction by Lionel Banks and Walter Holscher. Set Decoration by Joseph Kish. Costume Design by Walter Plunkett. Assistant Director: Robert Saunders. Sound by Lodge Cunningham. Original Music by John Leipold, Henry Myers, Jule Styne. John Blackburn, Edward Eliscu.

Lyrics by Sammy Cahn (with Fabian Andre, Edward Eliscu, Jay Gorney, Harry Myers). Musical Director: Yasha Bunchuck.

Cast: Mae West as Fay Lawrence, Victor Moore as Hubert Bainbridge, William Gaxton as Tony Ferris, Alan Dinehart as Forrest Stanton, Lloyd Bridges as Andy Walker, Lester Allen as Mouse Beller, Almira Sessions as Hannah Bainbridge, Mary Roche as Janey Bainbridge, Hazel Scott as Herself, Leon Belasco as Shore the Agent, Sam Aash as Frank, with David Lichine, Joan Thorsen, Edward Earle, Roy Engel, Eddie Hall, Harry Harvey, Jack Owen, Lina Romay, Harry Shannon, Leonard Sues, Ray Teal, Harry Tyler.

Released February 1944. 80 minutes.

Further Stage Plays – 1933–61

Plays written anonymously for Jim Timony's Hollytown Theatre (scripts in AMPAS-MW collection):

Loose Women

Dated December 1933. Performed 1935 under title *Ladies by Request*, attributed to writer Tom Kavin.

Clean Beds

Dated 1936. Attributed to Youacca G. Satovsky (??) or George S. George. Début appearance of actor Anthony Quinn, who attributed play to Mae West. Authorship unclear. Produced by Jim Timony as Cled Inc. Opened John Golden Theatre, New York 25 May 1939. 4 performances.

Havana Cruise

Date uncertain – late 1930s. Credit: by 'Jane Mast'. Details of performance unknown.

Other stage plays

It Takes Love

Undated. Credited to Jane Mast, Beverly Arden and Lee Lawrence. Details of performance unknown.

Catherine Was Great

Shubert Theatre and Royale Theatre, opened 2 August 1944. Written by Mae West. Produced by Michael Todd. Staged by Roy Hargrave. Scenic design by Howard Bay. Costumes by Mary Percy Schenck and Ernest Schrapps. 191 performances.

Cast: Mae West as Empress Catherine II, Philip Cary Jones as Captain Dronsky, Coburn Goodwin as Count Nikolai Mirovich, Don de Leo as Murad Pasha, Henry Vincent as English Ambassador, Owen Coll as

Choiseul, Don Gibson as captain Danilov, Hubert Long as Orloff, Charles
Gerrard as Panin, Joel Ashley as Prince Potemkin, John Stephen as
Chamberlain, Elinor Counts as Varvara, Ray Bourbon as Florian, John
Parrish as Suvorov, Gene Barry as Lieutenant Bunin, Bernard Hoffman as
Pugachev, with Leon Hamilton, Harry Bodin, Michael Bey, Victor Finney,
William Malone, Frank Baxter, Dayton Lummis, Lester Towne.

Come On Up (a.k.a. Ring Twice Tonight, Embassy Row, etc.)
First tour, 1945–6. Credited to Miles Mander, Fred Schiller and Thomas
Dunphy. Produced by the Select Operating Corporation. Staged by Russell
Fillmore. Gowns by Peter Johnson. Number of performances unknown.
Cast: Mae West as Carliss Dale, Charles La Torre as General Quantillo,
Michael Ames as Jeff Bentley, John Doucette as Krafft, Cleo Desmond as
Lottie, Francesca Rotoli as Annette, with Roy Gordon, Charles G. Martin,
Joe McTurk, Harold Bostwick, George Spelvin.

Diamond Lil – revivals:
British Tour: September 1947 to May 1948. Opened Palace Theatre,
Manchester, then Blackpool, Birmingham, Glasgow and London, Prince of
Wales Theatre, January 1948. Presented by Tom Arnold and Val Parnell.
Directed by William Mollison.
Cast: Mae West as Diamond Lil, Richard Bailey as Cummings, David
Davies as Gus Jordan, Francis de Wolff as Dan Flynn, Noele Gordon as
Rita, Bruno Barnabe as Juarez, Hal Gould as Chick Clarke, Margaret
Stallard as Sally, Danny Green as Kane, Victor Hagen as Mike George
Pughe as Doheny, Jack D'Ormonde as Pete the Dope.

US revivals:
Coronet Theater, New York, opened 5 February 1949. Written by Mae
West, based on a play by Jack Linder. Produced by Albert H. Rosen and
Herbert J. Freeyer. Directed by Charles K. Freeman. Scenic Design by
William De Forest and Ben Edwards. Costumes by Paul Du Pont. Closed
26 February. Reopened September 1949 at Plymouth Theater, total perfor-
mances 182.
Cast: Mae West as Diamond Lil, Richard Coogan as Cummings, Walter
Petrie as Gus Jordan, Charles G. Martin as Flynn, Miriam Goldina as Rita,
Steve Cochran as Juarez, Sylvia Sims as Flo, with Billy Van, Jack Howard,
Dick Arnold, George Warren, Harriet Nelson, Mike Keene, Peter Chan,
Margaret Magennis, Frances Arons, Lester Laurence, Ralph Chambers.

Broadway Theater, opened 14 September 1951. Produced by George
Brandt. Staged by Charles K. Freeman.

Cast: Mae West as Diamond Lil, Dan Matthews as Captain Cummings, Charles G. Martin as Flynn, Walter Petrie as Gus Jordan, Zolya Talma as Rita, James Courtney as Juarez, with Sheila Trent, Linda King, Helen Waters, Patsy Perroni, James Fallon, Louis Nussbaum, Harry Kadison, Lois Harmon, Lester Laurence, Val Gould.

5 April 1954: death of Jim Timony.

Las Vegas and Nightclub Acts – 1954–9

1954–6 itinerary

1954:
Sahara, Las Vegas, July
Reno, August
Latin Quarter club, Boston, September
Town Casino Buffalo, September
Latin Quarter club, New York, October
Sahara Las Vegas, December

1955:
Copa City Miami, January
Chez Paree, Chicago, Casino Royale, Washington, February
Latin Casino, Philadelphia, Italian Village, San Francisco, March
Twin Coaches, Pittsburgh, Chase Hotel, St Louis, April
Ciro's, Los Angeles, May
Biltmore, Taho, July

1956:
Latin Casino, Philadelphia, Latin Quarter, New York, April
Three Rivers, NY, 10 days
Casino Royale, Washington, 1 week.

Mae West's Last Play

Sextette (a.k.a. Sextet)
Edgewater Beach Playhouse, opened 7 July 1961. Number of performances unknown. Kenley Players production. Written by Mae West, 'based on a story idea' by Charlotte Francis. With Mae West, Francis Bethencourt, Jack La Rue, Michael Fox, Kitt Marshall, Brad Olson, Paul Novak.

Radio and TV Appearances (partial list)

Rudy Vallee Show – 1933?
Chase and Sanborn Hour, 12 December 1937, NBC Radio, with Edgar

Bergen, Charlie McCarthy and Don Ameche. 'Adam and Eve' sketch by Arch Oboler.
Chesterfield Supper Club with Perry Como, January 1949.
Chesterfield Supper Club with Perry Como, 16 February 1950.
1958 Academy Awards Ceremony, TV producer Jerry Wald.
CBS interview with Jack Collingwood, *Person to Person*, 4 October 1959.
Red Skelton Show, CBS TV, 1 March 1960.
CBS TV, *Mister Ed*. Episode 102, directed by Arthur Lubin, 15 March 1964.
A Night With Mae West at Universal City Studios, 14 May 1968.
American Forces Radio Service Christmas Shows, 1971 and 1972.

Discography (partial)

1966: *Way Out West, Wild Christmas*
1968: *Great Balls of Fire*. MGM records. Produced by Ian Whitcomb.
Includes songs: 'Light My Fire', 'Happy Birthday 21', 'Rock Around the Clock'. Released 1972.
The Fabulous Mae West, MCA records.
Mae West – I'm No Angel, soundtrack songs, CD, Jasmine Records.
Mae West Sings Sultry Songs, CD, Rosetta Records, includes: 'Come Up and See Me Sometime', 'Slow Down', 'Easy Rider', 'Memphis Blues', 'My Old Flame', 'St. Louis Woman', 'They Call Me Sister Honky Tonk', 'I'm an Occidental Woman', 'Mademoiselle Fifi', 'That's All Brother', 'My Daddy Rocks Me', etc.
Mae West On the Air – rare recordings 1934–60, CD.
Mae West, Original Radio Broadcasts, record, Mark 56 Records.

The Comeback Movies

Myra Breckinridge
Twentieth Century Fox, 1970. Produced by Robert Fryer. Directed by Michael Sarne. Written by Michael Sarne, David Giler, from the novel by Gore Vidal. Cinematography by Richard Moore. Assistant Camera: Thomas Del Ruth. Special Effects by Art Cruickshank and L. B. Abbott. Art Direction by Fred Harpman, Jack Martin, Jack Martin Smith. Costume Design by Edith Head and Theadora Van Runkle. Make-up by Edith Lindon, Daniel C. Striepeke, William Tuttle. Set Construction by Greg C. Jensen. Production Manager: William Eckhardt. Assistant Director: Dick Glassman. Stunts by Donna Garrett and Russ McCubbin. Choreography by Ralph Beaumont. Music Supervisor: Lionel Newman. Orchestrators: Jack Elliott, Lyn Murray, Allyn Ferguson. Unit Publicist: Don Prince. Cast: Mae West as Leticia (Letitia) Van Allen, Raquel Welch as Myra Breckinridge, Rex Reed as Myron, John Huston as Buck Loner, Farrah

Fawcett as Mary Ann Pringle, Roger Herren as Rusty Godowski, Roger C. Carmel as Dr Randolph Spencer Montag, George Furth as Charlie Flager Junior, Calvin Lockhart as Irving Amadeus, John Carradine as Surgeon, Jim Backus as Doctor, Andy Devine as Coyote Bill, Grady Sutton as Kid Barlow, Skip Ward as Chance, Kathleen Freeman as Bobby Dean Loner, Tom Selleck as Selected Stud, with B. S. Pulley, Monty Landis, Buck Kartalian, Peter Ireland, Nelson Sardelli, Calvin Bartlett, William Hopper, Miel Saan. Michael Sarne (as acting-school student), Svetlana as Extra, Genevive Waite as Dental Patient.
Released July 1970. 95 minutes.

Sextette
Crown International Pictures, 1976. Produced by Daniel Briggs and Robert Sullivan. Director: Ken Hughes. Executive Producer: Warner G. Toub. Written by Mae West and Herbert Baker. Cinematography by James Crabe. Camera Operator: Jack Willoughby. Edited by Art J. Nelson. Casting by Marvin Paige. Production Design by Thad Prescott. Art Direction by James F. Clayton. Set Decoration by Reg Allen. Costume Design by Edith Head. Hair Stylist: Evelyn Preece. Make-up Artist: Ron Snyder. Production Manager: Gene Marum. Assistant Directors: Gene Marum and Gary LaPoten. Music Supervisor: Michael Arciaga. Boom Operator: Raul A. Bruce. Music Editor: Dan Carlin. Dance Foleys: Jerry Trent. Choreography by Marc Breaux. Gaffer: Earl Gilbert. Grip: Loren Lambrecht. Script Supervisor: Terry Terrill. Titles: Phil Norman.
Cast: Mae West as Marlo Manners, Timothy Dalton as Sir Michael Barrington, Dom DeLuise as Dan Turner, Ringo Starr as Laslo Karolny, Tony Curtis as Alexei, George Hamilton as Vance Norton, Keith Moon as Dress Designer, Alice Cooper as Waiter, George Raft as Secret Agent, Walter Pidgeon as Chambers, Regis Philbin as Himself, Gil Stratton as Himself, Keith Allison as Waiter, Rona Barrett as Herself, Ed Beheler as President Jimmy Carter, with Van McCoy, Harry Weiss, Rick Leonard, June Fairchild, George E. Carey, Derek Murcott, Ed Ness, Jay B. Larson, Richard Peel, Ian Abercrombie, James Bacon, Peter Alexander, Jill Freeman, Jason Cooper, Calvin Bartlett, Klair Bybee. US Olympic Team: Brent Williams, Brian Abadie, Ric Drasin, Denny Gable, Reg Lewis, Jim Morris, Karl Szkalak, Jim Tarleton, John Austin, Roger Callard.
First released March 1976. 91 minutes.

Late Milestones

1975: Publication of *Mae West on Sex, Health and ESP*, W. H. Allen, London.

1975: Publication of third novel, *The Pleasure Man* (with Lawrence Lee), Dell Books.

[Writing of unpublished novel, *Margy Lamont*, date unknown, manuscript in AMPAS-MW.]

1976: TV appearance on *Dick Cavett's Backlot USA*, directed by Dwight Hemon, with Dick Cavett (host), Gene Kelly, Mickey Rooney, John Wayne and Mae West.

November 1978: Mae West personal appearance at San Francisco première of *Sextet* – 'Mae West is a legend still living . . .'

August 1980: Mae West is hospitalized.

22 November 1980: Mae West departs.

March 1982: death of Beverly West.

October 1998: ghost of Mae West haunts Ravenswood apartment.

Unpublished Scripts, Treatments, Synopses and Fragments in Mae West AMPAS Collection (partial list)

'Love for Sale': 'Story by Mae West' – early version of *Sex* or treatment for prospective film script. Twenty-nine pages.

'Mae West in Knights of Love', thirteen-page sketch, for nightclub acts.

'Lady Godiva's Modesty': a Farce-Comedy in One Act, nineteen pages. For nightclub acts?

'Madame Pompadour': sketch for sister Beverly, nightclub acts.

'The Bowery Beaut': four-page synopsis, date unknown.

'The Lady with the Pen' (a.k.a. 'A Woman of Desires', 'Madame Montmartre'); forty-one page treatment for play or movie, submitted by Orsatti Agency (probably 1950s): 'Lucille Bennett, a young woman teaching in Paris Vermont is fired because it turns out she has published a torrid book, taken as ms by her colleague to a publisher. Dubbed as a *Confessions of Casanova* by a woman, the book takes her to New York where she is fêted in society as a French woman from the real Paris. Although the deception takes her into various scrapes she eventually finds true love . . .'

'A Woman of Much Importance': story synopsis, version of *Embassy Row*, a.k.a. *Come On Up*.

'Too Many Husbands', partly hand-, partly typewritten fragments: 'Della Roscoe, beautiful but crude, intelligent but on the lower rung of Society's ladder, has been going "steady" with Jack Thurston for some time – to both their object is marriage – that is if they can stop quarreling long enough to have the ceremony performed . . .'

'St Louis Woman': synopsis set in 1890s: 'That St. Louis woman has been travelin' from Coast to Coast and everywhere she stops why she's the town's hot toast . . . '

'Perfectly Innocent': synopsis, yet another version of *Come On Up*, etc.

'Vaudeville' by Jane Mast: cover heading for file which contains film script of *Flame of the Yukon*, could have contained early version of *The Pleasure Man*?

Untitled script similar to *The Constant Sinner*, Mae as 'Mavis', gangster characters Duke, George, Monk, Darky.

'Imaginary Conversation between Mae West and George Bernard Shaw' (sketch):

MAE WEST: Mr Shaw, I know you're considered one of the world's greatest playwrights. How would you feel about making a – that is – I mean – writing a play for me?

SHAW: Miss West, don't you think that in writing a play for you, too much importance is placed on sex?

MAE WEST: If you think sex is unimportant, Mr Shaw, try writing an important play sometime – about two eunuchs!

'Mae West Meets Hitler and Vice Versa' (sketch).

'Mae West Meeting with Milton Berle', written by George Saylor (sketch).

'Censor Skit': eleven pages, for nightclub act.

'Fatima', forty-two pages: film (TV) script for Mae West Museum series.

'Sheherezade' ('Saylor-made for Miss West'): sketch, further story for Mae West Museum?

Cleopatra (The Gal Who Made her Mark) ditto, musclemen period – 'underneath the Sphinx's nose / up until the sun arose / we made hanky pank all night in tight embrace / Tho those desert sands were hot / Let's say Mark and I forgot / That's what put the smile upon the Sphinx's face . . .'

Sketch on dying Camille (ditto?).

'The Day of a Star' – A Stage Sketch by Mae West (nine pages).

Film script versions of *The Drag*, *The Pleasure Man*, *Catherine Was Great*.

Margy Lamont, unpublished novelization of *Sex* (date unknown).

Select Bibliography

Books by Mae West

Babe Gordon, a.k.a. *The Constant Sinner*, Macaulay, New York, 1930, 1931.
Diamond Lil, Macaulay, New York, 1932 (later reissued as *She Done Him Wrong*).
Goodness Had Nothing to Do with It, autobiography, Prentice-Hall Inc, Englewood Cliffs, NJ, 1959.
Mae West on Sex, Health and ESP, W. H. Allen, London and New York, 1975.
Pleasure Man, Dell Publishing Co., New York, 1975.
Three Plays by Mae West – Sex, The Drag, The Pleasure Man, Lillian Schlissel (ed.), Routledge, New York, 1997.

Biographies, Studies on Mae West

Bavar, Michael, *Mae West*, Pyramid Publications, New York, 1975.
Cashin, Fergus, *Mae West*, W. H. Allen and Co., London, 1982.
Curry, Ramona, *Too Much of a Good Thing: Mae West as Cultural Icon*, University of Minnesota Press, Minneapolis, London, 1996.
Eels, George, and Musgrove, Stanley, *Mae West, The Lies, The Legends, The Truth*, Morrow, New York, 1982; Robson Books, London, 1984.
Hamilton, Marybeth, *The Queen of Camp: Mae West, Sex and Popular Culture*, Harper Collins, New York, 1995.
Leider, Emily Wortis, *Becoming Mae West*, Da Capo Press, Farrar Straus and Giroux, New York, 2000.
Leonard, Maurice, *Mae West, Empress of Sex*, Carol Publishing Group, Birch Lane Press, New York, 1992.
Malachosky, Tim, *Mae West*, Empire Publishing, Lancaster, California, 1993 (photographs).
Sochen, June, *Mae West: She Who Laughs, Lasts*, Harlan Davidson Inc., Arlington Heights, Illinois, 1992.
Tuska, John, *The Films of Mae West*, Citadel Press, Secaucus, NJ, 1973.
Ward, Carol M., *Mae West, A Bio-Bibliography*, Greenwood Press, Westport, 1985.
Watts, Jill, Mae West, *An Icon in Black and White*, Oxford University Press, Oxford and New York, 2001.

Related Books on Mae West, Film History and Hollywood, Jazz Era

Allen, Frederick Lewis, *Only Yesterday, An Informal History of the 1920's*, Harper and Row, 1931,

Bergman, Andrew, *We're in the Money: Depression America and Its Films*, Elephant Paperbacks, Chicago, 1992.

Bordman, Gerald, *American Musical Theatre*, Oxford, 1978.

Bradford, Perry, *Born with the Blues*, Oak Publications, New York, 1965.

Brownlow, Kevin, *Behind the Mask of Innocence*, Jonathan Cape, London, 1990.

Burrows, Edwin G. and Wallace, Mike, *Gotham: A History of New York to 1898*, Oxford University Press, 1999.

Chandler, Charlotte, *The Ultimate Seduction*, Doubleday and Co. New York, 1984.

Cohn, Art, *The Nine Lives of Michael Todd*, Random House, New York, 1958.

Doherty, Thomas, *Pre-Code Hollywood, Sex, Immorality and Insurrection in American Cinema 1930–1934*, Columbia University Press, New York, 1999.

Douglas, Ann, *Terrible Honesty, Mongrel Manhattan in the 1920's*, Farrar Straus and Giroux, 1995.

Durgnat, Raymond, *The Crazy Mirror, Hollywood Comedy and the American Image*, Faber and Faber, London, 1969.

Fields, Ronald, *W. C. Fields by Himself*, Prentice-Hall, Englefield, NJ, 1973.

Friedrich, Otto, *City of Nets; A Portrait of Hollywood in the 1940's*, University of California Press, 1997.

Gabler, Neil, *An Empire of their Own: How the Jews Invented Hollywood*, Crown Publishers, New York, 1988.

Kobal, John, *People Will Talk, Conversations*, Knopf, New York, 1986.

Lasky, Jesse, *I Blow My Own Horn* (with Don Weldon), Victor Gollancz, London, 1951.

Leff, Leonard J. and Simmons, Jerold L., *The Dame in the Kimono, Hollywood, Censorship and the Production Code From the 1920's to the 1960's*, Grove Weidenfeld, Anchor Books, Doubleday, 1990.

Louvish, Simon, *Man on the Flying Trapeze: The Life and Times of W. C. Fields*, Faber and Faber, 1997.

Louvish, Simon, *Monkey Business: The Lives and Legends of the Marx Brothers*, Faber and Faber, 1999.

Miller, Frank, *Censored Hollywood*, Turner Publishing, 1994.

Richman, Harry (with Richard Gehman), *A Hell of a Life*, Duell, Sloan and Pearce, New York, 1966.

Shipton, Allen, *A New History of Jazz*, Continuum, London, New York, 2001.
Singer, Barry, *Black and Blue: The Life and Lyrics of Andy Razaf*, Schirmer Books (Macmillan), New York, 1982.
Sklar, Robert, *Movie-Made America*, Vintage, New York, 1975, 1994.
Stearns, Jean and Stearns, Marshall, *Jazz Dance: The Story of American Vernacular Dance*, Da Capo Press, New York, 1994.
Thomson, David, *A Biographical Dictionary of Film*, Andre Deutsch, London, 1994.
Tirro, Frank, *Jazz: A History*, W. W. Norton, New York, 1977.
Walker, Alexander, *Sex in the Movies*, Penguin, London, 1968.
Weintraub, Joseph (ed.), *The Wit and Wisdom of Mae West*, Avon Books, NY, 1967.
Wertheim, Arthur Frank, *Radio Comedy*, Oxford University Press, 1979.
Yablonsky, Lewis, *George Raft*, McGraw-Hill, New York, 1974.

Books on Vaudeville, Minstrel, Early Theatre

Allen, Fred, *Much Ado About Me*, Little Brown and Co., Boston, Toronto, 1956.
Atkinson, Brooks, *Broadway*, Limelight, 1985.
Burns, George, *All My Best Friends*, G. P. Putnam's Sons, New York, 1989.
Cockrell, Dale, *Demons of Disorder: Early Blackface Minstrels and Their World*, Cambridge University Press, 1997.
Corio, Ann, with Joseph DiMona, *This Was Burlesque*, Grossettt and Dunlap, New York, 1968.
Gilbert, Douglas, *American Vaudeville*, McGraw-Hill, New York, 1940.
Green, Abel and Laurie, John, *Show Biz from Vaude to Video*, Henry Holt and Co., New York, 1951.
Green, Abel and Laurie, John, *Vaudeville: From the Honky Tonks to the Palace*, Henry Holt and Co., 1953.
Mahar, William J., *Behind the Burnt Cork Mask: Early Blackface Minstrelsy and Antebellum American Popular Culture*, University of Illinois Press, Urbana and Chicago, 1999.
Nathan, Hans, *Dan Emmett and the Rise of Early Negro Minstrelsy*, University of Oklahoma Press, 1962.
Rowland, Mabel (ed.), *Bert Williams: Son of Laughter*, English Crafters, NY, 1923.
Slide, Anthony, *The Vaudevillians: A Dictionary of Vaudeville Performers*, Arlington House, 1981.
Sobel, Bernard, *A Pictorial History of Burlesque*, Bonanza Books, New York, 1956.

Sobel, Bernard, *Burleycue: An Underground History of Burlesque*, Farrar and Reinhart, New York, 1931
Toll, Robert C., *Blacking Up: The Minstrel Show in 19th Century America*, Oxford University Press, 1974

Acknowledgements

Extended quotations from Mae West's works used by permission of the Mae West Estate. Major thanks and accolades must go to the staff of the Margaret Herrick Library at the Academy of Motion Picture Arts and Sciences in Los Angeles, to Barbara Hall, Howard Prouty and Warren Sherk, diligent and most generous archivists. Also many thanks to Ned Comstock at the University of Southern California's Doheny Library, to Rod Bladel and staff at the Billy Rose Theatre Collection at the New York Public Library of the Performing Arts, to Maryan Schach and staff at the Shubert Archive in New York, and to staff of the Brooklyn Public Library. Also to staff at the Manuscript and Motion Picture Divisions of the Library of Congress, Washington, and the British Film Institute Library in London. Thanks, too, to Miles Kreuger, keeper of the Institute of the American Musical in Los Angeles, and to Emily Wortis Leider, Don and Maya Peretz, Joel Finler, Oren Moverman, Stuart Schaar, Rick Mitz, Walter Donohue, Richard Kelly and, of course, Mairi, who came up to see me some time.

Index

This index is compiled on a word-by-word rather than a letter-by-letter basis so that, for example, de Leo, Don precedes *Dean Martin Show, The.* All Mae West's films, theatre productions, songs, and original plays, novels, and other of her writings will be found under West, Mae. References to illustrations are in **bold** type.

Hays Office
  Board of Directors, 212–13, 251,
    252, 255–7, 290, 295
  Breen's regime, 258–9, 261
  Fields and, 341
  first involvement with West, 200
  Go West, Young Man, 305–6
  Goin' to Town, 278–9
  Heat Is On, The, 352
  Klondike Annie, 288, 290, 295
  Paramount, 217, 254–8, 260, 287,
    288, 298
  Production Code, 250–1, 253
  Roosevelt, 211
  'Ruby Red' script, 212
  sharpens up, 238–9, 251
  She Done Him Wrong, 213
  West with Fields, 340
Hayworth, Rita, 293–4, 347
Head, Edith, 221, 401
Hearn, Ed, 168
Hearst, William Randolph, 251, 260,
  287, 298–301, 303, 304
Hecht, Ben, 210
Held, Anna, 18
Hell of a Life, A (Harry Richman and
  Richard Gehman), 97
Hell's Kitchen Gophers, 106
Hemion, Dwight, 411
Henderson, W. J., 23
Hepburn, Katharine, 270–1, 277
Herbert, Victor, 41
Hersholt, Jean, 165
Herzbrun, Bernard, 262
Hill, Gus, 126
Hines, Florence, 22
Hiroshima, 364
Hirschfeld, Al, 322, 361, 374
His Girl Friday (Howard Hawks),
  210
His Majesty the American (Joseph
  Henabery), 82
Hitler, Adolf, 335, 351, 359
Hodkinson, W. W., 39
Hoffman, Gertrude, 17
Hogan, Ernest, 23
Hogan, William, 26, 27, 30

Hollywood Confidential, 128, 173,
  382–5
Hollywood Ten, 347
Hopper, Dennis, 397
Horne, Lena, 107
Houdini, xvii, 16, 28, 67, 72, 126
House of Secrets (Edmund Lawrence),
  94
How to Write Moving Picture Plays
  (William Lewis Gordon), 63
Howard, Gertrude, 233
Hoyt, Charles, 50
Huber, Harold, 288
Hubert's Flea Circus, 185
Hudson, Rochelle, 219
Hudson, Rock, 128, 385
Hudson Theatre, 42
Hughes, Ken, 413
Humphrey, Hal, 380
Hurley, Harold, 212, 213
Huston, Anjelica, 195–6, 411
Huston, John, 196, 401
Huston, Walter, 347
Hyers sisters, 22

I Am a Fugitive from a Chain Gang
  (Mervyn LeRoy), 345
I Blow My Own Horn (Jesse Lasky),
  40
I'll Say She Is, 105
Ince, Thomas, 139
Industrial Recovery Act, 250
Intermezzo- A Love Story (Gregory
  Ratoff), 352
International House (Edward
  Sutherland), 317
Interstate circuit, 104
Intimidade (Perry Salles and Michael
  Sarne), 407
Ireland, Dr Richard, 401, 408
Iron Horse, The (John Ford), 103
Irwin, May, 23
It Happened One Night (Frank
  Capra), 302
It's the Old Army Game (Edward
  Sutherland), 317